[redacted]

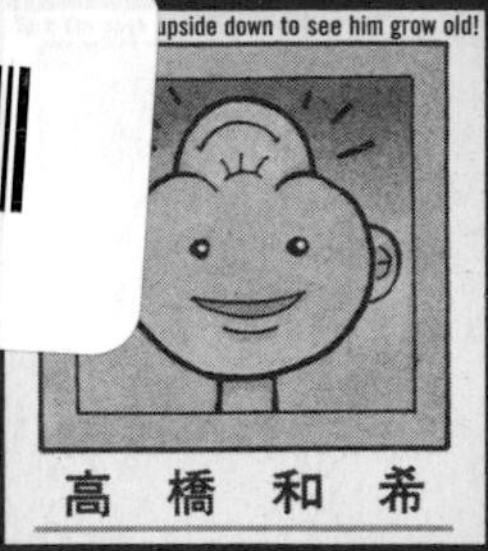
upside down to see him grow old!
高 橋 和 希

A MANGA CANNOT BE CREATED BY JUST ONE PERSON. FIRST I CREATE THE *NAME* (STORYBOARD) AND DISCUSS THE CONTENT WITH MY EDITOR. THEN I DRAW THE CHARACTERS AND MONSTERS. THEN MY STAFF DRAWS THE BACKGROUNDS AND EFFECTS (LIKE SPEED LINES) TO FINISH IT UP. IF I DID ALL THIS WORK ALONE, THERE'S NO WAY I COULD DO A WEEKLY SERIAL COMIC.
—KAZUKI TAKAHASHI, 2000

Artist/author Kazuki Takahashi first tried to break into the manga business in 1982, but success eluded him until **Yu-Gi-Oh!** debuted in the Japanese **Weekly Shonen Jump** magazine in 1996. **Yu-Gi-Oh!**'s themes of friendship and fighting, together with Takahashi's weird and wonderful art, soon became enormously successful, spawning a real-world card game, video games, and two anime series. A lifelong gamer, Takahashi enjoys Shogi (Japanese chess), Mahjong, card games, and tabletop RPGs, among other games.

YU-GI-OH!: DUELIST VOL. 17
The SHONEN JUMP Manga Edition

STORY AND ART BY
KAZUKI TAKAHASHI

Translation & English Adaptation/Joe Yamazaki
Touch-up Art & Lettering/Eric Erbes
Design/Andrea Rice
Editor/Jason Thompson

Managing Editor/Frances E. Wall
Editorial Director/Elizabeth Kawasaki
VP & Editor in Chief/Yumi Hoashi
Sr. Director of Acquisitions/Rika Inouye
Sr. Vice President of Marketing/Liza Coppola
Exec. VP of Sales & Marketing/John Easum
Publisher/Hyoe Narita

In the original Japanese edition, YU-GI-OH!, YU-GI-OH!: DUELIST and
YU-GI-OH!: MILLENNIUM WORLD are known collectively as YU-GI-OH!.
The English YU-GI-OH!: DUELIST was originally volumes 8-31
of the Japanese YU-GI-OH!.

Printed in the U.S.A.

Published by VIZ Media, LLC
P.O. Box 77010
San Francisco, CA 94107

SHONEN JUMP Manga Edition
10 9 8 7 6 5 4 3 2 1
First printing, October 2006

www.viz.com

PARENTAL ADVISORY
RATED T TEEN
YU-GI-OH!: DUELIST is rated T for Teen
and is recommended for ages 13 and
up. Contains fantasy violence.

THE WORLD'S
MOST POPULAR MANGA

SHONEN JUMP
www.shonenjump.com

SHONEN JUMP MANGA

YU-GI-OH!™ DUELIST

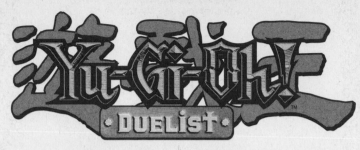

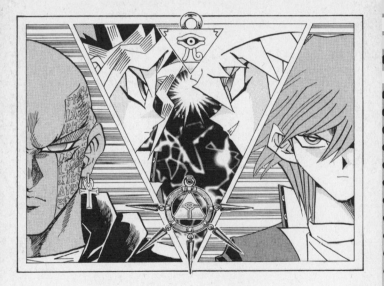

Vol. 17

ONE-TURN KILL

STORY AND ART BY

KAZUKI TAKAHASHI

THE STORY SO FAR...

**YUGI MUTOU/
YU-GI-OH**

When 10th grader Yugi solved the Millennium Puzzle, another spirit took up residence in his body...Yu-Gi-Oh, the King of Games, a dark avenger who challenges evildoers to "Shadow Games" of life and death!

YUGI FACES DEADLY ENEMIES!

Using his gaming skills, Yugi fights ruthless adversaries like Maximillion Pegasus, multimillionaire creator of the collectible card game "Duel Monsters," and Ryo Bakura, whose friendly personality turns evil when he is possessed by the spirit of the Millennium Ring. But Yugi's greatest rival is Seto Kaiba, the world's second-greatest gamer—and the ruthless teenage president of Kaiba Corporation. At first, Kaiba and Yugi are bitter enemies, but after fighting against a common adversary—Pegasus—they come to respect one another. But for all his powers, there is one thing Yu-Gi-Oh cannot do: remember who he is and where he came from.

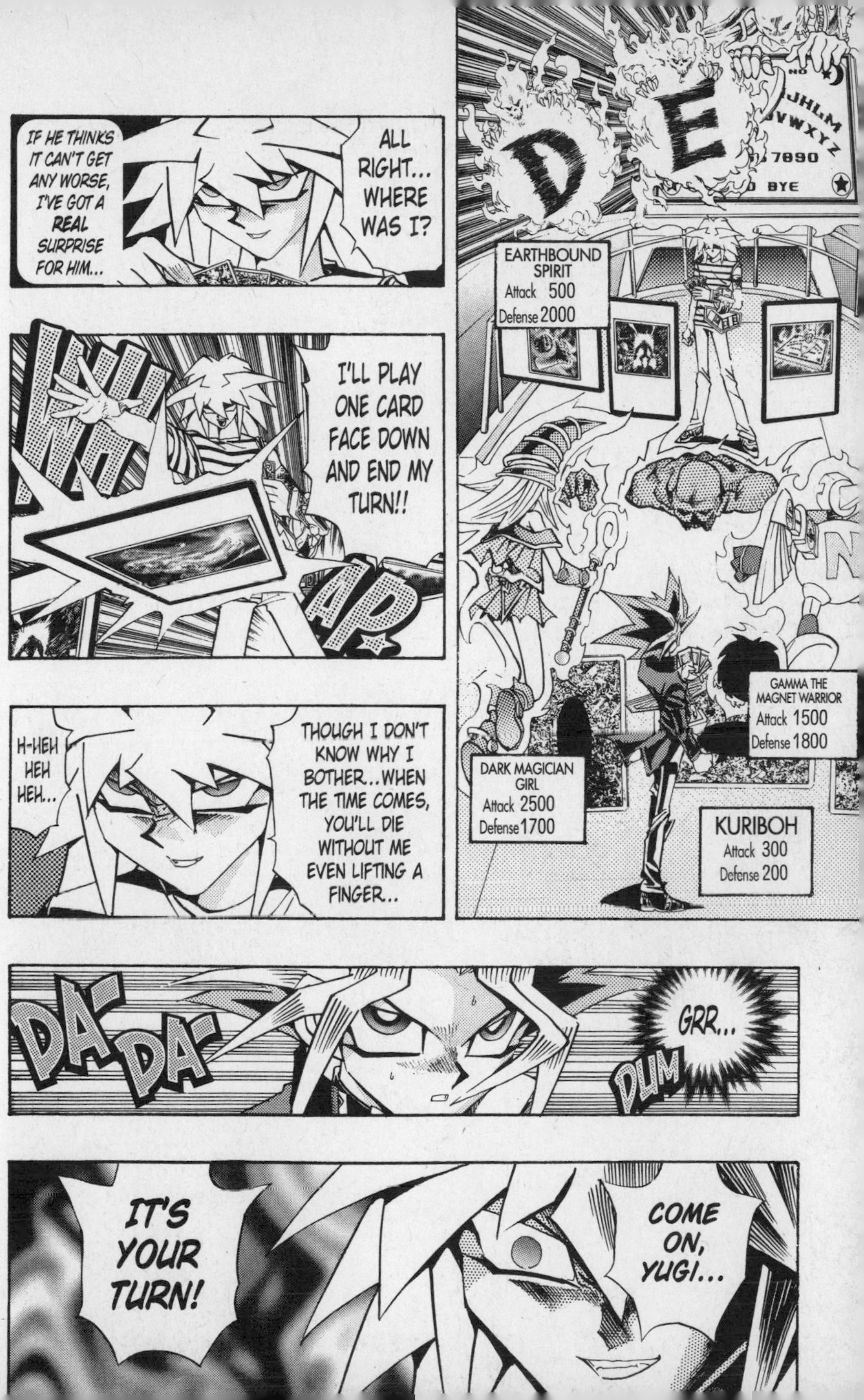
NO
JHLM
VWXYZ
7890
BYE
D
E
EARTHBOUND SPIRIT Attack 500 Defense 2000
GAMMA THE MAGNET WARRIOR Attack 1500 Defense 1800
DARK MAGICIAN GIRL Attack 2500 Defense 1700
KURIBOH Attack 300 Defense 200
ALL RIGHT... WHERE WAS I?
IF HE THINKS IT CAN'T GET ANY WORSE, I'VE GOT A REAL SURPRISE FOR HIM...
I'LL PLAY ONE CARD FACE DOWN AND END MY TURN!!
THOUGH I DON'T KNOW WHY I BOTHER...WHEN THE TIME COMES, YOU'LL DIE WITHOUT ME EVEN LIFTING A FINGER...
H-HEH HEH HEH...
GRR...
DUM
DA-
DA-
COME ON, YUGI...
IT'S YOUR TURN!

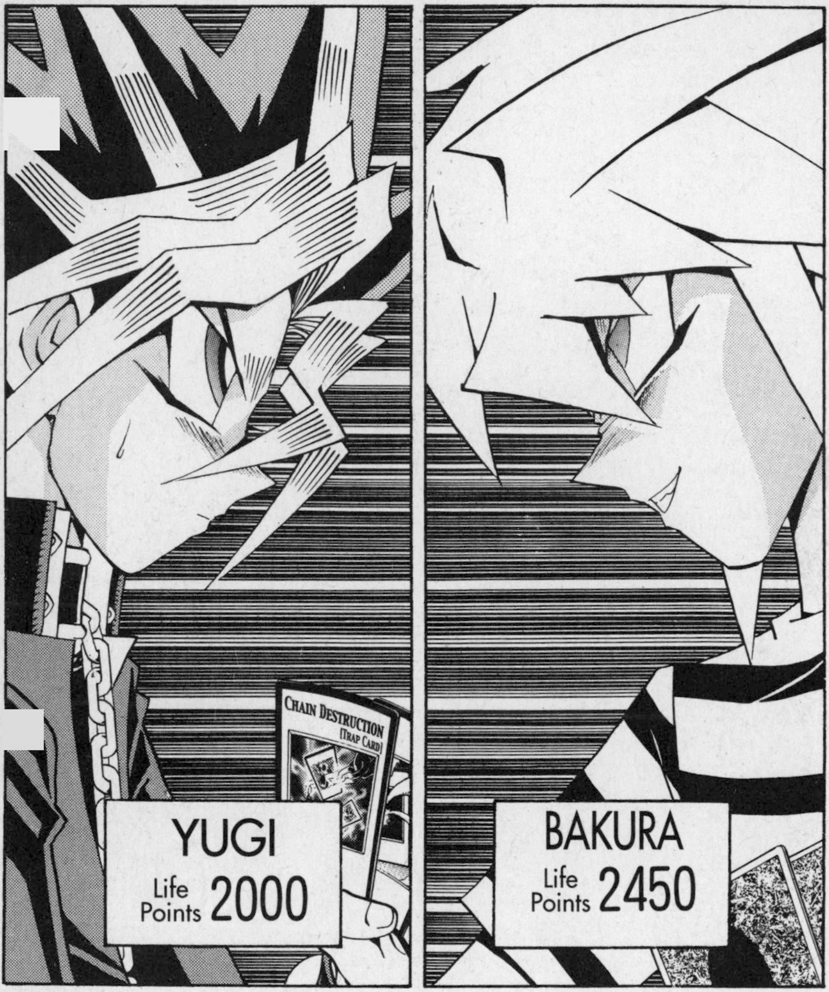
BAKURA
Life Points 2450
CHAIN DESTRUCTION
[TRAP CARD]
YUGI
Life Points 2000

DUEL 147: UNBREAKABLE SPIRIT!

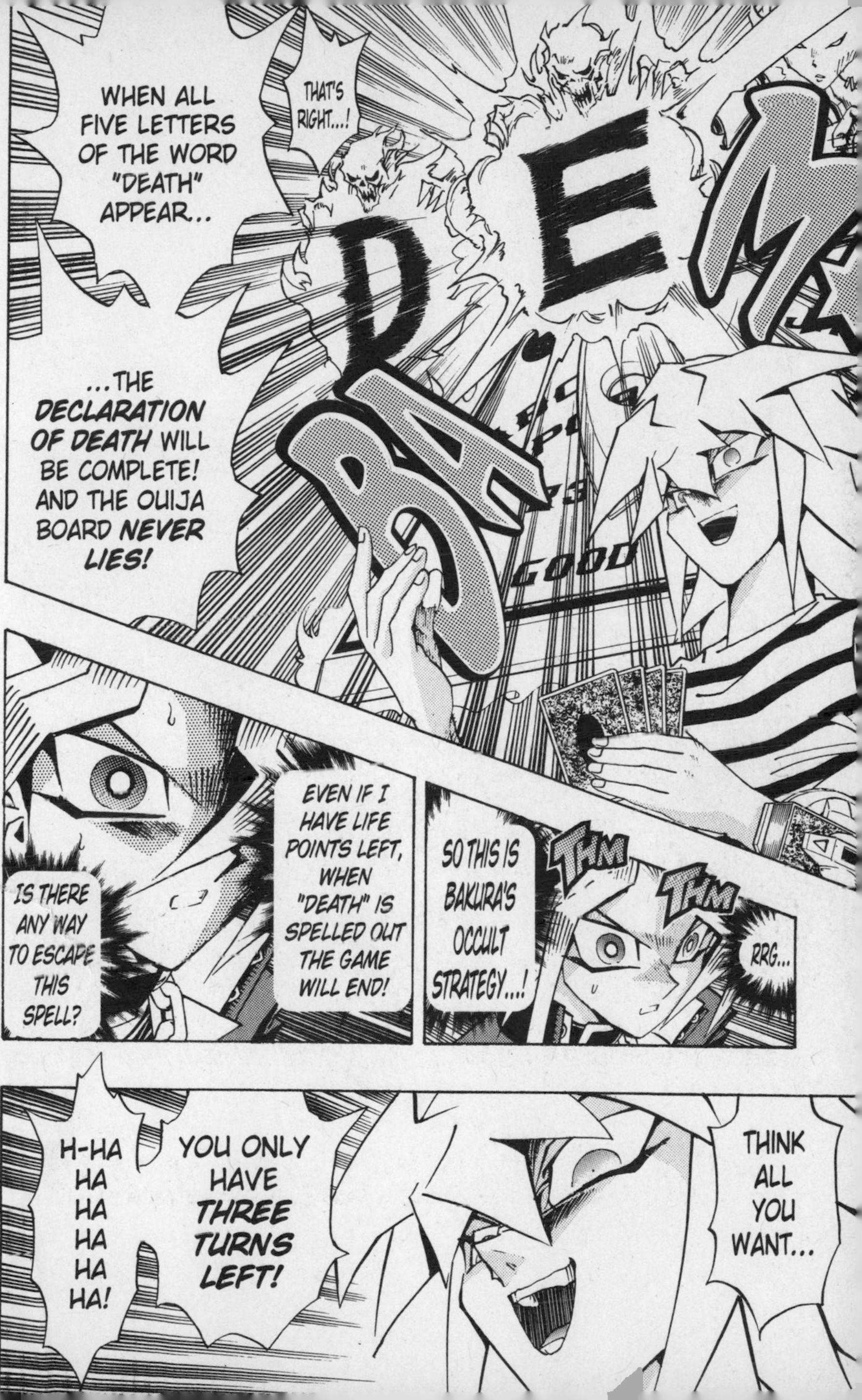
THAT'S RIGHT...!
WHEN ALL FIVE LETTERS OF THE WORD "DEATH" APPEAR...
...THE DECLARATION OF DEATH WILL BE COMPLETE! AND THE OUIJA BOARD NEVER LIES!
GOOD
THM
THM
RRG...
SO THIS IS BAKURA'S OCCULT STRATEGY...!
EVEN IF I HAVE LIFE POINTS LEFT, WHEN "DEATH" IS SPELLED OUT THE GAME WILL END!
IS THERE ANY WAY TO ESCAPE THIS SPELL?
THINK ALL YOU WANT...
YOU ONLY HAVE THREE TURNS LEFT!
H-HA HA HA HA HA HA!

Duel 147: Unbreakable Spirit!

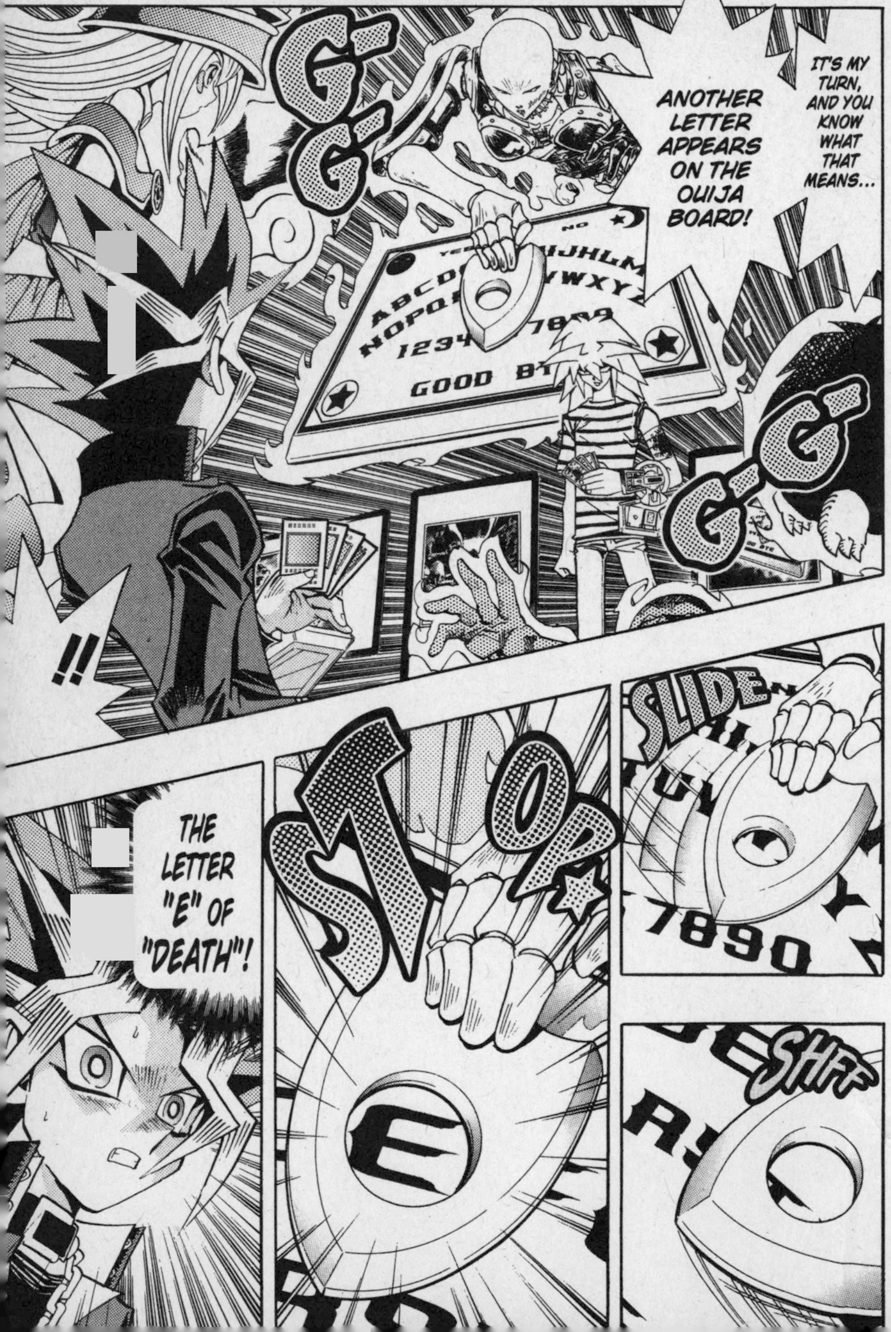
IT'S MY TURN, AND YOU KNOW WHAT THAT MEANS...
ANOTHER LETTER APPEARS ON THE OUIJA BOARD!
G-G
G-G
!!
SLIDE
STOP
THE LETTER "E" OF "DEATH"!
SHFF

Yu-Gi-Oh!

·DUELIST·

Vol. 17

CONTENTS

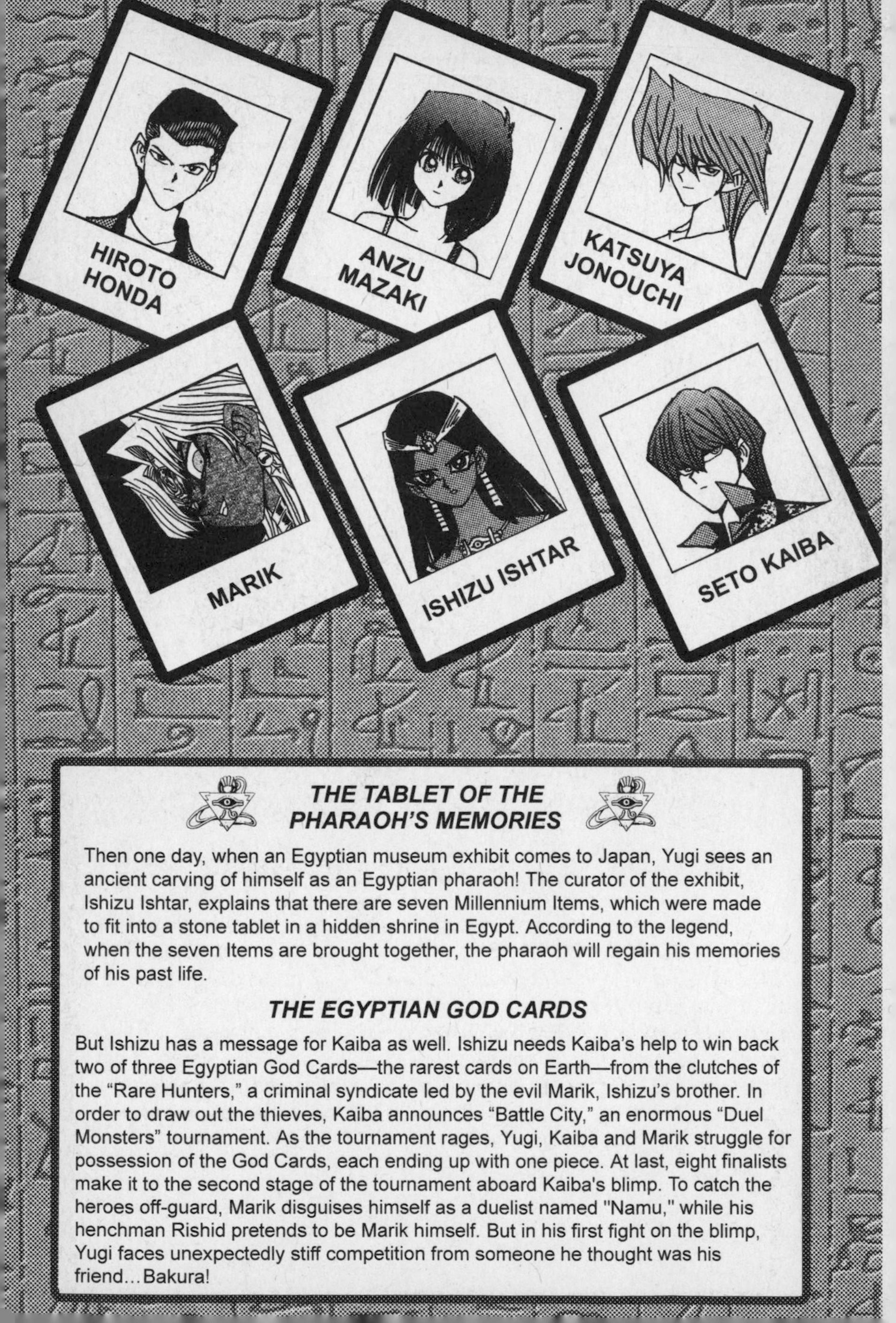
HIROTO HONDA
ANZU MAZAKI
KATSUYA JONOUCHI
MARIK
ISHIZU ISHTAR
SETO KAIBA

THE TABLET OF THE PHARAOH'S MEMORIES

Then one day, when an Egyptian museum exhibit comes to Japan, Yugi sees an ancient carving of himself as an Egyptian pharaoh! The curator of the exhibit, Ishizu Ishtar, explains that there are seven Millennium Items, which were made to fit into a stone tablet in a hidden shrine in Egypt. According to the legend, when the seven Items are brought together, the pharaoh will regain his memories of his past life.

THE EGYPTIAN GOD CARDS

But Ishizu has a message for Kaiba as well. Ishizu needs Kaiba's help to win back two of three Egyptian God Cards—the rarest cards on Earth—from the clutches of the "Rare Hunters," a criminal syndicate led by the evil Marik, Ishizu's brother. In order to draw out the thieves, Kaiba announces "Battle City," an enormous "Duel Monsters" tournament. As the tournament rages, Yugi, Kaiba and Marik struggle for possession of the God Cards, each ending up with one piece. At last, eight finalists make it to the second stage of the tournament aboard Kaiba's blimp. To catch the heroes off-guard, Marik disguises himself as a duelist named "Namu," while his henchman Rishid pretends to be Marik himself. But in his first fight on the blimp, Yugi faces unexpectedly stiff competition from someone he thought was his friend... Bakura!

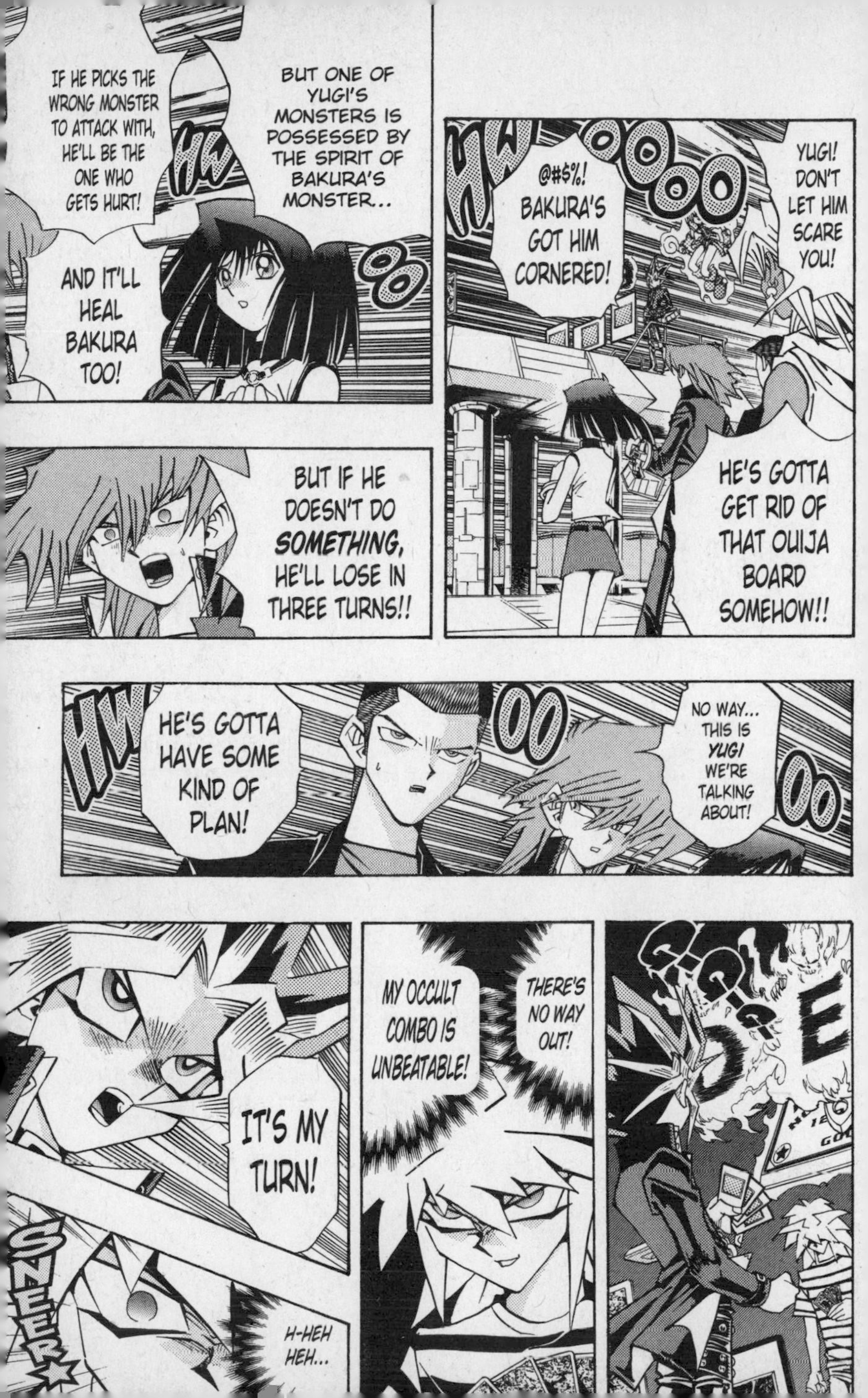
HWOOOOO
YUGI! DON'T LET HIM SCARE YOU!
@#$%! BAKURA'S GOT HIM CORNERED!
HE'S GOTTA GET RID OF THAT OUIJA BOARD SOMEHOW!!
HWOO
BUT ONE OF YUGI'S MONSTERS IS POSSESSED BY THE SPIRIT OF BAKURA'S MONSTER...
IF HE PICKS THE WRONG MONSTER TO ATTACK WITH, HE'LL BE THE ONE WHO GETS HURT!
AND IT'LL HEAL BAKURA TOO!
BUT IF HE DOESN'T DO SOMETHING, HE'LL LOSE IN THREE TURNS!!
HWOOOO
NO WAY... THIS IS YUGI WE'RE TALKING ABOUT!
HE'S GOTTA HAVE SOME KIND OF PLAN!
THERE'S NO WAY OUT!
MY OCCULT COMBO IS UNBEATABLE!
IT'S MY TURN!
H-HEH HEH...
SNEER

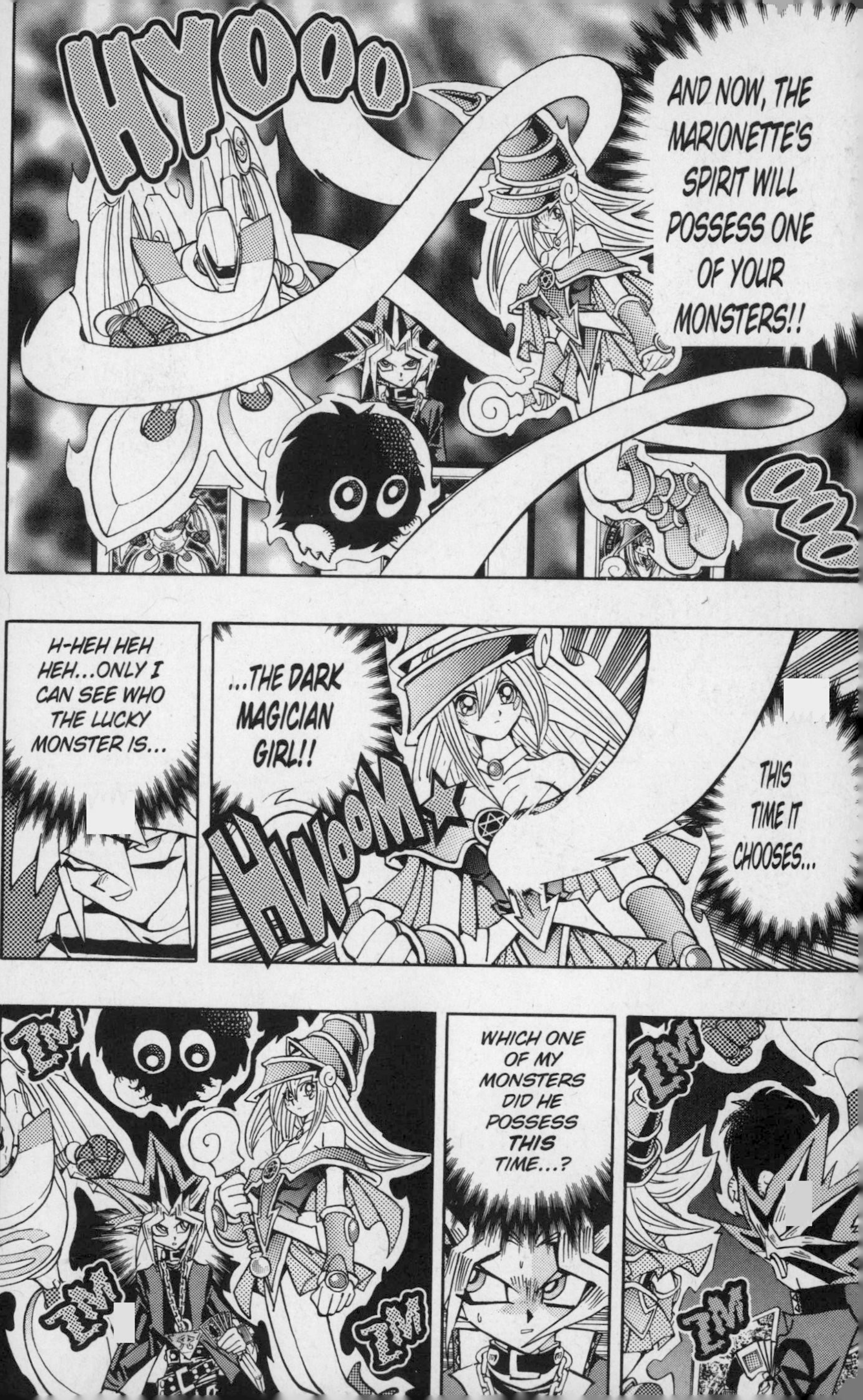
AND NOW, THE MARIONETTE'S SPIRIT WILL POSSESS ONE OF YOUR MONSTERS!!
HYOOO
OOO
THIS TIME IT CHOOSES...
...THE DARK MAGICIAN GIRL!!
HWOOM★
H-HEH HEH HEH...ONLY I CAN SEE WHO THE LUCKY MONSTER IS...
ZM
ZM
WHICH ONE OF MY MONSTERS DID HE POSSESS THIS TIME...?
ZM
ZM
ZM

READ THIS WAY

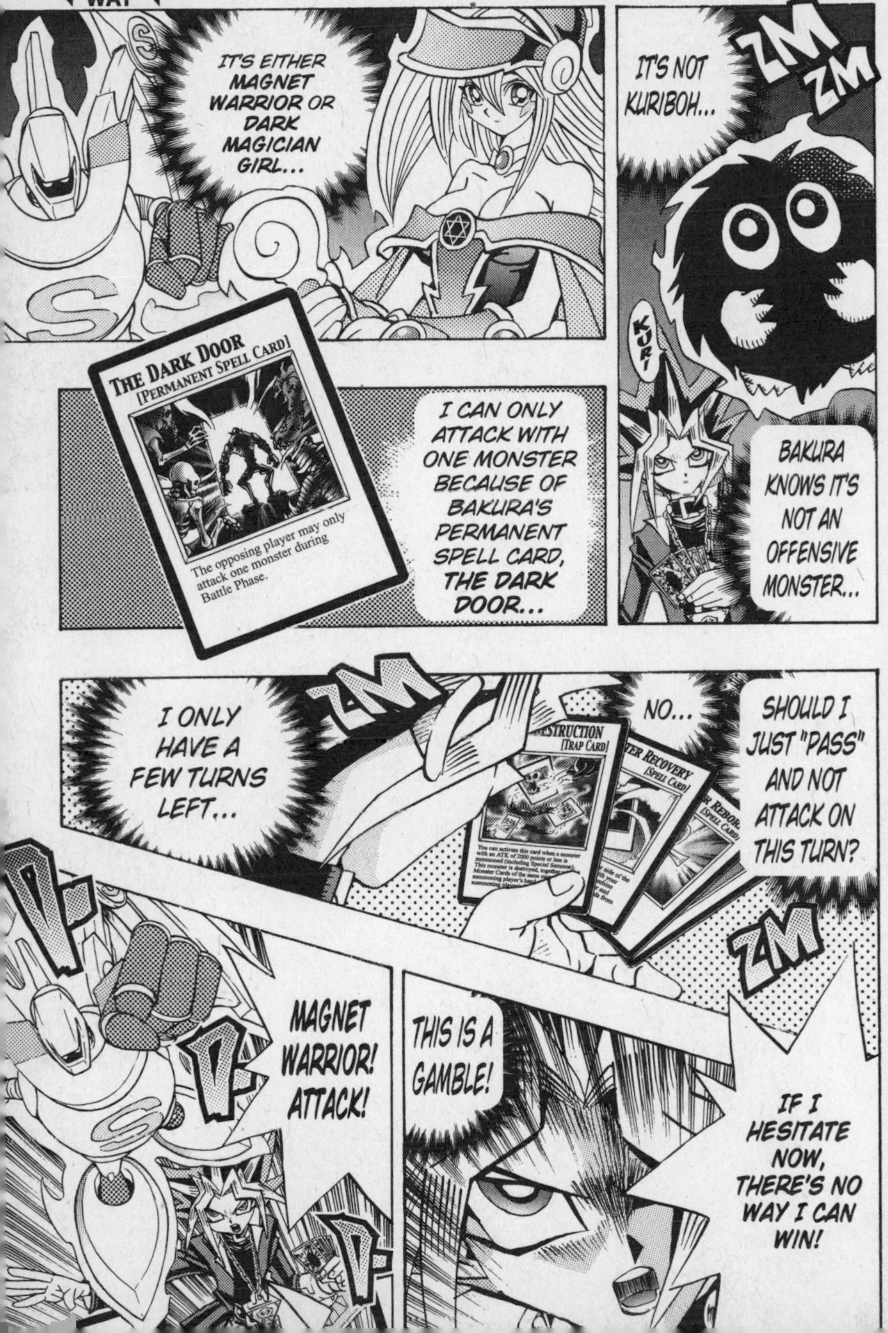
ZM ZM
IT'S NOT KURIBOH...
KURI
BAKURA KNOWS IT'S NOT AN OFFENSIVE MONSTER...
IT'S EITHER MAGNET WARRIOR OR DARK MAGICIAN GIRL...
THE DARK DOOR
[PERMANENT SPELL CARD]
The opposing player may only attack one monster during Battle Phase.
I CAN ONLY ATTACK WITH ONE MONSTER BECAUSE OF BAKURA'S PERMANENT SPELL CARD, THE DARK DOOR...
SHOULD I JUST "PASS" AND NOT ATTACK ON THIS TURN?
NO...
ZM
I ONLY HAVE A FEW TURNS LEFT...
ZM
THIS IS A GAMBLE!
IF I HESITATE NOW, THERE'S NO WAY I CAN WIN!
MAGNET WARRIOR! ATTACK!

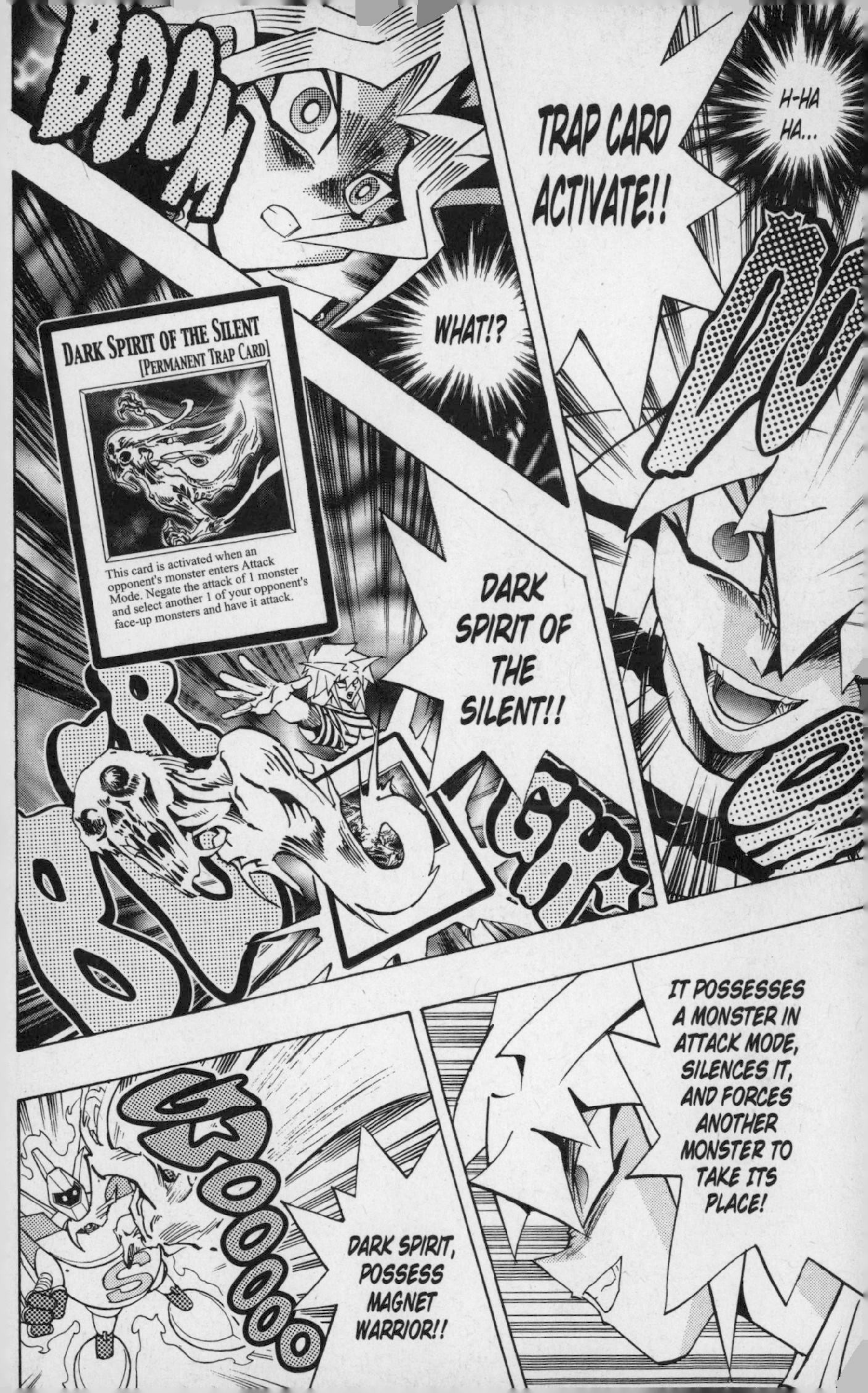
H-HA HA...
TRAP CARD ACTIVATE!!
BOOM
WHAT!?
DARK SPIRIT OF THE SILENT
[PERMANENT TRAP CARD]
This card is activated when an opponent's monster enters Attack Mode. Negate the attack of 1 monster and select another 1 of your opponent's face-up monsters and have it attack.
DARK SPIRIT OF THE SILENT!!
IT POSSESSES A MONSTER IN ATTACK MODE, SILENCES IT, AND FORCES ANOTHER MONSTER TO TAKE ITS PLACE!
DARK SPIRIT, POSSESS MAGNET WARRIOR!!

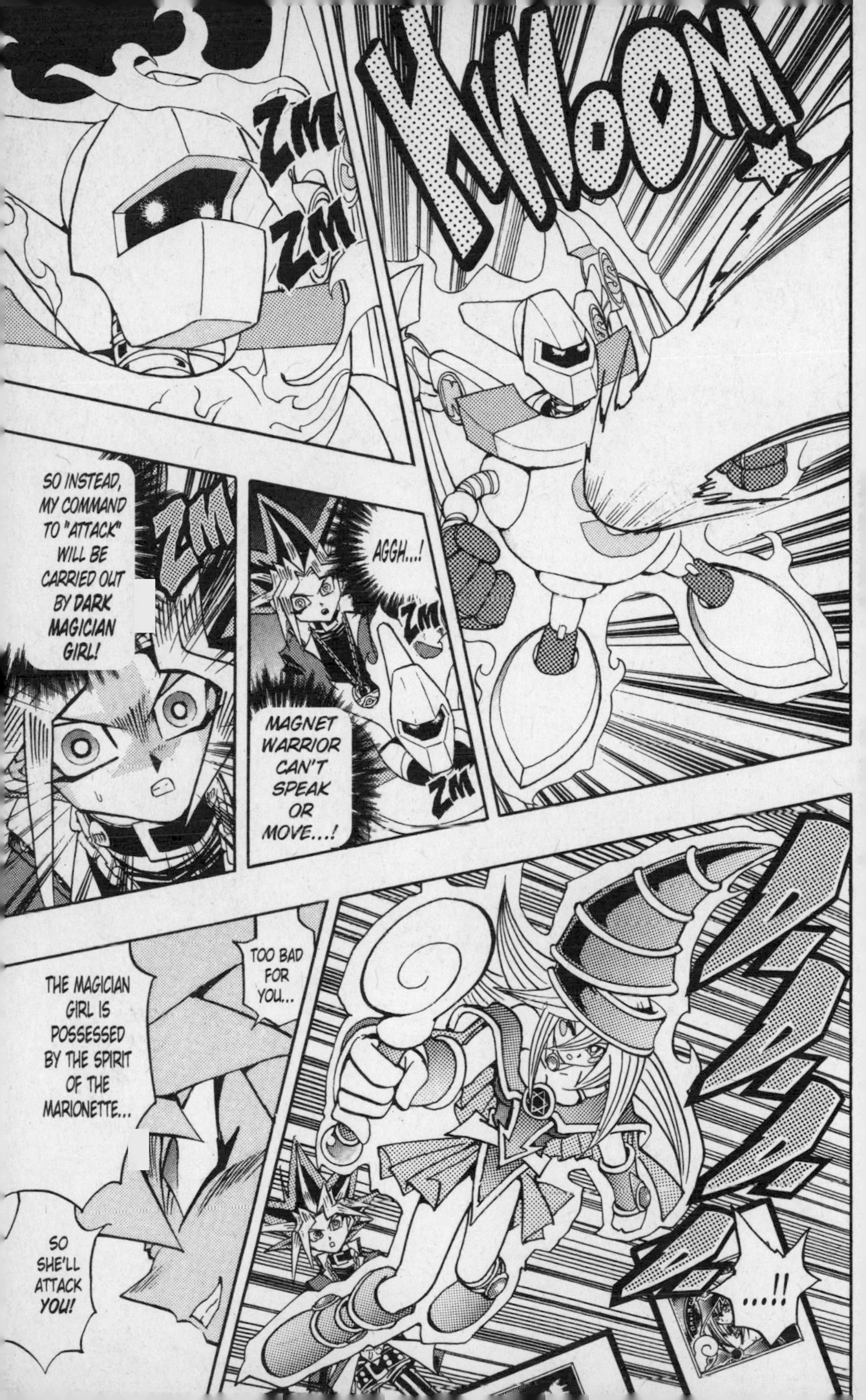
KWOOM!
ZM
ZM
AGGH...!
ZM
MAGNET WARRIOR CAN'T SPEAK OR MOVE...!
ZM
SO INSTEAD, MY COMMAND TO "ATTACK" WILL BE CARRIED OUT BY DARK MAGICIAN GIRL!
ZM
...!!
TOO BAD FOR YOU...
THE MAGICIAN GIRL IS POSSESSED BY THE SPIRIT OF THE MARIONETTE...
SO SHE'LL ATTACK YOU!

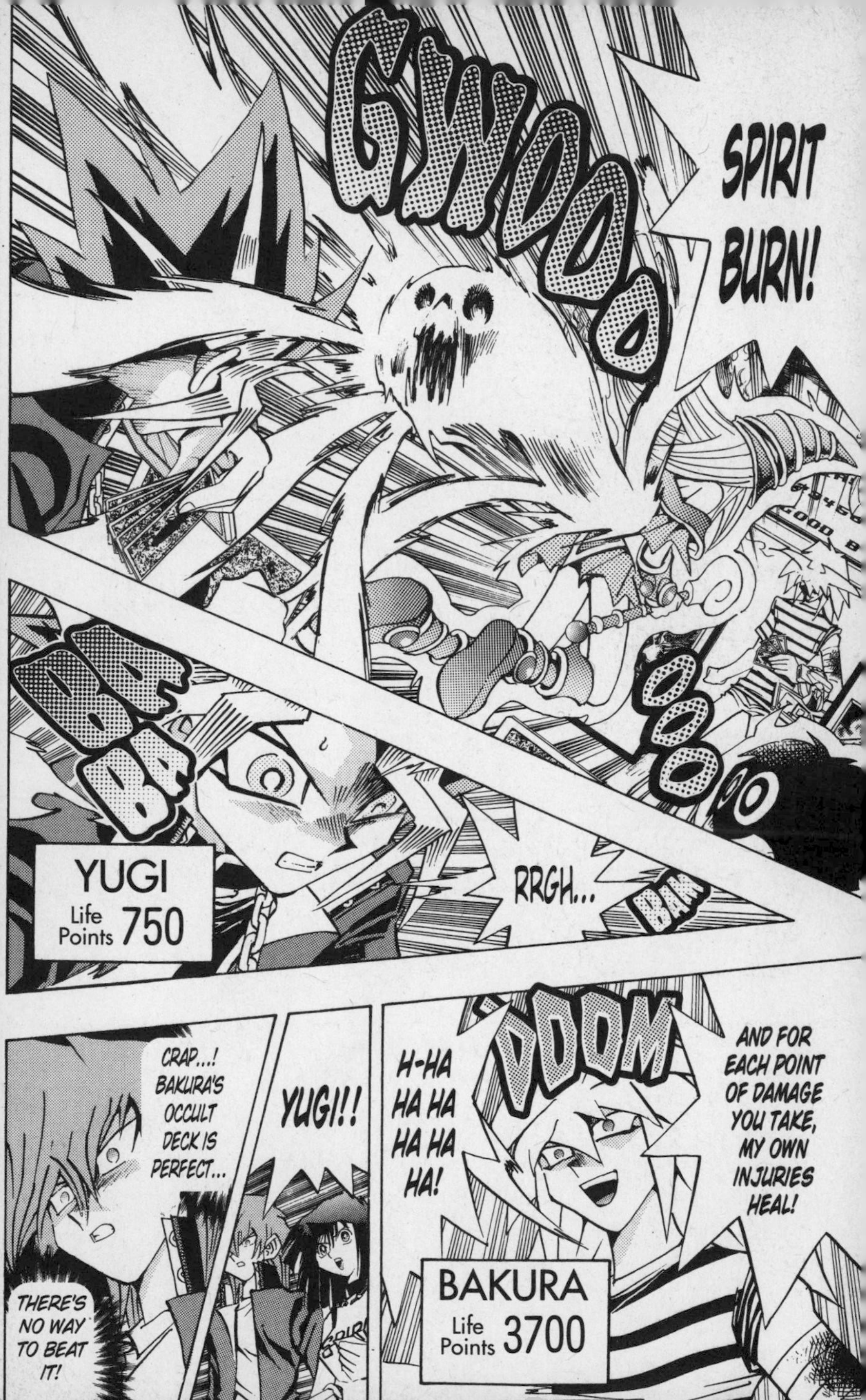
GWOOOO
SPIRIT BURN!
YUGI
Life Points 750
RRGH...
AND FOR EACH POINT OF DAMAGE YOU TAKE, MY OWN INJURIES HEAL!
DOOM
H-HA HA HA HA HA HA!
BAKURA
Life Points 3700
YUGI!!
CRAP...! BAKURA'S OCCULT DECK IS PERFECT...
THERE'S NO WAY TO BEAT IT!

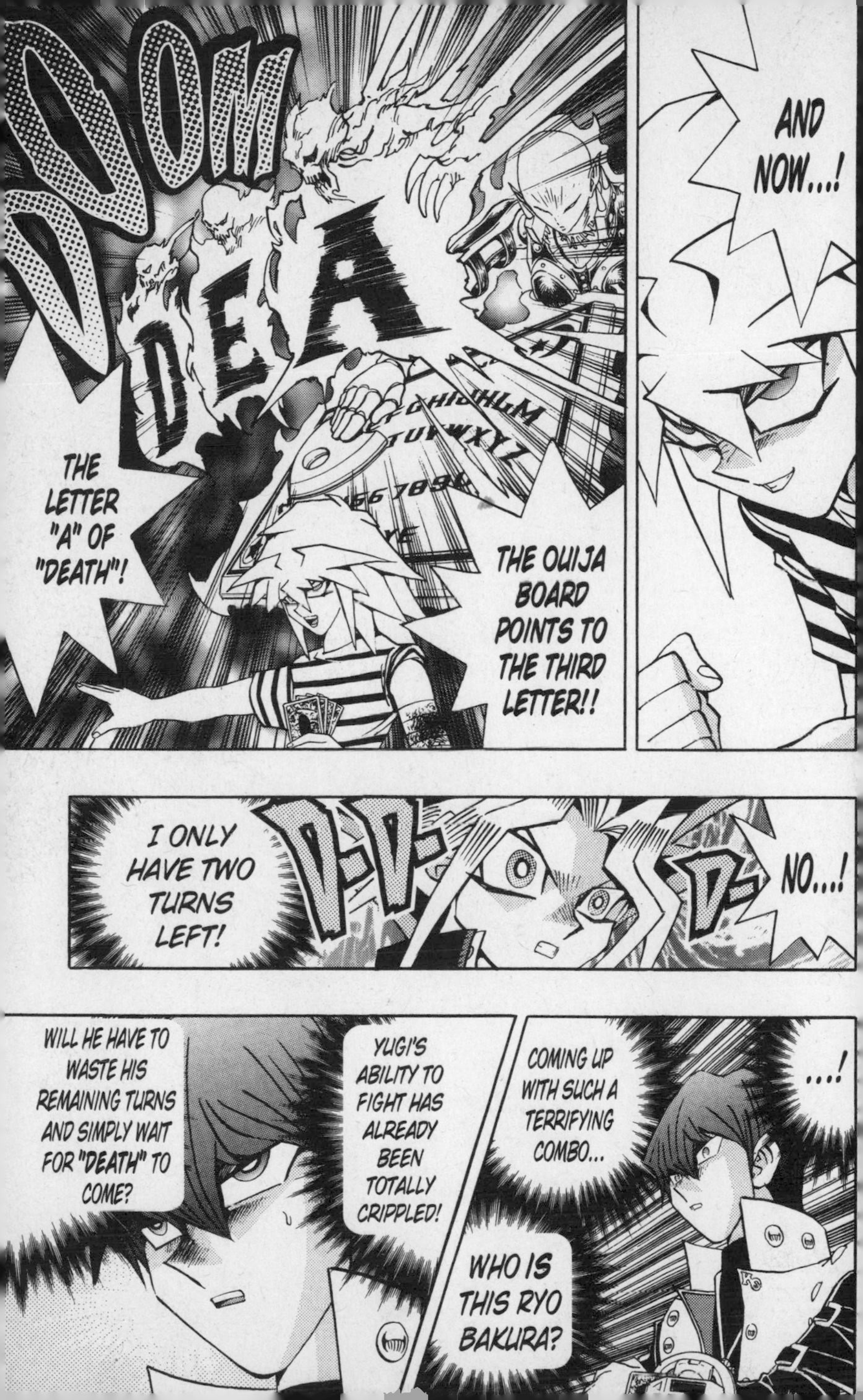
AND NOW...!
DOOM
DEA
THE OUIJA BOARD POINTS TO THE THIRD LETTER!!
THE LETTER "A" OF "DEATH"!
NO...!
D-
D-D-
I ONLY HAVE TWO TURNS LEFT!
...!
COMING UP WITH SUCH A TERRIFYING COMBO...
WHO IS THIS RYO BAKURA?
YUGI'S ABILITY TO FIGHT HAS ALREADY BEEN TOTALLY CRIPPLED!
WILL HE HAVE TO WASTE HIS REMAINING TURNS AND SIMPLY WAIT FOR "DEATH" TO COME?

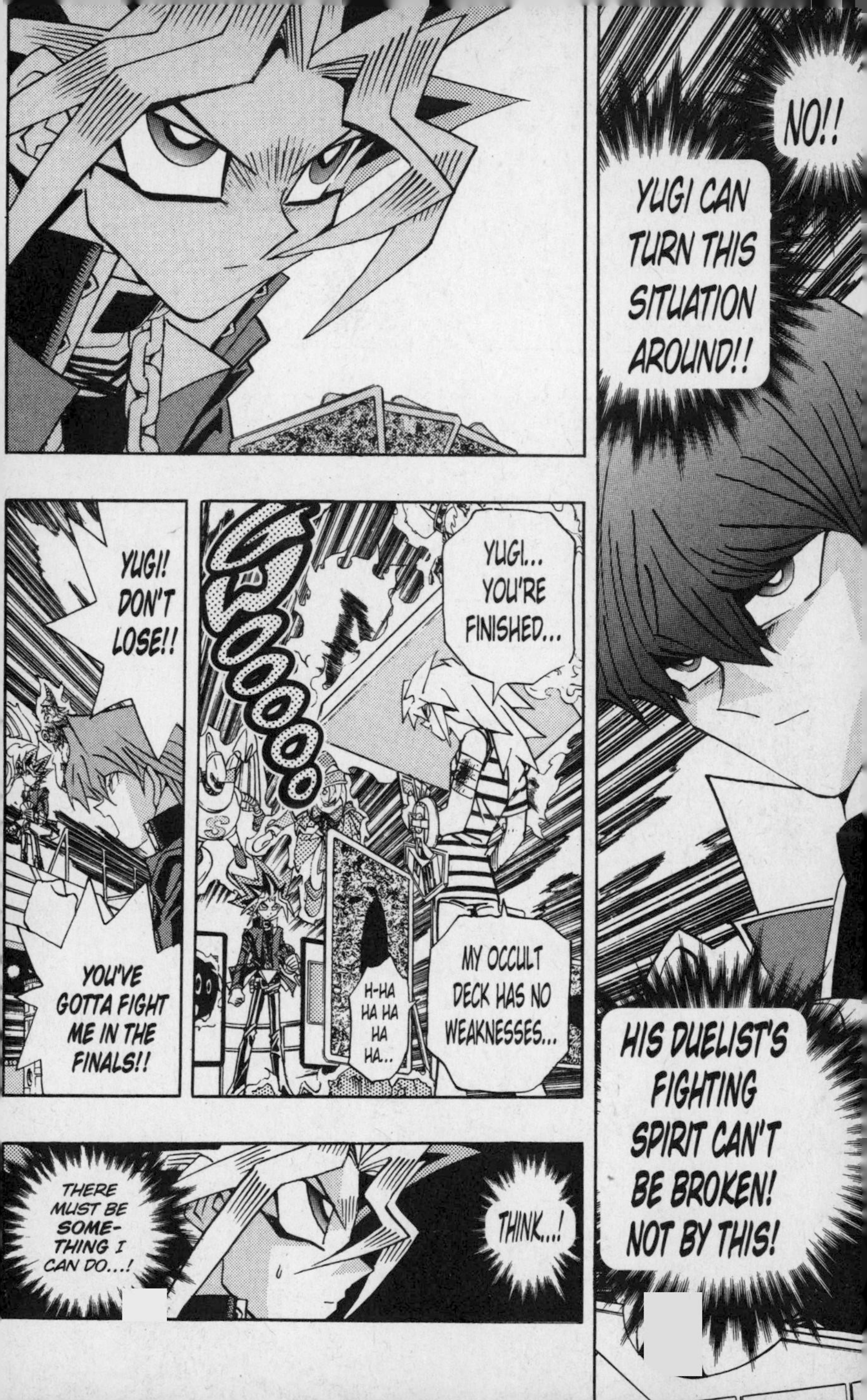
NO!!
YUGI CAN TURN THIS SITUATION AROUND!!
HIS DUELIST'S FIGHTING SPIRIT CAN'T BE BROKEN! NOT BY THIS!
YUGI... YOU'RE FINISHED...
MY OCCULT DECK HAS NO WEAKNESSES...
H-HA HA HA HA HA...
YUGI! DON'T LOSE!!
YOU'VE GOTTA FIGHT ME IN THE FINALS!!
THINK...!
THERE MUST BE SOME-THING I CAN DO...!

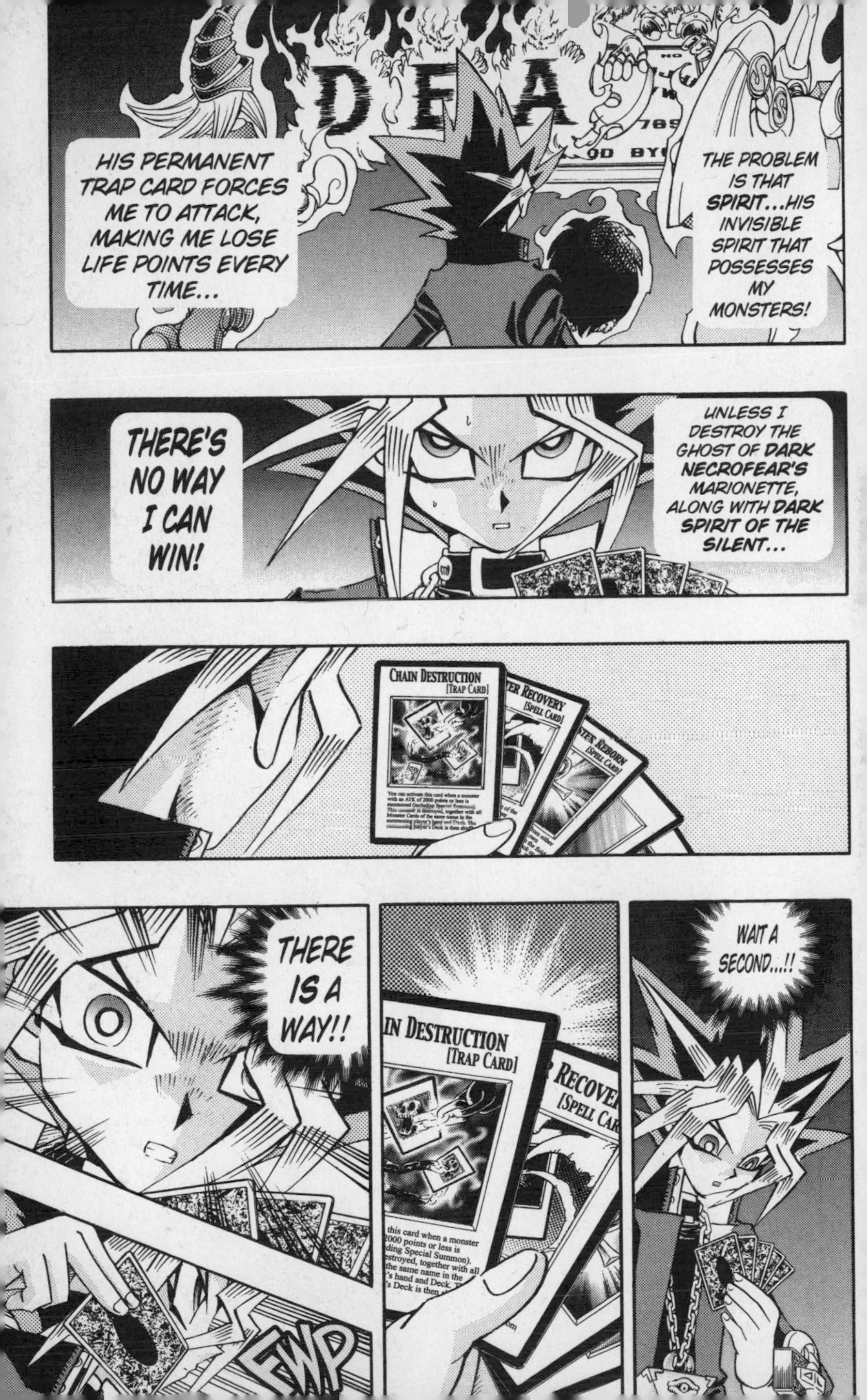
THE PROBLEM IS THAT SPIRIT...HIS INVISIBLE SPIRIT THAT POSSESSES MY MONSTERS!
HIS PERMANENT TRAP CARD FORCES ME TO ATTACK, MAKING ME LOSE LIFE POINTS EVERY TIME...
UNLESS I DESTROY THE GHOST OF DARK NECROFEAR'S MARIONETTE, ALONG WITH DARK SPIRIT OF THE SILENT...
THERE'S NO WAY I CAN WIN!
CHAIN DESTRUCTION
[TRAP CARD]
WAIT A SECOND...!!
THERE IS A WAY!!
FWP

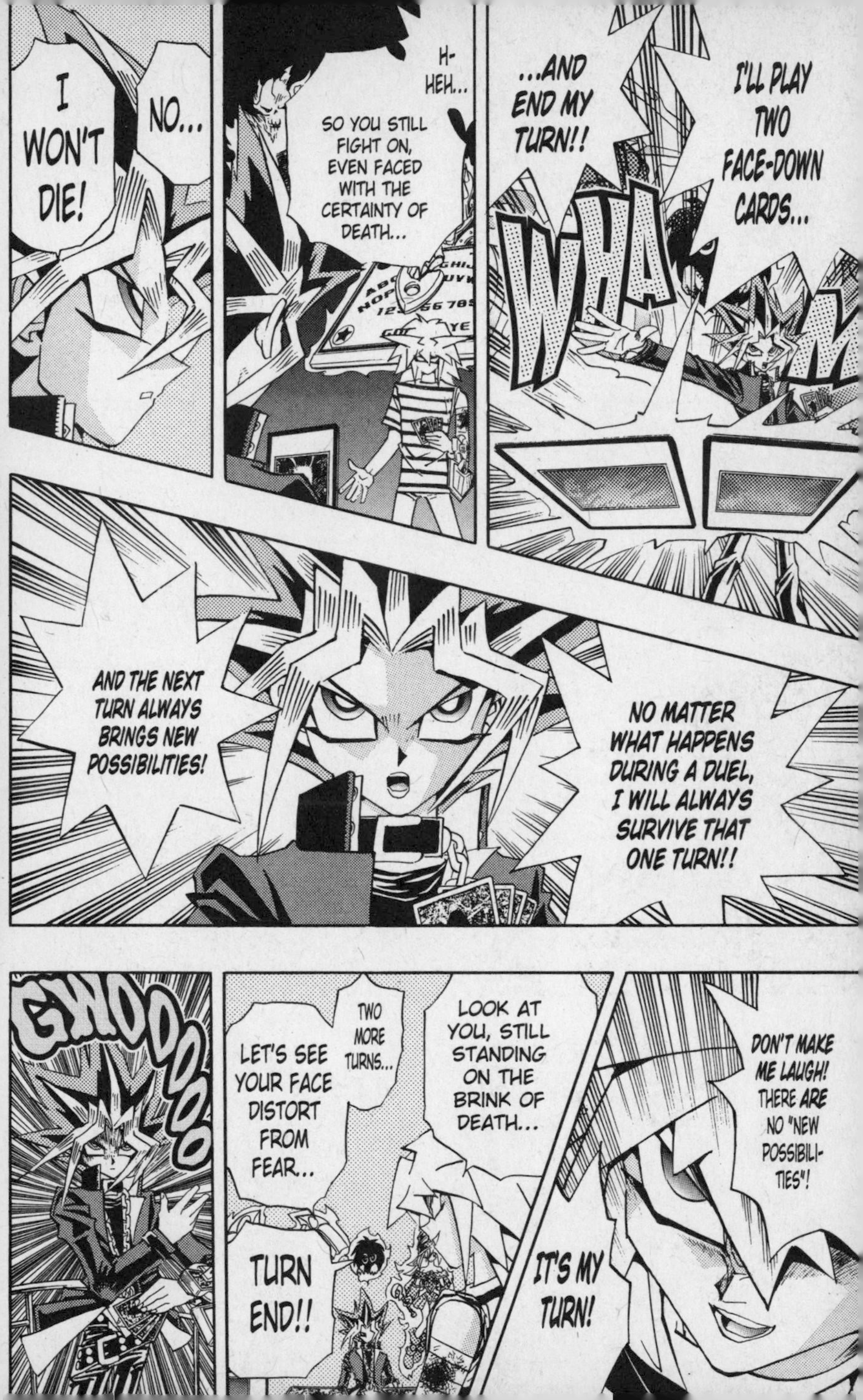
I'LL PLAY TWO FACE-DOWN CARDS...
...AND END MY TURN!!
WHAM
H-HEH...
SO YOU STILL FIGHT ON, EVEN FACED WITH THE CERTAINTY OF DEATH...
NO...
I WON'T DIE!
NO MATTER WHAT HAPPENS DURING A DUEL, I WILL ALWAYS SURVIVE THAT ONE TURN!!
AND THE NEXT TURN ALWAYS BRINGS NEW POSSIBILITIES!
DON'T MAKE ME LAUGH! THERE ARE NO "NEW POSSIBILITIES"!
IT'S MY TURN!
LOOK AT YOU, STILL STANDING ON THE BRINK OF DEATH...
TWO MORE TURNS...
LET'S SEE YOUR FACE DISTORT FROM FEAR...
TURN END!!
GHOOOOO

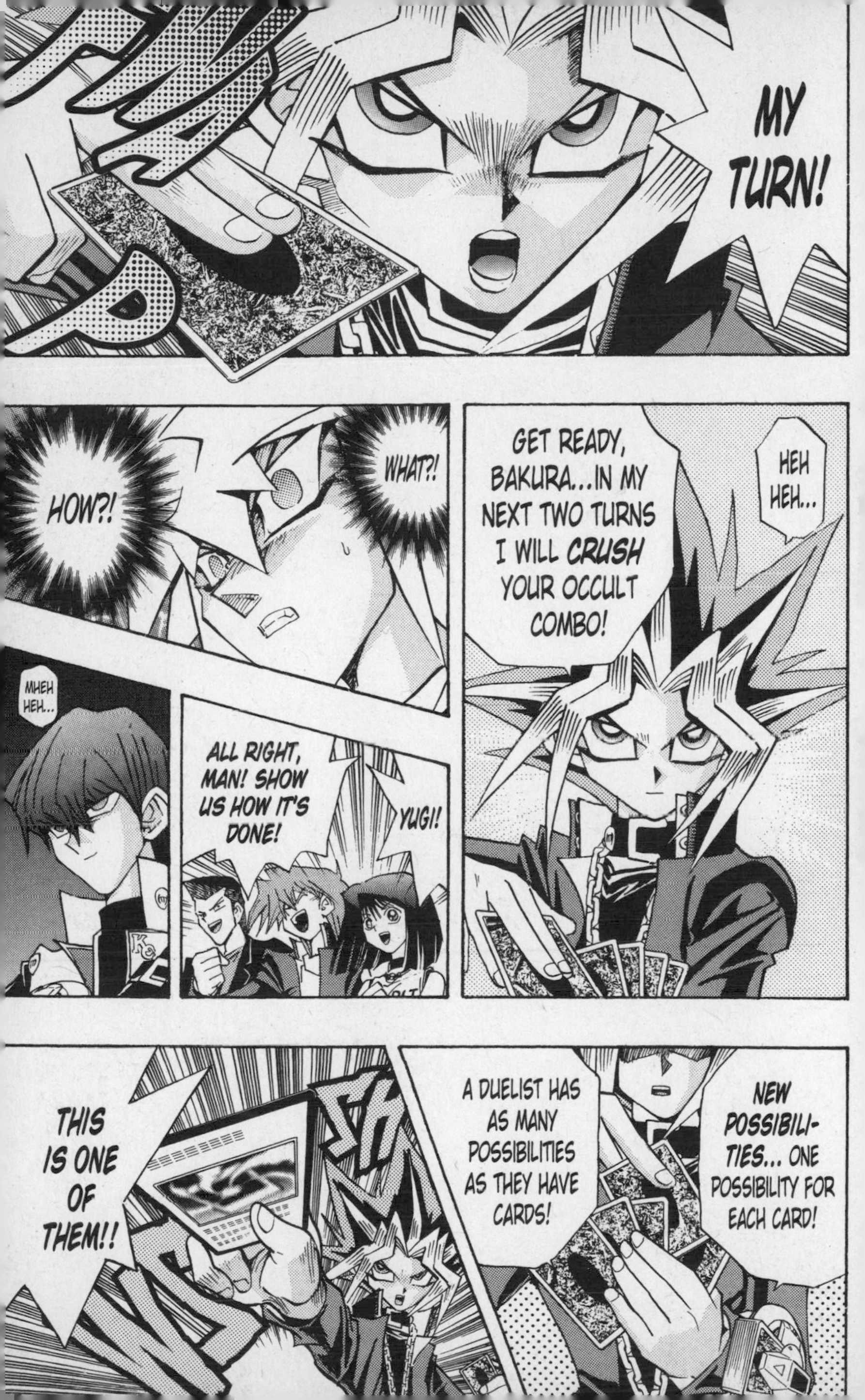
MY TURN!
HEH HEH...
GET READY, BAKURA...IN MY NEXT TWO TURNS I WILL **CRUSH** YOUR OCCULT COMBO!
WHAT?!
HOW?!
YUGI!
ALL RIGHT, MAN! SHOW US HOW IT'S DONE!
MHEH HEH...
NEW POSSIBILI-TIES... ONE POSSIBILITY FOR EACH CARD!
A DUELIST HAS AS MANY POSSIBILITIES AS THEY HAVE CARDS!
THIS IS ONE OF THEM!!

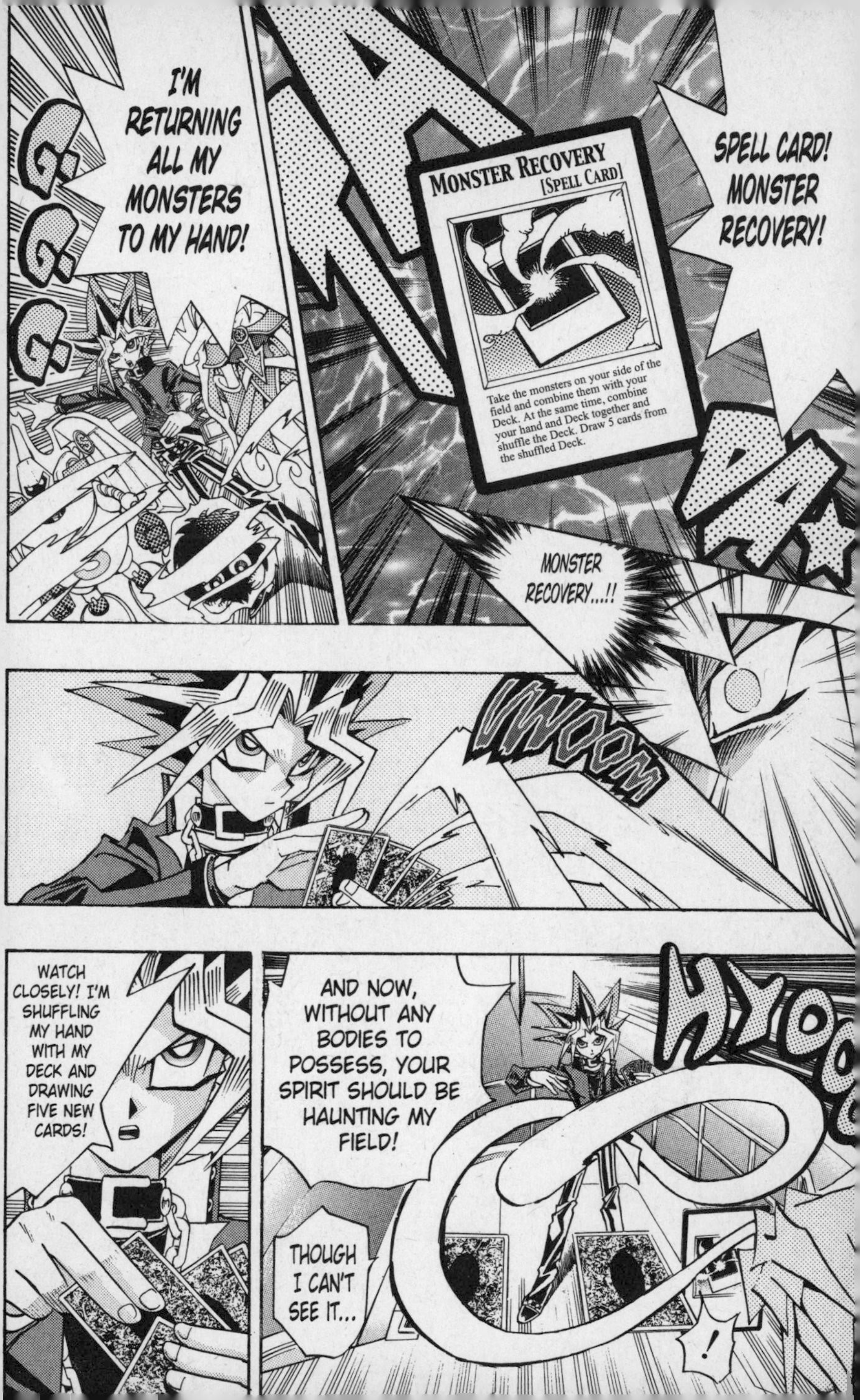
SPELL CARD! MONSTER RECOVERY!
MONSTER RECOVERY
[SPELL CARD]
Take the monsters on your side of the field and combine them with your Deck. At the same time, combine your hand and Deck together and shuffle the Deck. Draw 5 cards from the shuffled Deck.
I'M RETURNING ALL MY MONSTERS TO MY HAND!
MONSTER RECOVERY...!!
VWOOM
AND NOW, WITHOUT ANY BODIES TO POSSESS, YOUR SPIRIT SHOULD BE HAUNTING MY FIELD!
THOUGH I CAN'T SEE IT...
!
WATCH CLOSELY! I'M SHUFFLING MY HAND WITH MY DECK AND DRAWING FIVE NEW CARDS!

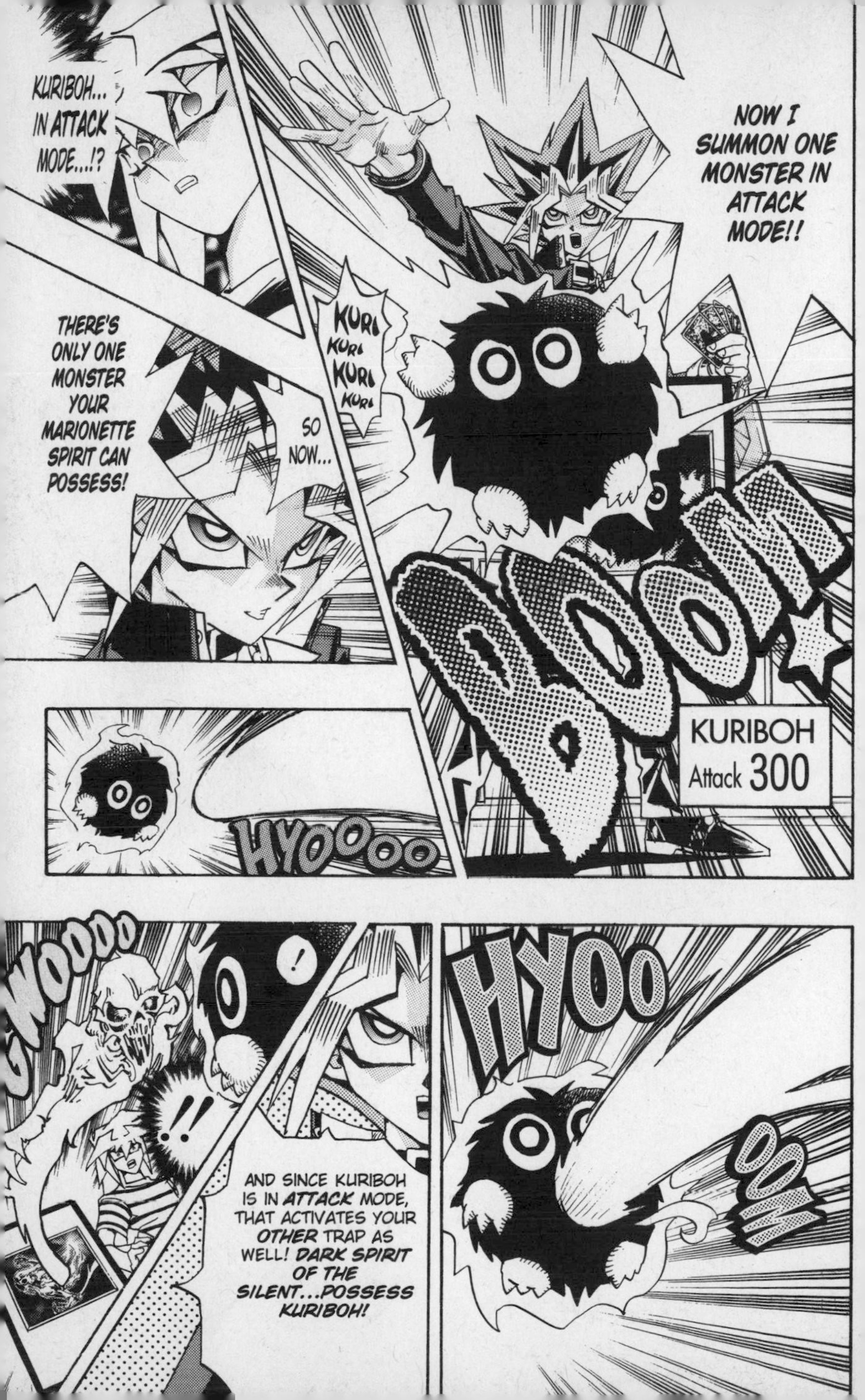
NOW I SUMMON ONE MONSTER IN ATTACK MODE!!
KURI KURI KURI KURI
BOOM
KURIBOH Attack 300
KURIBOH... IN ATTACK MODE...!?
THERE'S ONLY ONE MONSTER YOUR MARIONETTE SPIRIT CAN POSSESS!
SO NOW...
HYOOOOO
HYOO
OOOM
GWOOOO
!
!!
AND SINCE KURIBOH IS IN *ATTACK* MODE, THAT ACTIVATES YOUR *OTHER* TRAP AS WELL! *DARK SPIRIT OF THE SILENT...POSSESS KURIBOH!*

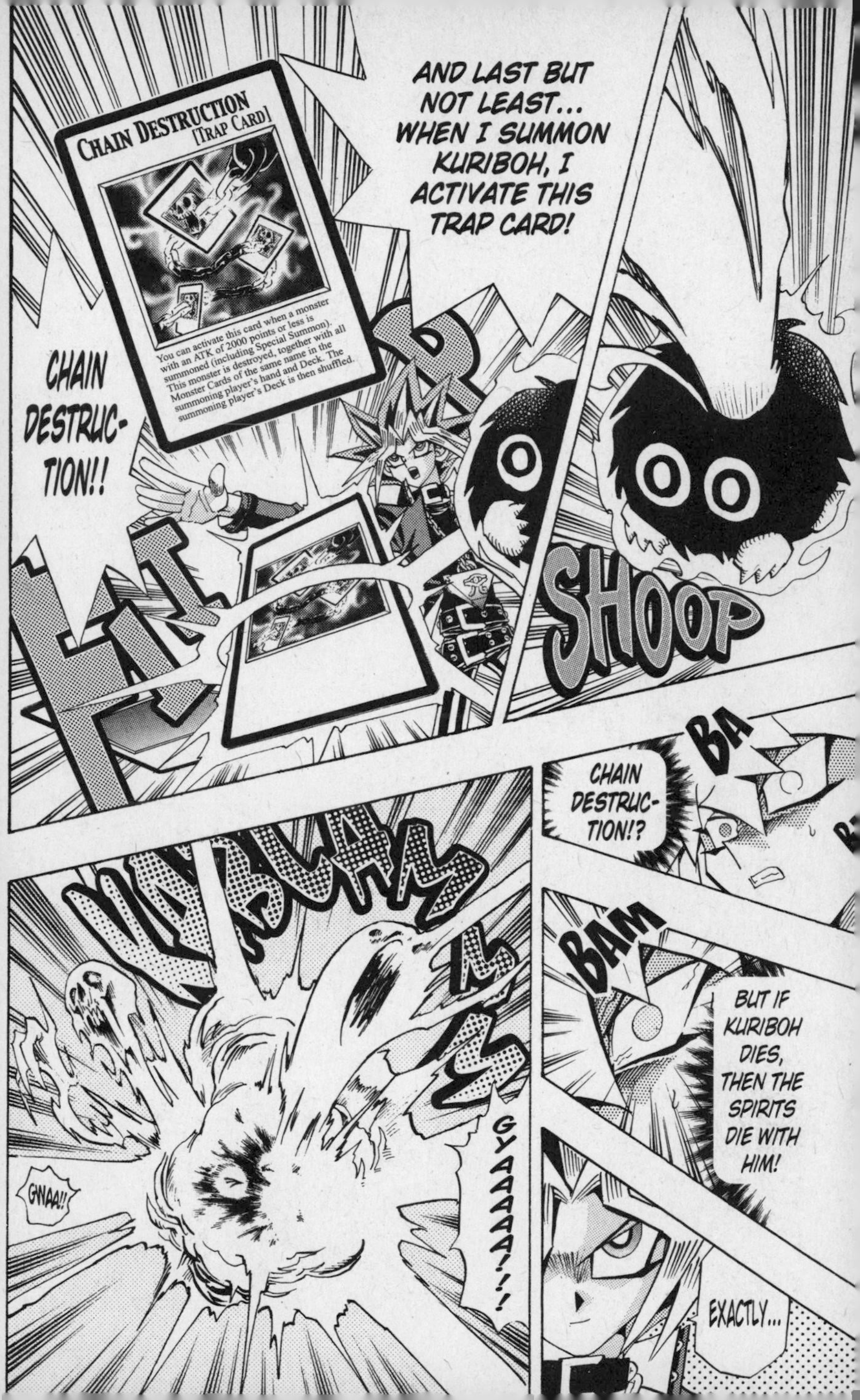

SHOOP
AND LAST BUT NOT LEAST... WHEN I SUMMON KURIBOH, I ACTIVATE THIS TRAP CARD!
CHAIN DESTRUCTION
[TRAP CARD]
You can activate this card when a monster with an ATK of 2000 points or less is summoned (including Special Summon). This monster is destroyed, together with all Monster Cards of the same name in the summoning player's hand and Deck. The summoning player's Deck is then shuffled.
CHAIN DESTRUCTION!!
BA
CHAIN DESTRUCTION!?
BAM
BUT IF KURIBOH DIES, THEN THE SPIRITS DIE WITH HIM!
EXACTLY...
GYAAAAA!!!
GWAA!!

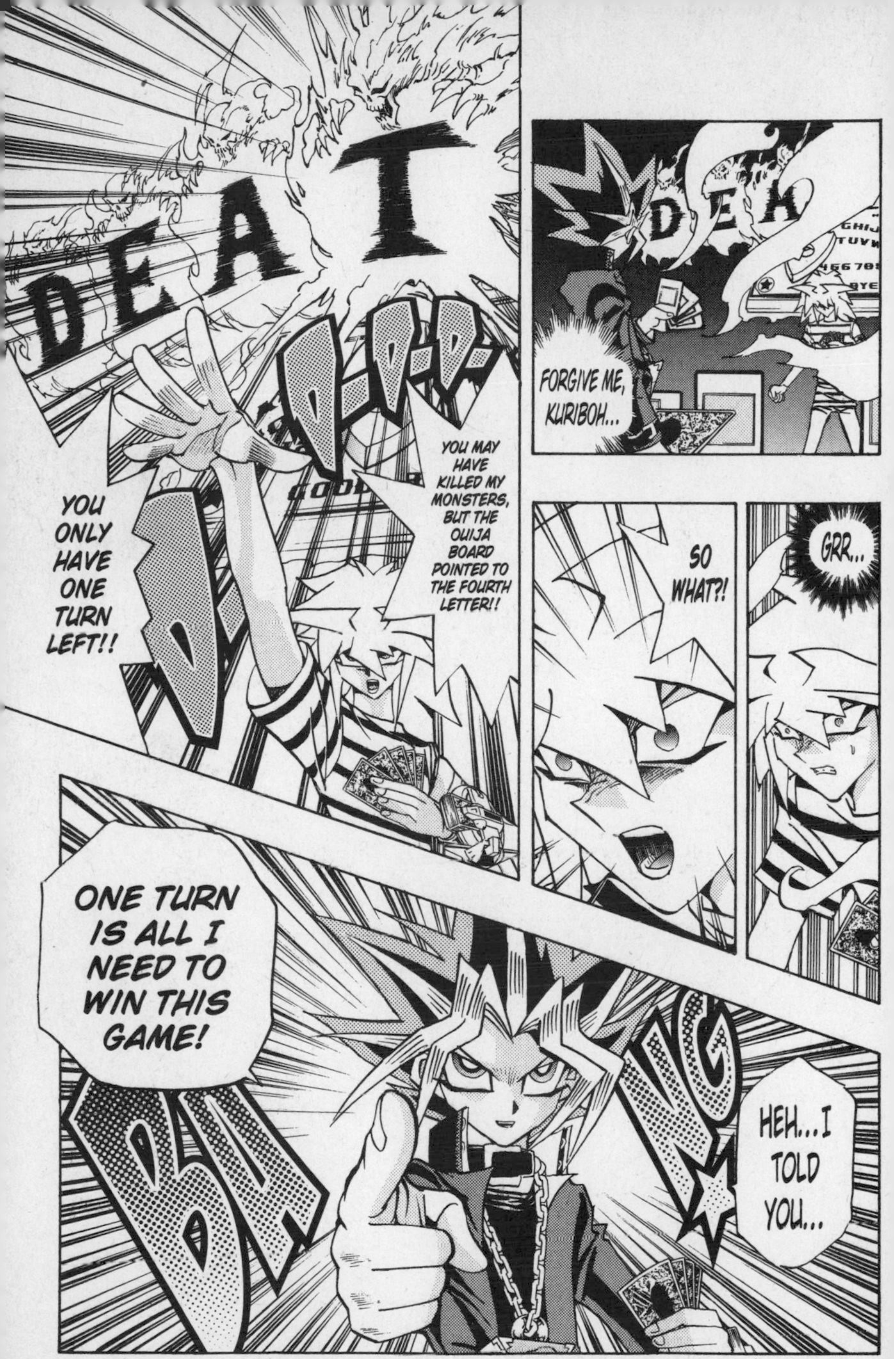
DEA
FORGIVE ME, KURIBOH...
GRR...
SO WHAT?!
DEAT
D-D-D-
YOU MAY HAVE KILLED MY MONSTERS, BUT THE OUIJA BOARD POINTED TO THE FOURTH LETTER!!
YOU ONLY HAVE ONE TURN LEFT!!
D-
HEH...I TOLD YOU...
BANG
ONE TURN IS ALL I NEED TO WIN THIS GAME!

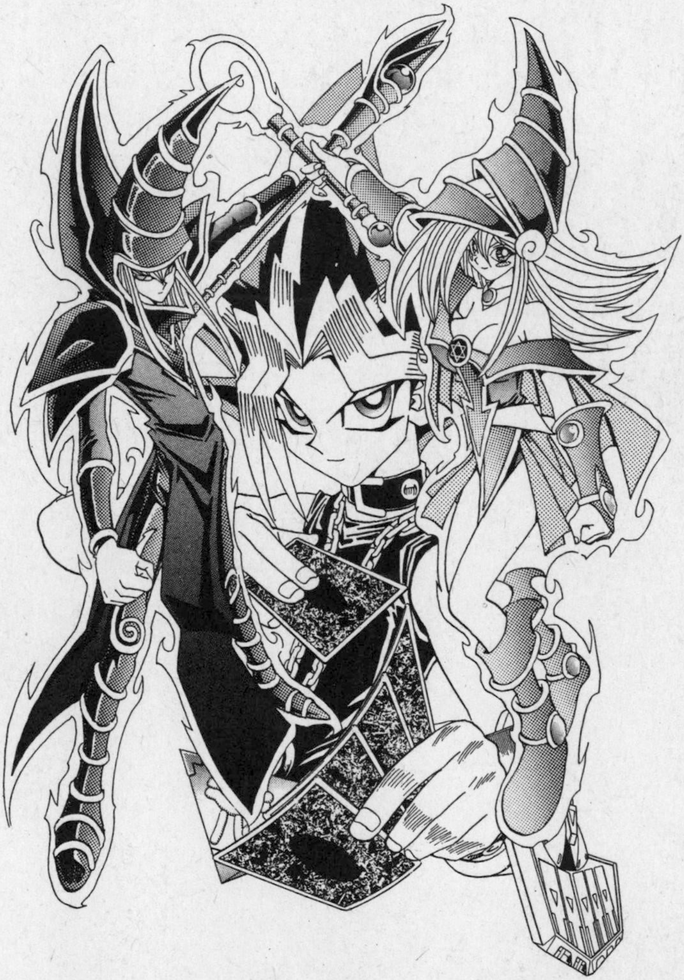

Duel 148: One-Turn Kill!

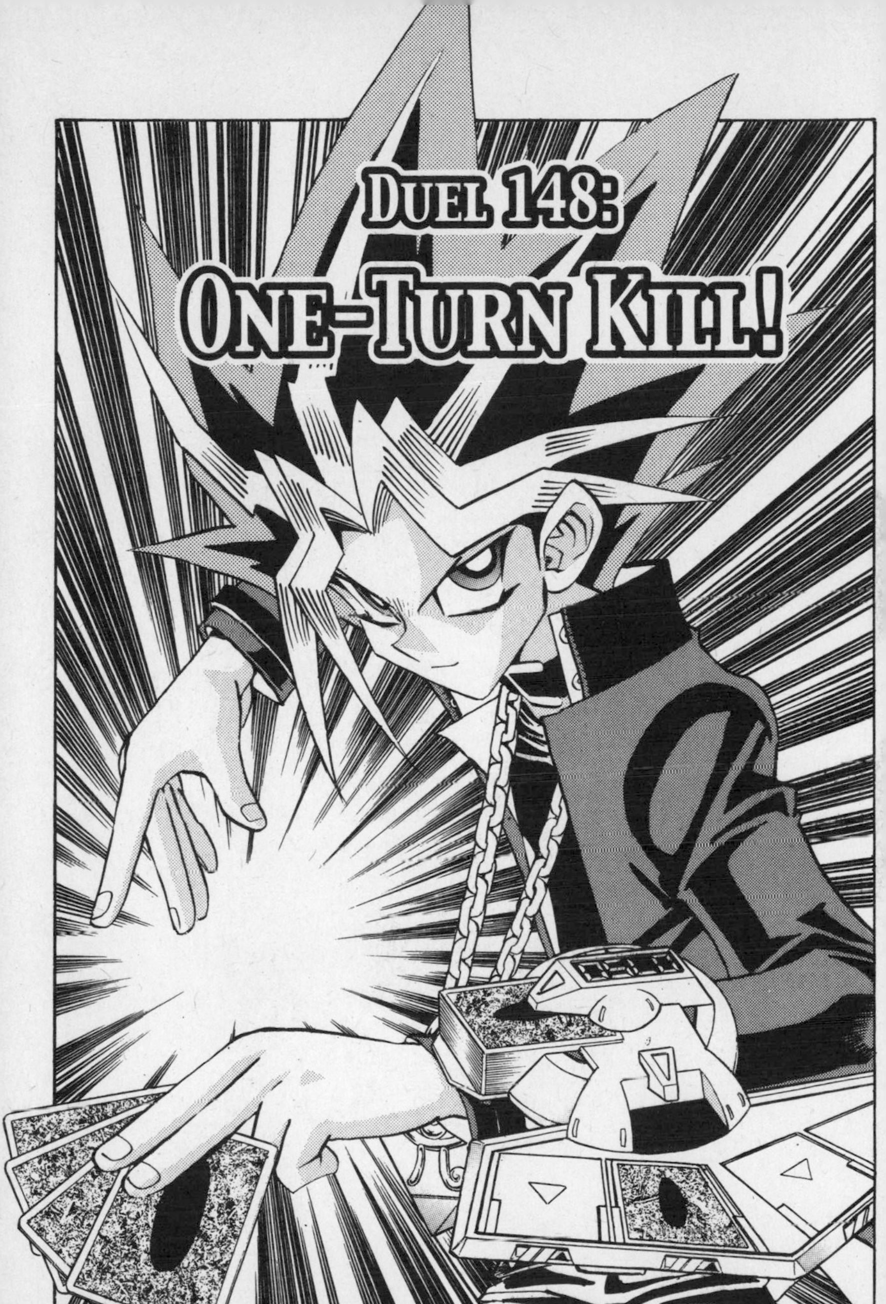

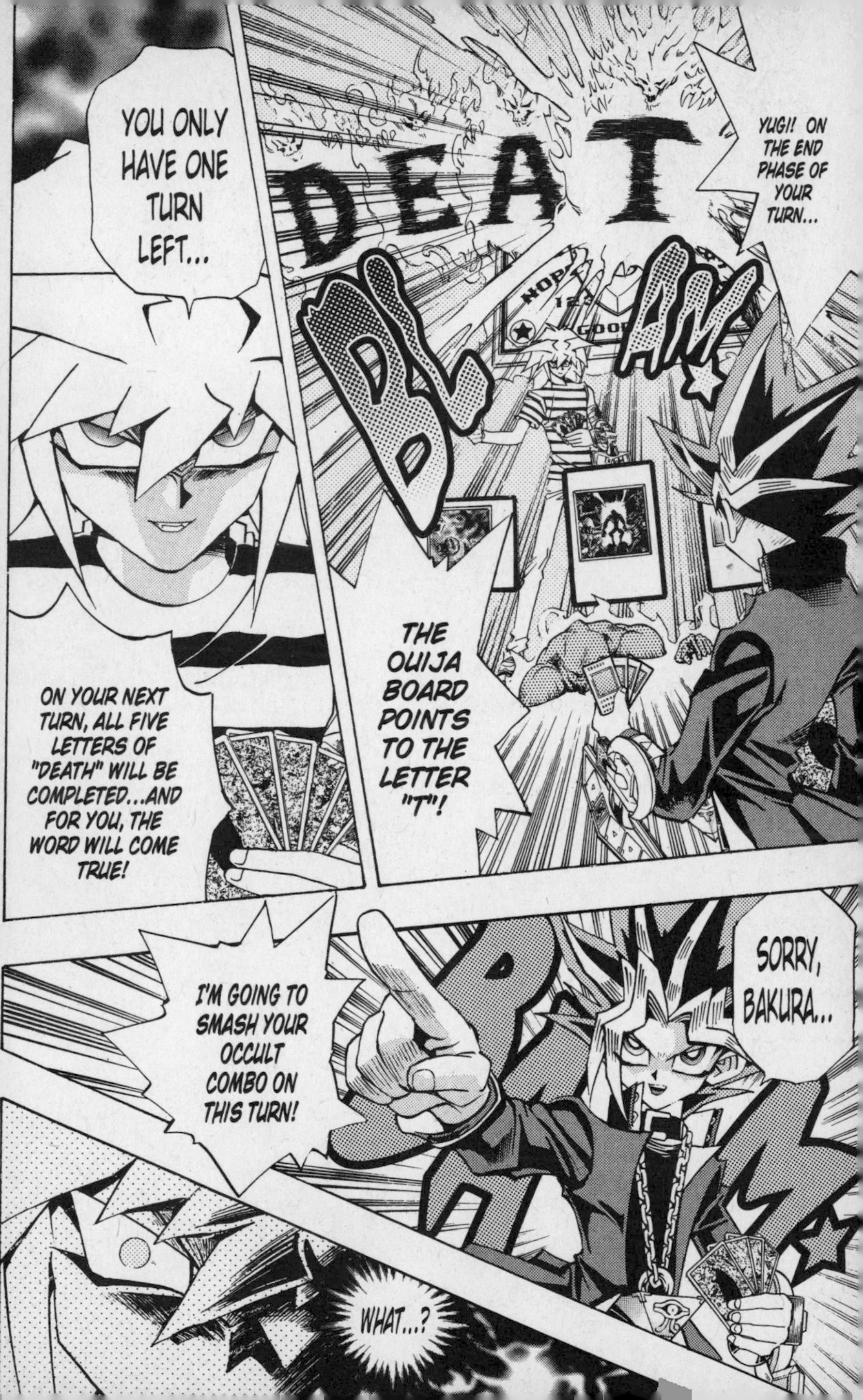
YUGI! ON THE END PHASE OF YOUR TURN...
DEAT
BLAM!
THE OUIJA BOARD POINTS TO THE LETTER "T"!
YOU ONLY HAVE ONE TURN LEFT...
ON YOUR NEXT TURN, ALL FIVE LETTERS OF "DEATH" WILL BE COMPLETED...AND FOR YOU, THE WORD WILL COME TRUE!
SORRY, BAKURA...
I'M GOING TO SMASH YOUR OCCULT COMBO ON THIS TURN!
WHAT...?

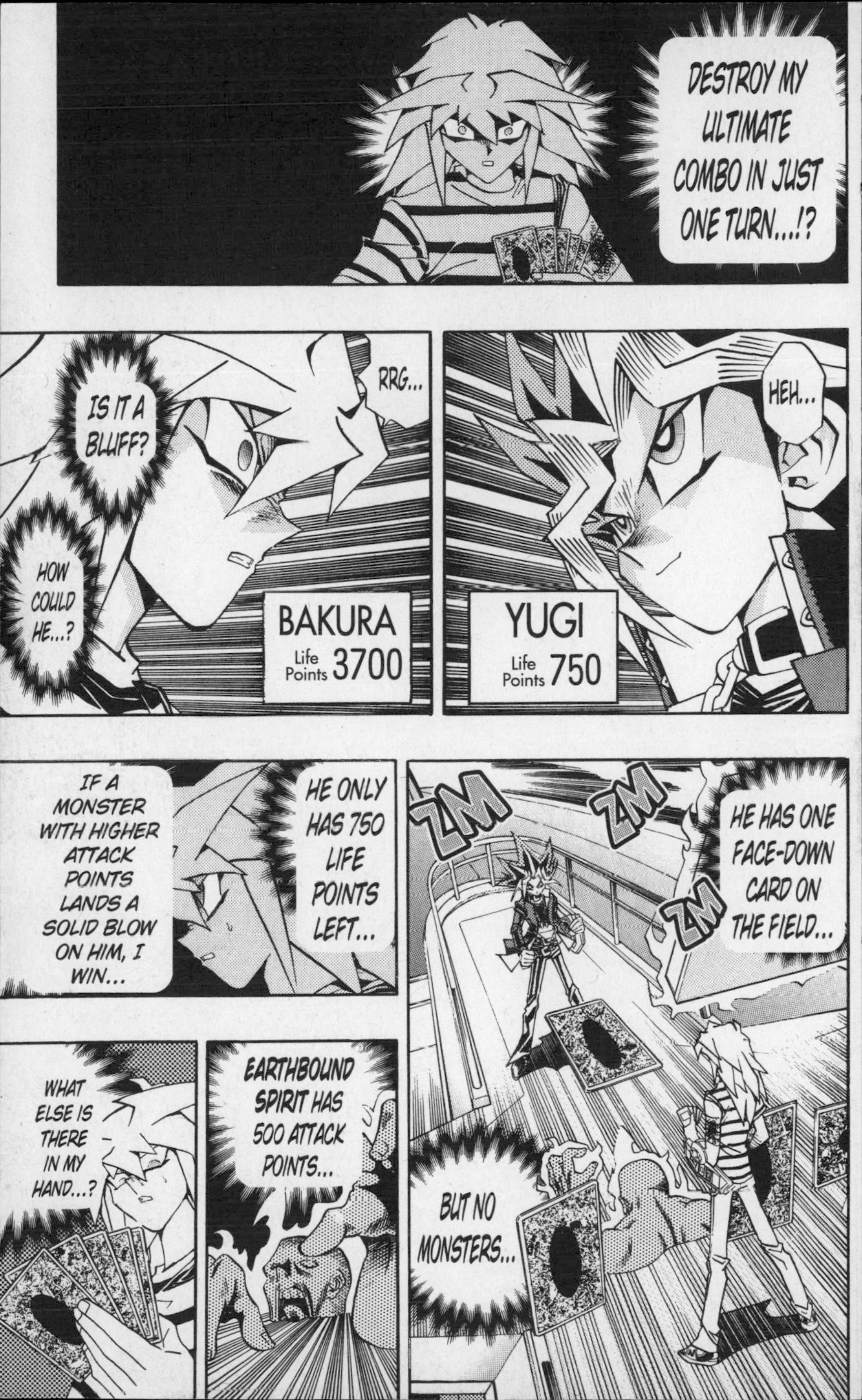
DESTROY MY ULTIMATE COMBO IN JUST ONE TURN...!?
HEH...
YUGI
Life Points 750
RRG...
IS IT A BLUFF?
HOW COULD HE...?
BAKURA
Life Points 3700
ZM
ZM
HE HAS ONE FACE-DOWN CARD ON THE FIELD...
ZM
BUT NO MONSTERS...
HE ONLY HAS 750 LIFE POINTS LEFT...
IF A MONSTER WITH HIGHER ATTACK POINTS LANDS A SOLID BLOW ON HIM, I WIN...
EARTHBOUND SPIRIT HAS 500 ATTACK POINTS...
WHAT ELSE IS THERE IN MY HAND...?

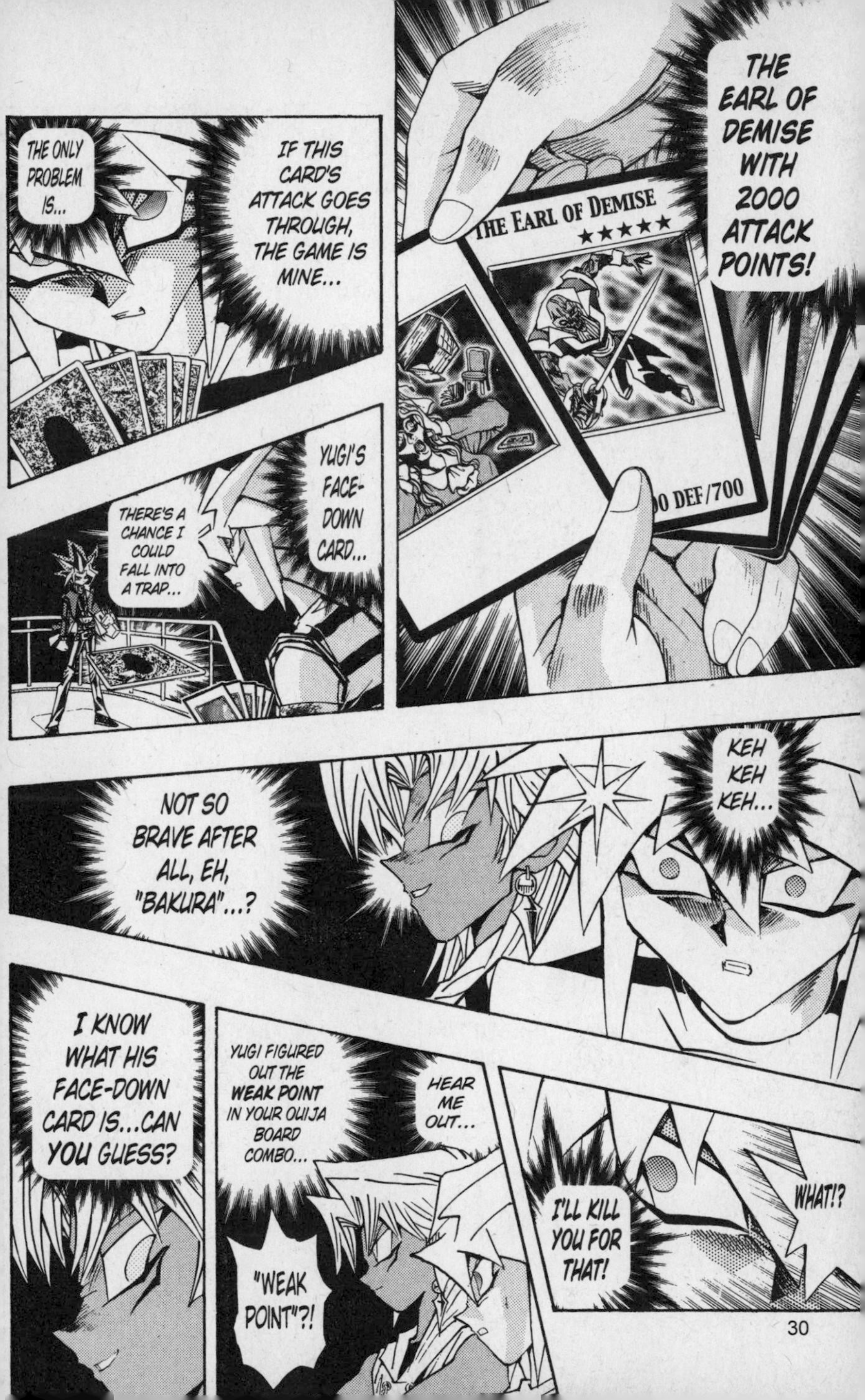
THE EARL OF DEMISE WITH 2000 ATTACK POINTS!
THE EARL OF DEMISE
00 DEF/700
IF THIS CARD'S ATTACK GOES THROUGH, THE GAME IS MINE...
THE ONLY PROBLEM IS...
YUGI'S FACE-DOWN CARD...
THERE'S A CHANCE I COULD FALL INTO A TRAP...
KEH KEH KEH...
NOT SO BRAVE AFTER ALL, EH, "BAKURA"...?
WHAT!?
I'LL KILL YOU FOR THAT!
HEAR ME OUT...
YUGI FIGURED OUT THE WEAK POINT IN YOUR OUIJA BOARD COMBO...
"WEAK POINT"?!
I KNOW WHAT HIS FACE-DOWN CARD IS...CAN YOU GUESS?

READ THIS WAY

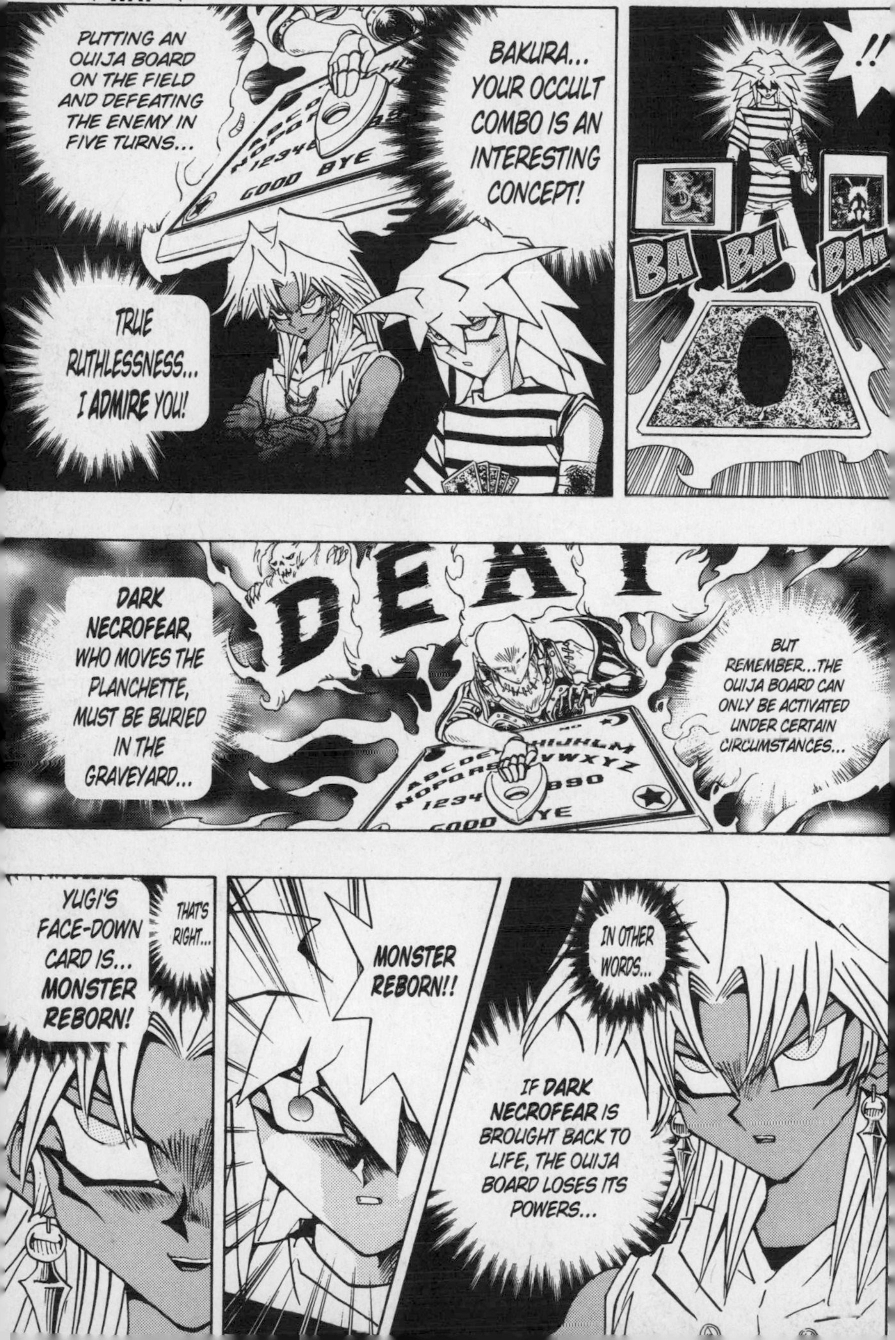
!!
BA BA BAM
BAKURA... YOUR OCCULT COMBO IS AN INTERESTING CONCEPT!
PUTTING AN OUIJA BOARD ON THE FIELD AND DEFEATING THE ENEMY IN FIVE TURNS...
GOOD BYE
TRUE RUTHLESSNESS... I ADMIRE YOU!
BUT REMEMBER...THE OUIJA BOARD CAN ONLY BE ACTIVATED UNDER CERTAIN CIRCUMSTANCES...
DEAT
DARK NECROFEAR, WHO MOVES THE PLANCHETTE, MUST BE BURIED IN THE GRAVEYARD...
IN OTHER WORDS...
IF DARK NECROFEAR IS BROUGHT BACK TO LIFE, THE OUIJA BOARD LOSES ITS POWERS...
MONSTER REBORN!!
THAT'S RIGHT...
YUGI'S FACE-DOWN CARD IS... MONSTER REBORN!

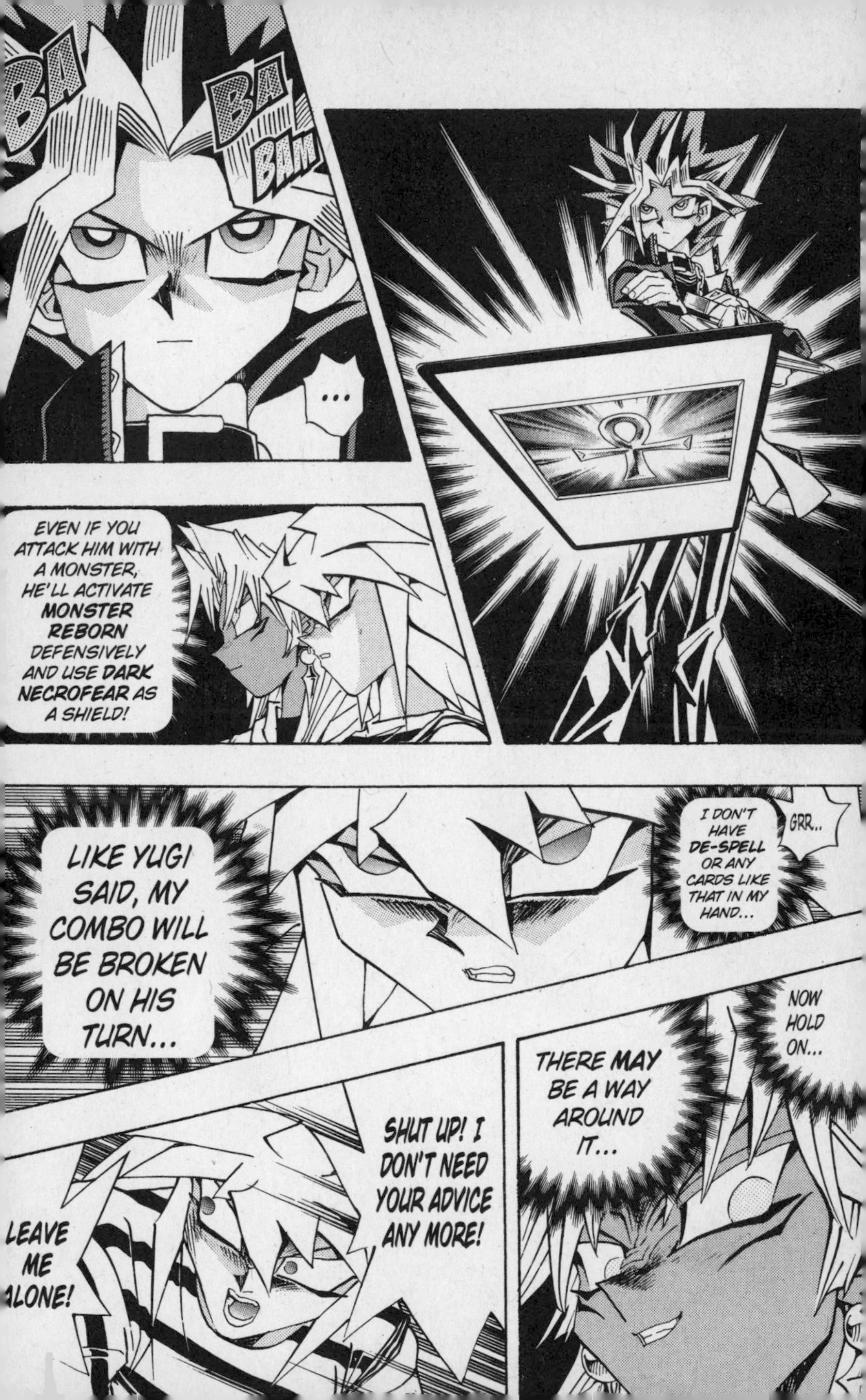

BA
BA BAM
...
EVEN IF YOU ATTACK HIM WITH A MONSTER, HE'LL ACTIVATE **MONSTER REBORN** DEFENSIVELY AND USE **DARK NECROFEAR** AS A SHIELD!
GRR...
I DON'T HAVE **DE-SPELL** OR ANY CARDS LIKE THAT IN MY HAND...
LIKE YUGI SAID, MY COMBO WILL BE BROKEN ON HIS TURN...
NOW HOLD ON...
THERE MAY BE A WAY AROUND IT...
SHUT UP! I DON'T NEED YOUR ADVICE ANY MORE!
LEAVE ME ALONE!

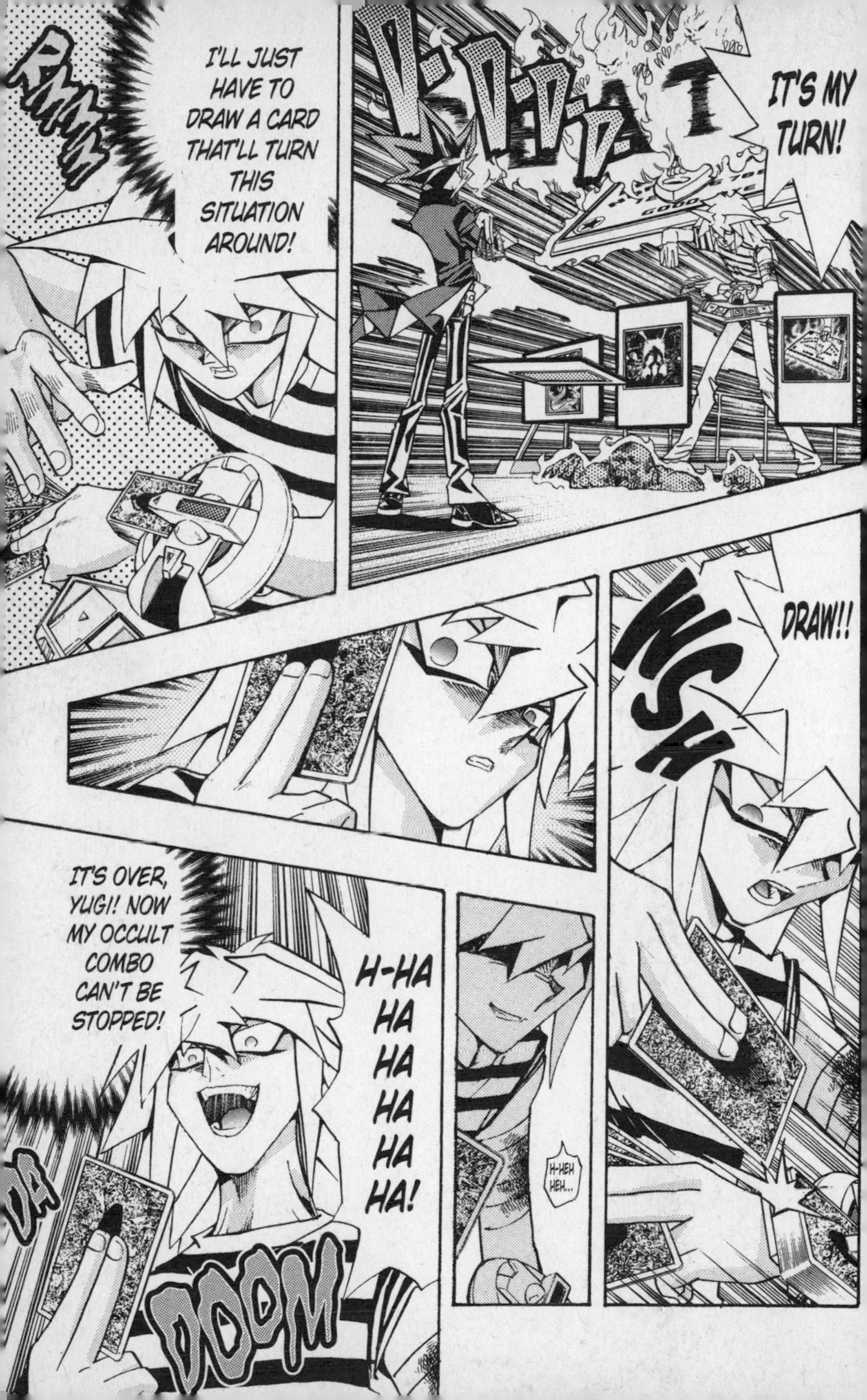
IT'S MY TURN!
D-D-D-DAT
RMMM
I'LL JUST HAVE TO DRAW A CARD THAT'LL TURN THIS SITUATION AROUND!
DRAW!!
WSH
H-HEH HEH...
IT'S OVER, YUGI! NOW MY OCCULT COMBO CAN'T BE STOPPED!
H-HA HA HA HA HA HA HA!
DOOM

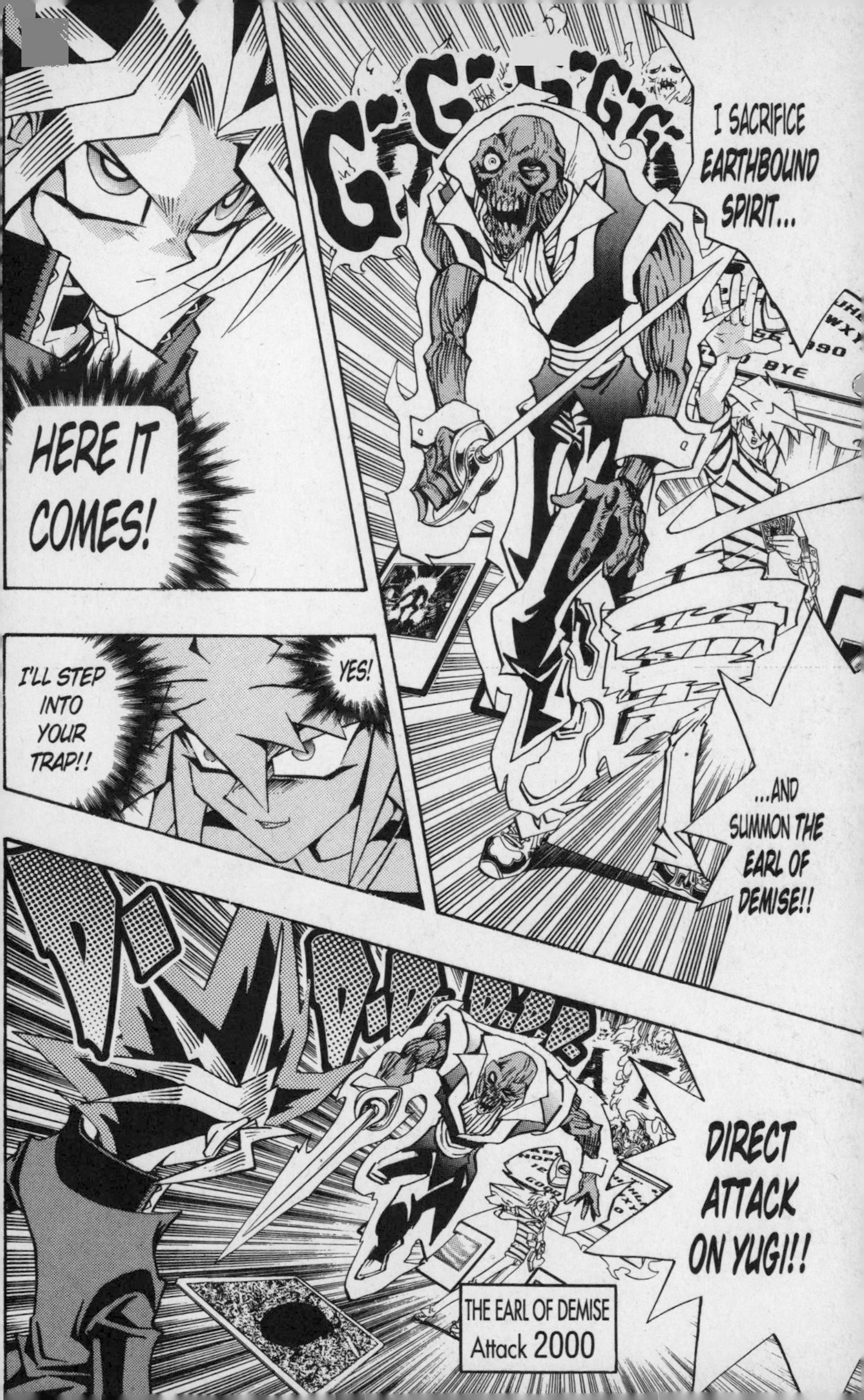
I SACRIFICE EARTHBOUND SPIRIT...
...AND SUMMON THE EARL OF DEMISE!!
HERE IT COMES!
YES!
I'LL STEP INTO YOUR TRAP!!
DIRECT ATTACK ON YUGI!!
THE EARL OF DEMISE
Attack 2000

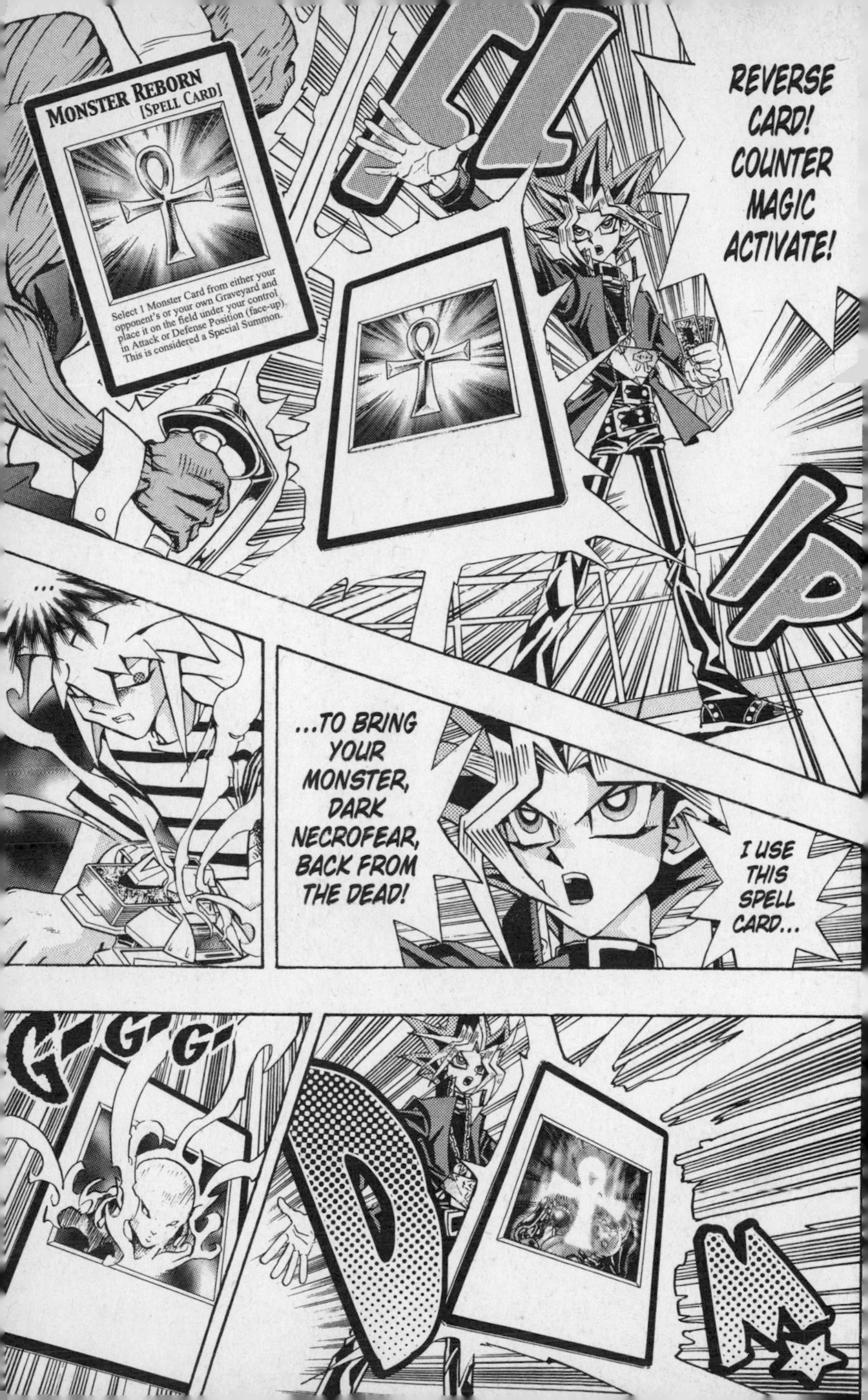
CLIP
REVERSE CARD! COUNTER MAGIC ACTIVATE!
MONSTER REBORN
[SPELL CARD]
Select 1 Monster Card from either your opponent's or your own Graveyard and place it on the field under your control in Attack or Defense Position (face-up). This is considered a Special Summon.
I USE THIS SPELL CARD...
...TO BRING YOUR MONSTER, DARK NECROFEAR, BACK FROM THE DEAD!
...
G-G-G-

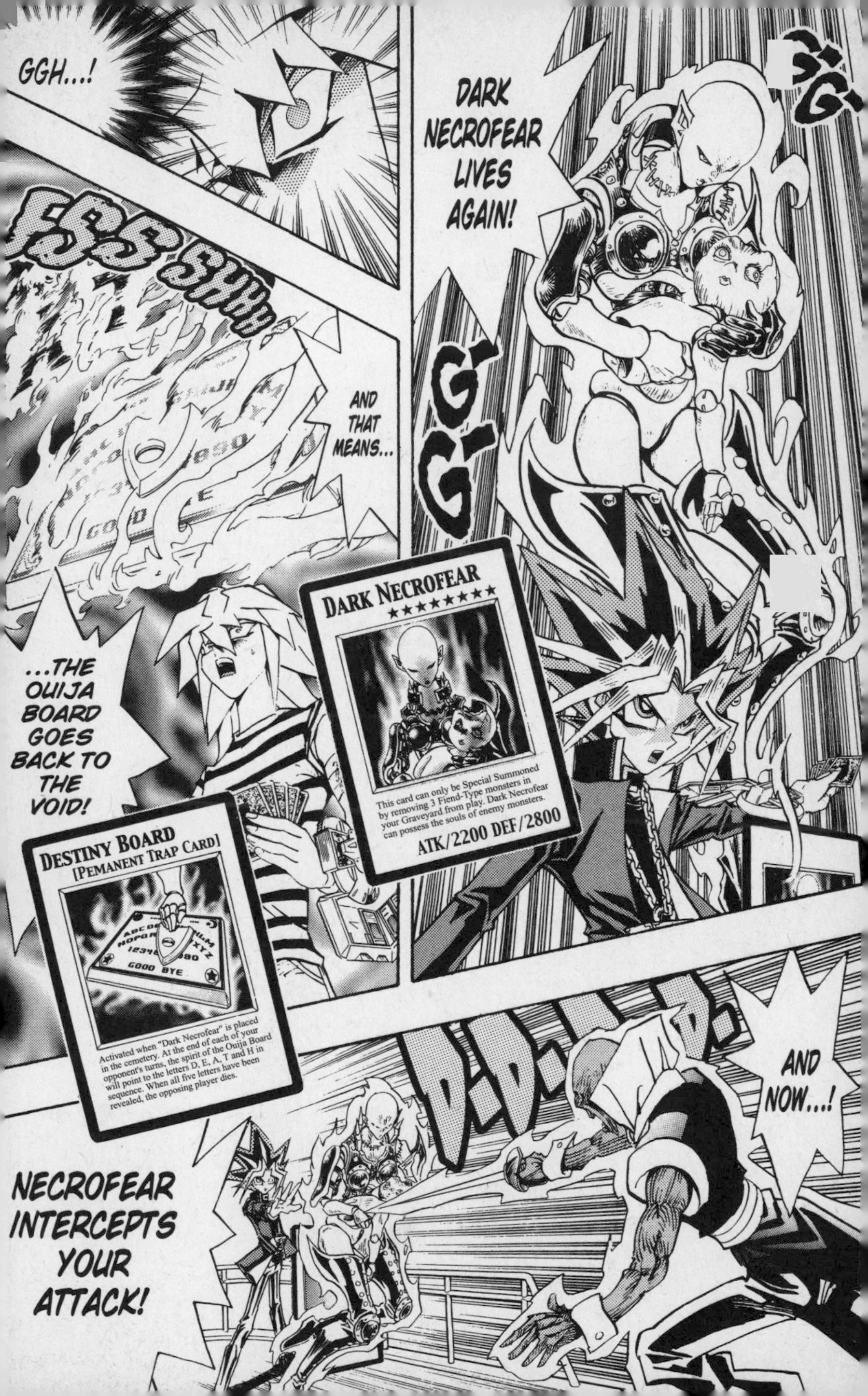

DARK NECROFEAR LIVES AGAIN!
G-G-
G-G-
GGH...!
FSSSHHH
AND THAT MEANS...
...THE OUIJA BOARD GOES BACK TO THE VOID!
DARK NECROFEAR
★★★★★★★★
This card can only be Special Summoned by removing 3 Fiend-Type monsters in your Graveyard from play. Dark Necrofear can possess the souls of enemy monsters.
ATK/2200 DEF/2800
DESTINY BOARD
[PEMANENT TRAP CARD]
GOOD BYE
Activated when "Dark Necrofear" is placed in the cemetery. At the end of each of your opponent's turns, the spirit of the Ouija Board will point to the letters D, E, A, T and H in sequence. When all five letters have been revealed, the opposing player dies.
AND NOW...!
D.D...
NECROFEAR INTERCEPTS YOUR ATTACK!

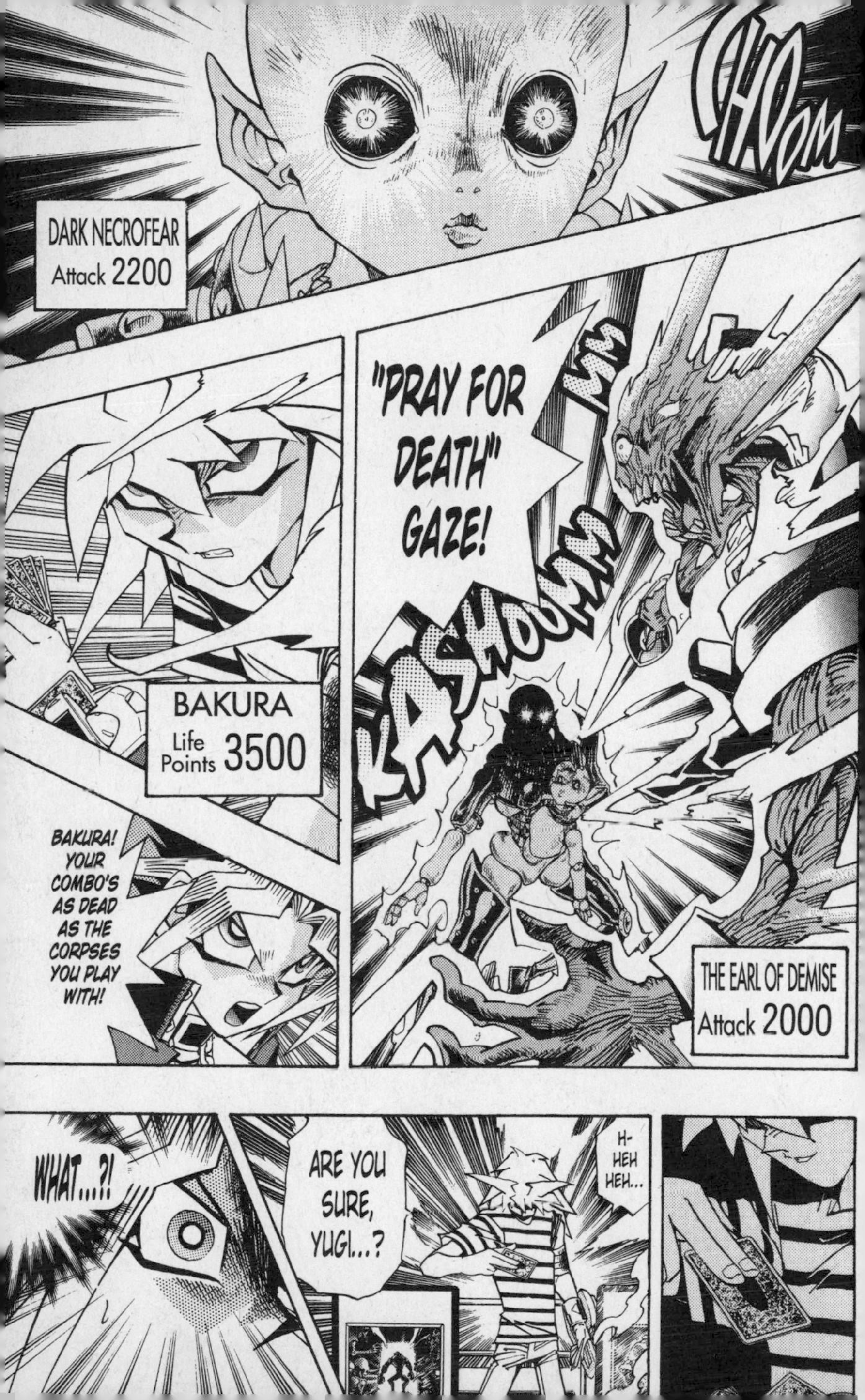

CHOOM
DARK NECROFEAR Attack 2200
"PRAY FOR DEATH" GAZE!
KASHOOMMM
THE EARL OF DEMISE Attack 2000
BAKURA Life Points 3500
BAKURA! YOUR COMBO'S AS DEAD AS THE CORPSES YOU PLAY WITH!
H-HEH HEH...
ARE YOU SURE, YUGI...?
WHAT...?!

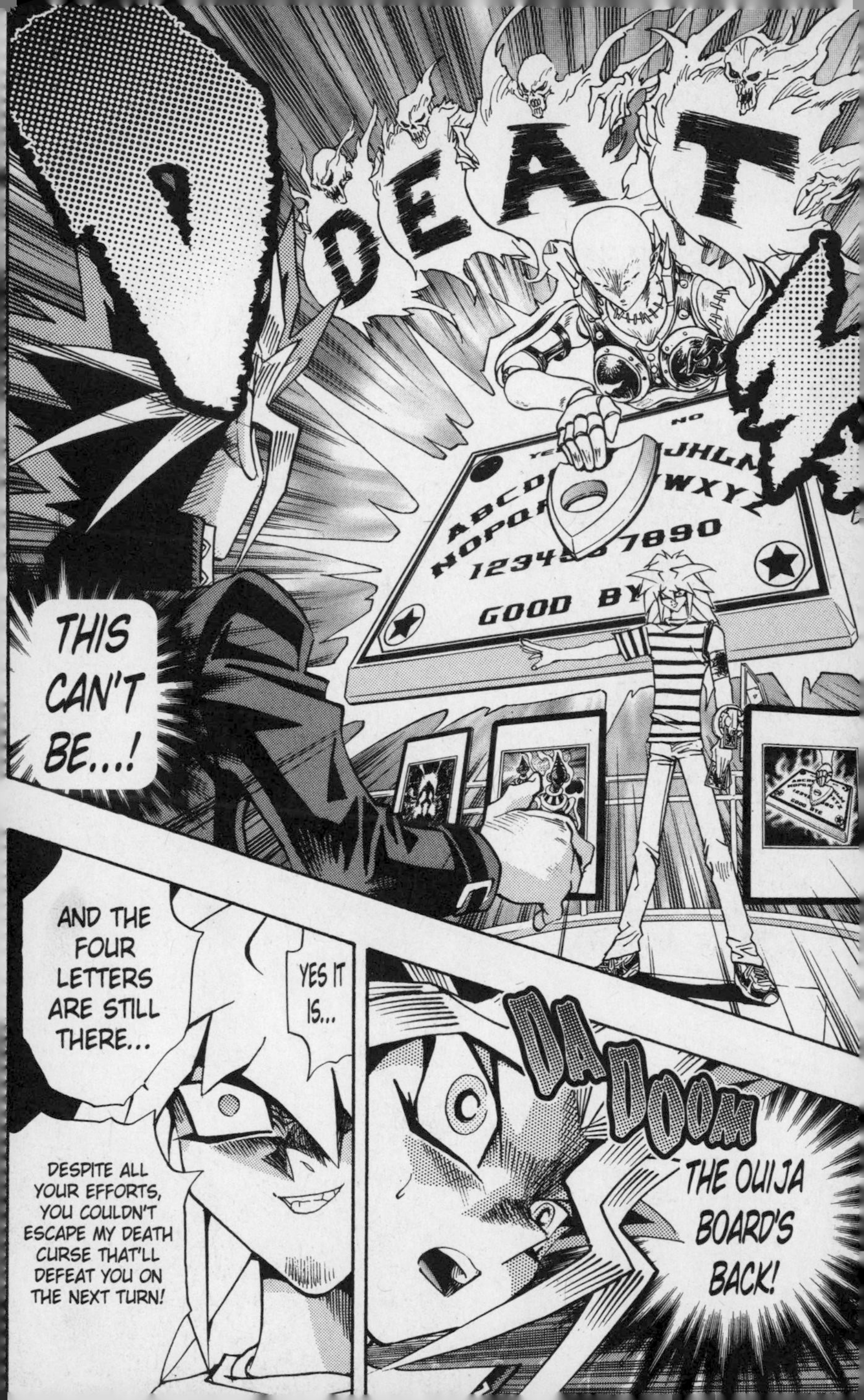
DEAT
THIS CAN'T BE...!
DA DOOM
THE OUIJA BOARD'S BACK!
YES IT IS...
AND THE FOUR LETTERS ARE STILL THERE...
DESPITE ALL YOUR EFFORTS, YOU COULDN'T ESCAPE MY DEATH CURSE THAT'LL DEFEAT YOU ON THE NEXT TURN!

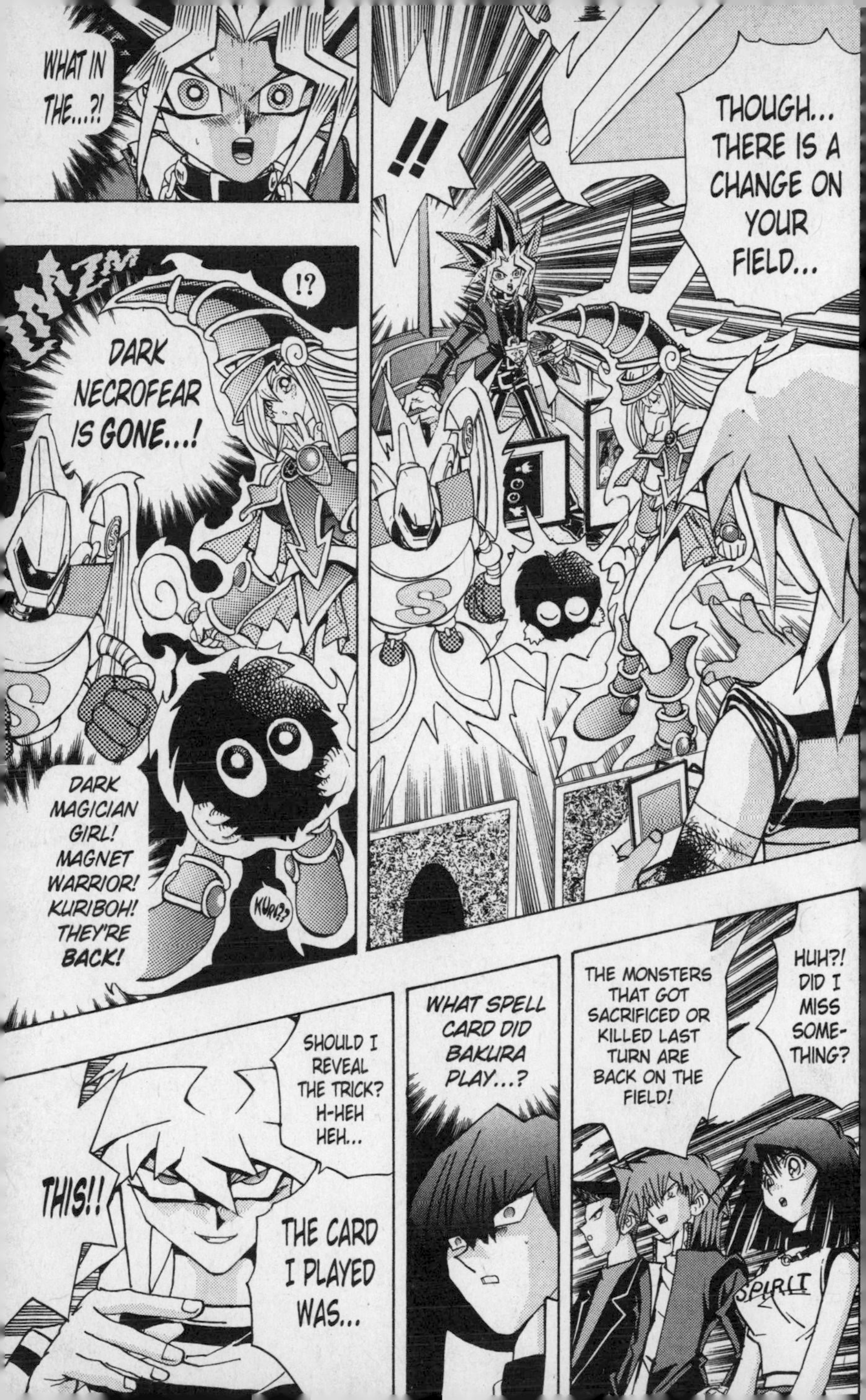

THOUGH... THERE IS A CHANGE ON YOUR FIELD...
!!
WHAT IN THE...?!
!?
DARK NECROFEAR IS GONE...!
DARK MAGICIAN GIRL! MAGNET WARRIOR! KURIBOH! THEY'RE BACK!
KURI!?
HUH?! DID I MISS SOME-THING?
THE MONSTERS THAT GOT SACRIFICED OR KILLED LAST TURN ARE BACK ON THE FIELD!
WHAT SPELL CARD DID BAKURA PLAY...?
SHOULD I REVEAL THE TRICK? H-HEH HEH...
THE CARD I PLAYED WAS...
THIS!!

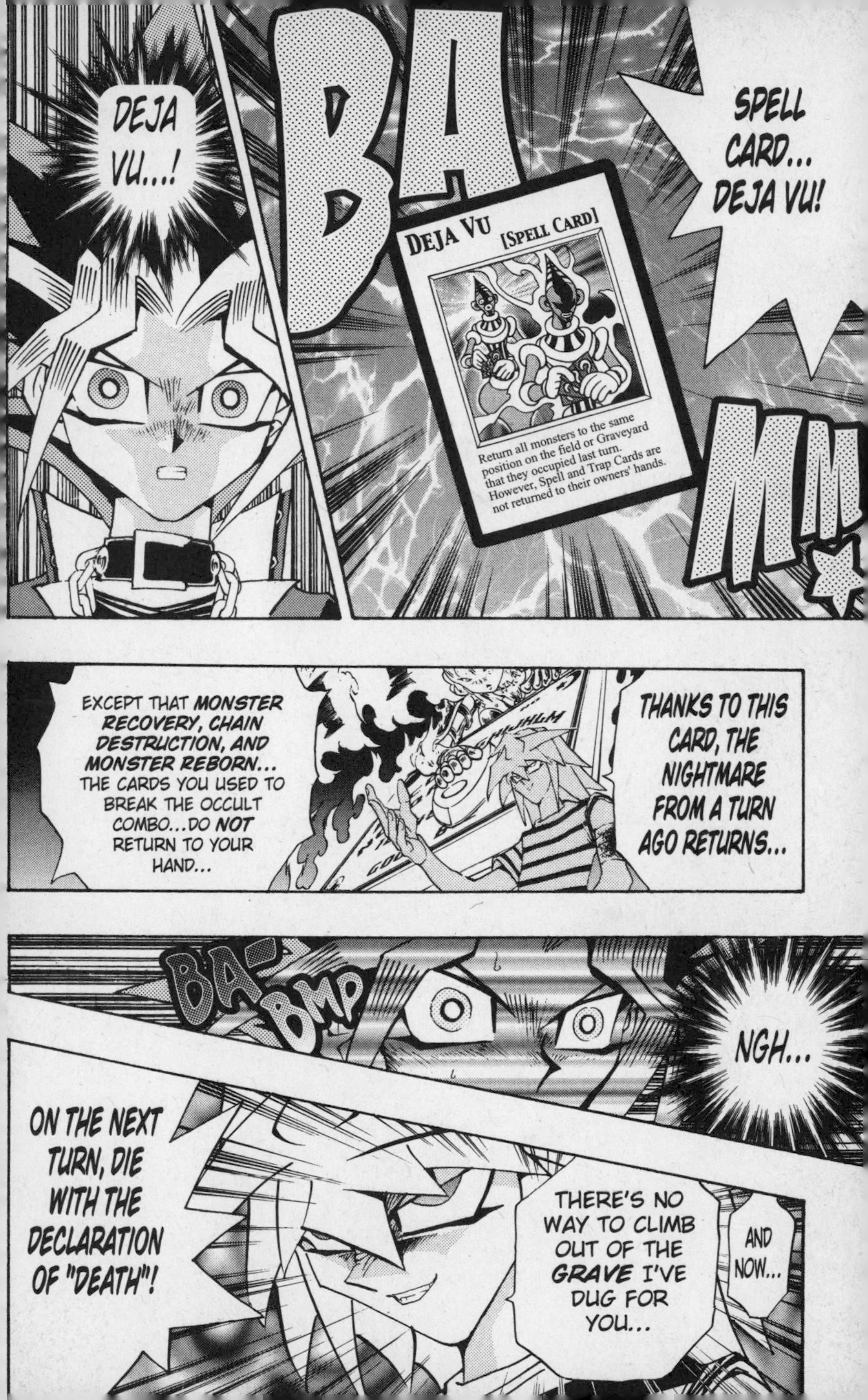
SPELL CARD... DEJA VU!
BA
DEJA VU [SPELL CARD]
Return all monsters to the same position on the field or Graveyard that they occupied last turn. However, Spell and Trap Cards are not returned to their owners' hands.
MM!!
DEJA VU...!
THANKS TO THIS CARD, THE NIGHTMARE FROM A TURN AGO RETURNS...
EXCEPT THAT MONSTER RECOVERY, CHAIN DESTRUCTION, AND MONSTER REBORN... THE CARDS YOU USED TO BREAK THE OCCULT COMBO...DO NOT RETURN TO YOUR HAND...
NGH...
BA-BMP
AND NOW...
THERE'S NO WAY TO CLIMB OUT OF THE GRAVE I'VE DUG FOR YOU...
ON THE NEXT TURN, DIE WITH THE DECLARATION OF "DEATH"!

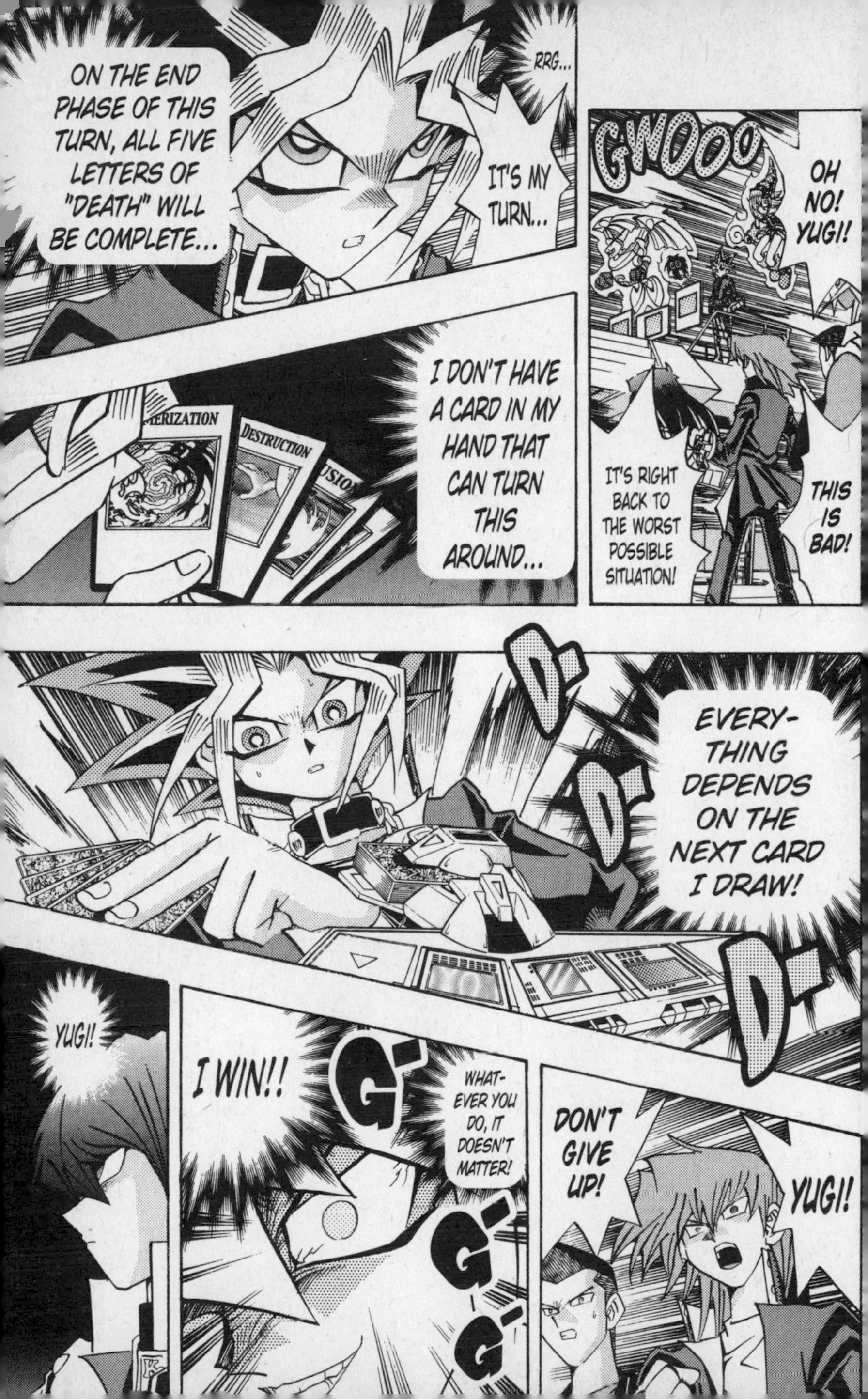
GWOOO
OH NO! YUGI!
THIS IS BAD!
IT'S RIGHT BACK TO THE WORST POSSIBLE SITUATION!
ON THE END PHASE OF THIS TURN, ALL FIVE LETTERS OF "DEATH" WILL BE COMPLETE...
RRG...
IT'S MY TURN...
DESTRUCTION
I DON'T HAVE A CARD IN MY HAND THAT CAN TURN THIS AROUND...
D
EVERYTHING DEPENDS ON THE NEXT CARD I DRAW!
D
D
YUGI!
DON'T GIVE UP!
WHATEVER YOU DO, IT DOESN'T MATTER!
G
G
G
I WIN!!
YUGI!

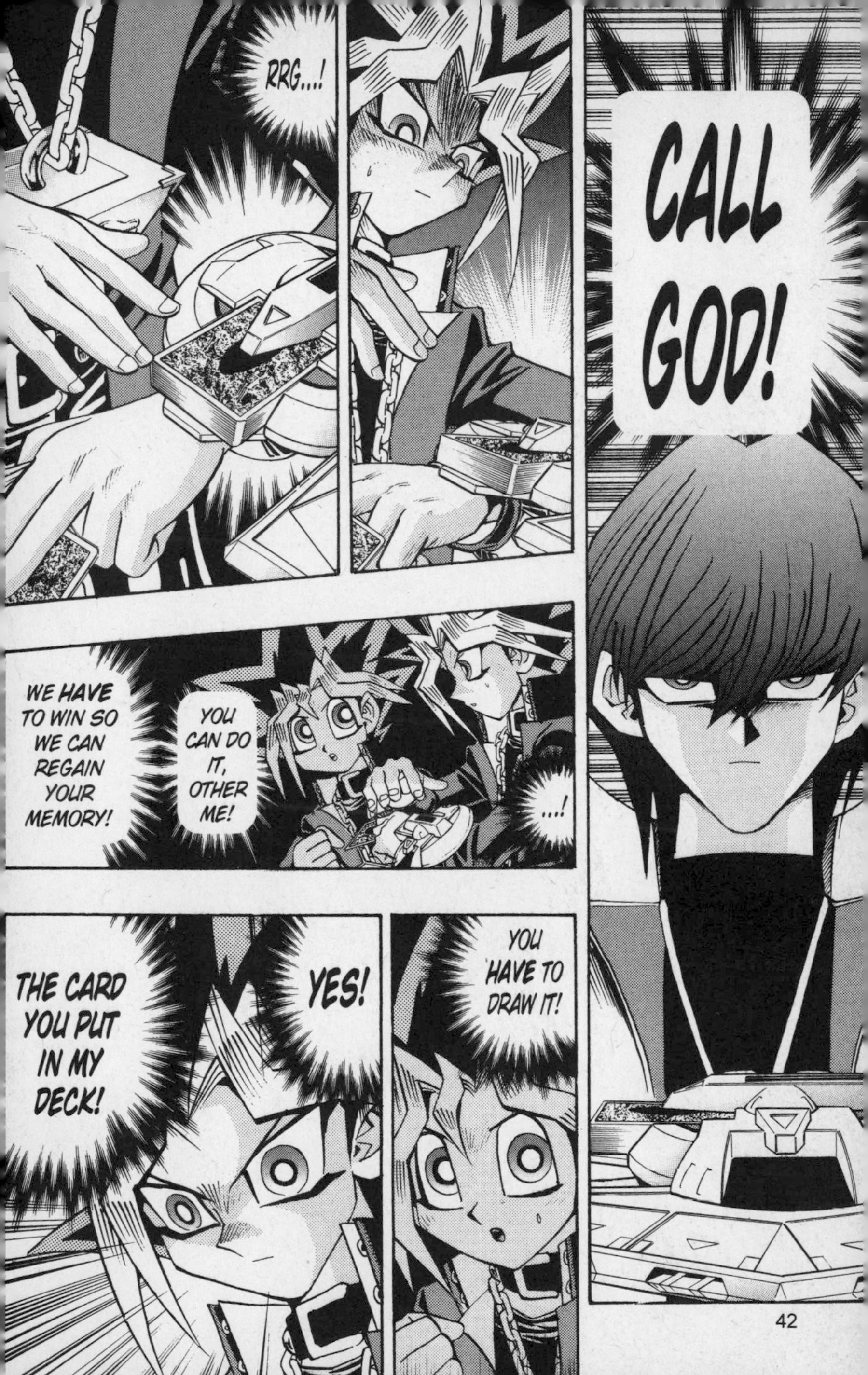
CALL GOD!
RRG...!
...!
YOU CAN DO IT, OTHER ME!
WE HAVE TO WIN SO WE CAN REGAIN YOUR MEMORY!
YOU HAVE TO DRAW IT!
YES!
THE CARD YOU PUT IN MY DECK!

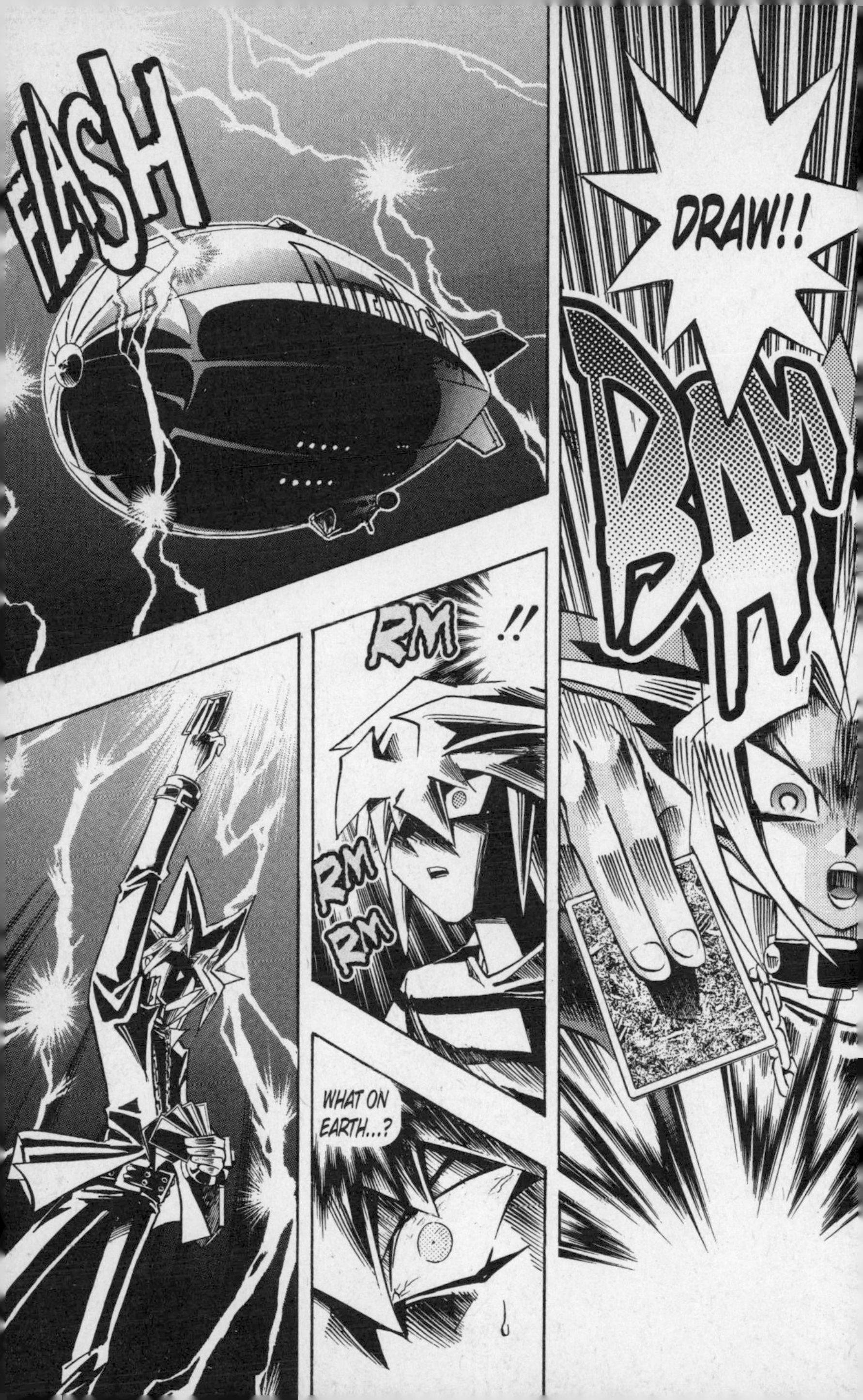
DRAW!!
BAM
FLASH
RM
!!
RM
RM
WHAT ON EARTH...?

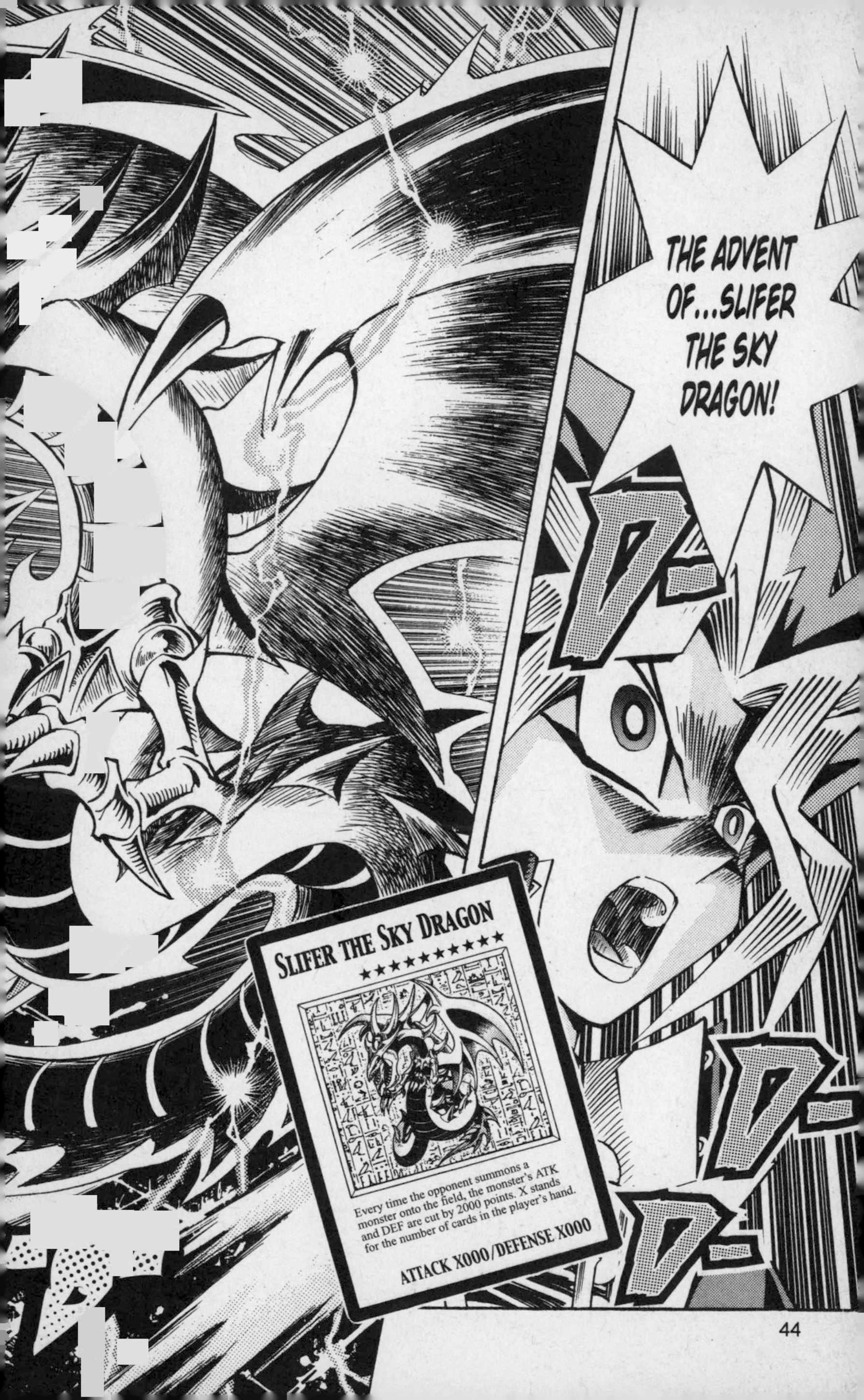
THE ADVENT OF...SLIFER THE SKY DRAGON!
D-
D-
D-
SLIFER THE SKY DRAGON
★★★★★★★★★★
Every time the opponent summons a monster onto the field, the monster's ATK and DEF are cut by 2000 points. X stands for the number of cards in the player's hand.
ATTACK X000/DEFENSE X000

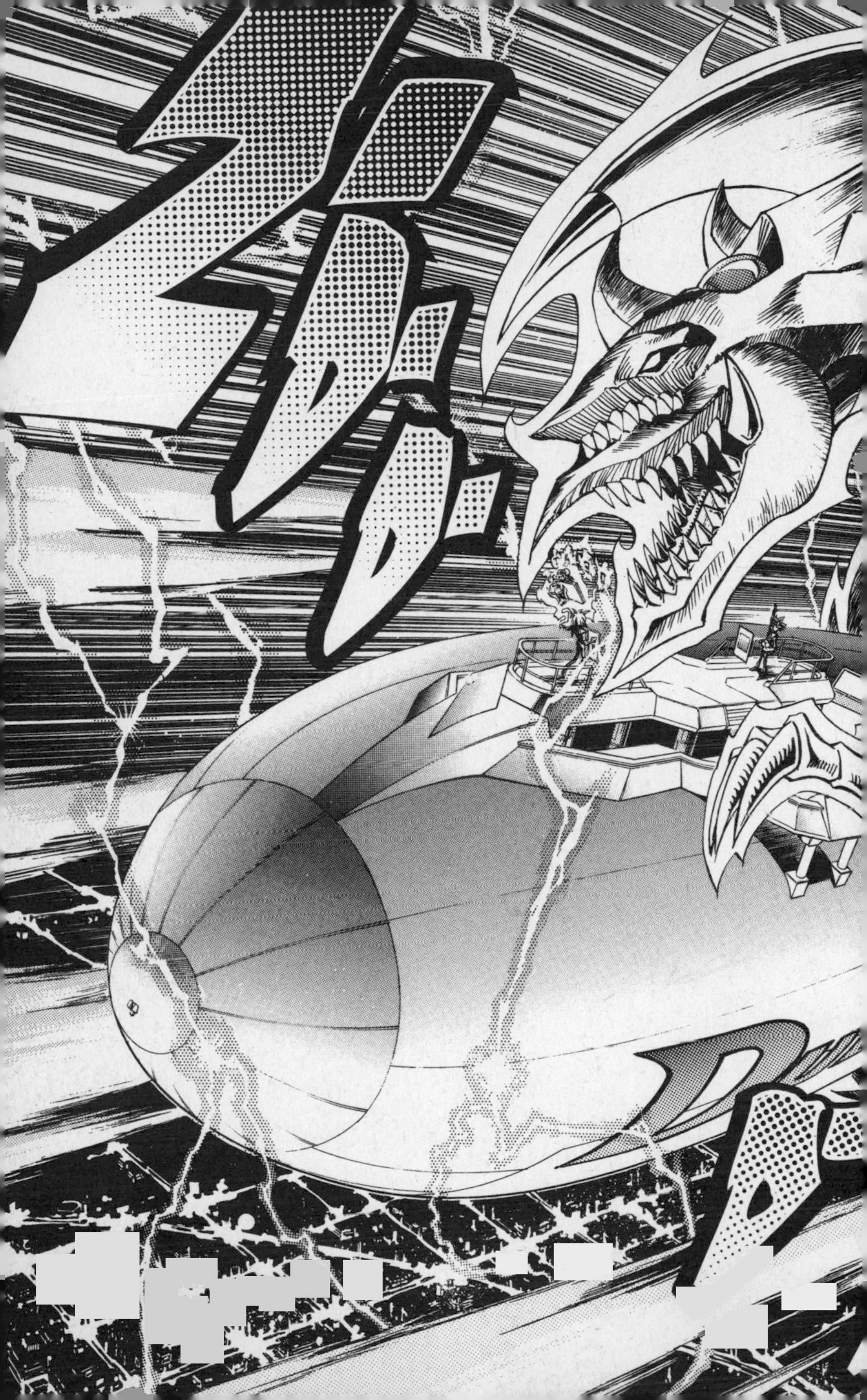

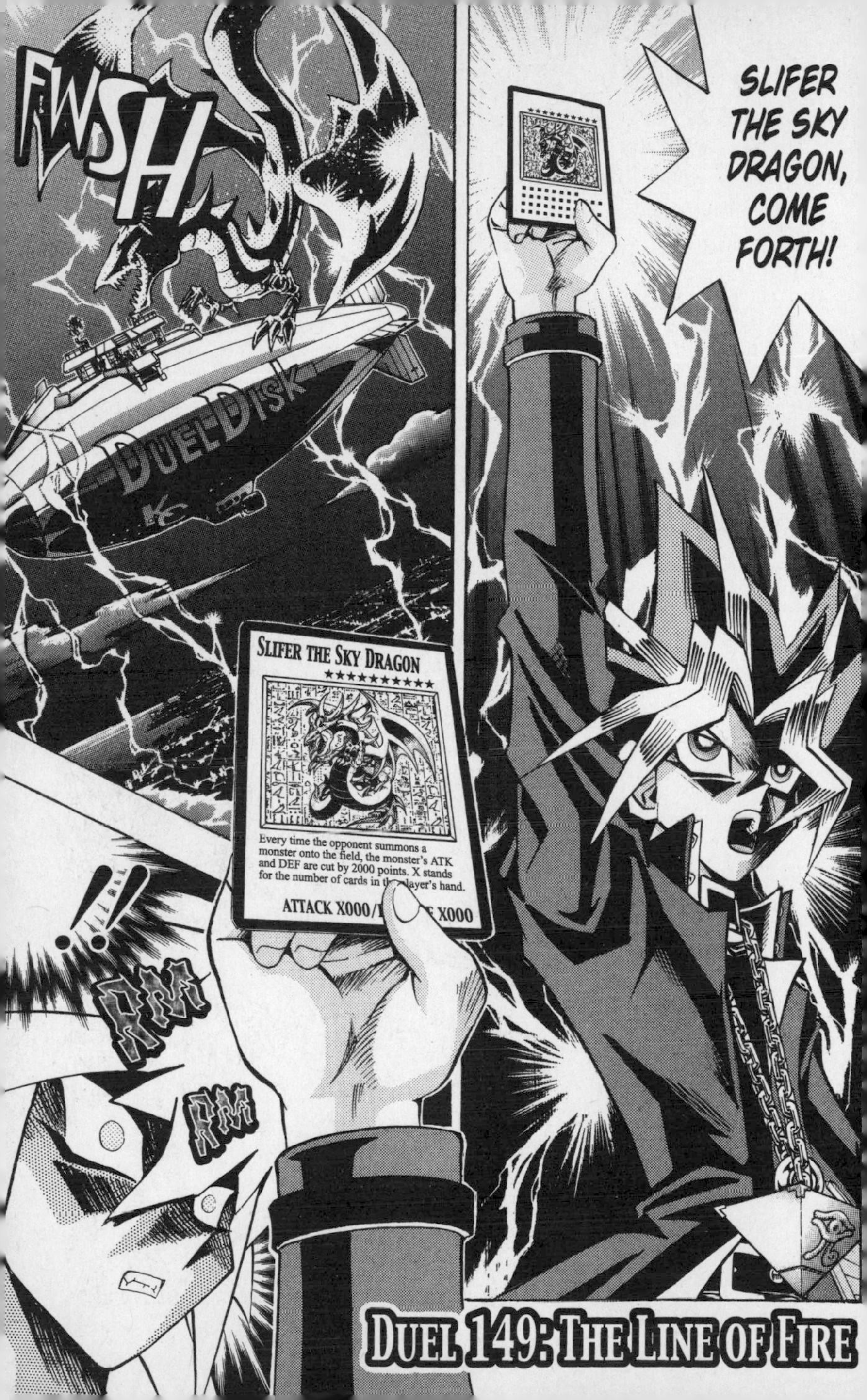
SLIFER THE SKY DRAGON, COME FORTH!
DUEL 149: THE LINE OF FIRE
FWSH
DUEL DISK
SLIFER THE SKY DRAGON
Every time the opponent summons a monster onto the field, the monster's ATK and DEF are cut by 2000 points. X stands for the number of cards in th layer's hand.
ATTACK X000/
X000
!!
RM
RM

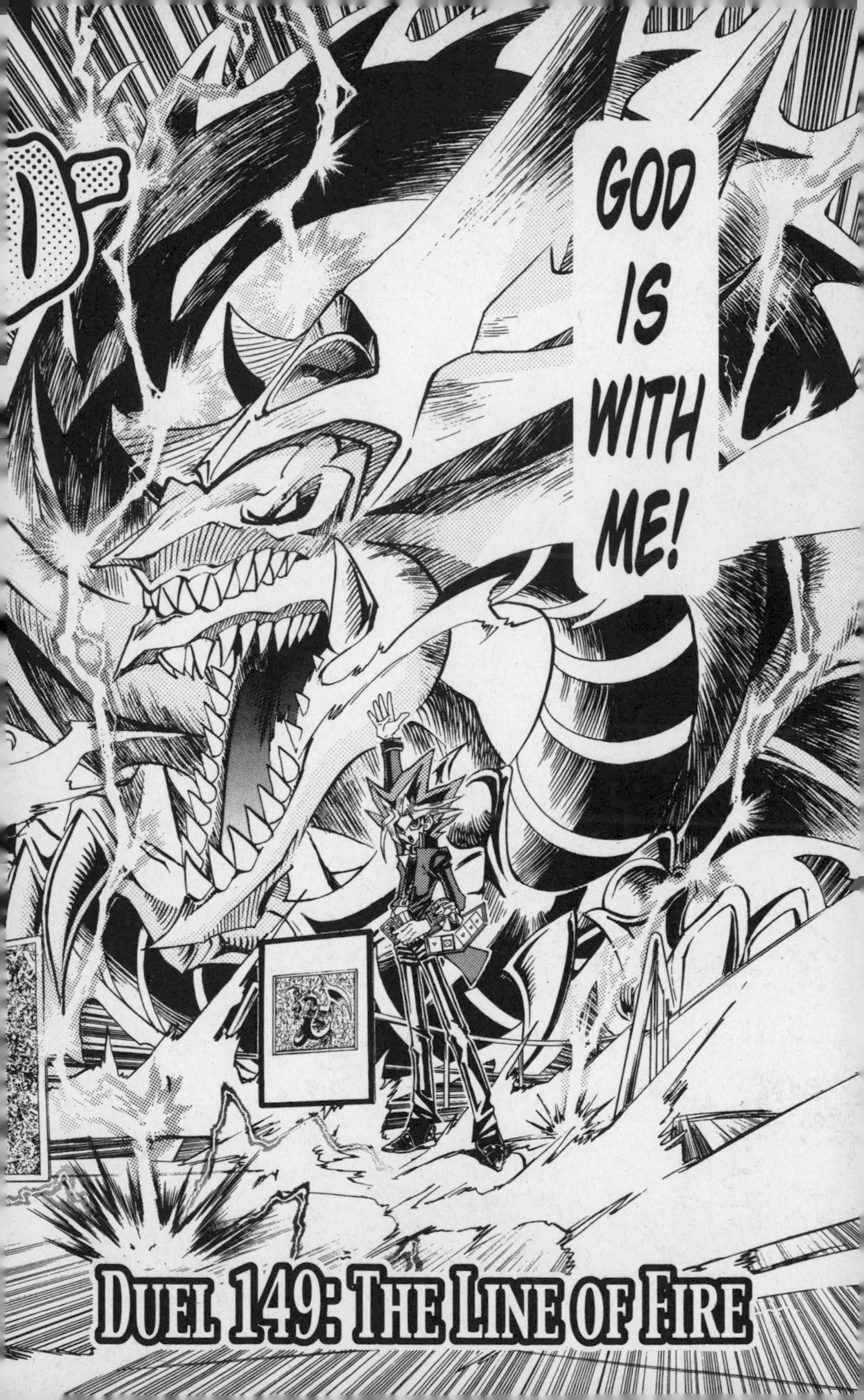
GOD IS WITH ME!
DUEL 149: THE LINE OF FIRE

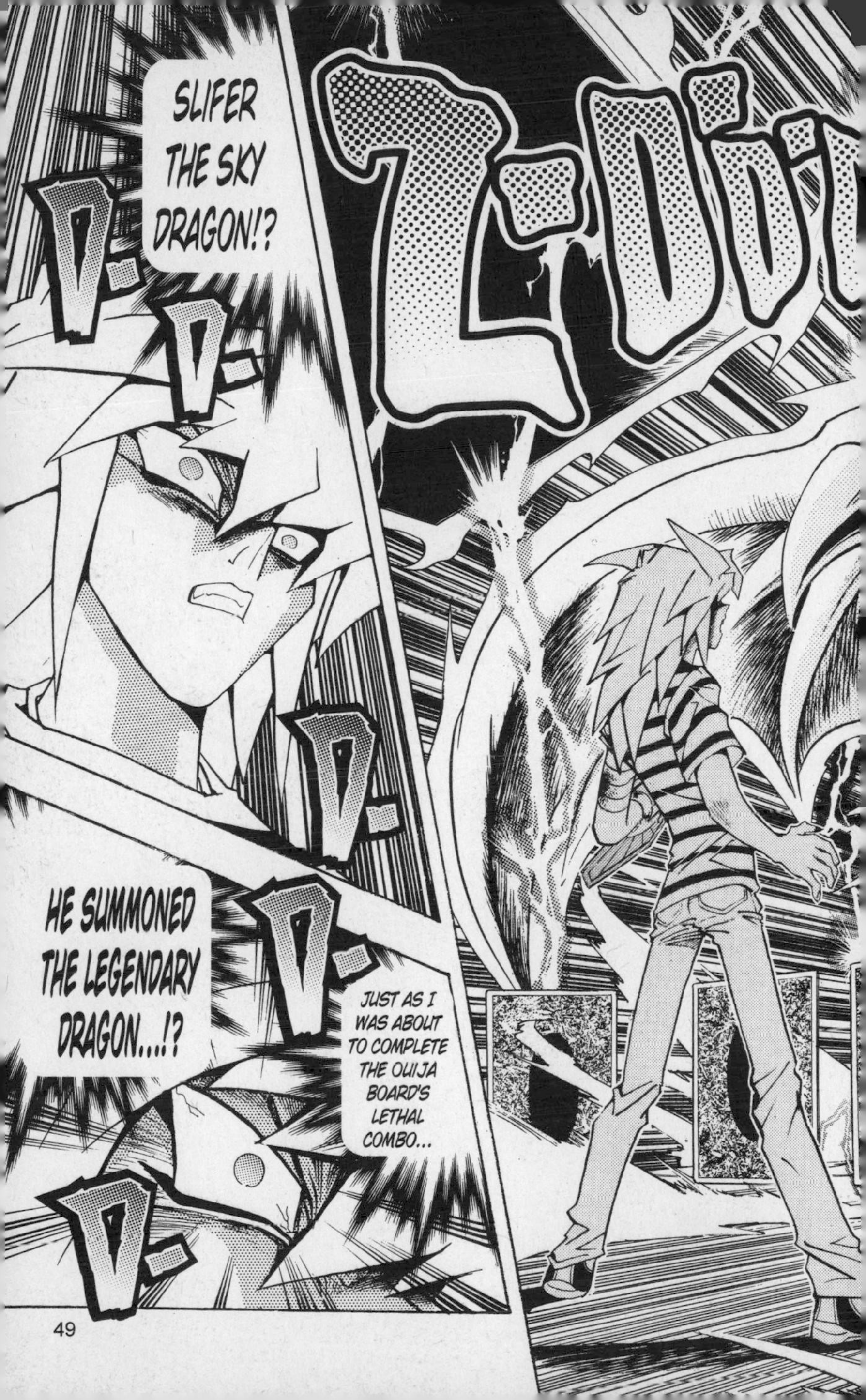
SLIFER THE SKY DRAGON!?
D-D-
D-D-
JUST AS I WAS ABOUT TO COMPLETE THE OUIJA BOARD'S LETHAL COMBO...
HE SUMMONED THE LEGENDARY DRAGON...!?

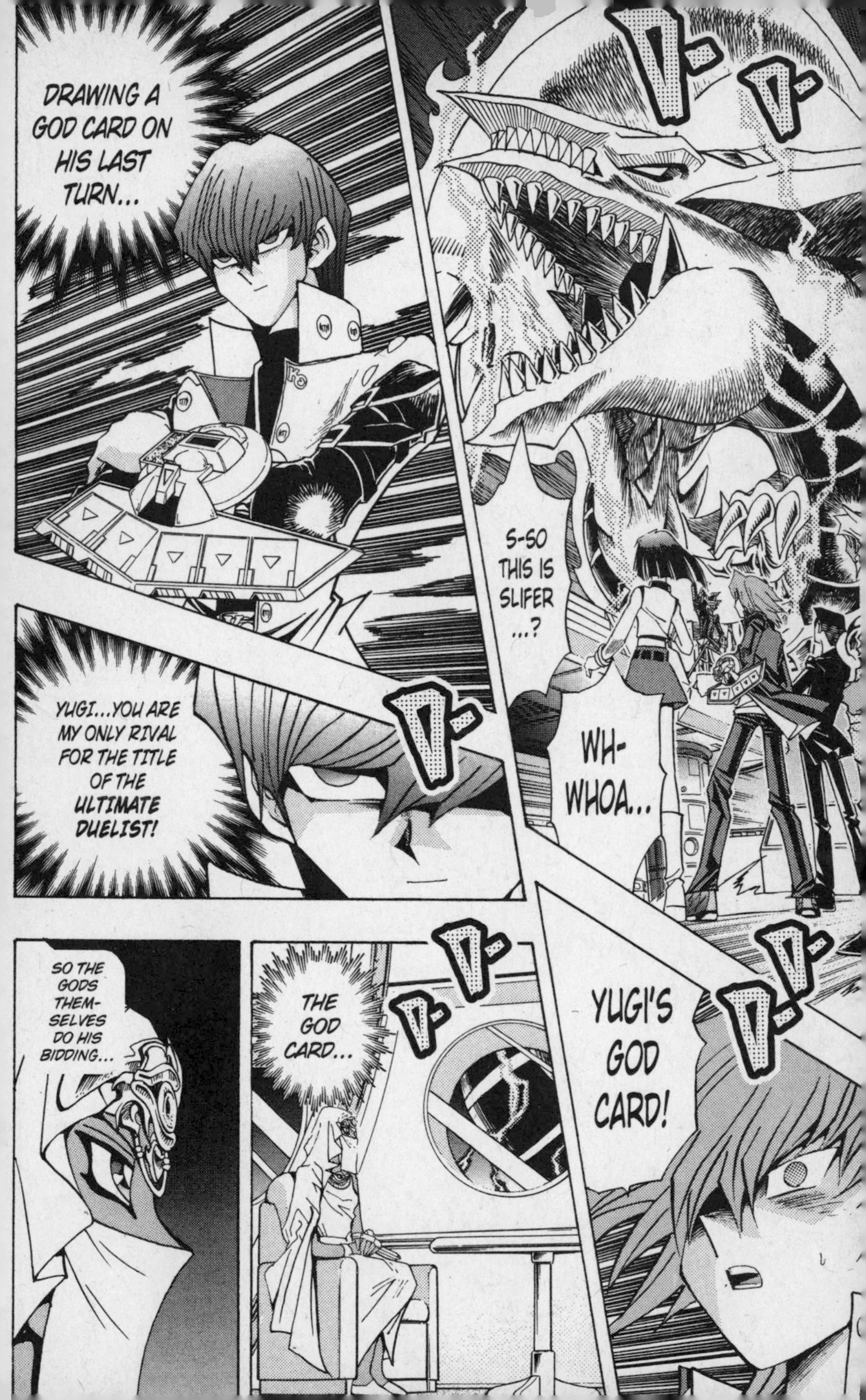
S-SO THIS IS SLIFER ...?
WH-WHOA...
DRAWING A GOD CARD ON HIS LAST TURN...
YUGI...YOU ARE MY ONLY RIVAL FOR THE TITLE OF THE ULTIMATE DUELIST!
YUGI'S GOD CARD!
THE GOD CARD...
SO THE GODS THEM-SELVES DO HIS BIDDING...

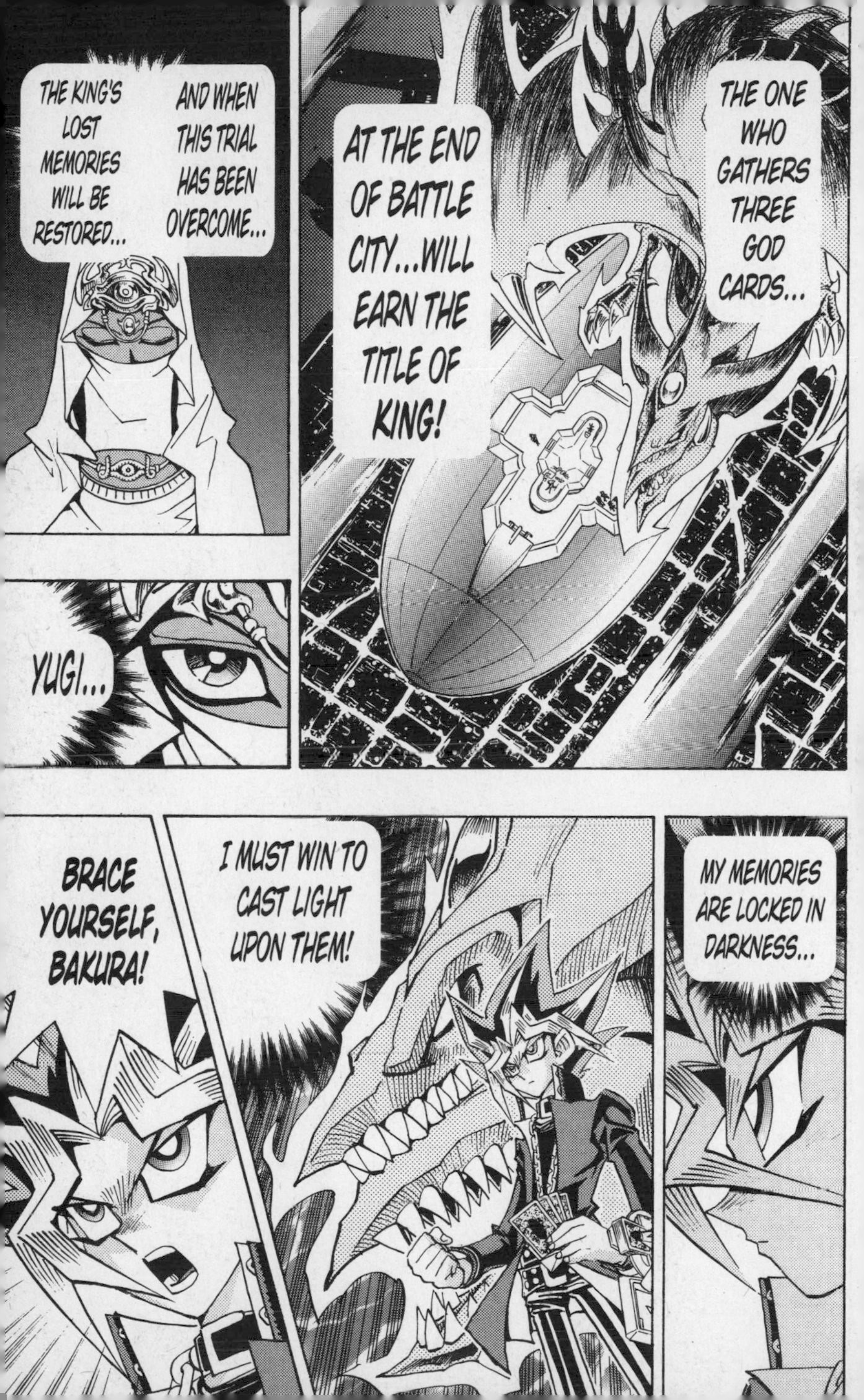
THE ONE WHO GATHERS THREE GOD CARDS...
AT THE END OF BATTLE CITY...WILL EARN THE TITLE OF KING!
AND WHEN THIS TRIAL HAS BEEN OVERCOME...
THE KING'S LOST MEMORIES WILL BE RESTORED...
YUGI...
MY MEMORIES ARE LOCKED IN DARKNESS...
I MUST WIN TO CAST LIGHT UPON THEM!
BRACE YOURSELF, BAKURA!

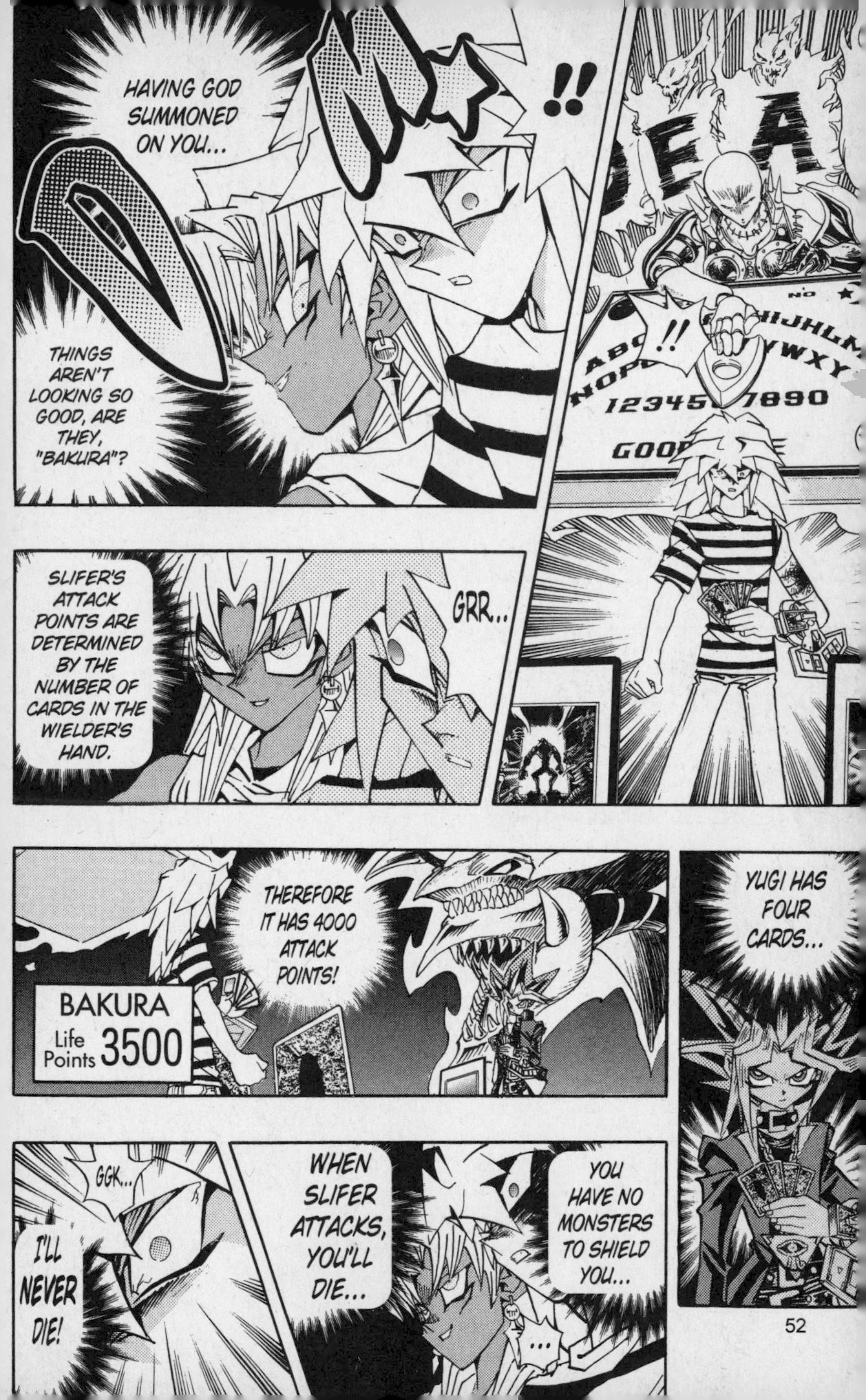
!!
HAVING GOD SUMMONED ON YOU...
!!
THINGS AREN'T LOOKING SO GOOD, ARE THEY, "BAKURA"?
GRR...
SLIFER'S ATTACK POINTS ARE DETERMINED BY THE NUMBER OF CARDS IN THE WIELDER'S HAND.
YUGI HAS FOUR CARDS...
THEREFORE IT HAS 4000 ATTACK POINTS!
BAKURA
Life Points 3500
YOU HAVE NO MONSTERS TO SHIELD YOU...
WHEN SLIFER ATTACKS, YOU'LL DIE...
...
GGK...
I'LL NEVER DIE!

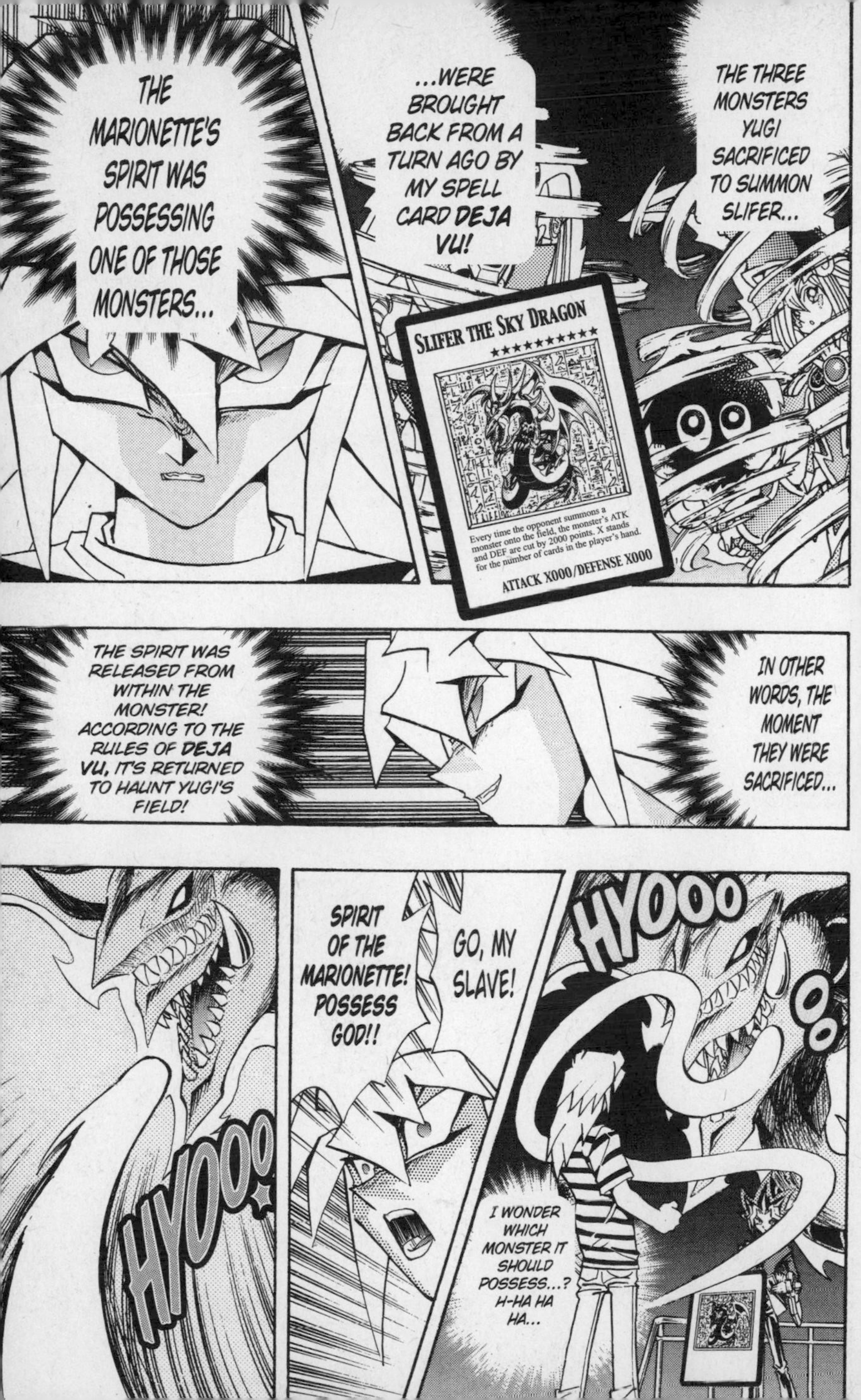
THE THREE MONSTERS YUGI SACRIFICED TO SUMMON SLIFER...
...WERE BROUGHT BACK FROM A TURN AGO BY MY SPELL CARD DEJA VU!
SLIFER THE SKY DRAGON
Every time the opponent summons a monster onto the field, the monster's ATK and DEF are cut by 2000 points. X stands for the number of cards in the player's hand.
ATTACK X000/DEFENSE X000
THE MARIONETTE'S SPIRIT WAS POSSESSING ONE OF THOSE MONSTERS...
IN OTHER WORDS, THE MOMENT THEY WERE SACRIFICED...
THE SPIRIT WAS RELEASED FROM WITHIN THE MONSTER! ACCORDING TO THE RULES OF DEJA VU, IT'S RETURNED TO HAUNT YUGI'S FIELD!
HYOOOOO
I WONDER WHICH MONSTER IT SHOULD POSSESS...? H-HA HA HA...
GO, MY SLAVE!
SPIRIT OF THE MARIONETTE! POSSESS GOD!!
HYOOO!

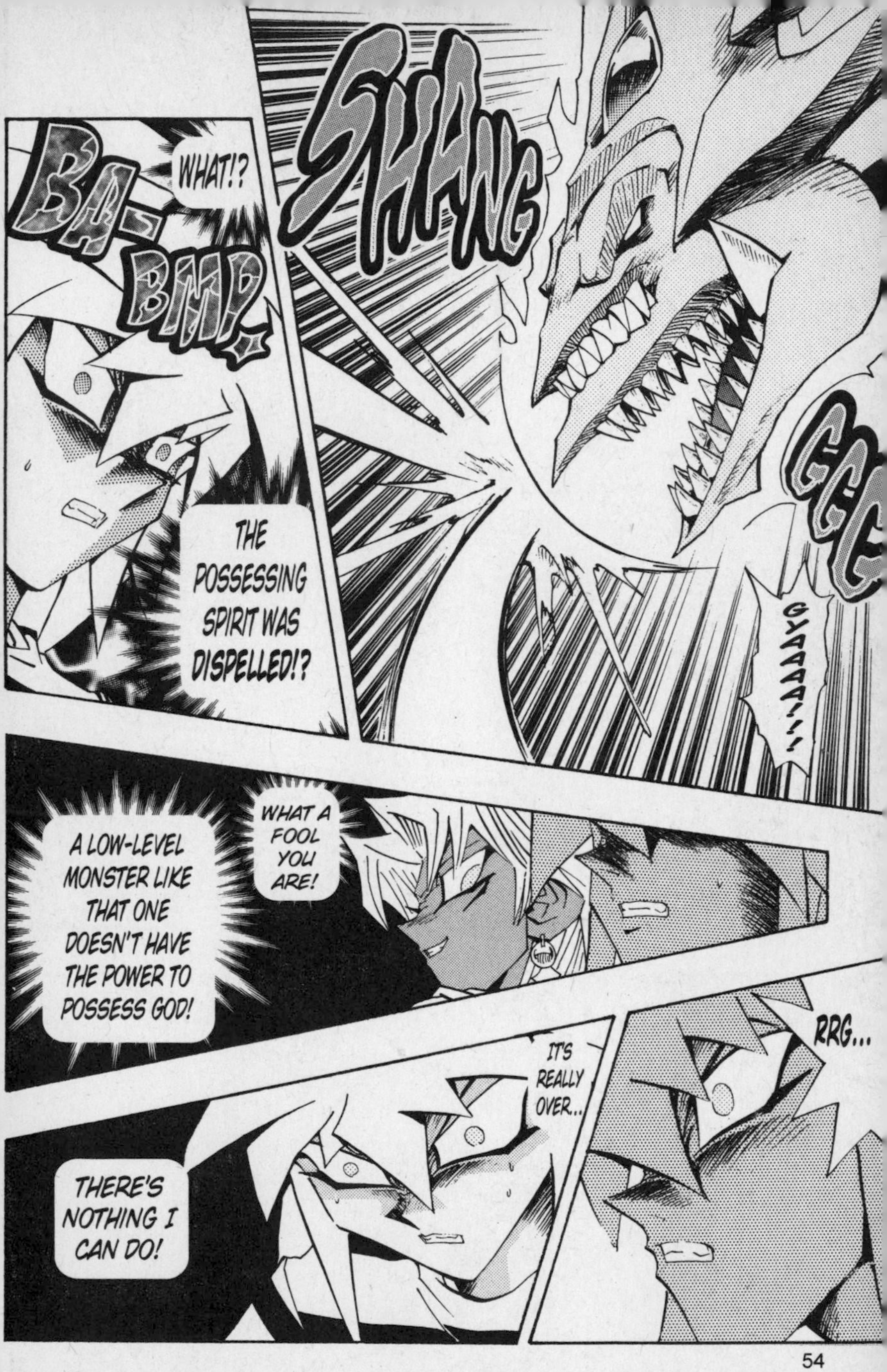
SHANG
GGG
GYAAAA!!!
BA-BMP
WHAT!?
THE POSSESSING SPIRIT WAS DISPELLED!?
WHAT A FOOL YOU ARE!
A LOW-LEVEL MONSTER LIKE THAT ONE DOESN'T HAVE THE POWER TO POSSESS GOD!
RRG...
IT'S REALLY OVER...
THERE'S NOTHING I CAN DO!

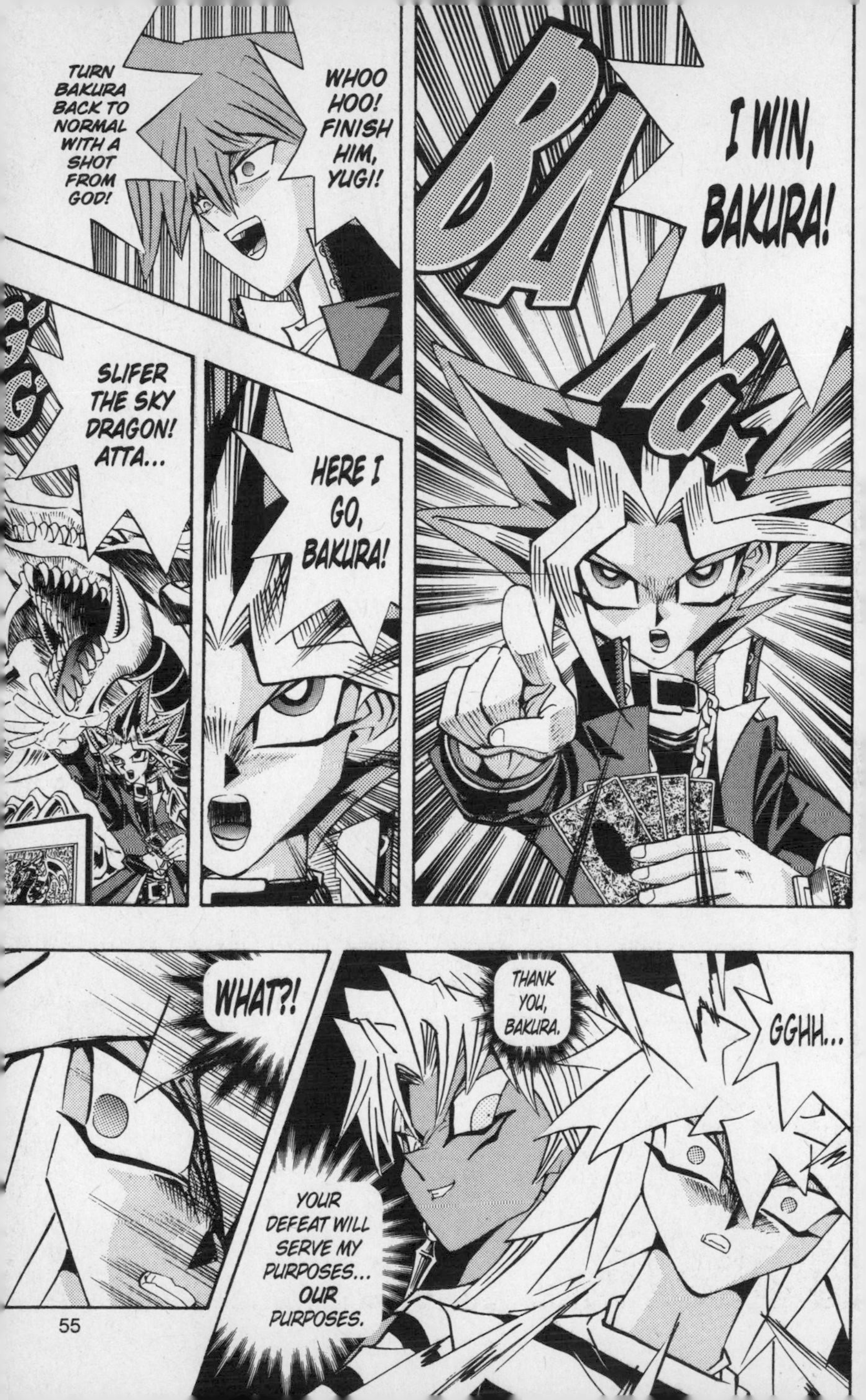
BANG!
I WIN, BAKURA!
WHOO HOO! FINISH HIM, YUGI!
TURN BAKURA BACK TO NORMAL WITH A SHOT FROM GOD!
HERE I GO, BAKURA!
SLIFER THE SKY DRAGON! ATTA...
GGHH...
THANK YOU, BAKURA.
YOUR DEFEAT WILL SERVE MY PURPOSES... OUR PURPOSES.
WHAT?!

IT'S HIM!

ZWMMM

!!

MARIK...!!

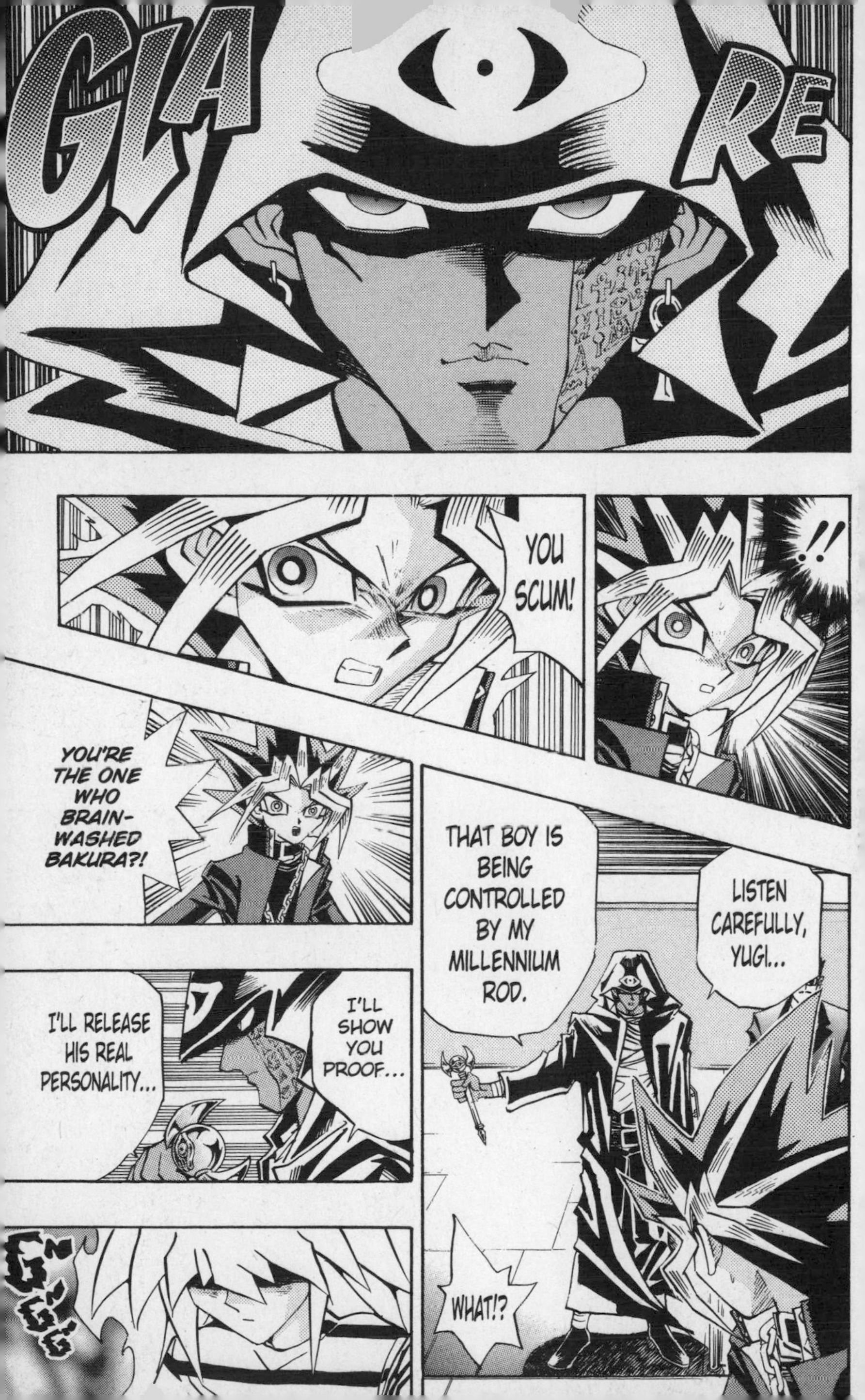
GLARE
!!
YOU SCUM!
YOU'RE THE ONE WHO BRAIN-WASHED BAKURA?!
LISTEN CAREFULLY, YUGI...
THAT BOY IS BEING CONTROLLED BY MY MILLENNIUM ROD.
WHAT!?
I'LL SHOW YOU PROOF...
I'LL RELEASE HIS REAL PERSONALITY...

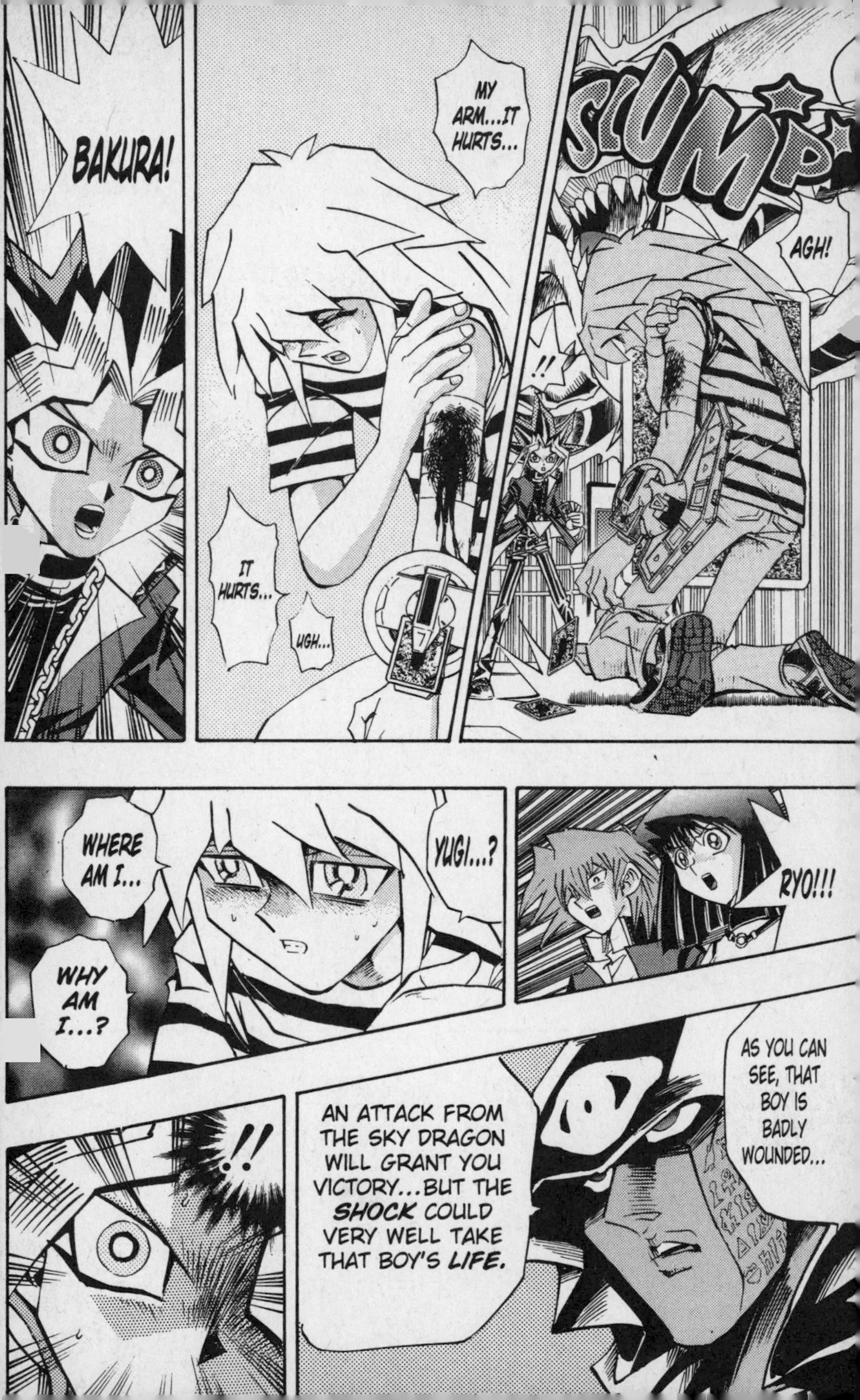
SLUMP
AGH!
!!
MY ARM...IT HURTS...
IT HURTS...
UGH...
BAKURA!
RYO!!!
YUGI...?
WHERE AM I...
WHY AM I...?
AS YOU CAN SEE, THAT BOY IS BADLY WOUNDED...
AN ATTACK FROM THE SKY DRAGON WILL GRANT YOU VICTORY...BUT THE SHOCK COULD VERY WELL TAKE THAT BOY'S LIFE.
!!

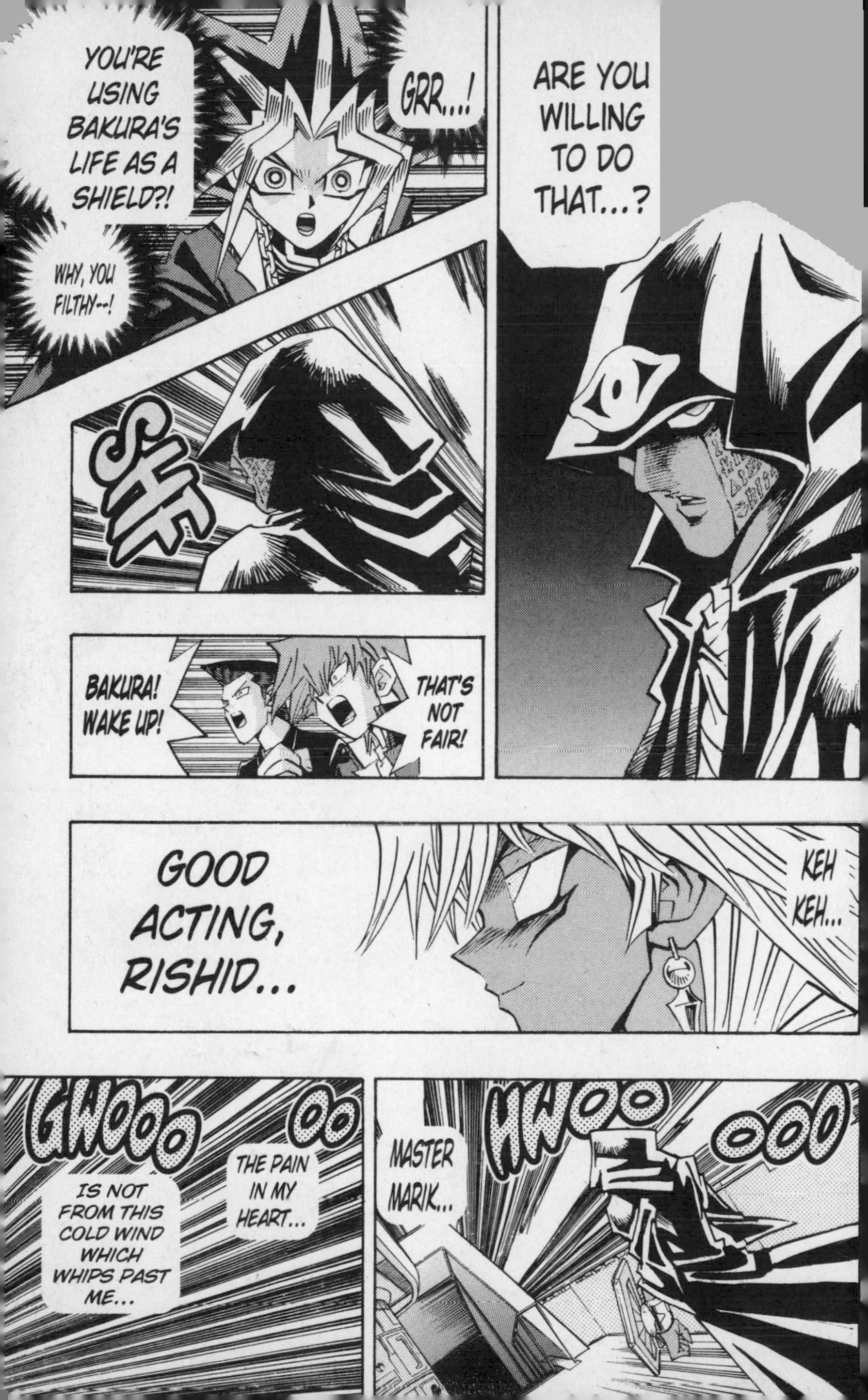
ARE YOU WILLING TO DO THAT...?
GRR...!
YOU'RE USING BAKURA'S LIFE AS A SHIELD?!
WHY, YOU FILTHY--!
SHF
THAT'S NOT FAIR!
BAKURA! WAKE UP!
KEH KEH...
GOOD ACTING, RISHID...
HWOO OOO
MASTER MARIK...
GWOOOO OO
THE PAIN IN MY HEART...
IS NOT FROM THIS COLD WIND WHICH WHIPS PAST ME...

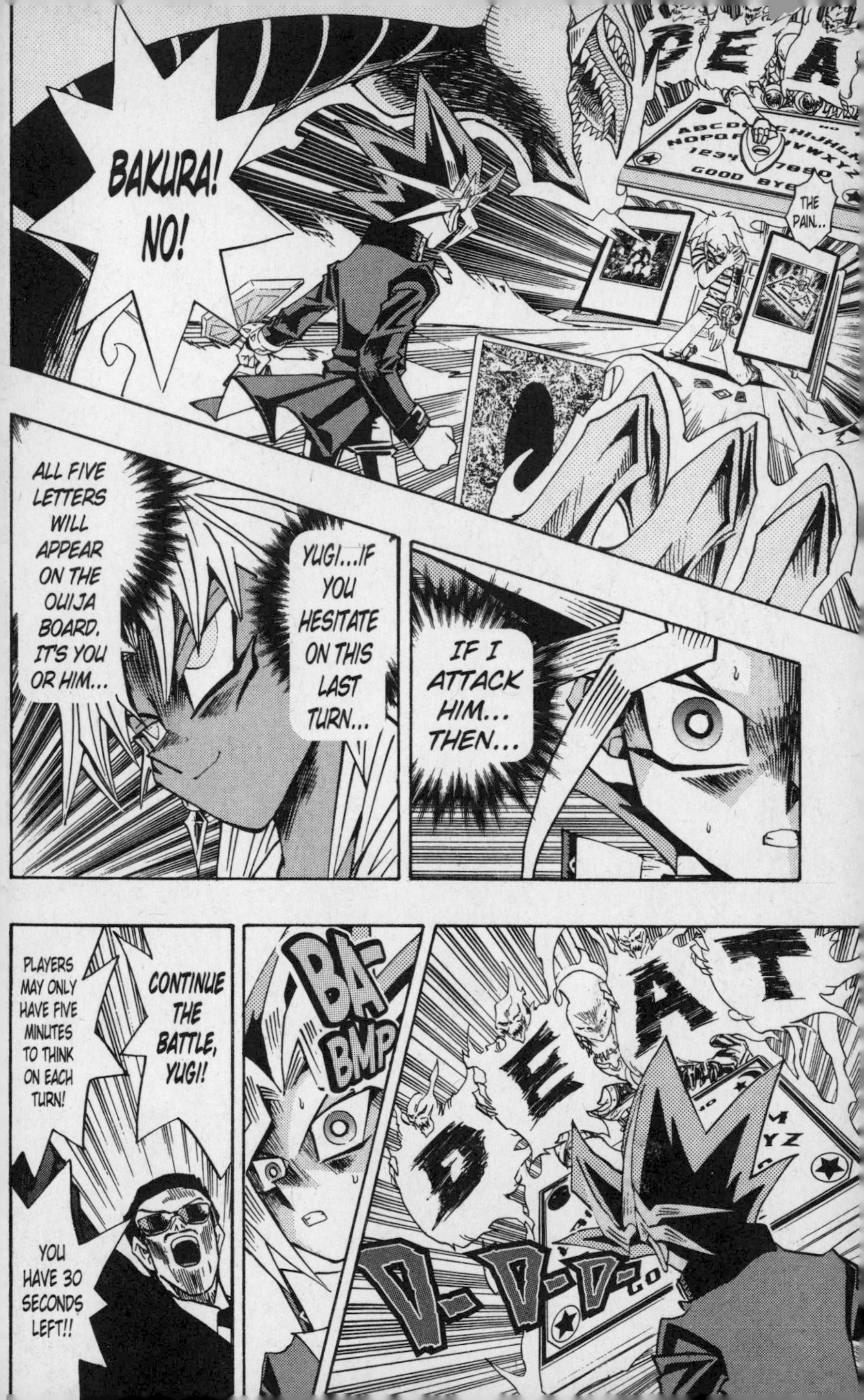
PEA
THE PAIN...
BAKURA! NO!
IF I ATTACK HIM... THEN...
YUGI...IF YOU HESITATE ON THIS LAST TURN...
ALL FIVE LETTERS WILL APPEAR ON THE OUIJA BOARD. IT'S YOU OR HIM...
DEAT
D-D-D-
BA-BMP
CONTINUE THE BATTLE, YUGI!
PLAYERS MAY ONLY HAVE FIVE MINUTES TO THINK ON EACH TURN!
YOU HAVE 30 SECONDS LEFT!!

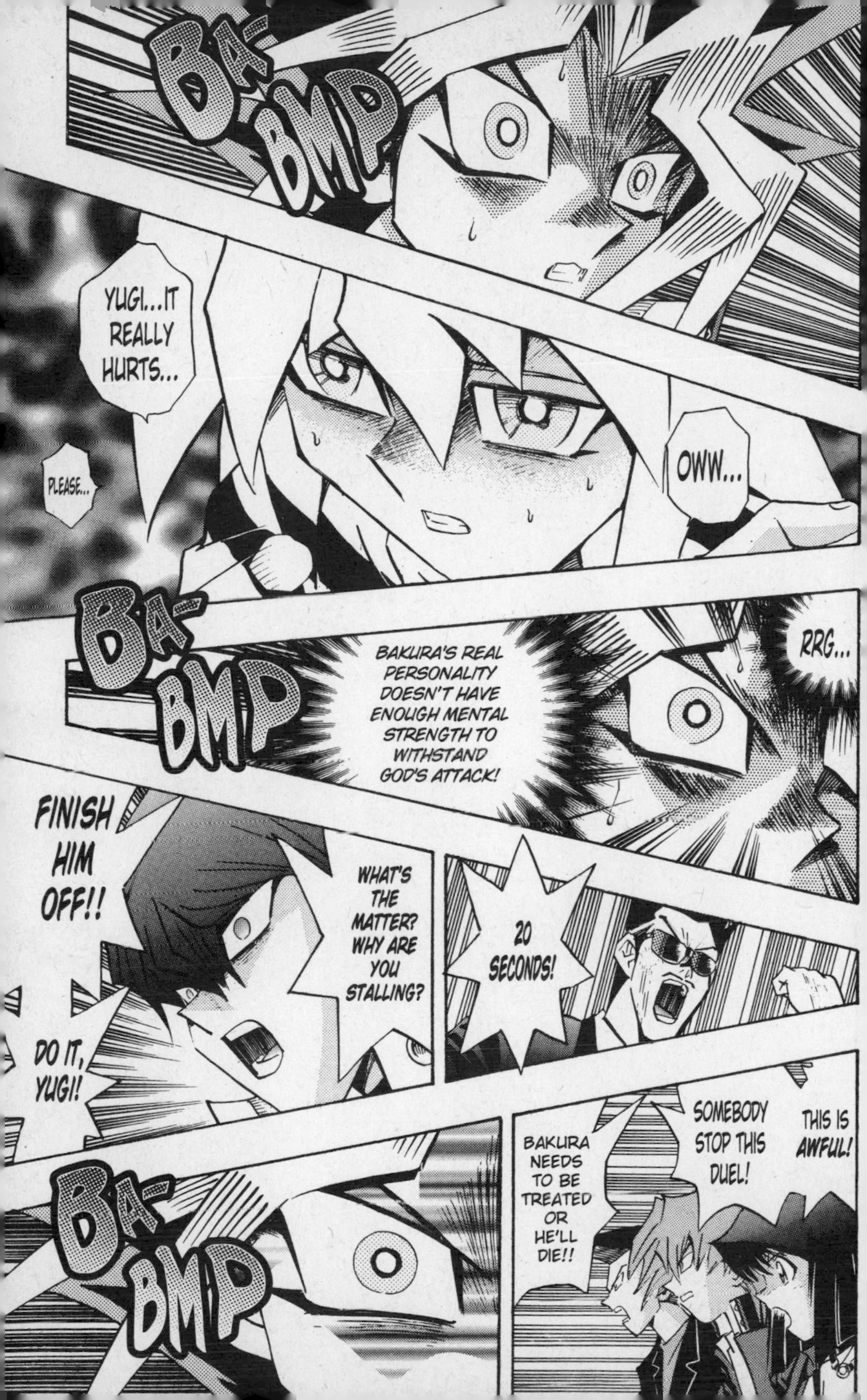
BA-BMP
OWW...
YUGI...IT REALLY HURTS...
PLEASE...
RRG...
BAKURA'S REAL PERSONALITY DOESN'T HAVE ENOUGH MENTAL STRENGTH TO WITHSTAND GOD'S ATTACK!
BA-BMP
20 SECONDS!
WHAT'S THE MATTER? WHY ARE YOU STALLING?
FINISH HIM OFF!!
DO IT, YUGI!
THIS IS AWFUL!
SOMEBODY STOP THIS DUEL!
BAKURA NEEDS TO BE TREATED OR HE'LL DIE!!
BA-BMP

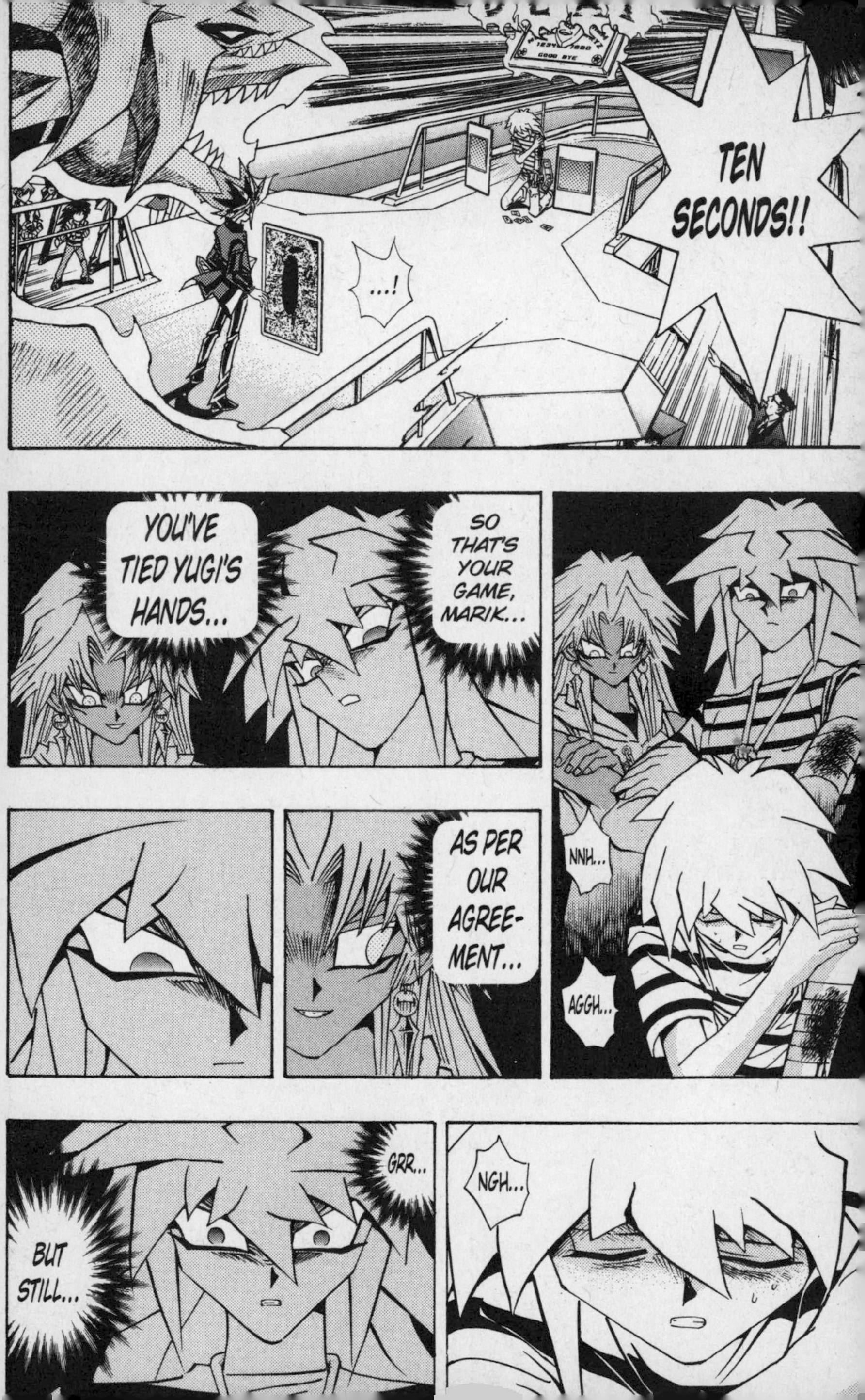
TEN SECONDS!!
...!
NNH...
AGGH...
SO THAT'S YOUR GAME, MARIK...
YOU'VE TIED YUGI'S HANDS...
AS PER OUR AGREEMENT...
NGH...
GRR...
BUT STILL...

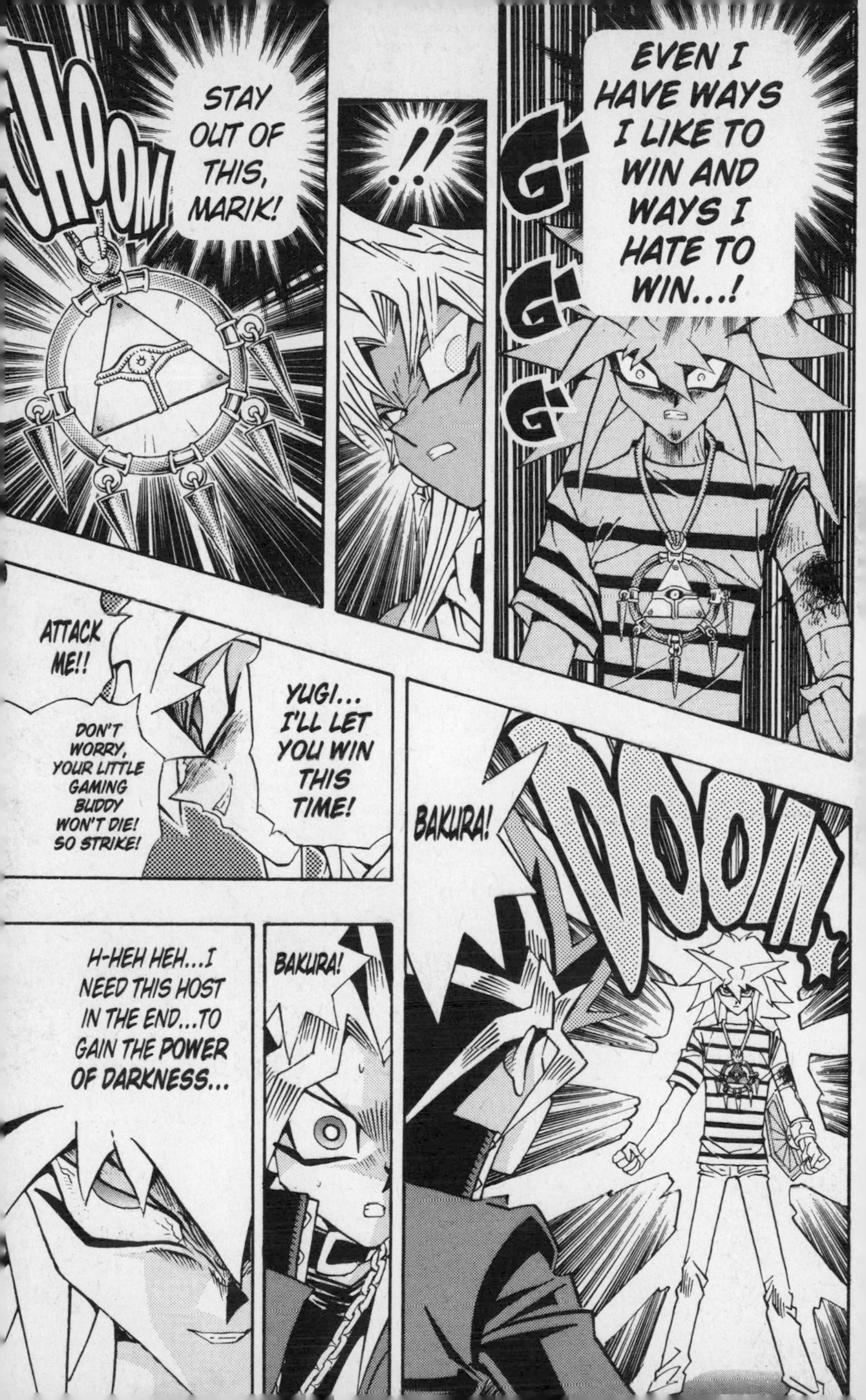
G
G
G
EVEN I HAVE WAYS I LIKE TO WIN AND WAYS I HATE TO WIN...!
!!
CHOOM
STAY OUT OF THIS, MARIK!
DOOM
BAKURA!
YUGI... I'LL LET YOU WIN THIS TIME!
ATTACK ME!!
DON'T WORRY, YOUR LITTLE GAMING BUDDY WON'T DIE! SO STRIKE!
BAKURA!
H-HEH HEH...I NEED THIS HOST IN THE END...TO GAIN THE POWER OF DARKNESS...

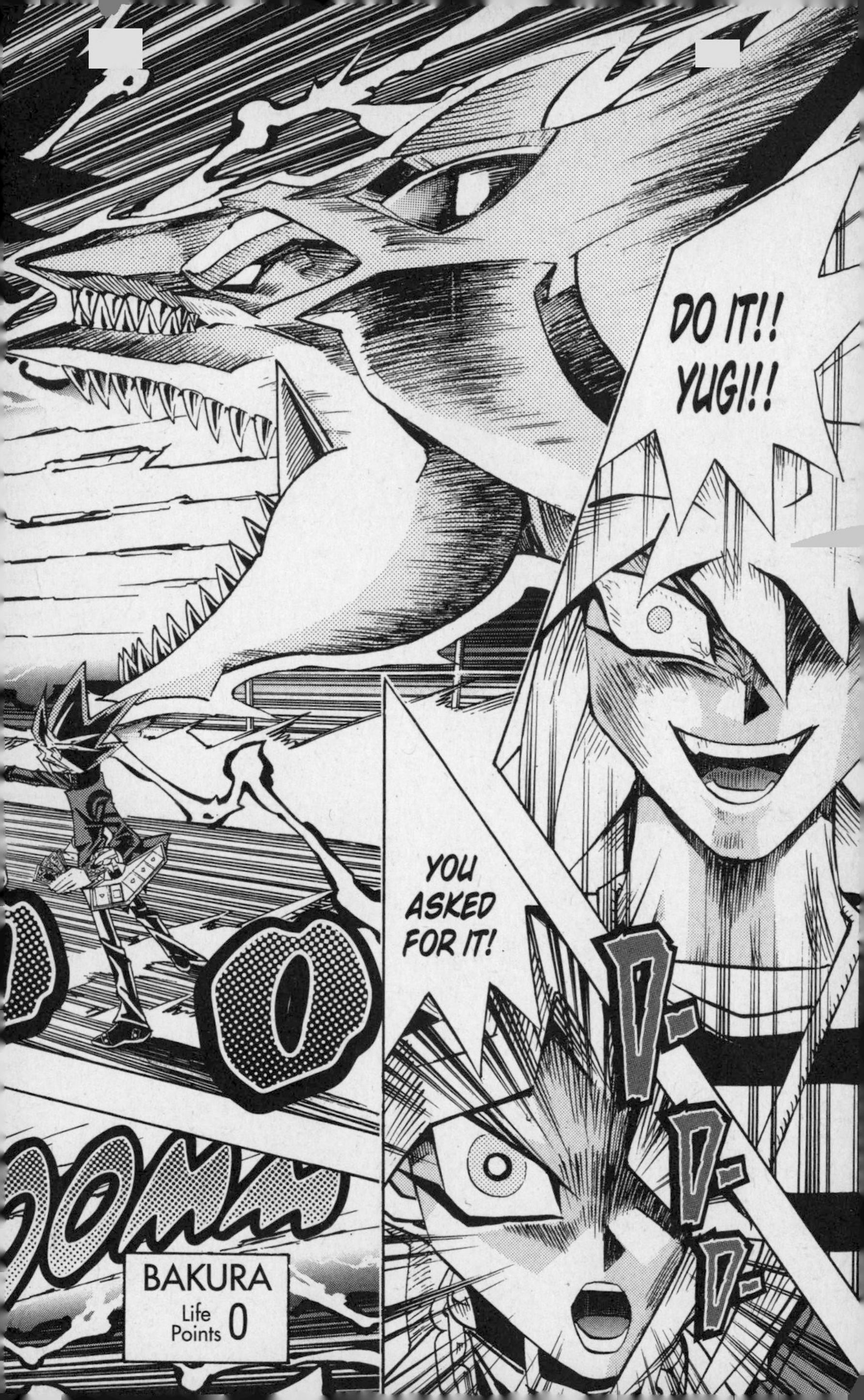
DO IT!! YUGI!!
YOU ASKED FOR IT!
D- D- D-
BAKURA
Life Points 0

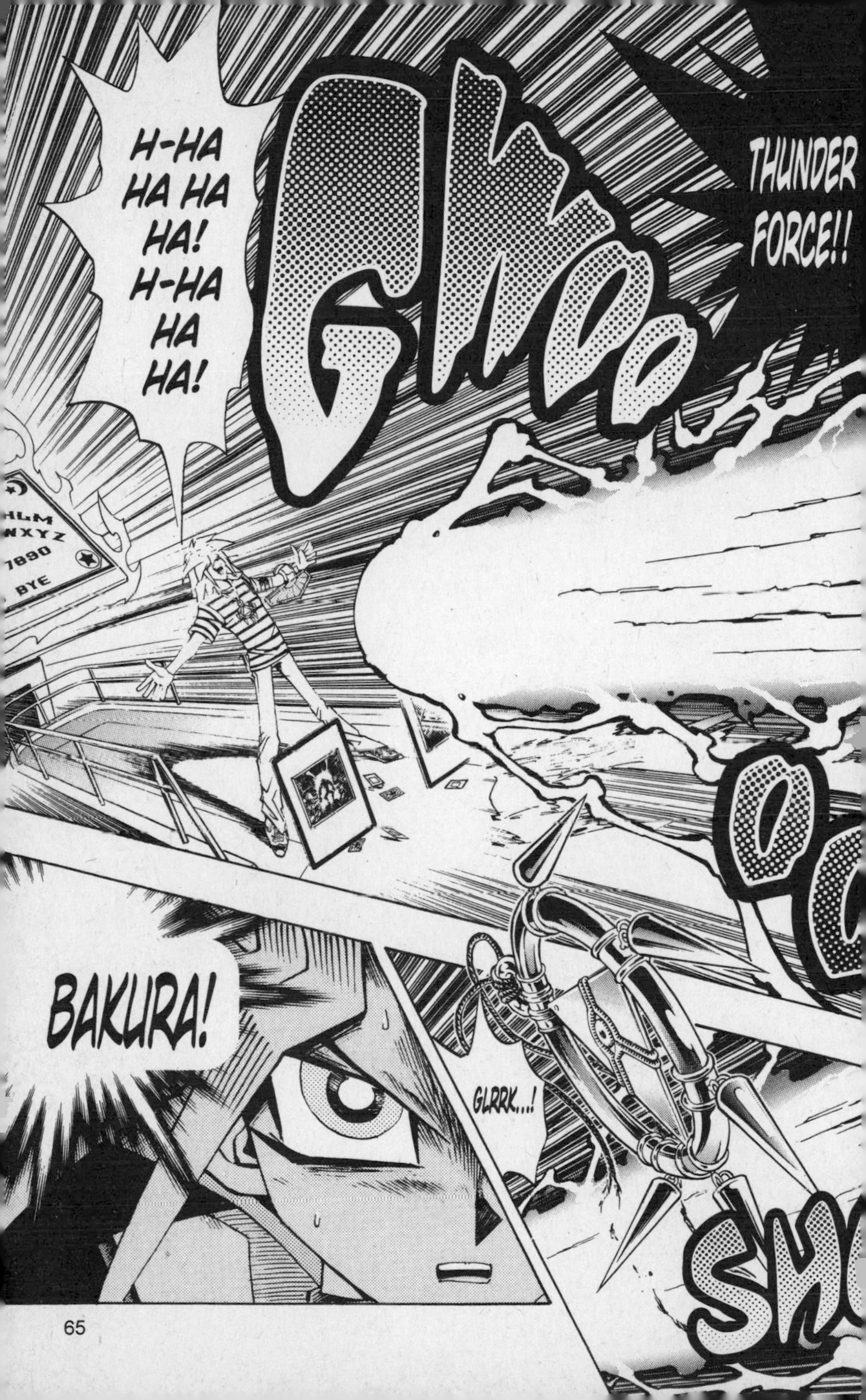
THUNDER FORCE!!
H-HA HA HA HA! H-HA HA HA HA!
GLRRK...!
BAKURA!

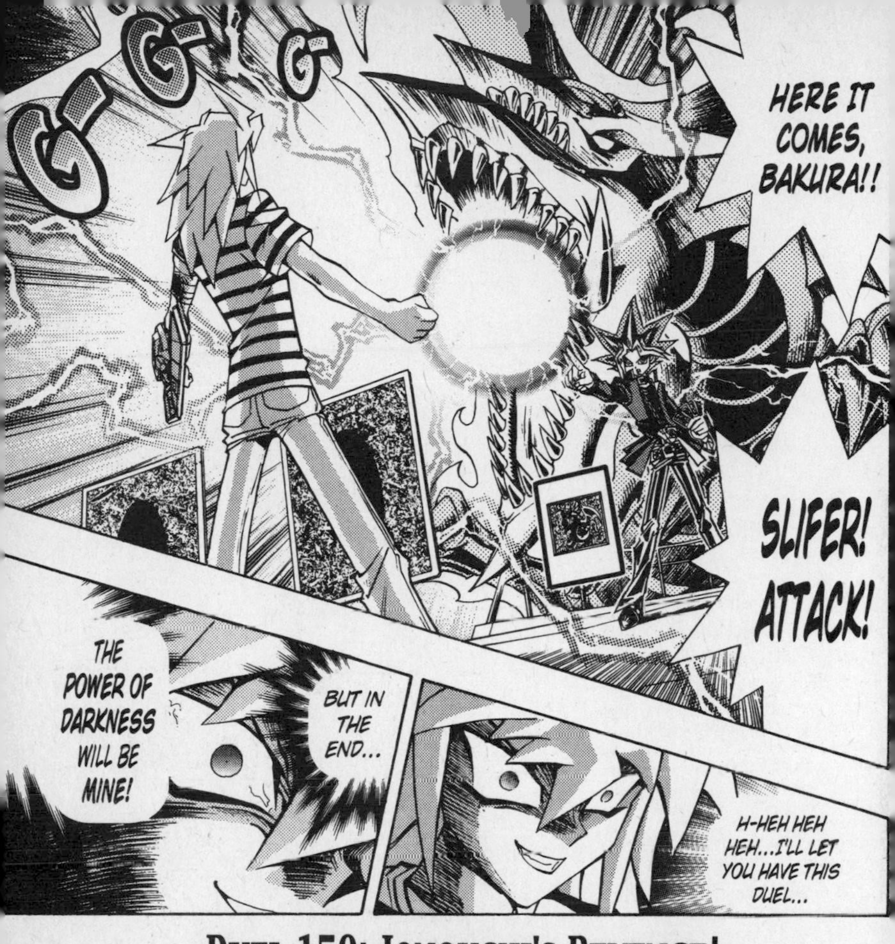
HERE IT COMES, BAKURA!!
SLIFER! ATTACK!
G-G-G
H-HEH HEH HEH...I'LL LET YOU HAVE THIS DUEL...
BUT IN THE END...
THE POWER OF DARKNESS WILL BE MINE!

DUEL 150: JONOUCHI'S REVENGE!

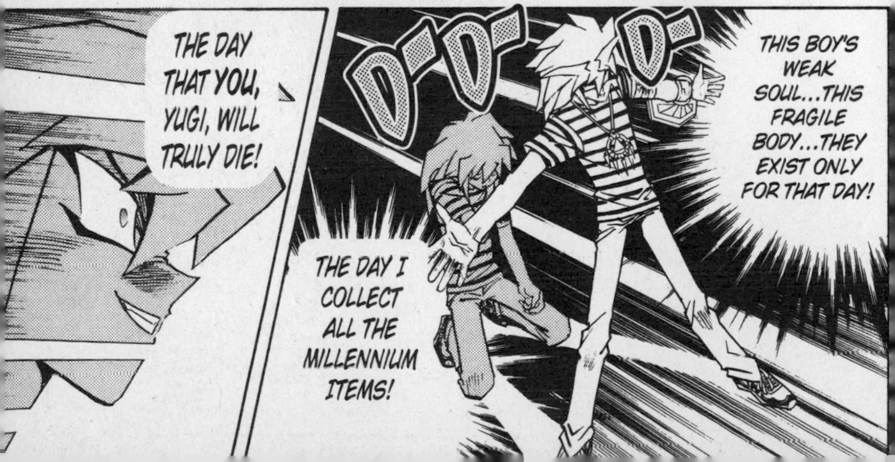
THIS BOY'S WEAK SOUL...THIS FRAGILE BODY...THEY EXIST ONLY FOR THAT DAY!
D-D-D
THE DAY I COLLECT ALL THE MILLENNIUM ITEMS!
THE DAY THAT YOU, YUGI, WILL TRULY DIE!

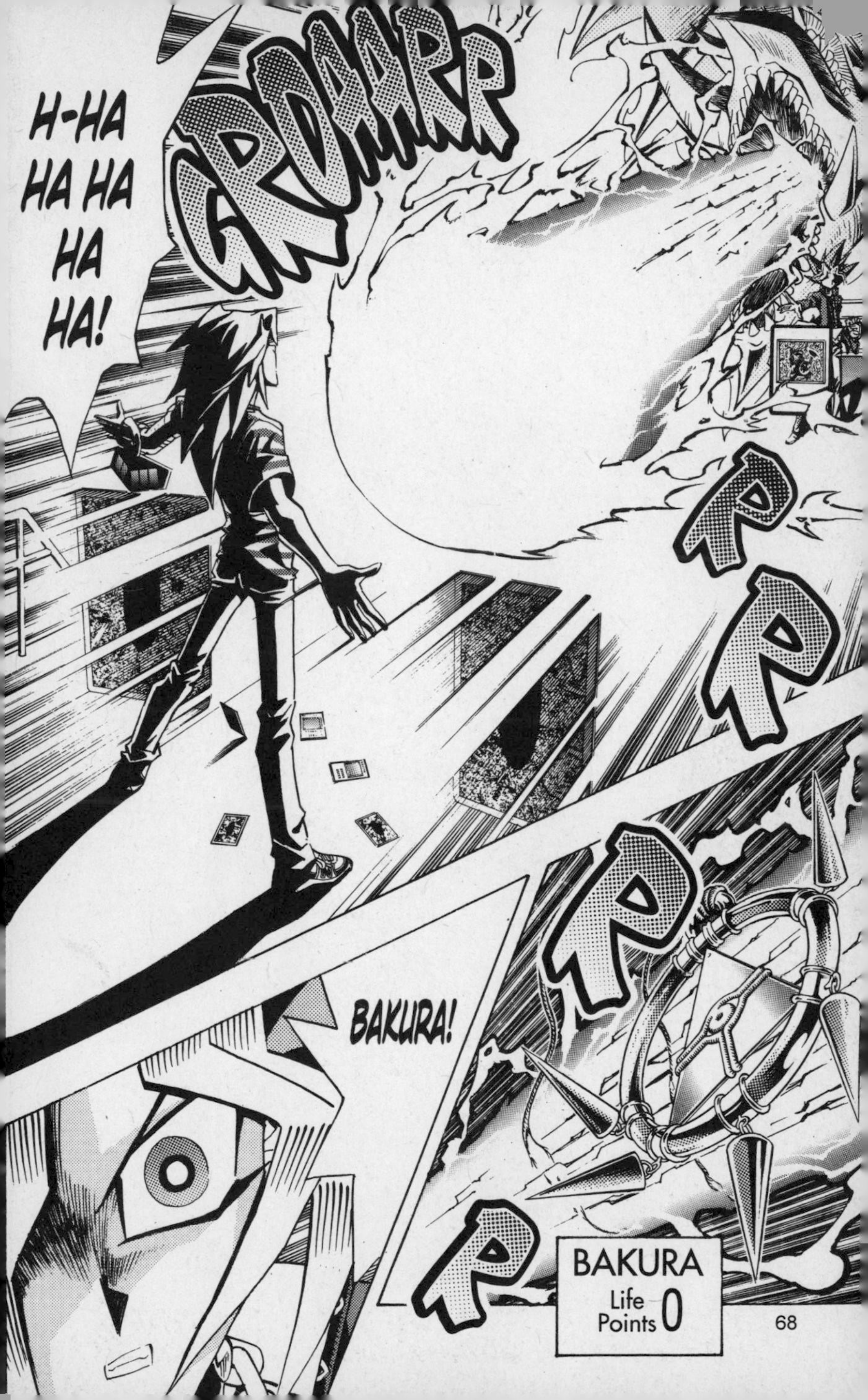
H-HA HA HA HA HA!
RRRRR
BAKURA
Life Points 0
BAKURA!

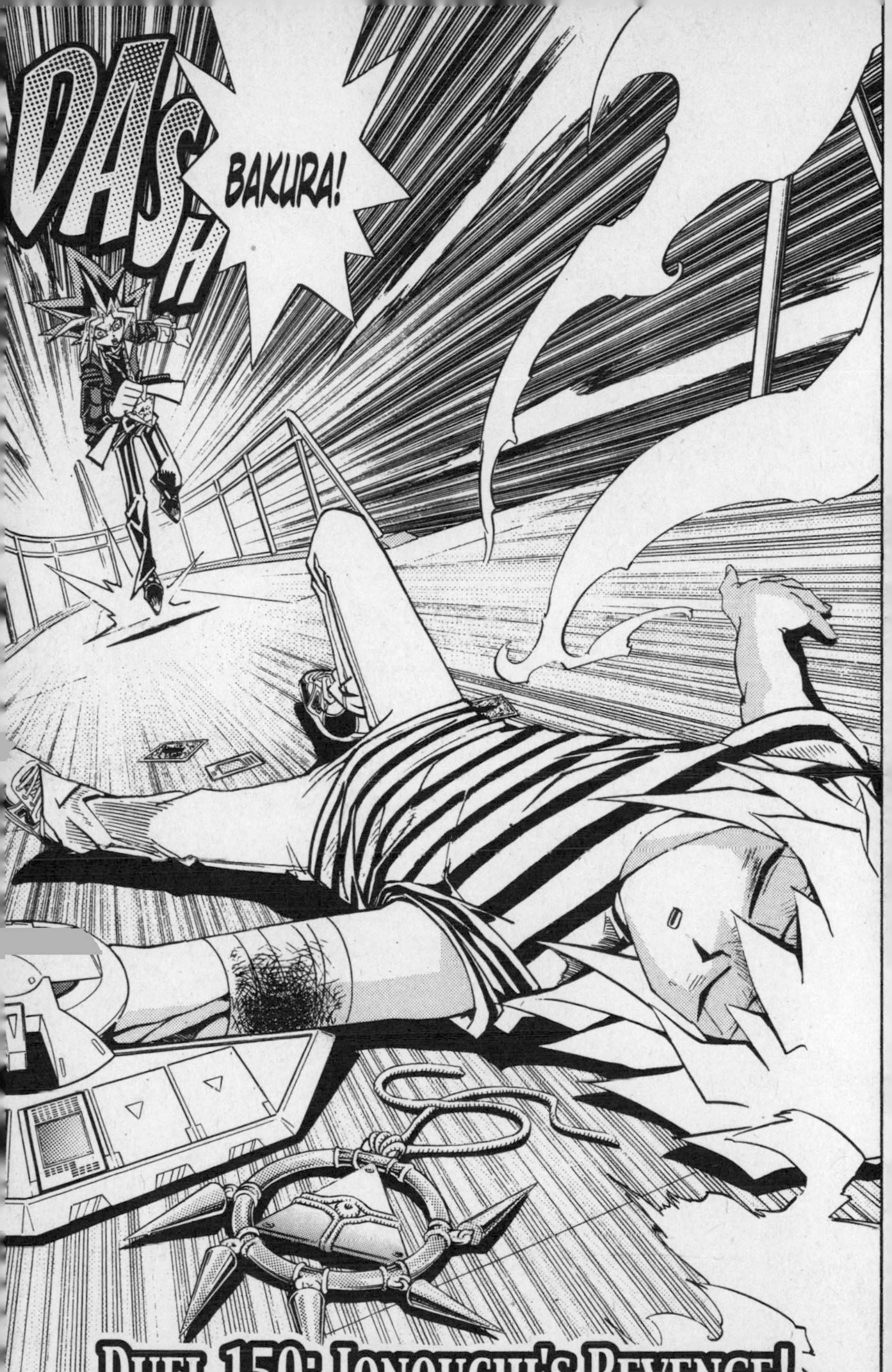
DASH
BAKURA!

Duel 150: Jonouchi's Revenge!

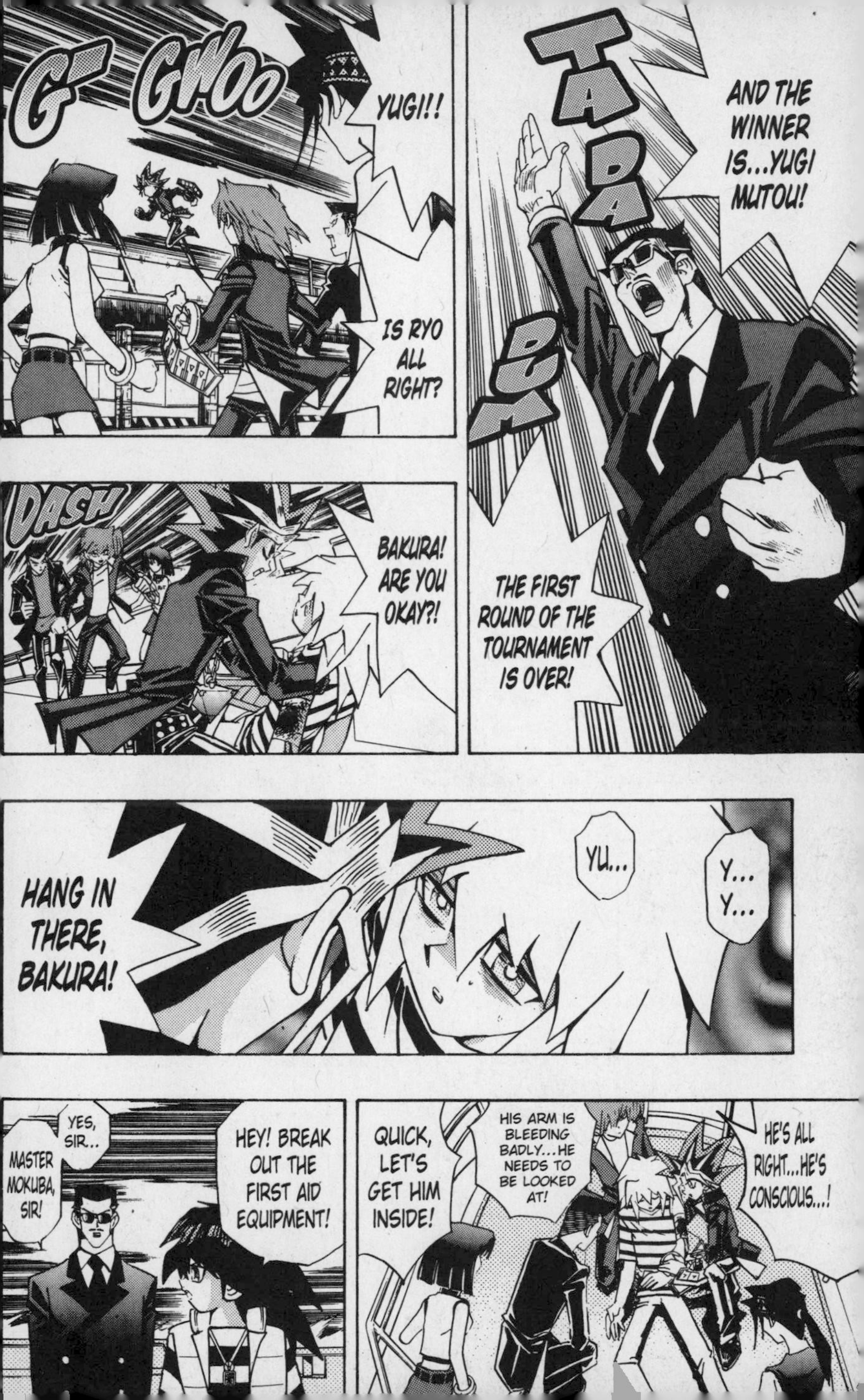
TADA
AND THE WINNER IS...YUGI MUTOU!
DUM
THE FIRST ROUND OF THE TOURNAMENT IS OVER!
G- GWOO
YUGI!!
IS RYO ALL RIGHT?
DASH
BAKURA! ARE YOU OKAY?!
Y... Y...
YU...
HANG IN THERE, BAKURA!
HE'S ALL RIGHT...HE'S CONSCIOUS...!
HIS ARM IS BLEEDING BADLY...HE NEEDS TO BE LOOKED AT!
QUICK, LET'S GET HIM INSIDE!
HEY! BREAK OUT THE FIRST AID EQUIPMENT!
YES, SIR...
MASTER MOKUBA, SIR!

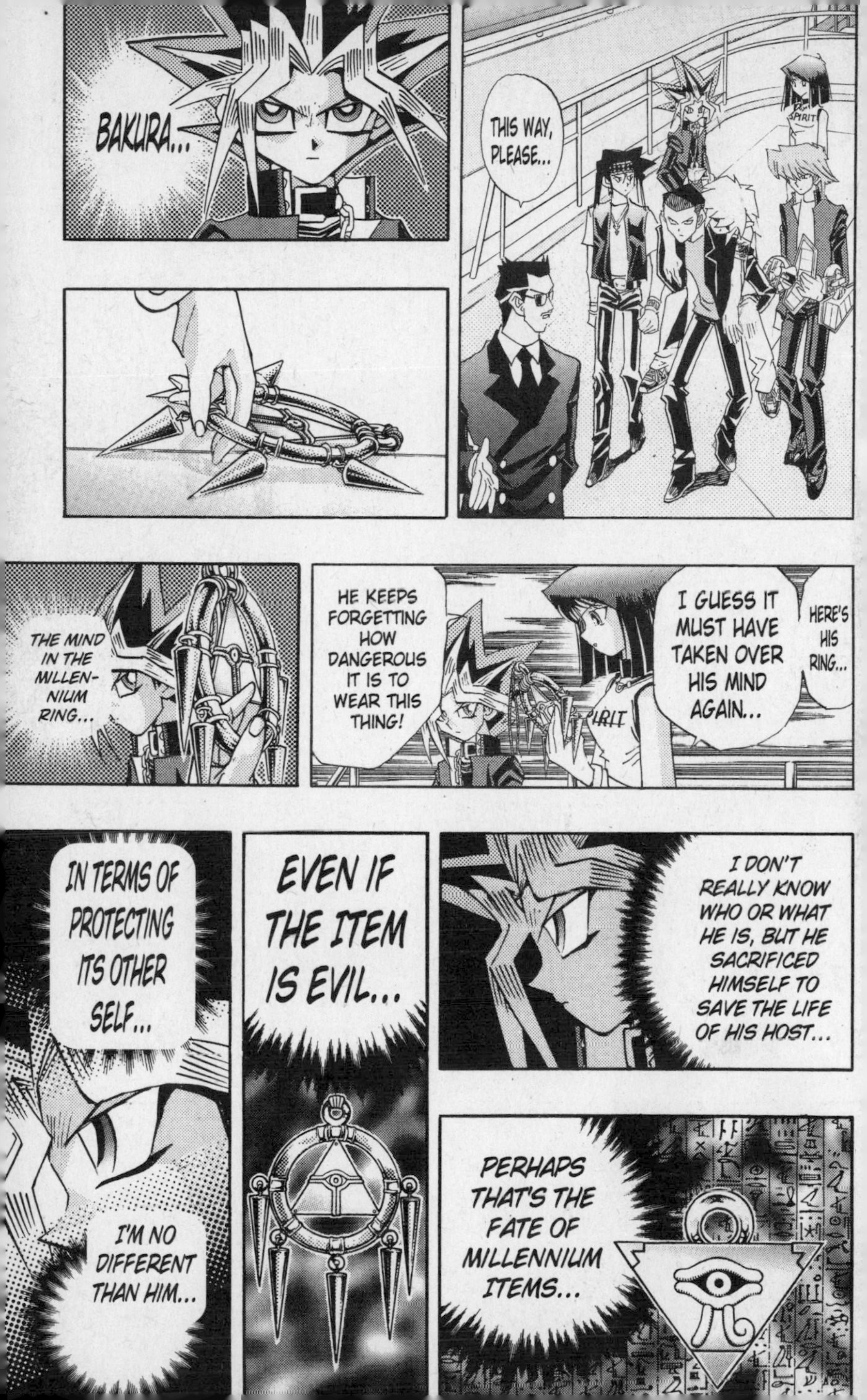
THIS WAY, PLEASE...
BAKURA...
HERE'S HIS RING...
I GUESS IT MUST HAVE TAKEN OVER HIS MIND AGAIN...
HE KEEPS FORGETTING HOW DANGEROUS IT IS TO WEAR THIS THING!
THE MIND IN THE MILLENNIUM RING...
I DON'T REALLY KNOW WHO OR WHAT HE IS, BUT HE SACRIFICED HIMSELF TO SAVE THE LIFE OF HIS HOST...
PERHAPS THAT'S THE FATE OF MILLENNIUM ITEMS...
EVEN IF THE ITEM IS EVIL...
IN TERMS OF PROTECTING ITS OTHER SELF...
I'M NO DIFFERENT THAN HIM...

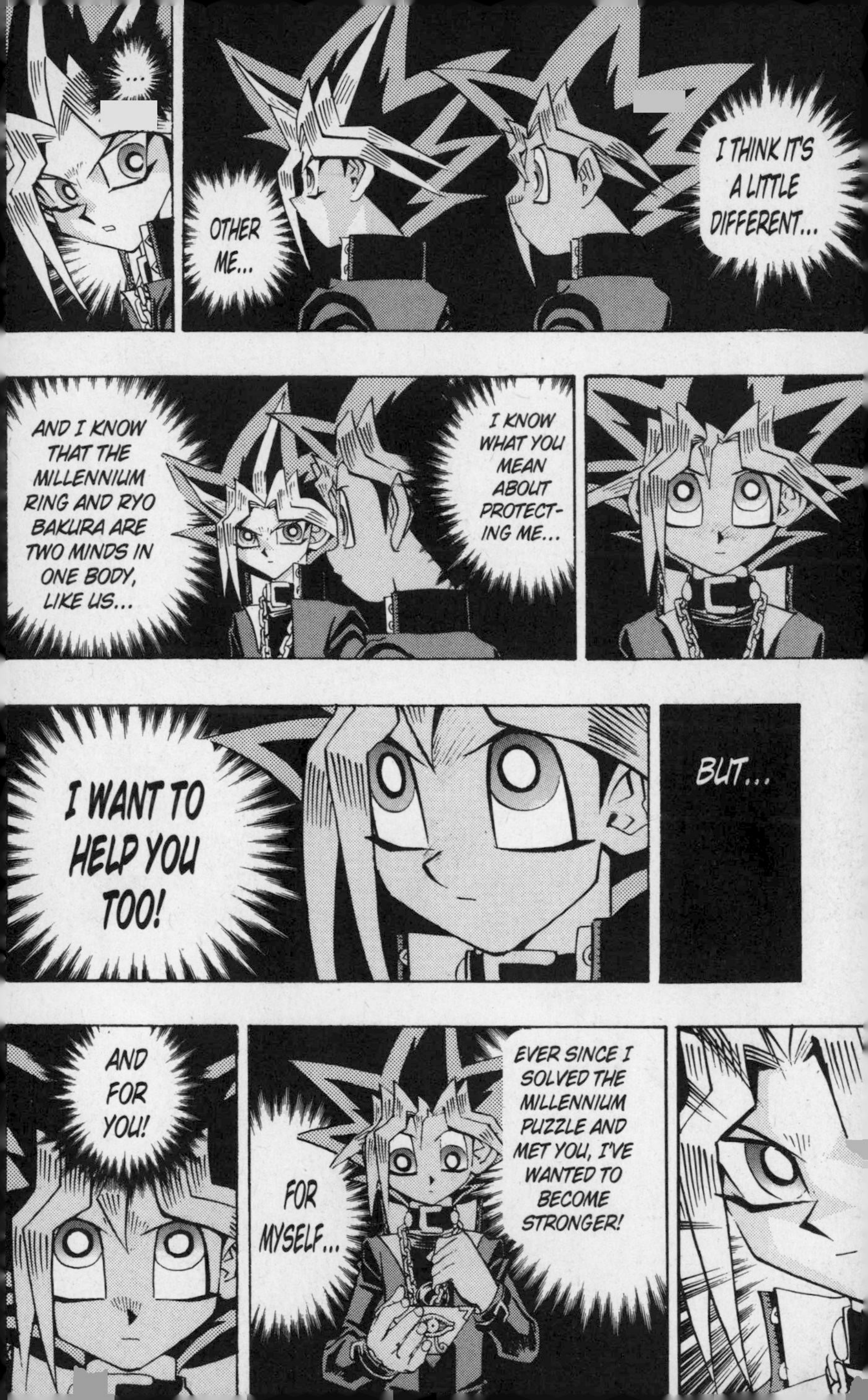
I THINK IT'S A LITTLE DIFFERENT...
OTHER ME...
...
I KNOW WHAT YOU MEAN ABOUT PROTECTING ME...
AND I KNOW THAT THE MILLENNIUM RING AND RYO BAKURA ARE TWO MINDS IN ONE BODY, LIKE US...
BUT...
I WANT TO HELP YOU TOO!
EVER SINCE I SOLVED THE MILLENNIUM PUZZLE AND MET YOU, I'VE WANTED TO BECOME STRONGER!
FOR MYSELF...
AND FOR YOU!

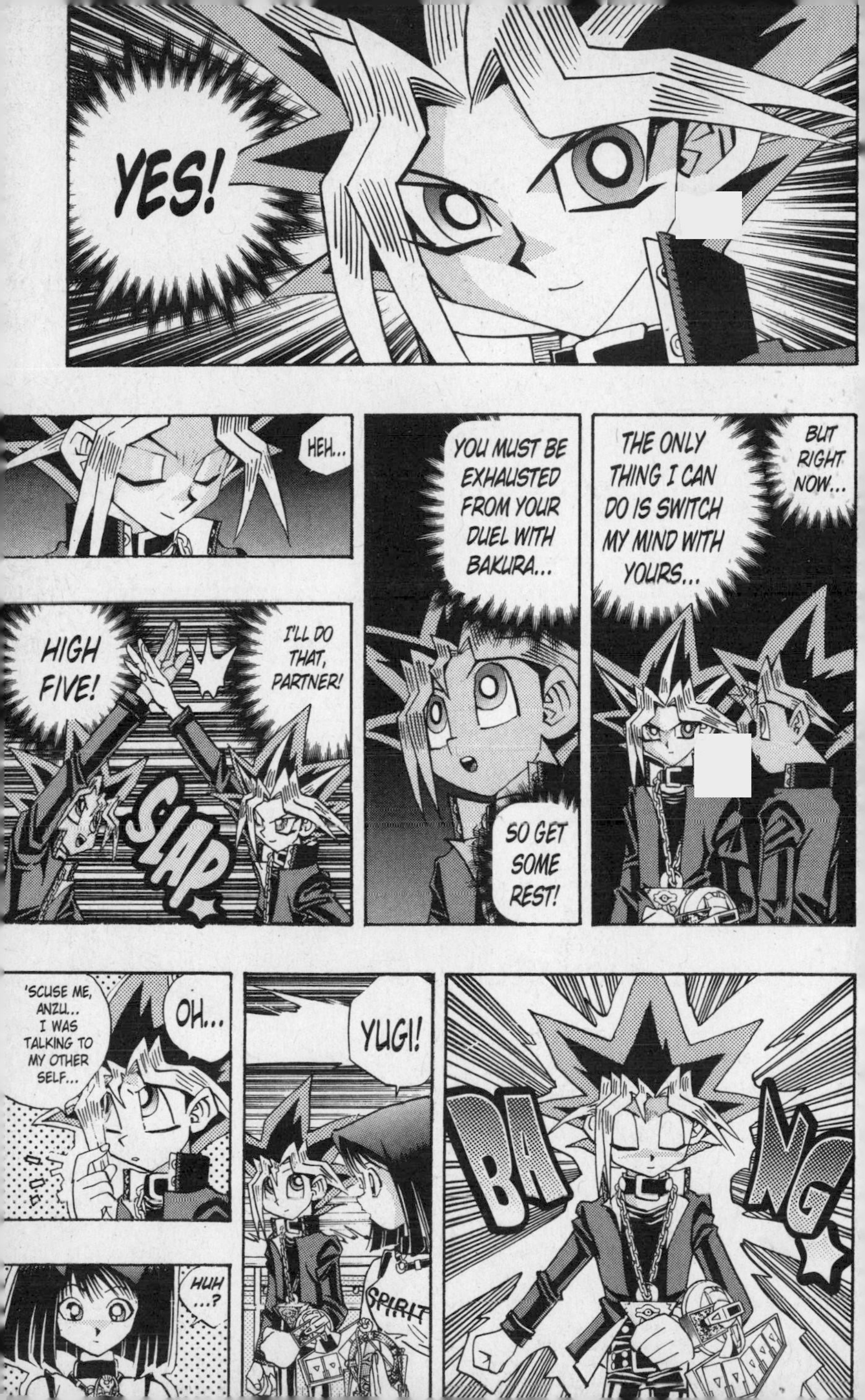
YES!
BUT RIGHT NOW...
THE ONLY THING I CAN DO IS SWITCH MY MIND WITH YOURS...
YOU MUST BE EXHAUSTED FROM YOUR DUEL WITH BAKURA...
SO GET SOME REST!
HEH...
I'LL DO THAT, PARTNER!
HIGH FIVE!
SLAP
BANG
YUGI!
SPIRIT
OH...
'SCUSE ME, ANZU... I WAS TALKING TO MY OTHER SELF...
HUH ...?

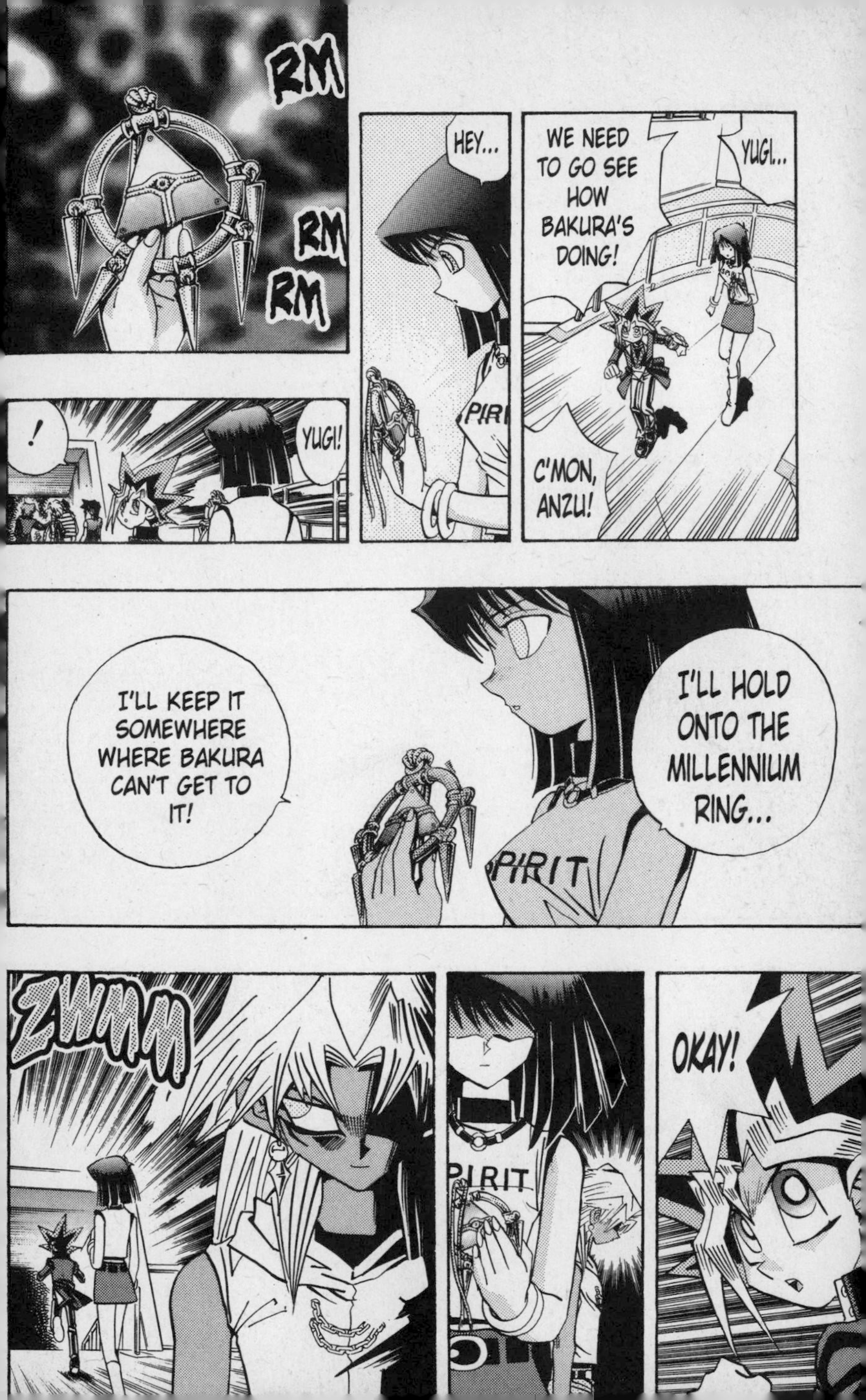
YUGI...
WE NEED TO GO SEE HOW BAKURA'S DOING!
C'MON, ANZU!
HEY...
RM
RM
RM
YUGI!
!
I'LL HOLD ONTO THE MILLENNIUM RING...
I'LL KEEP IT SOMEWHERE WHERE BAKURA CAN'T GET TO IT!
OKAY!
ZWMM

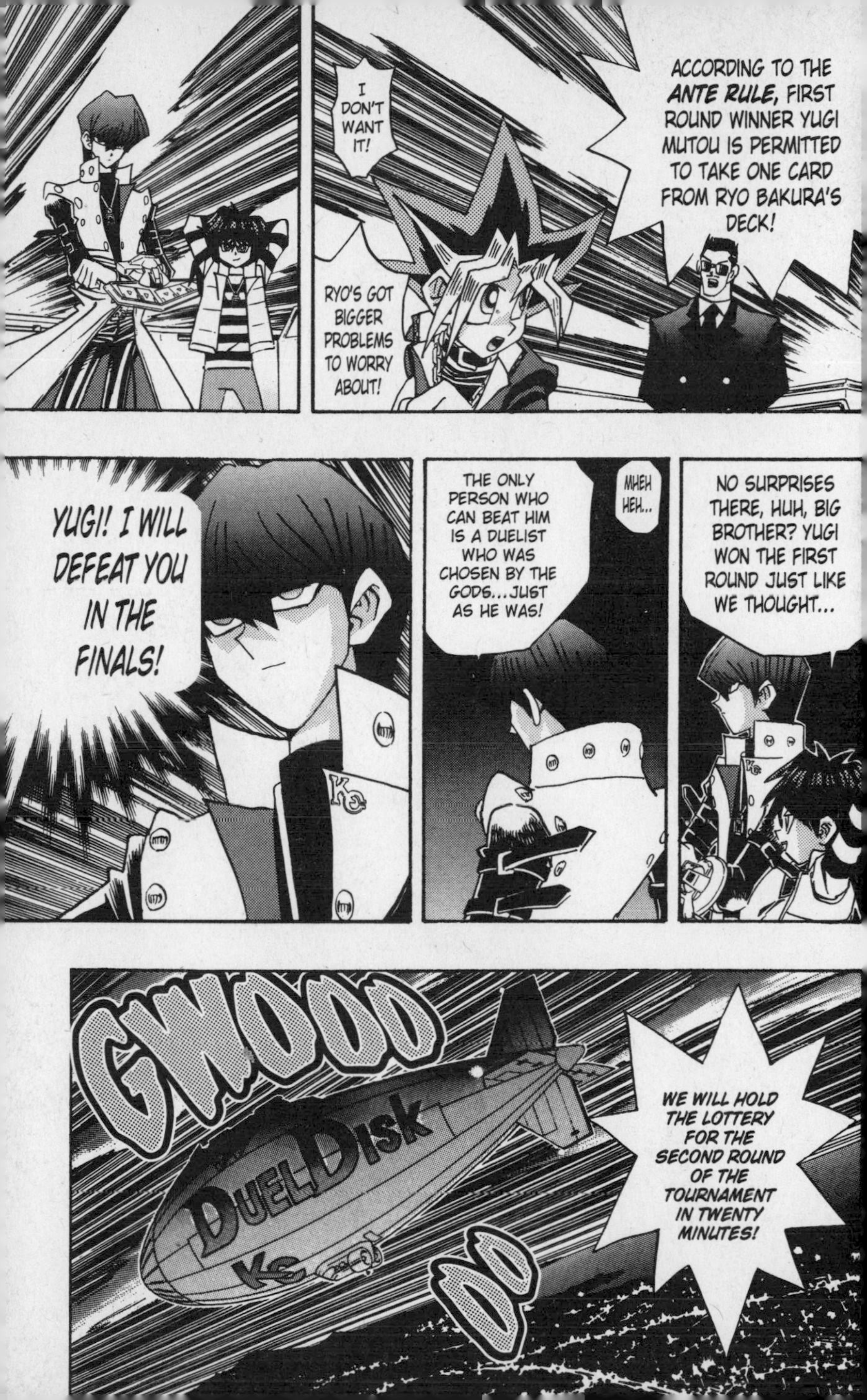
ACCORDING TO THE *ANTE RULE*, FIRST ROUND WINNER YUGI MUTOU IS PERMITTED TO TAKE ONE CARD FROM RYO BAKURA'S DECK!
I DON'T WANT IT!
RYO'S GOT BIGGER PROBLEMS TO WORRY ABOUT!
NO SURPRISES THERE, HUH, BIG BROTHER? YUGI WON THE FIRST ROUND JUST LIKE WE THOUGHT...
MHEH HEH...
THE ONLY PERSON WHO CAN BEAT HIM IS A DUELIST WHO WAS CHOSEN BY THE GODS...JUST AS HE WAS!
YUGI! I WILL DEFEAT YOU IN THE FINALS!
WE WILL HOLD THE LOTTERY FOR THE SECOND ROUND OF THE TOURNAMENT IN TWENTY MINUTES!
GWOOOOO
DUEL DISK

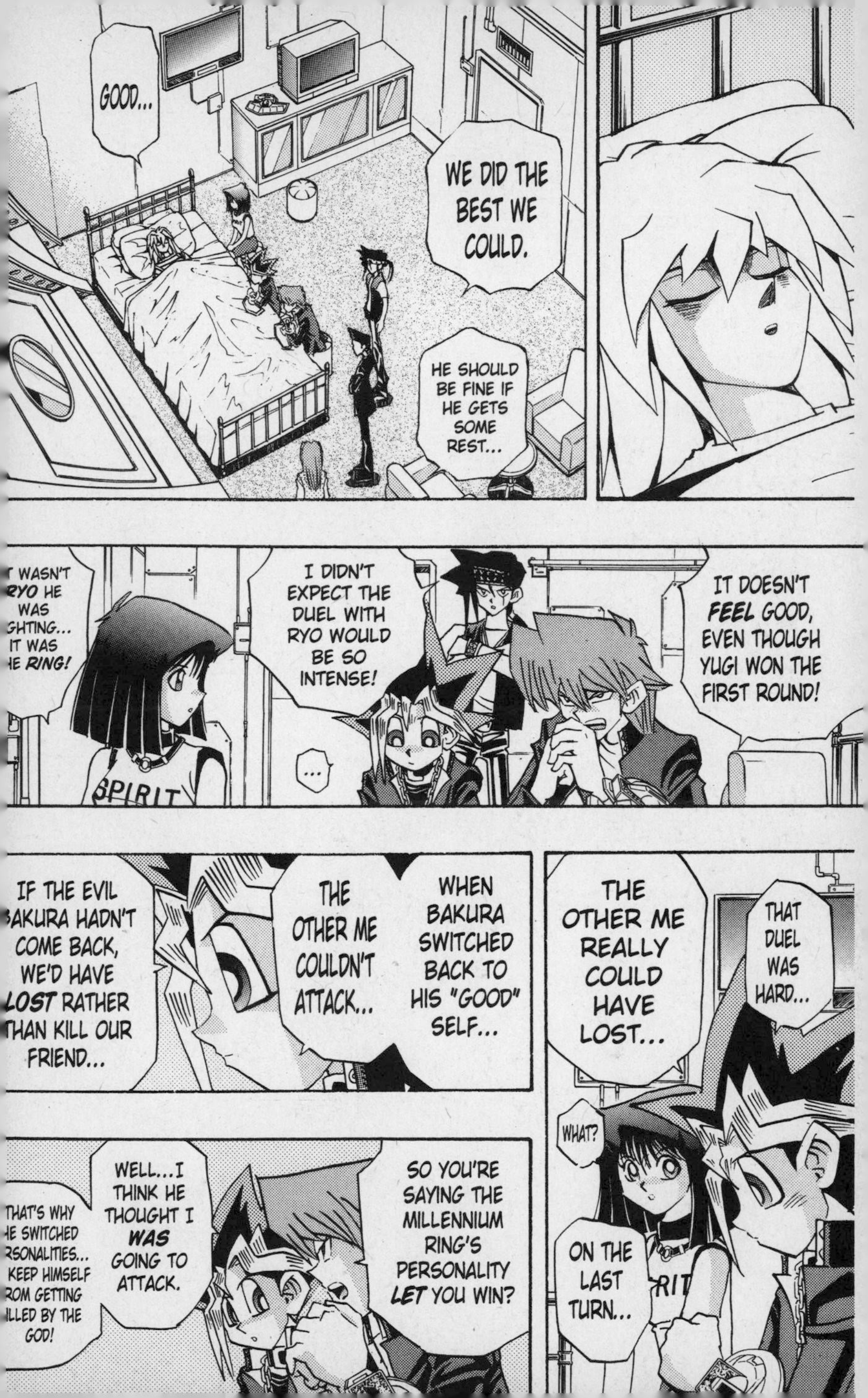
WE DID THE BEST WE COULD.
GOOD...
HE SHOULD BE FINE IF HE GETS SOME REST...
IT DOESN'T FEEL GOOD, EVEN THOUGH YUGI WON THE FIRST ROUND!
I DIDN'T EXPECT THE DUEL WITH RYO WOULD BE SO INTENSE!
...
T WASN'T RYO HE WAS GHTING... IT WAS HE RING!
THAT DUEL WAS HARD...
THE OTHER ME REALLY COULD HAVE LOST...
WHAT?
ON THE LAST TURN...
WHEN BAKURA SWITCHED BACK TO HIS "GOOD" SELF...
THE OTHER ME COULDN'T ATTACK...
IF THE EVIL BAKURA HADN'T COME BACK, WE'D HAVE LOST RATHER THAN KILL OUR FRIEND...
SO YOU'RE SAYING THE MILLENNIUM RING'S PERSONALITY LET YOU WIN?
WELL...I THINK HE THOUGHT I WAS GOING TO ATTACK.
THAT'S WHY HE SWITCHED RSONALITIES... KEEP HIMSELF ROM GETTING ILLED BY THE GOD!

READ THIS WAY

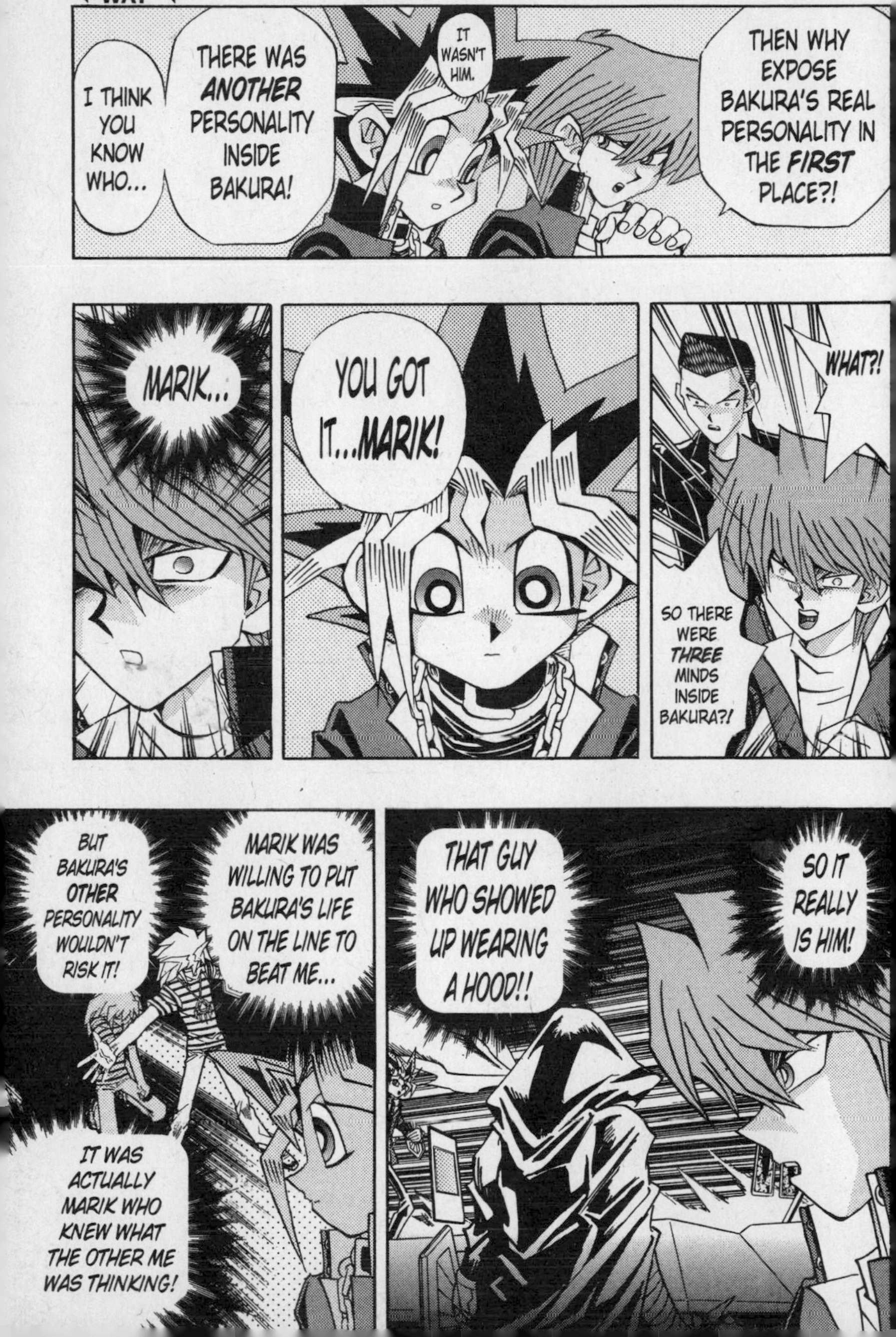
THEN WHY EXPOSE BAKURA'S REAL PERSONALITY IN THE FIRST PLACE?!
IT WASN'T HIM.
THERE WAS ANOTHER PERSONALITY INSIDE BAKURA!
I THINK YOU KNOW WHO...
WHAT?!
SO THERE WERE THREE MINDS INSIDE BAKURA?!
YOU GOT IT...MARIK!
MARIK...
SO IT REALLY IS HIM!
THAT GUY WHO SHOWED UP WEARING A HOOD!!
MARIK WAS WILLING TO PUT BAKURA'S LIFE ON THE LINE TO BEAT ME...
BUT BAKURA'S OTHER PERSONALITY WOULDN'T RISK IT!
IT WAS ACTUALLY MARIK WHO KNEW WHAT THE OTHER ME WAS THINKING!

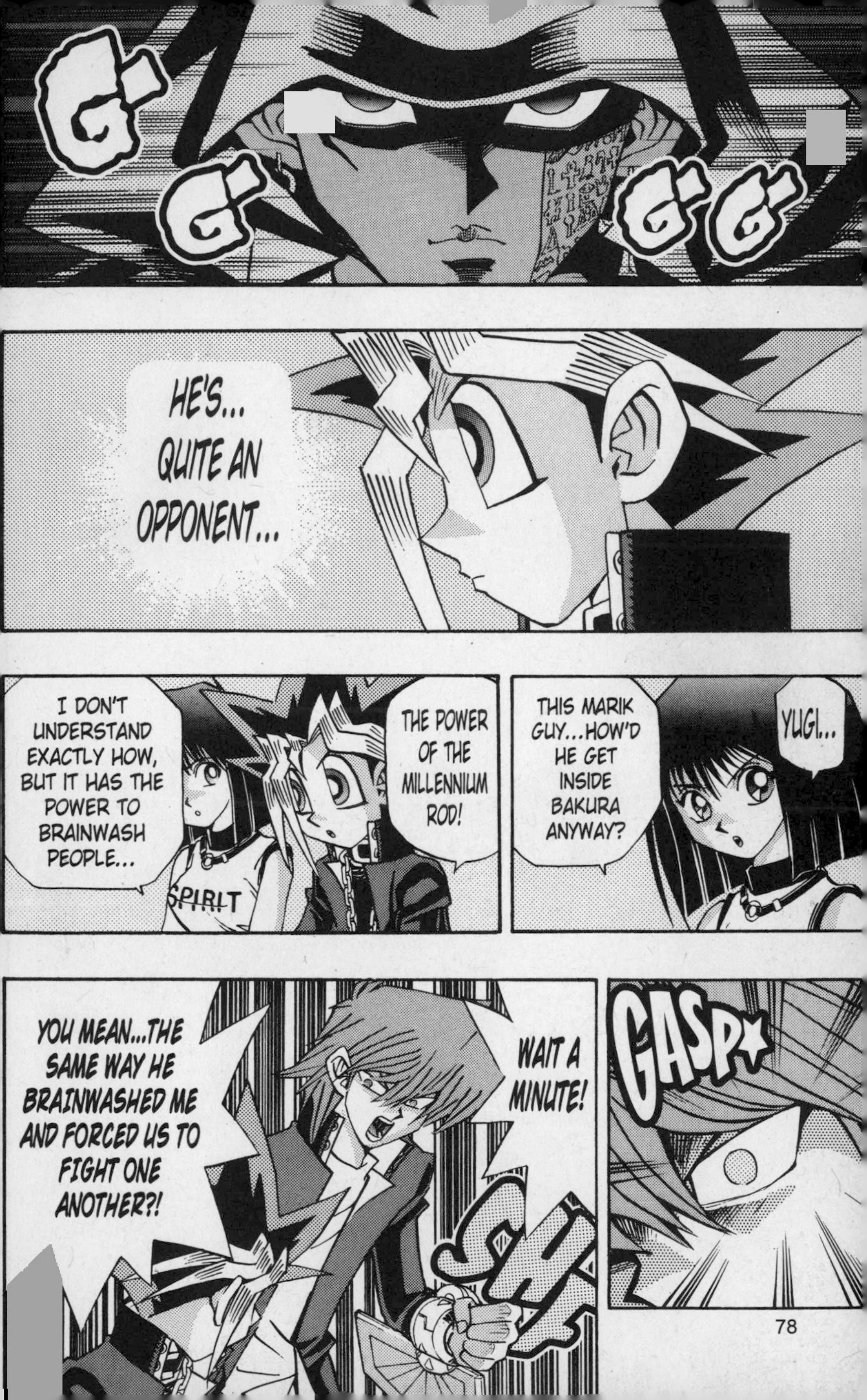
G G G G
HE'S... QUITE AN OPPONENT...
YUGI...
THIS MARIK GUY...HOW'D HE GET INSIDE BAKURA ANYWAY?
THE POWER OF THE MILLENNIUM ROD!
I DON'T UNDERSTAND EXACTLY HOW, BUT IT HAS THE POWER TO BRAINWASH PEOPLE...
SPIRIT
GASP
WAIT A MINUTE!
YOU MEAN...THE SAME WAY HE BRAINWASHED ME AND FORCED US TO FIGHT ONE ANOTHER?!

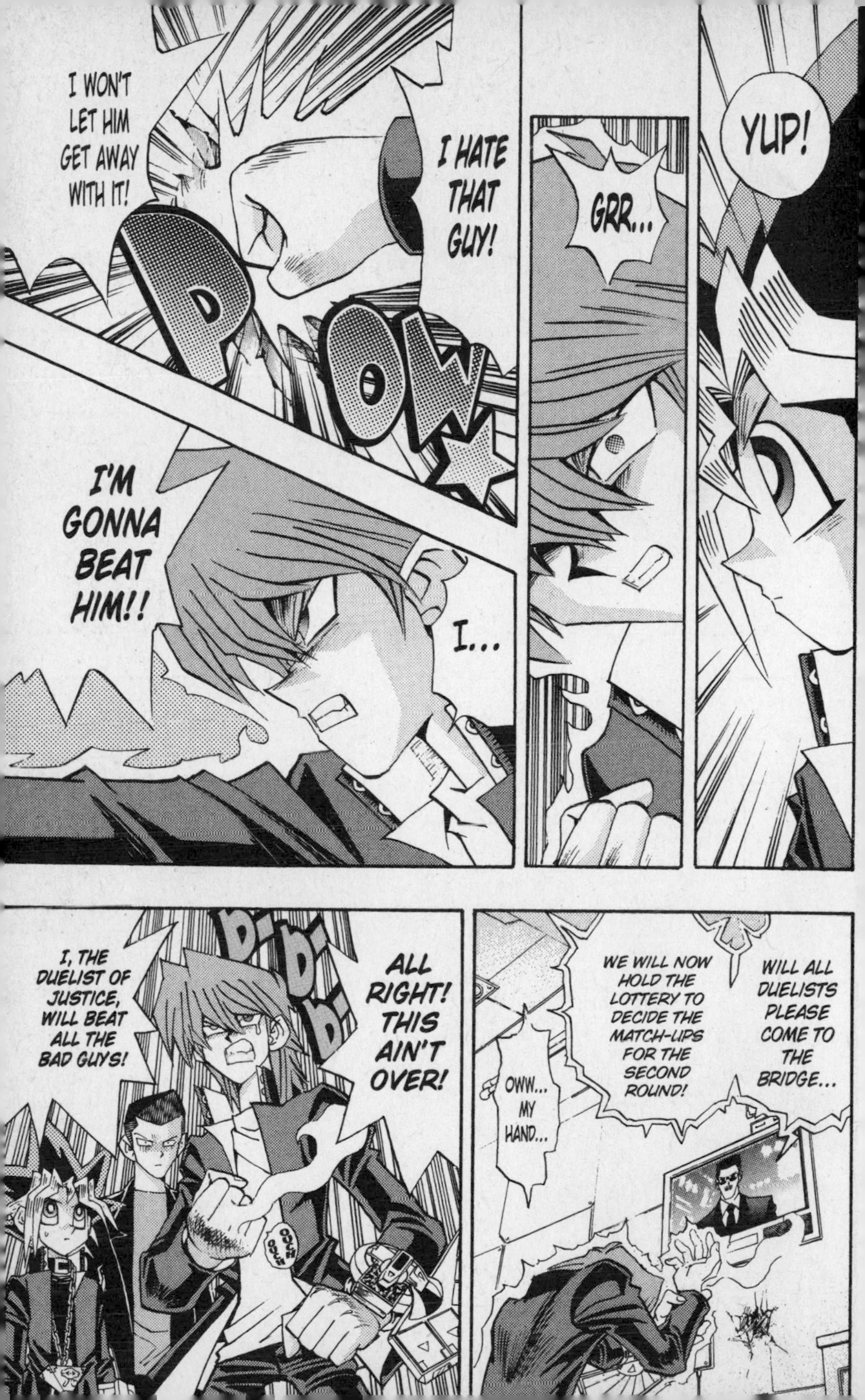
YUP!
GRR...
I HATE THAT GUY!
I WON'T LET HIM GET AWAY WITH IT!
POW
I...
I'M GONNA BEAT HIM!!
WILL ALL DUELISTS PLEASE COME TO THE BRIDGE...
WE WILL NOW HOLD THE LOTTERY TO DECIDE THE MATCH-UPS FOR THE SECOND ROUND!
OWW... MY HAND...
ALL RIGHT! THIS AIN'T OVER!
I, THE DUELIST OF JUSTICE, WILL BEAT ALL THE BAD GUYS!
OUCH OUCH

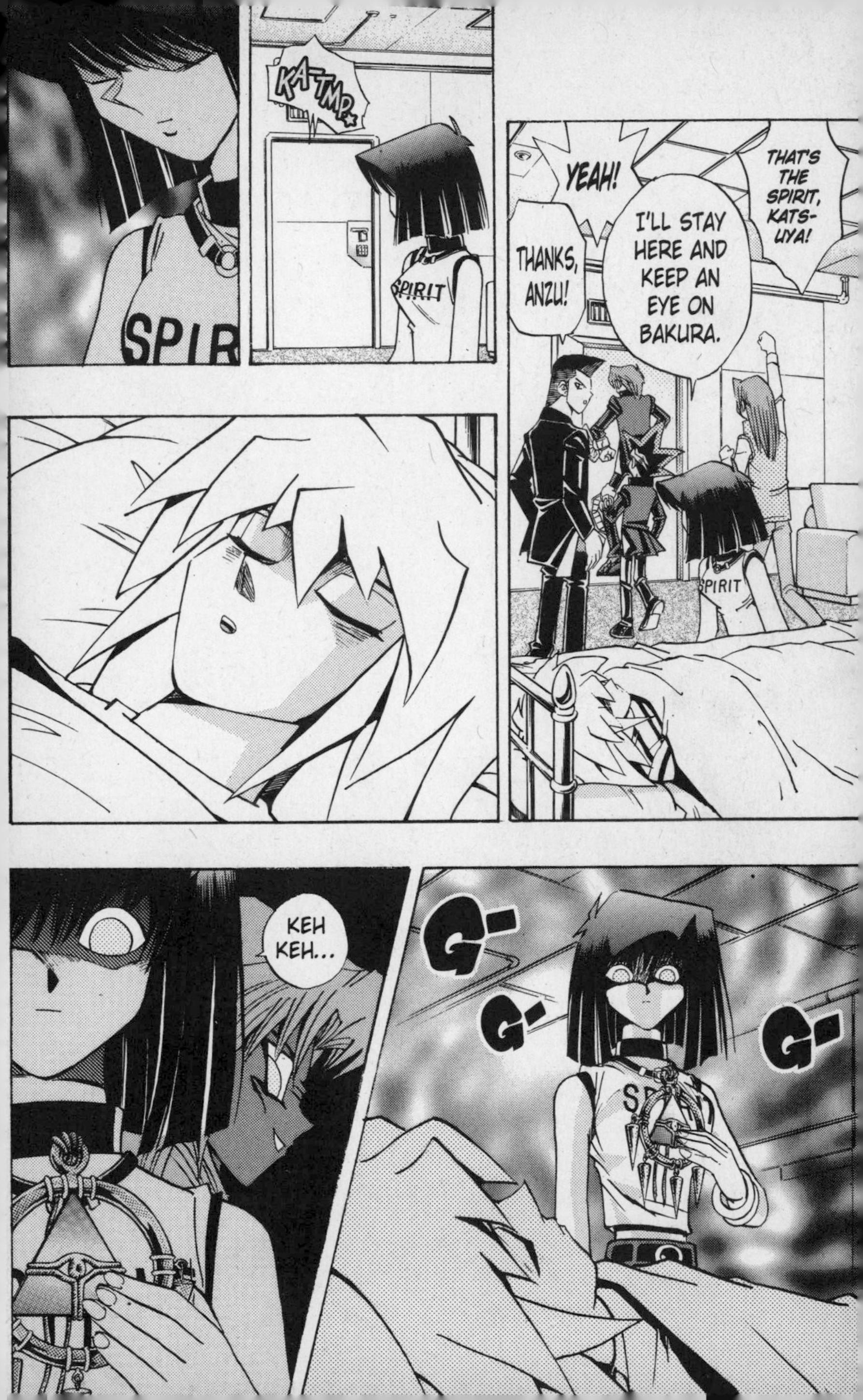
THAT'S THE SPIRIT, KATSUYA!
YEAH!
I'LL STAY HERE AND KEEP AN EYE ON BAKURA.
THANKS, ANZU!
SPIRIT
KA-TMP
SPIRIT
SPIR
G-
G-
G-
KEH KEH...

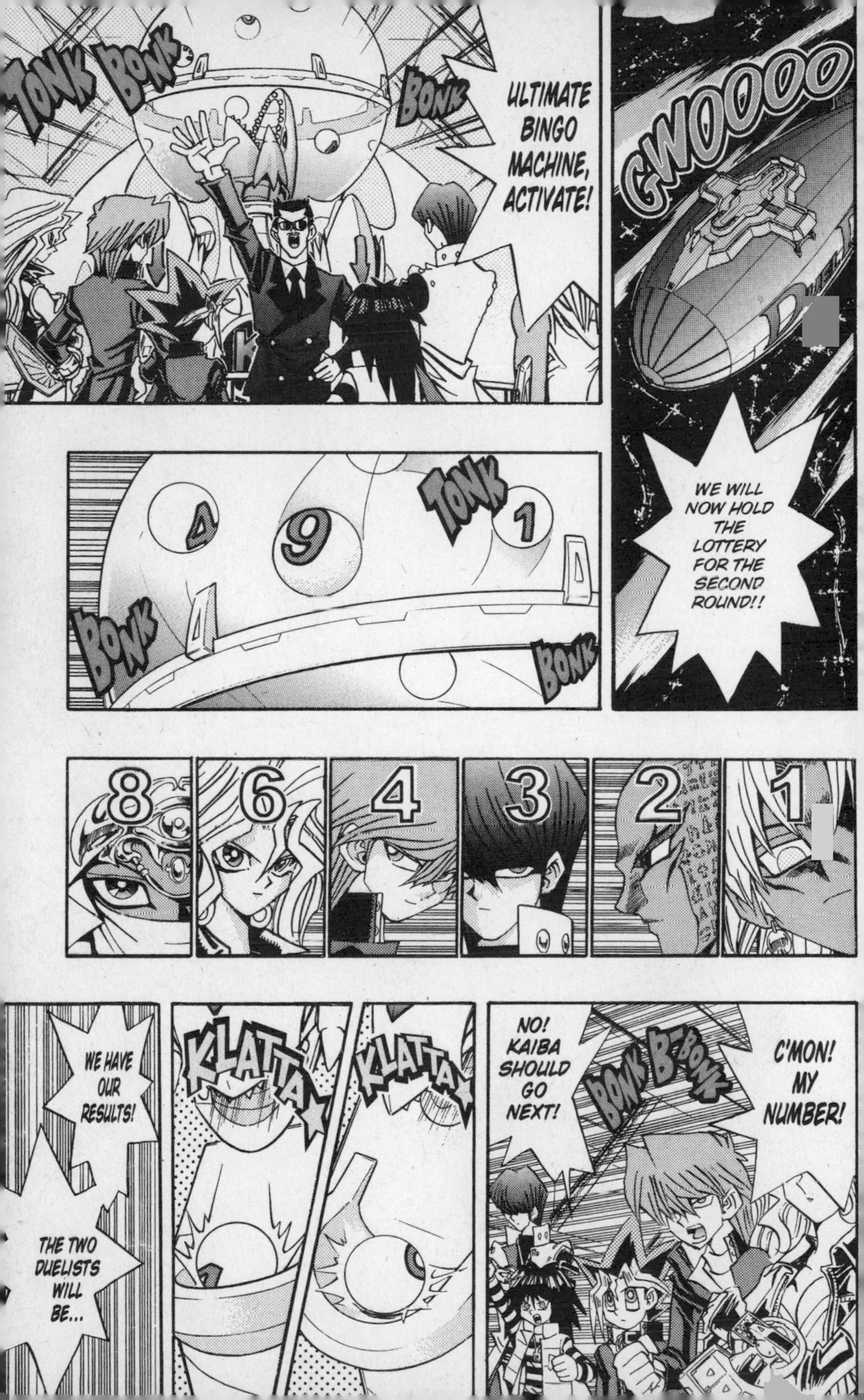
GWOOOO
WE WILL NOW HOLD THE LOTTERY FOR THE SECOND ROUND!!
ULTIMATE BINGO MACHINE, ACTIVATE!
BONK
TONK BONK
TONK
1
9
4
BONK
BONK
1
2
3
4
6
8
C'MON! MY NUMBER!
BONK B-BONK
NO! KAIBA SHOULD GO NEXT!
KLATTA
KLATTA
WE HAVE OUR RESULTS!
THE TWO DUELISTS WILL BE...

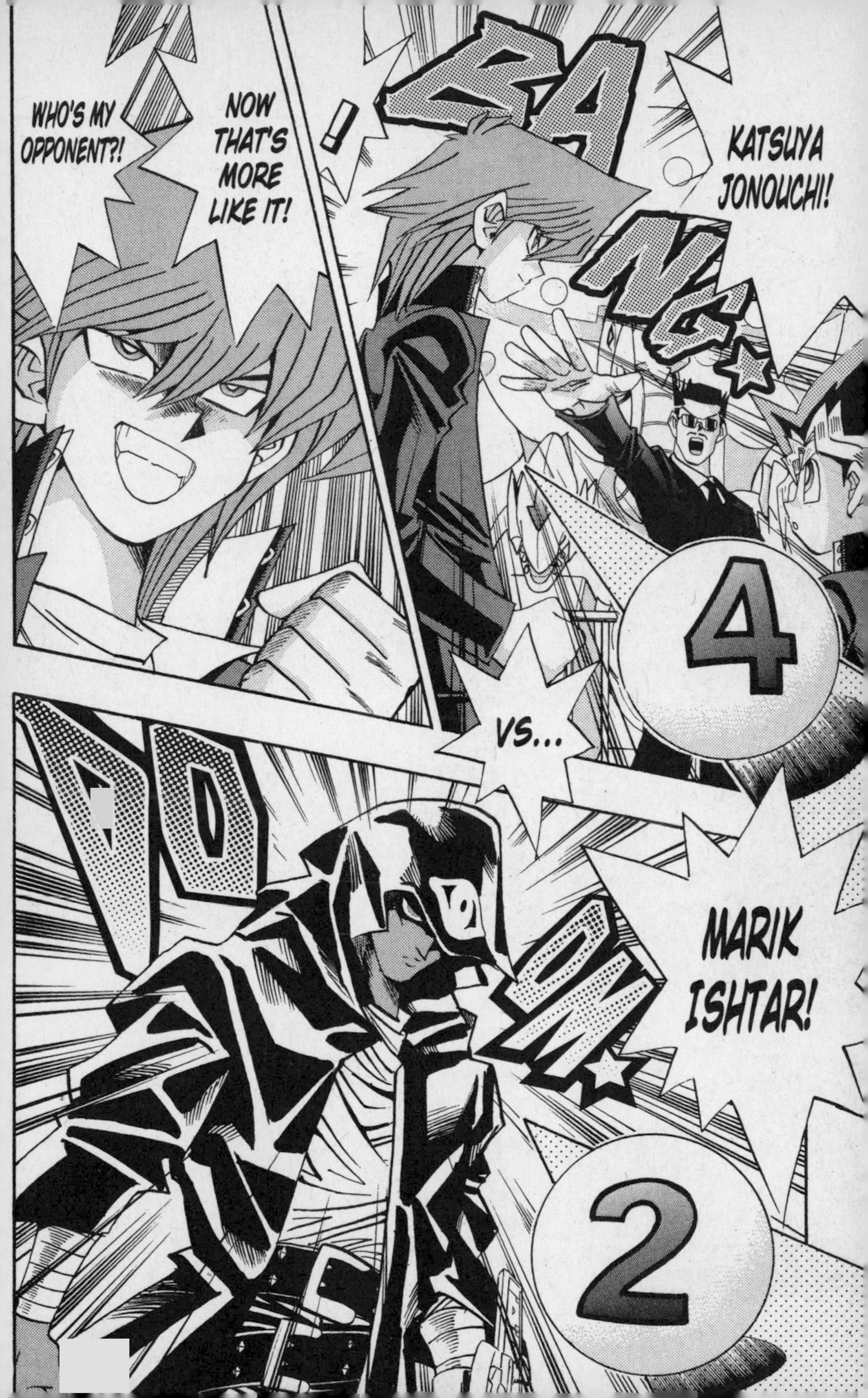
!
BANG
KATSUYA JONOUCHI!
4
NOW THAT'S MORE LIKE IT!
WHO'S MY OPPONENT?!
VS...
MARIK ISHTAR!
DODOM
2

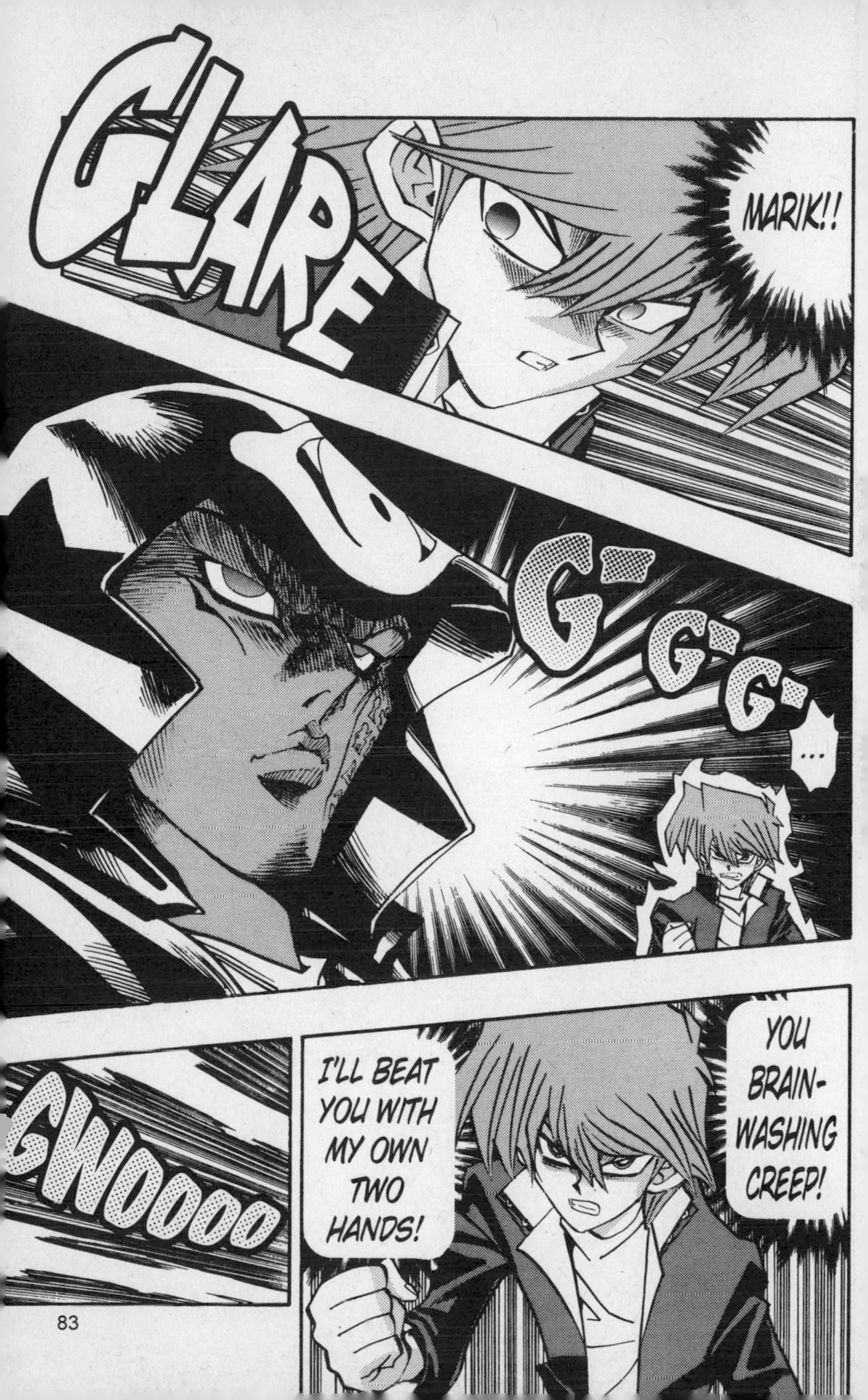
GLARE
MARIK!!
G-G-G-
...
YOU BRAIN-WASHING CREEP!
I'LL BEAT YOU WITH MY OWN TWO HANDS!
GNOOOOO

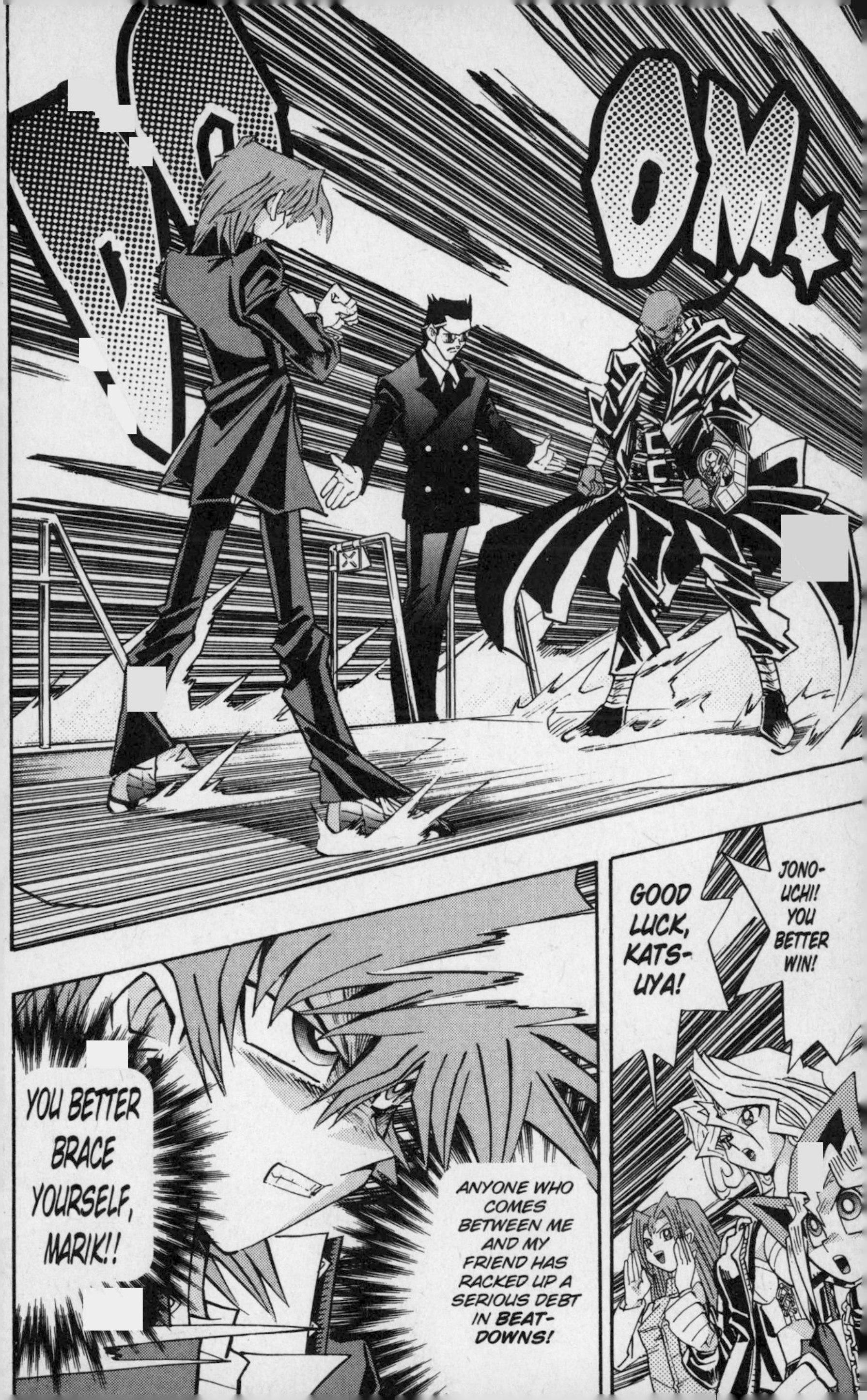
OM
JONO-UCHI! YOU BETTER WIN!
GOOD LUCK, KATS-UYA!
ANYONE WHO COMES BETWEEN ME AND MY FRIEND HAS RACKED UP A SERIOUS DEBT IN BEAT-DOWNS!
YOU BETTER BRACE YOURSELF, MARIK!!

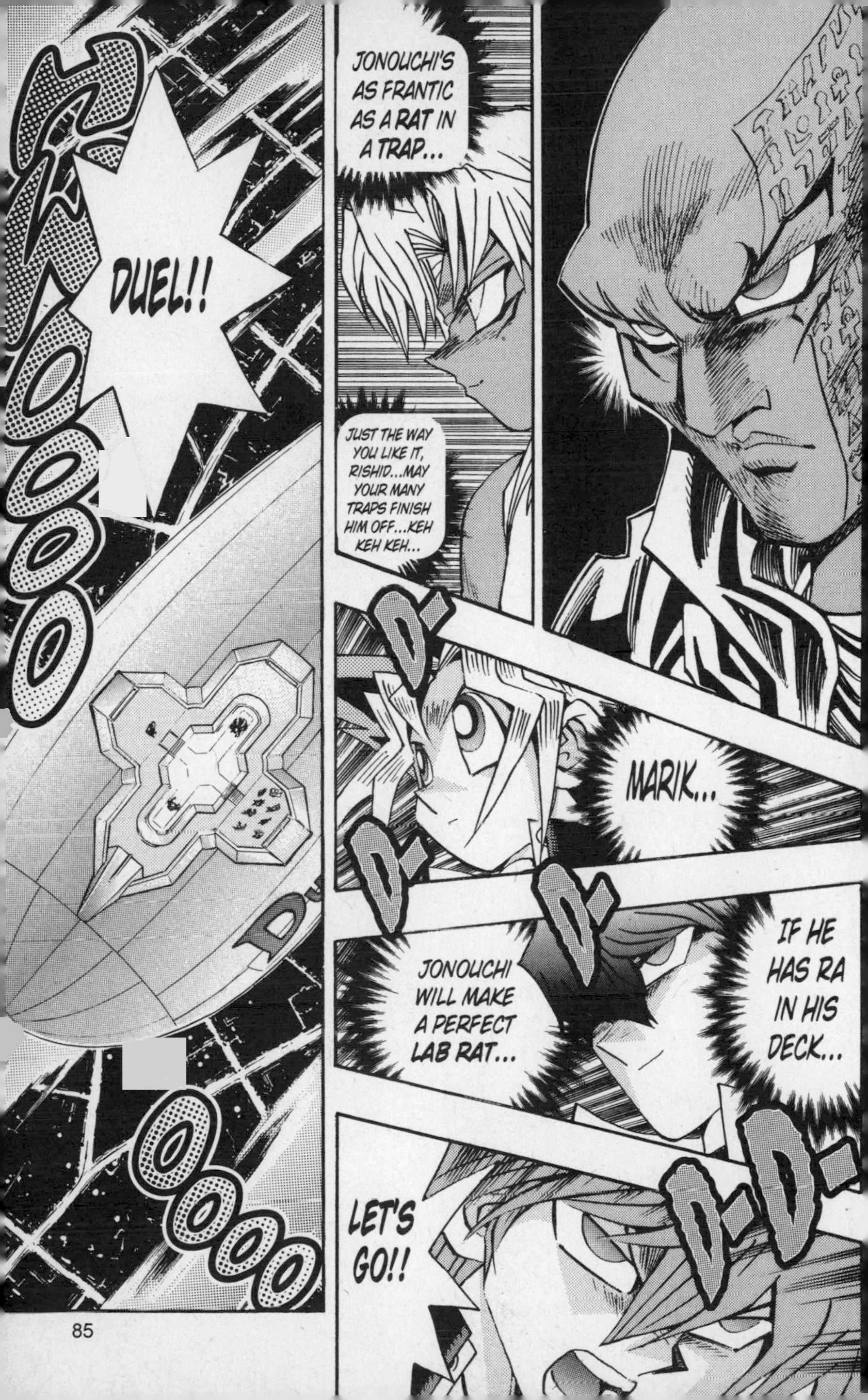
JONOUCHI'S AS FRANTIC AS A RAT IN A TRAP...
JUST THE WAY YOU LIKE IT, RISHID...MAY YOUR MANY TRAPS FINISH HIM OFF...KEH KEH KEH...
MARIK...
IF HE HAS RA IN HIS DECK...
JONOUCHI WILL MAKE A PERFECT LAB RAT...
LET'S GO!!
DUEL!!

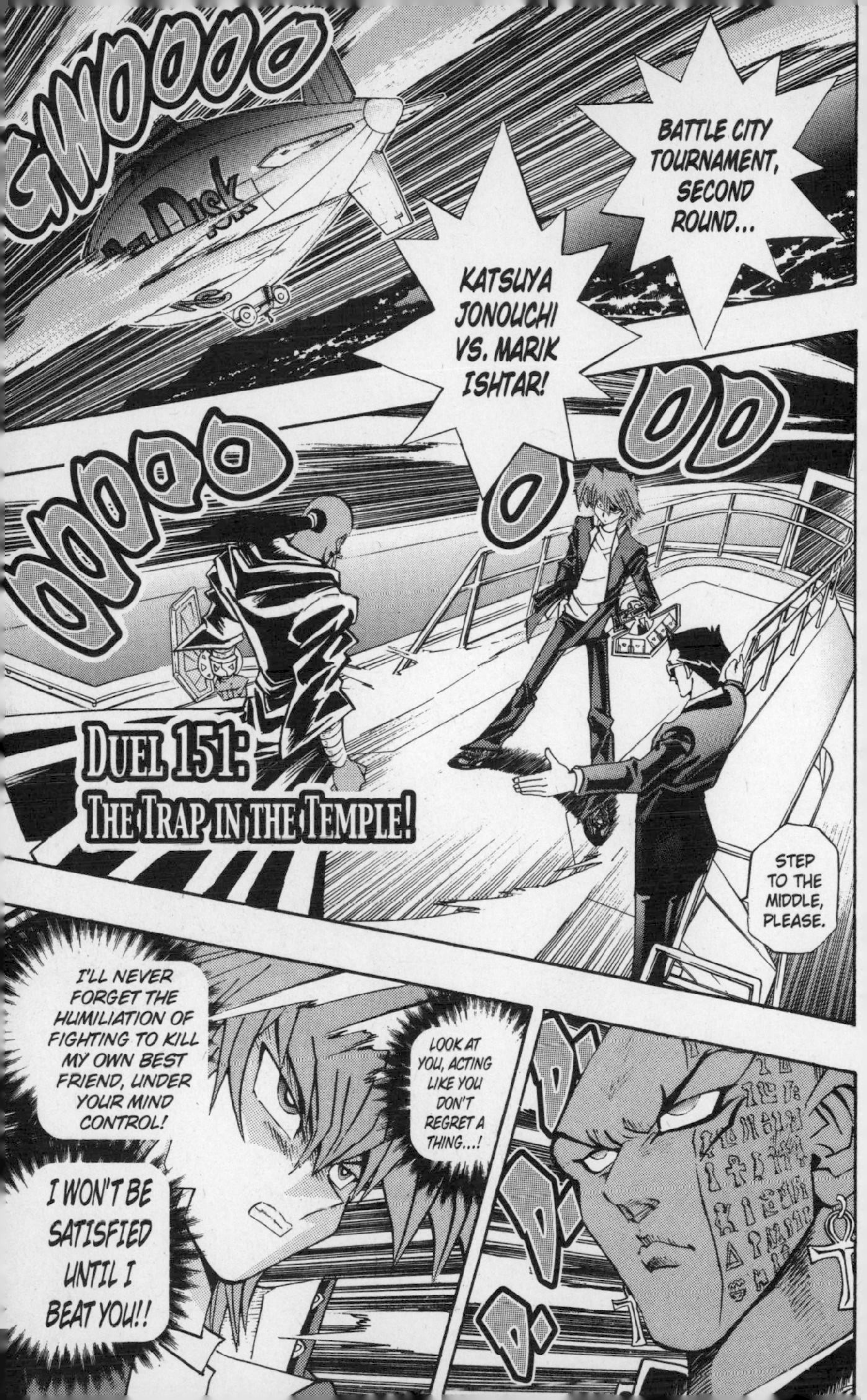
GWOOOOO
BATTLE CITY TOURNAMENT, SECOND ROUND...
KATSUYA JONOUCHI VS. MARIK ISHTAR!
OOOOOO
OOO
DUEL 151: THE TRAP IN THE TEMPLE!
STEP TO THE MIDDLE, PLEASE.
LOOK AT YOU, ACTING LIKE YOU DON'T REGRET A THING...!
I'LL NEVER FORGET THE HUMILIATION OF FIGHTING TO KILL MY OWN BEST FRIEND, UNDER YOUR MIND CONTROL!
I WON'T BE SATISFIED UNTIL I BEAT YOU!!

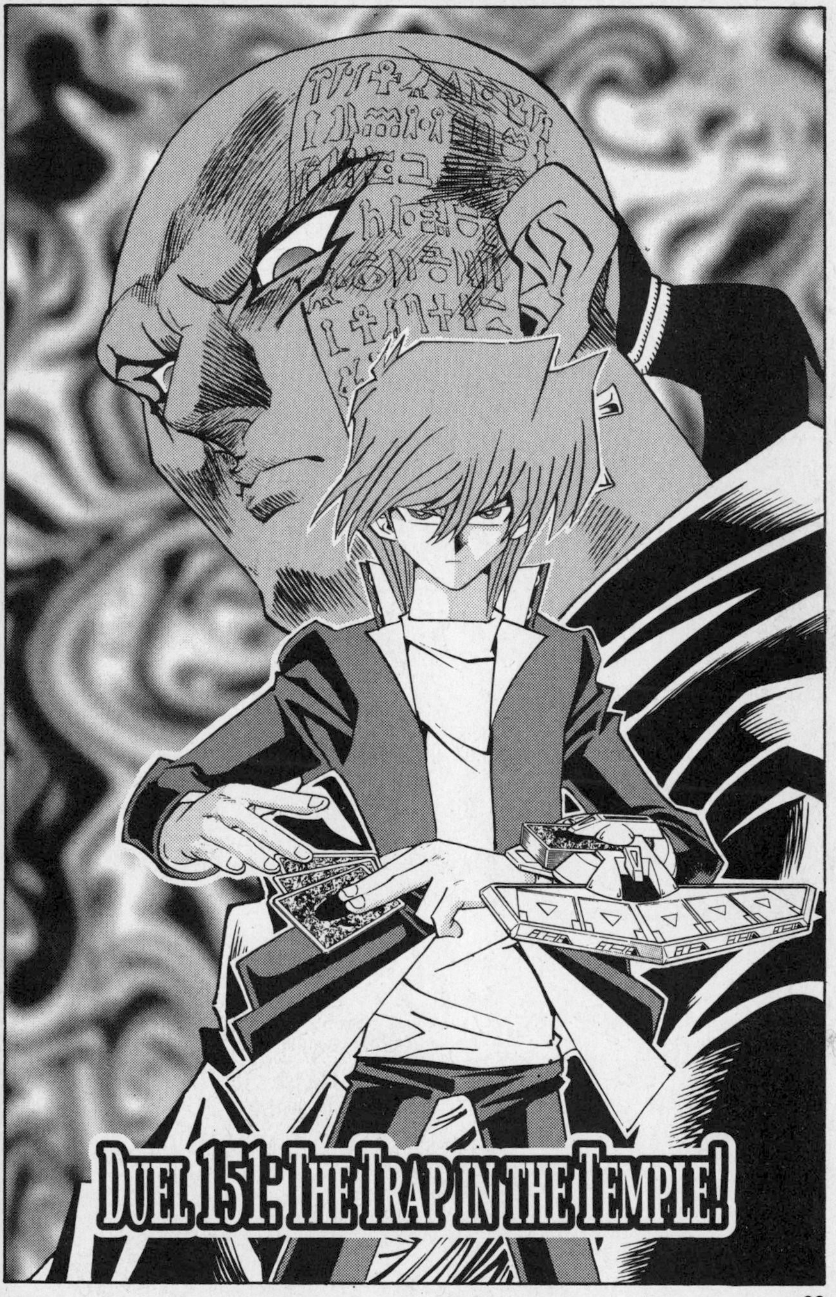
DUEL 151: THE TRAP IN THE TEMPLE!

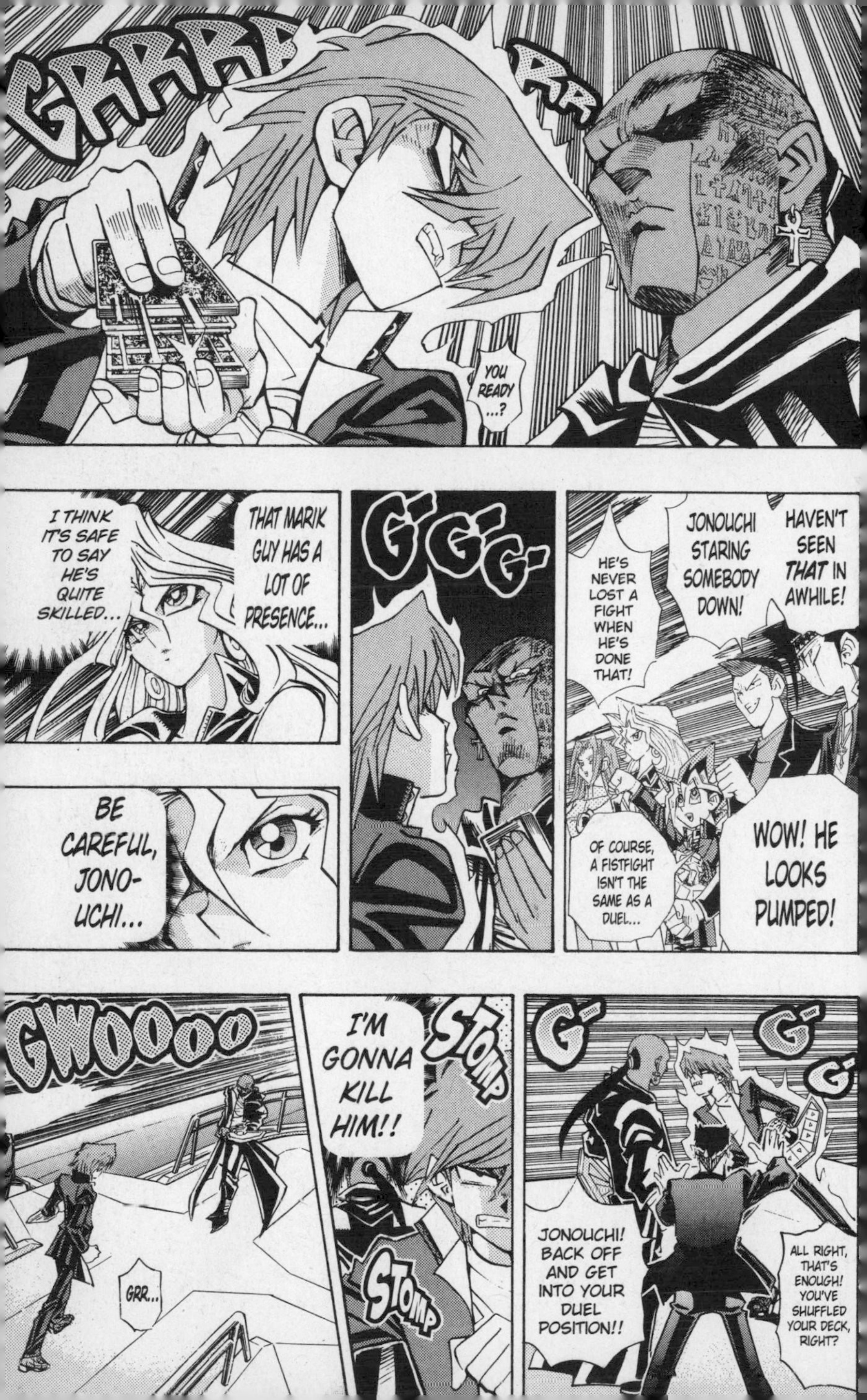
GRRRR
RR
YOU READY ...?
HAVEN'T SEEN THAT IN AWHILE!
JONOUCHI STARING SOMEBODY DOWN!
HE'S NEVER LOST A FIGHT WHEN HE'S DONE THAT!
WOW! HE LOOKS PUMPED!
OF COURSE, A FISTFIGHT ISN'T THE SAME AS A DUEL...
G'G'G'
THAT MARIK GUY HAS A LOT OF PRESENCE...
I THINK IT'S SAFE TO SAY HE'S QUITE SKILLED...
BE CAREFUL, JONO-UCHI...
G
G
G
ALL RIGHT, THAT'S ENOUGH! YOU'VE SHUFFLED YOUR DECK, RIGHT?
JONOUCHI! BACK OFF AND GET INTO YOUR DUEL POSITION!!
STOMP
I'M GONNA KILL HIM!!
STOMP
GWOOOOO
GRR...

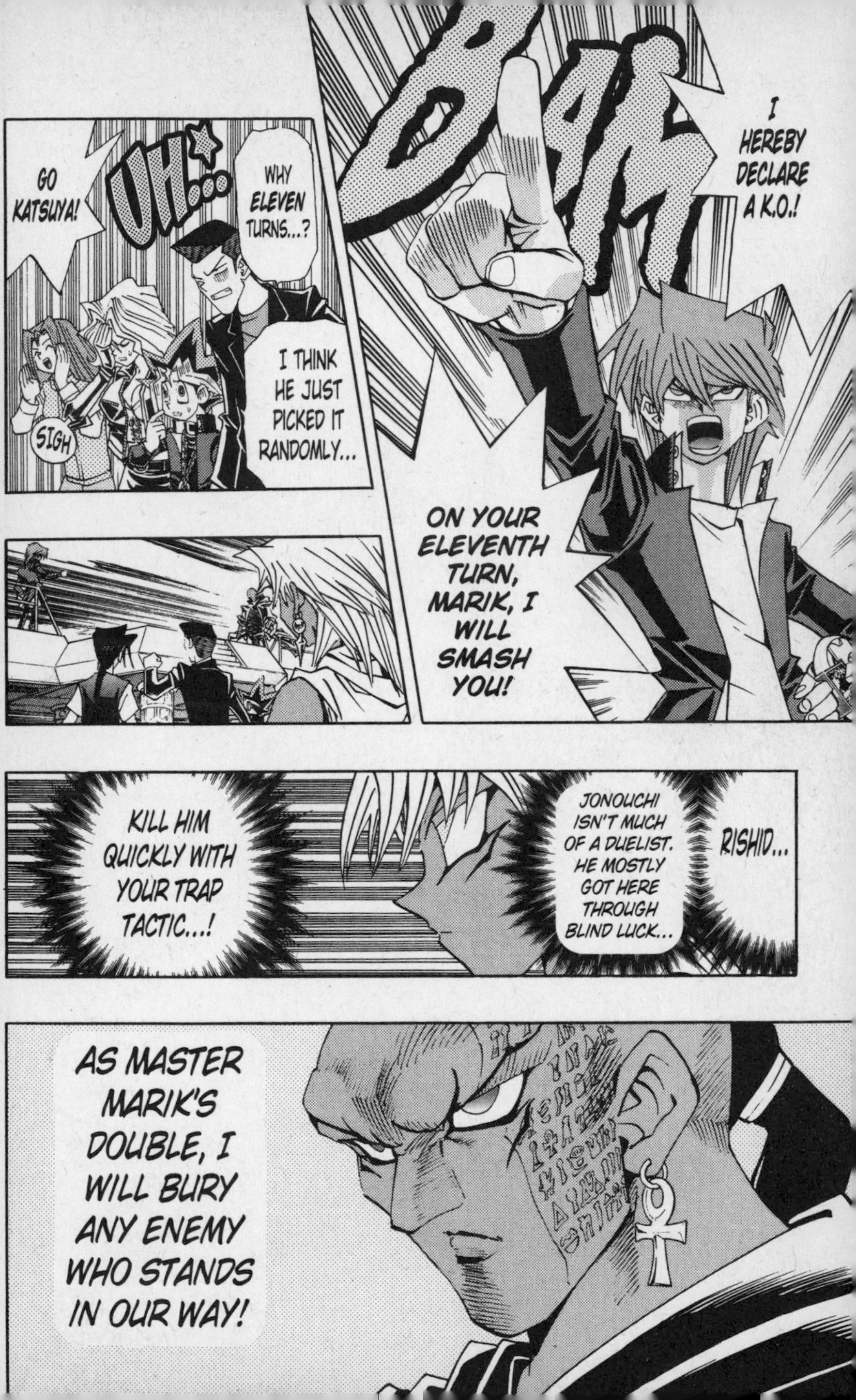
BAM
I HEREBY DECLARE A K.O.!
ON YOUR ELEVENTH TURN, MARIK, I WILL SMASH YOU!
WHY ELEVEN TURNS...?
UH!...
GO KATSUYA!
I THINK HE JUST PICKED IT RANDOMLY...
SIGH
RISHID...
JONOUCHI ISN'T MUCH OF A DUELIST. HE MOSTLY GOT HERE THROUGH BLIND LUCK...
KILL HIM QUICKLY WITH YOUR TRAP TACTIC...!
AS MASTER MARIK'S DOUBLE, I WILL BURY ANY ENEMY WHO STANDS IN OUR WAY!

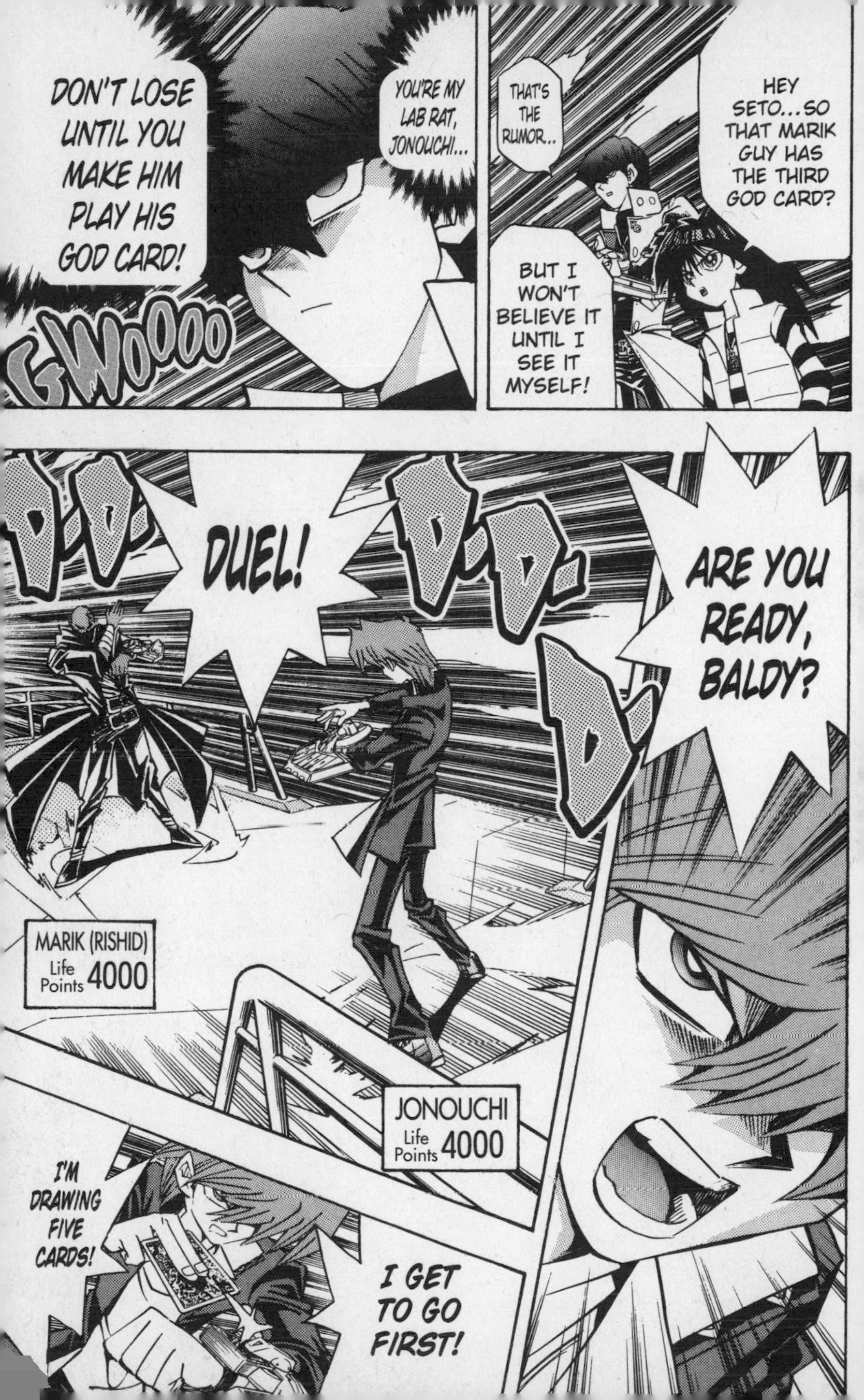

HEY SETO...SO THAT MARIK GUY HAS THE THIRD GOD CARD?
THAT'S THE RUMOR...
BUT I WON'T BELIEVE IT UNTIL I SEE IT MYSELF!
YOU'RE MY LAB RAT, JONOUCHI...
DON'T LOSE UNTIL YOU MAKE HIM PLAY HIS GOD CARD!
GWOOOO
ARE YOU READY, BALDY?
D.
D.D.
D.D.
DUEL!
MARIK (RISHID) Life Points 4000
JONOUCHI Life Points 4000
I GET TO GO FIRST!
I'M DRAWING FIVE CARDS!

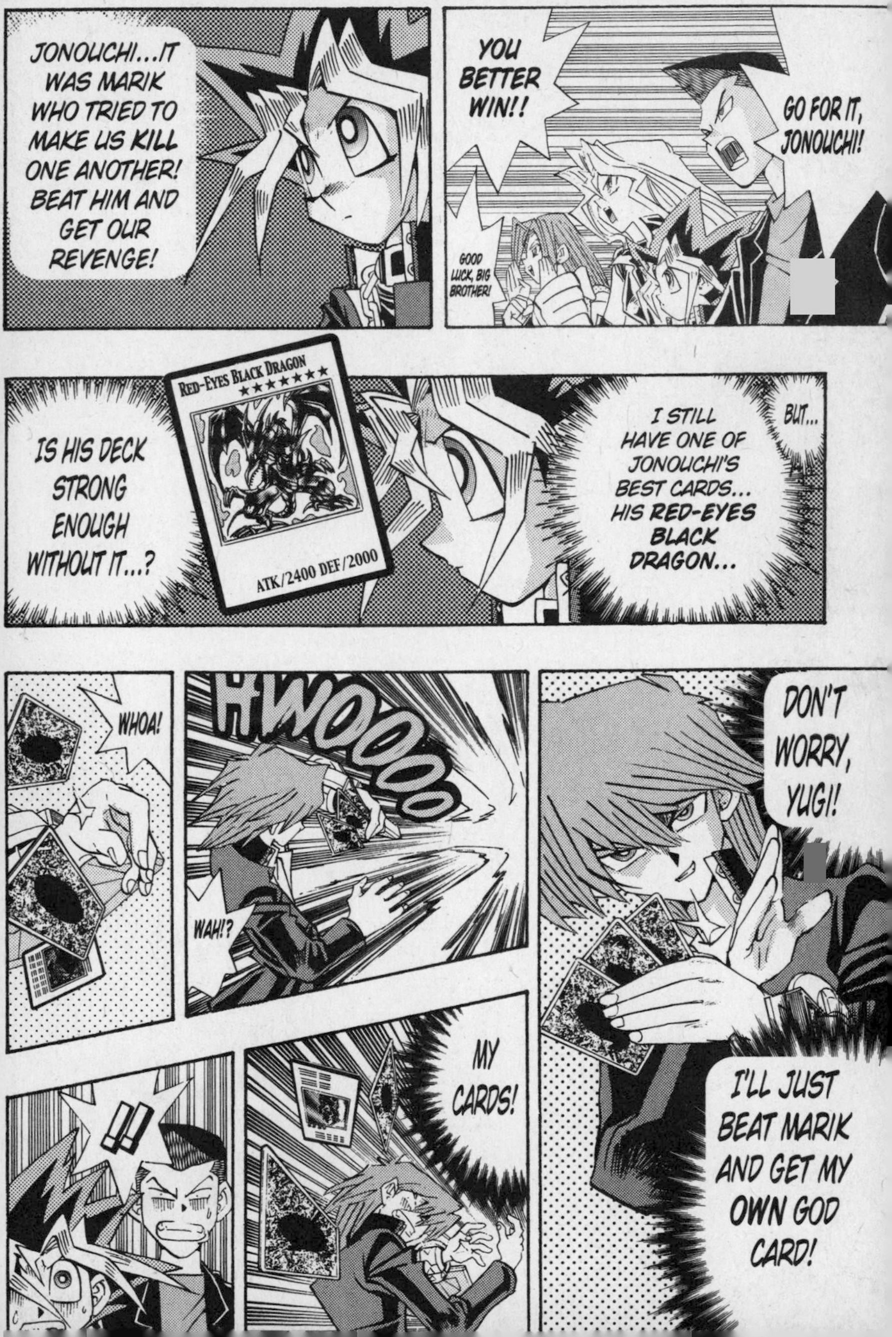
GO FOR IT, JONOUCHI!
YOU BETTER WIN!!
GOOD LUCK, BIG BROTHER!
JONOUCHI...IT WAS MARIK WHO TRIED TO MAKE US KILL ONE ANOTHER! BEAT HIM AND GET OUR REVENGE!
BUT...
I STILL HAVE ONE OF JONOUCHI'S BEST CARDS... HIS RED-EYES BLACK DRAGON...
RED-EYES BLACK DRAGON
ATK/2400 DEF/2000
IS HIS DECK STRONG ENOUGH WITHOUT IT...?
DON'T WORRY, YUGI!
I'LL JUST BEAT MARIK AND GET MY OWN GOD CARD!
HWOOOO
WAH!?
WHOA!
MY CARDS!
!!

READ THIS WAY

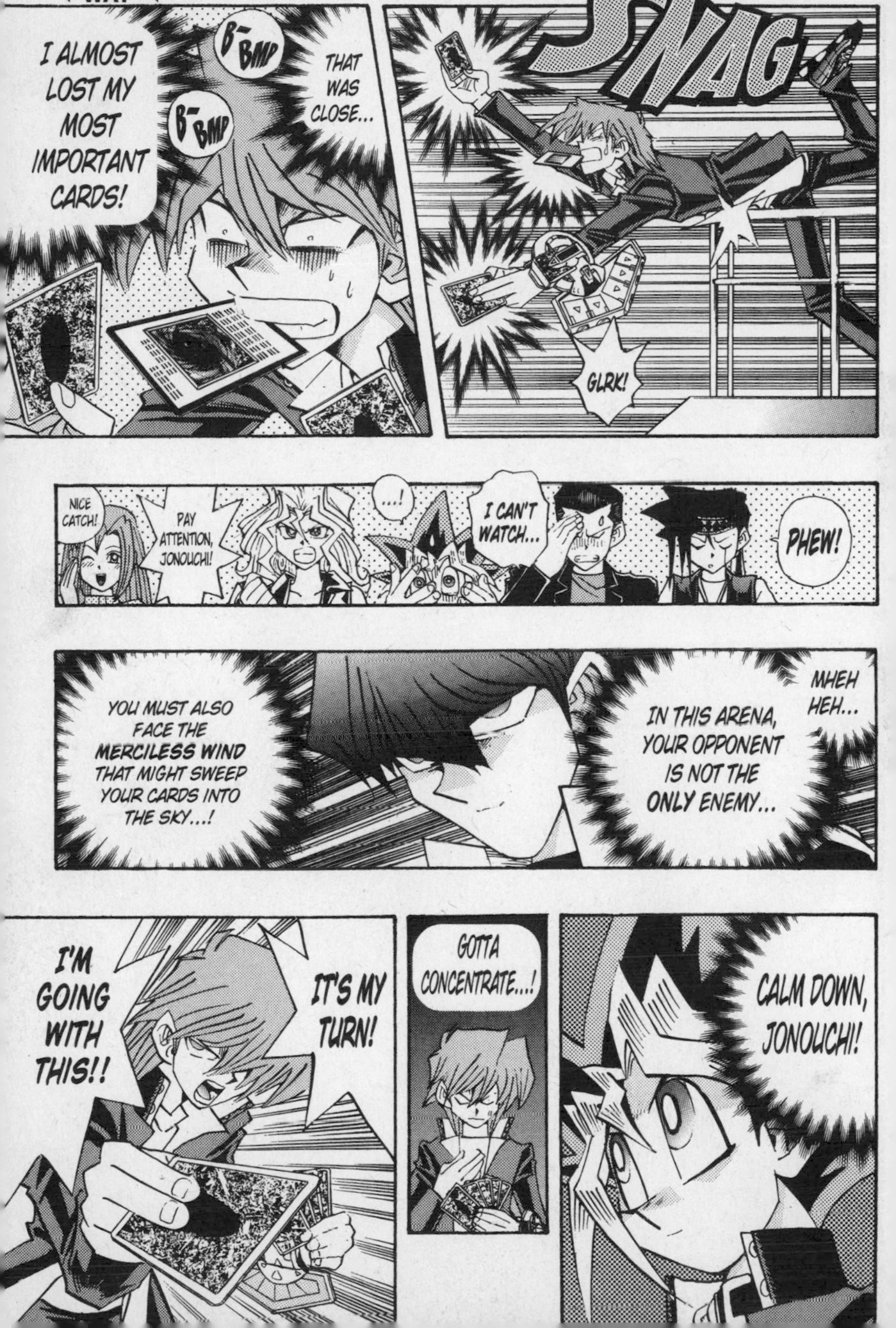
SNAG
GLRK!
THAT WAS CLOSE...
B-BMP
B-BMP
I ALMOST LOST MY MOST IMPORTANT CARDS!
PHEW!
I CAN'T WATCH...
...!
PAY ATTENTION, JONOUCHI!
NICE CATCH!
MHEH HEH...
IN THIS ARENA, YOUR OPPONENT IS NOT THE ONLY ENEMY...
YOU MUST ALSO FACE THE MERCILESS WIND THAT MIGHT SWEEP YOUR CARDS INTO THE SKY...!
CALM DOWN, JONOUCHI!
GOTTA CONCENTRATE...!
IT'S MY TURN!
I'M GOING WITH THIS!!

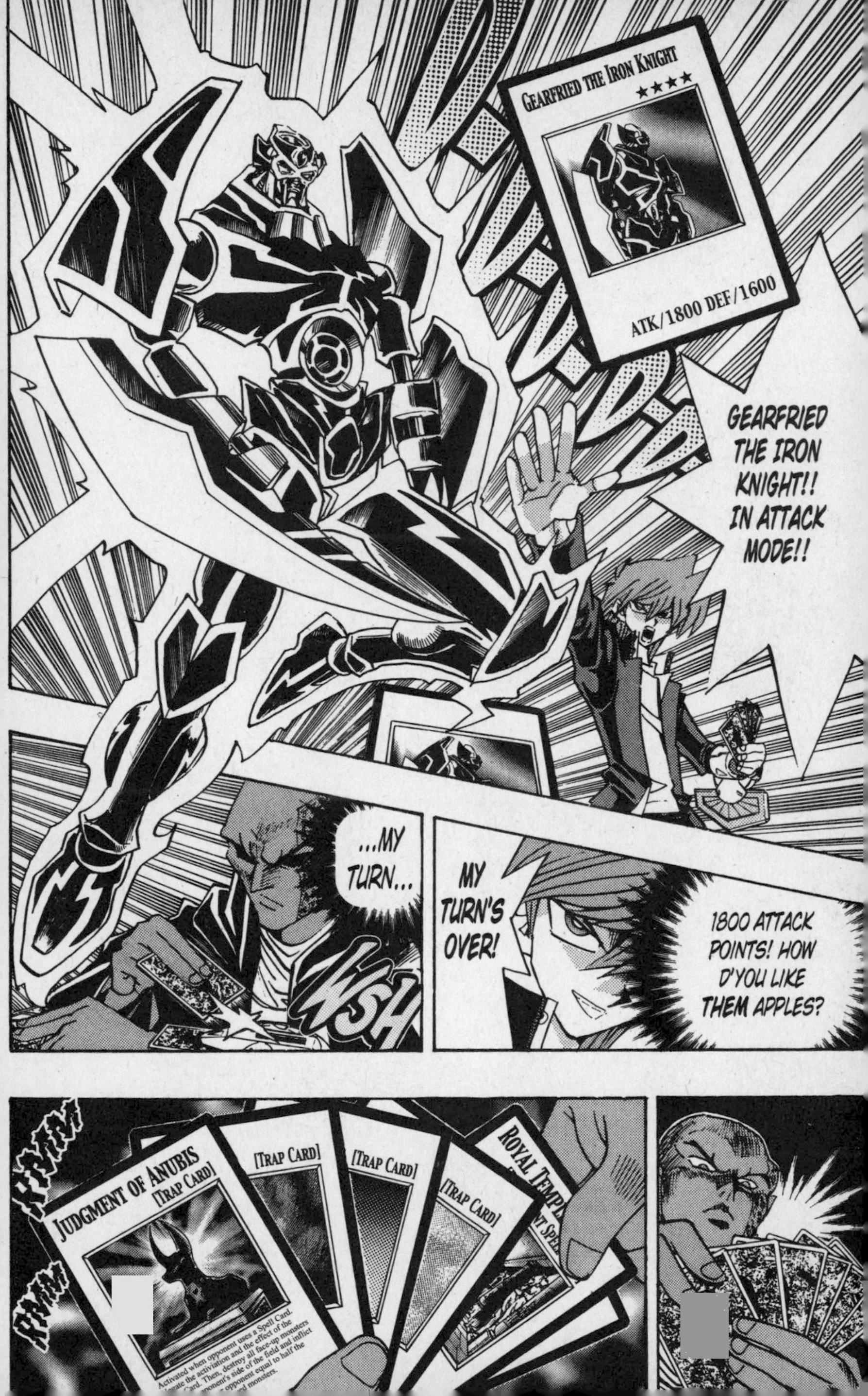

GEARFRIED THE IRON KNIGHT
★★★★
ATK/1800 DEF/1600
GEARFRIED THE IRON KNIGHT!! IN ATTACK MODE!!
1800 ATTACK POINTS! HOW D'YOU LIKE THEM APPLES?
MY TURN'S OVER!
...MY TURN...
WSH
JUDGMENT OF ANUBIS
[TRAP CARD]
[TRAP CARD]
[TRAP CARD]
[TRAP CARD]

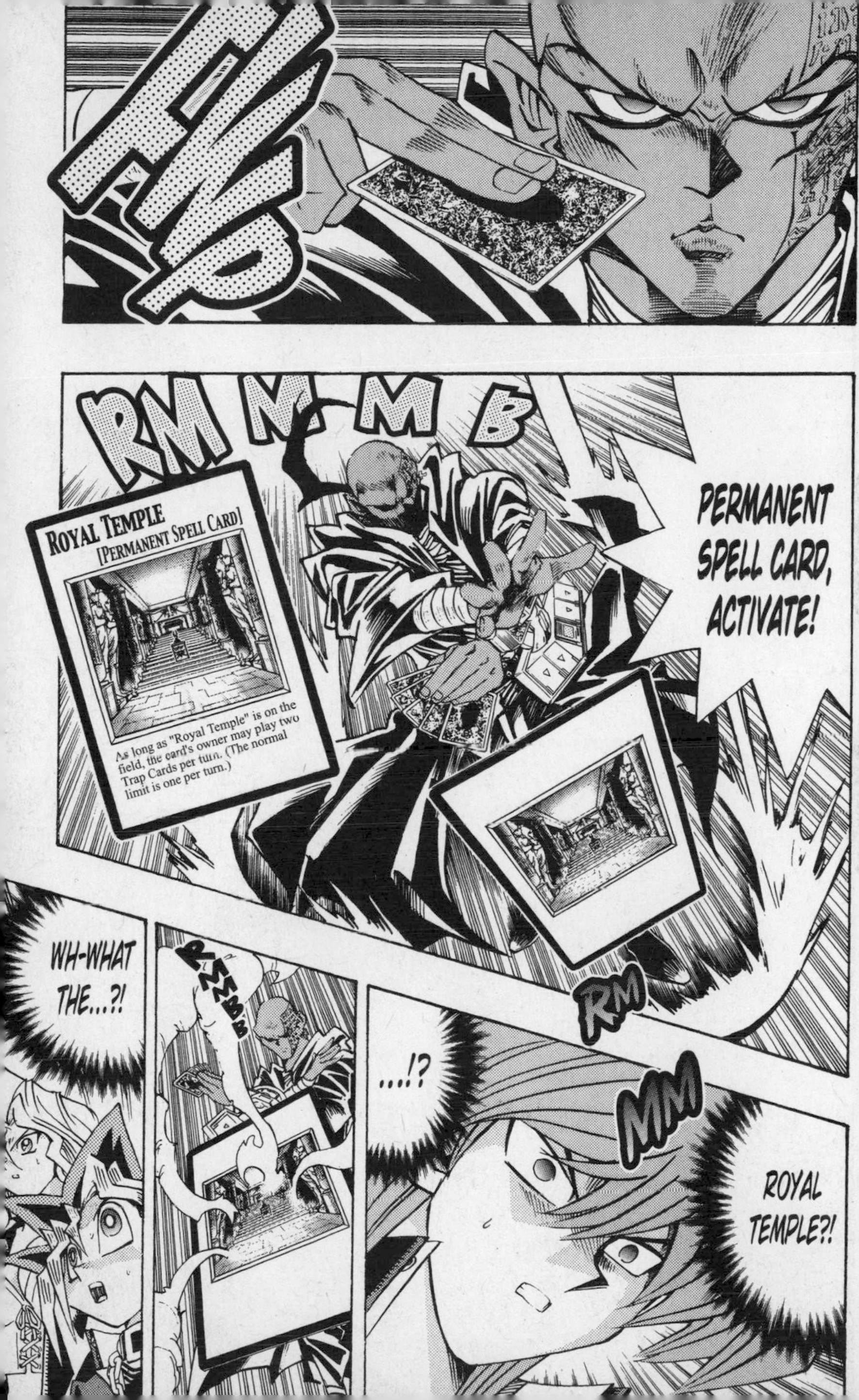
FLIP
RMMMB
ROYAL TEMPLE
[PERMANENT SPELL CARD]
As long as "Royal Temple" is on the field, the card's owner may play two Trap Cards per turn. (The normal limit is one per turn.)
PERMANENT SPELL CARD, ACTIVATE!
RM
...!?
MM
ROYAL TEMPLE?!
RMMBB
WH-WHAT THE...?!

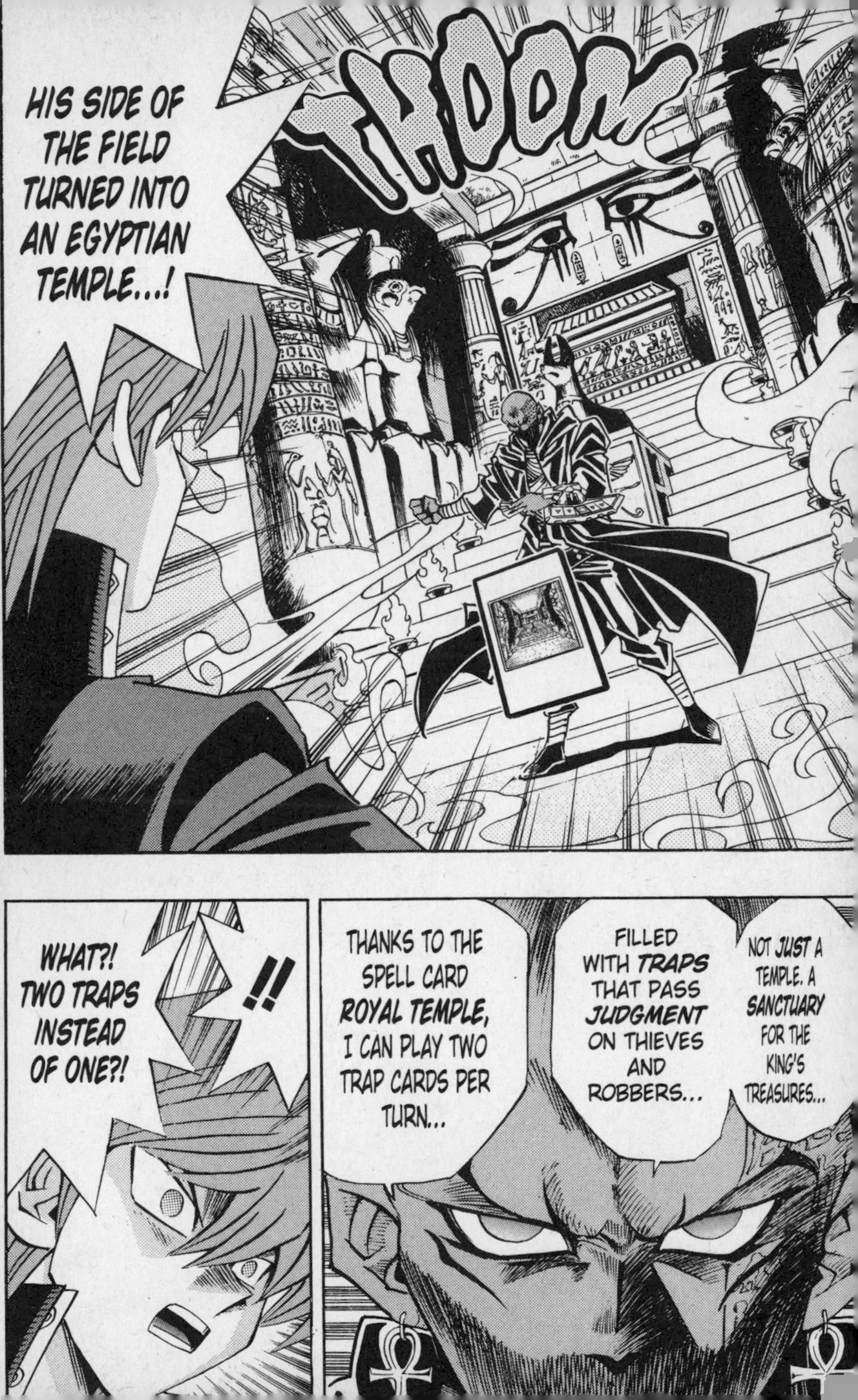
THOOM
HIS SIDE OF THE FIELD TURNED INTO AN EGYPTIAN TEMPLE...!
NOT JUST A TEMPLE. A SANCTUARY FOR THE KING'S TREASURES...
FILLED WITH TRAPS THAT PASS JUDGMENT ON THIEVES AND ROBBERS...
THANKS TO THE SPELL CARD ROYAL TEMPLE, I CAN PLAY TWO TRAP CARDS PER TURN...
!!
WHAT?! TWO TRAPS INSTEAD OF ONE?!

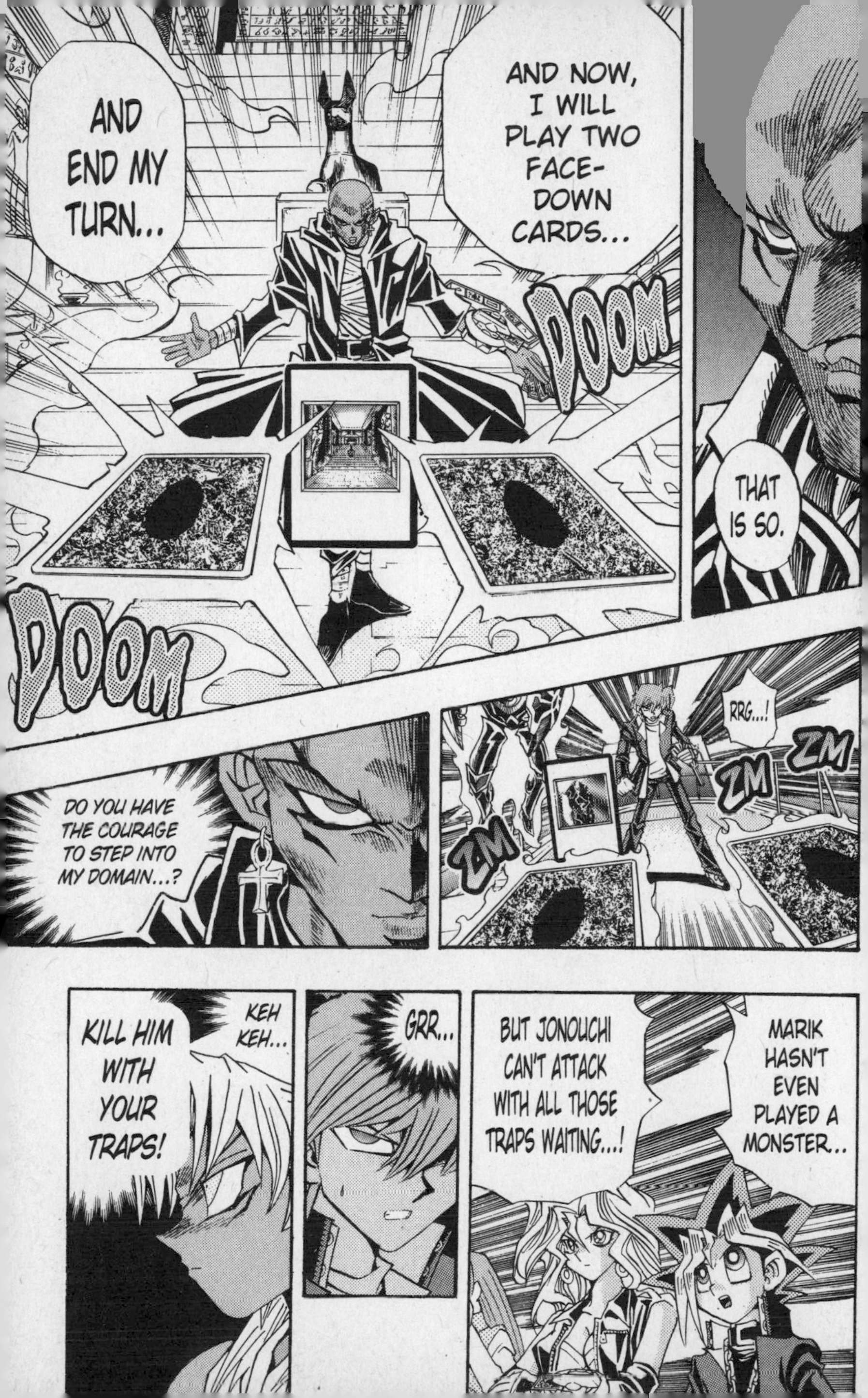
THAT IS SO.
AND NOW, I WILL PLAY TWO FACE-DOWN CARDS...
DOOM
AND END MY TURN...
DOOM
RRG...!
ZM
ZM
ZM
DO YOU HAVE THE COURAGE TO STEP INTO MY DOMAIN...?
MARIK HASN'T EVEN PLAYED A MONSTER...
BUT JONOUCHI CAN'T ATTACK WITH ALL THOSE TRAPS WAITING...!
GRR...
KEH KEH...
KILL HIM WITH YOUR TRAPS!

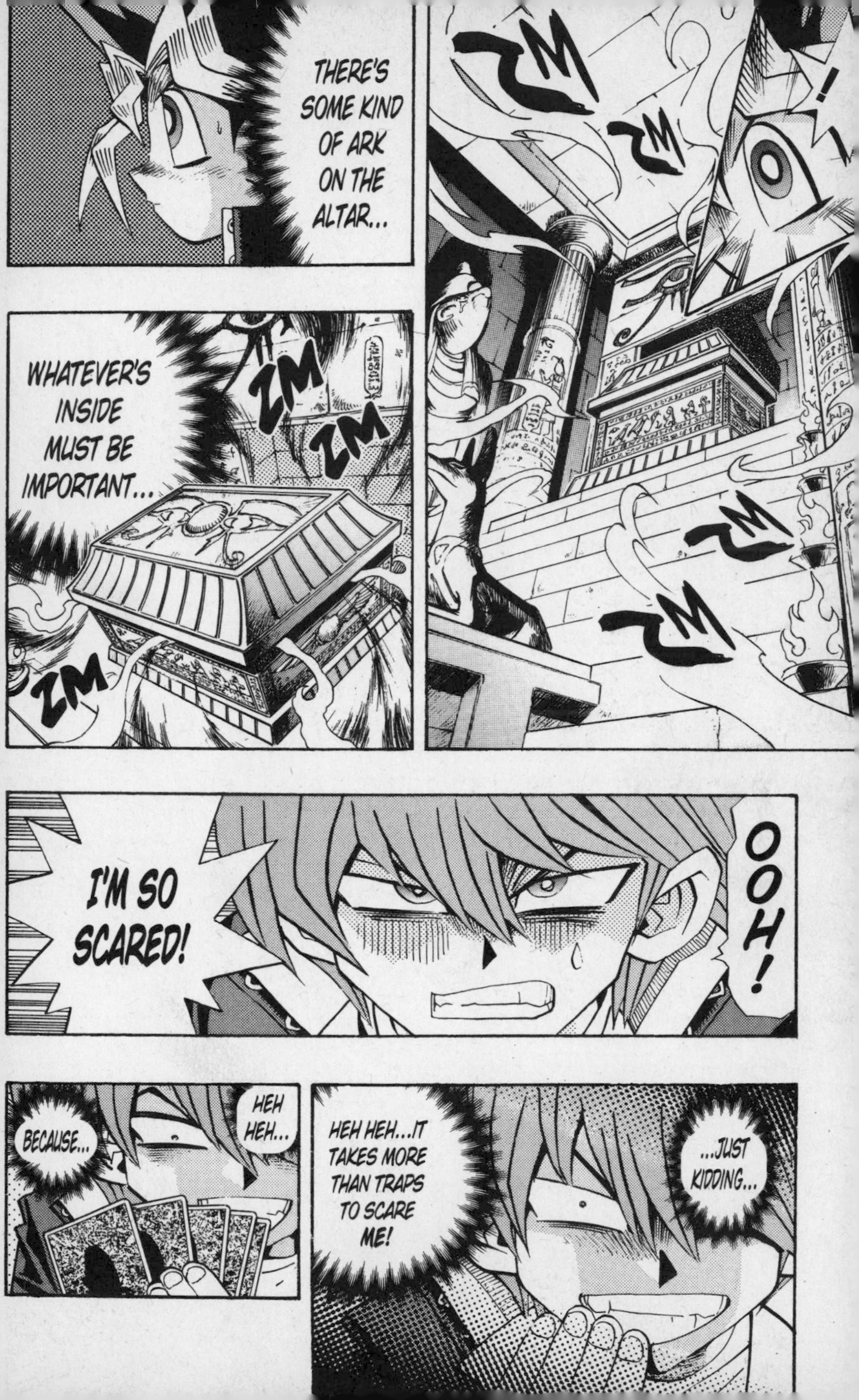
!
ZM
ZM
ZM
ZM
THERE'S SOME KIND OF ARK ON THE ALTAR...
WHATEVER'S INSIDE MUST BE IMPORTANT...
ZM
ZM
ZM
OOH!
I'M SO SCARED!
...JUST KIDDING...
HEH HEH...IT TAKES MORE THAN TRAPS TO SCARE ME!
HEH HEH...
BECAUSE...

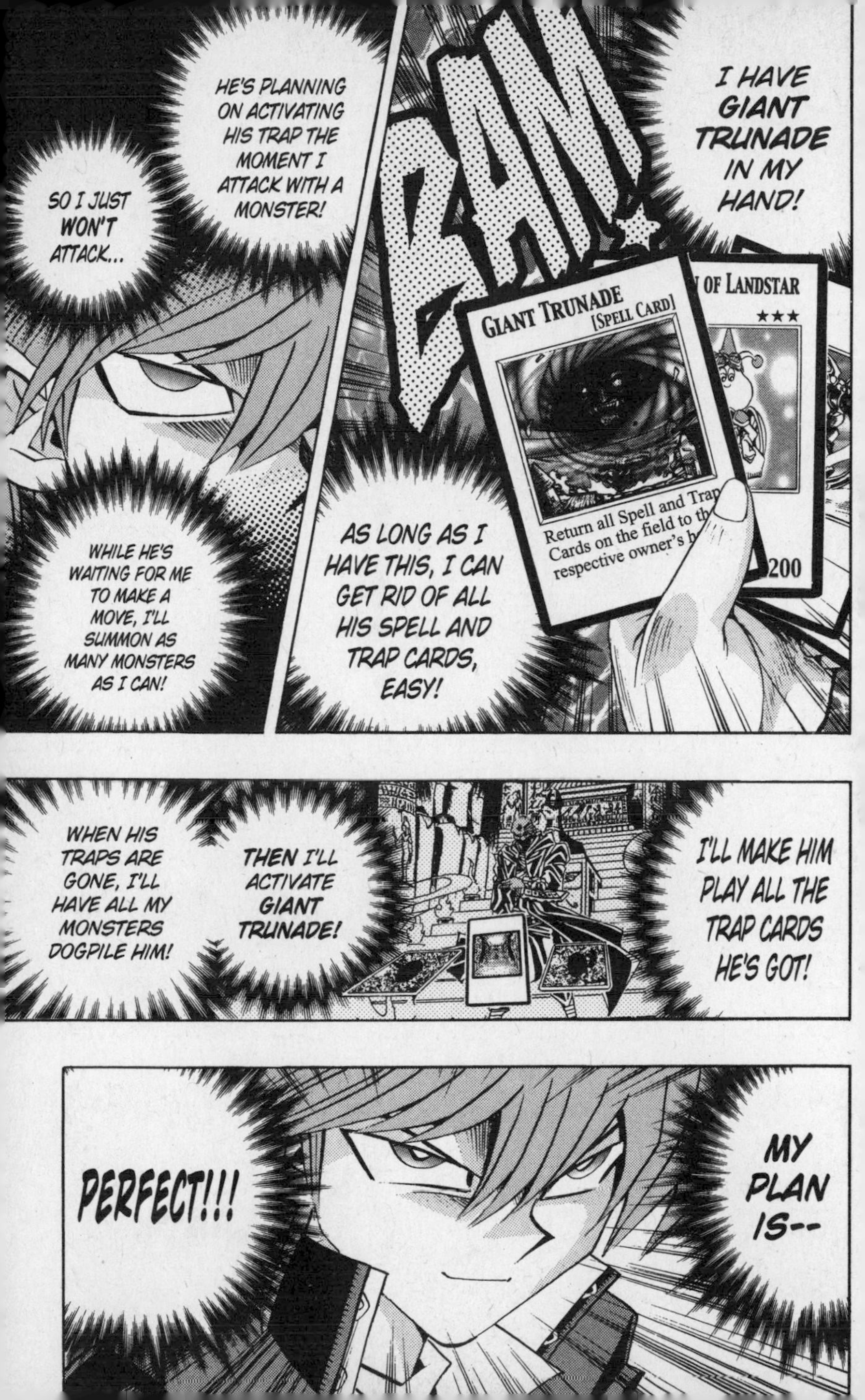

I HAVE GIANT TRUNADE IN MY HAND!
BAM!
GIANT TRUNADE [SPELL CARD]
Return all Spell and Trap Cards on the field to th respective owner's h
OF LANDSTAR
200
AS LONG AS I HAVE THIS, I CAN GET RID OF ALL HIS SPELL AND TRAP CARDS, EASY!
HE'S PLANNING ON ACTIVATING HIS TRAP THE MOMENT I ATTACK WITH A MONSTER!
SO I JUST WON'T ATTACK...
WHILE HE'S WAITING FOR ME TO MAKE A MOVE, I'LL SUMMON AS MANY MONSTERS AS I CAN!
I'LL MAKE HIM PLAY ALL THE TRAP CARDS HE'S GOT!
THEN I'LL ACTIVATE GIANT TRUNADE!
WHEN HIS TRAPS ARE GONE, I'LL HAVE ALL MY MONSTERS DOGPILE HIM!
MY PLAN IS--
PERFECT!!!

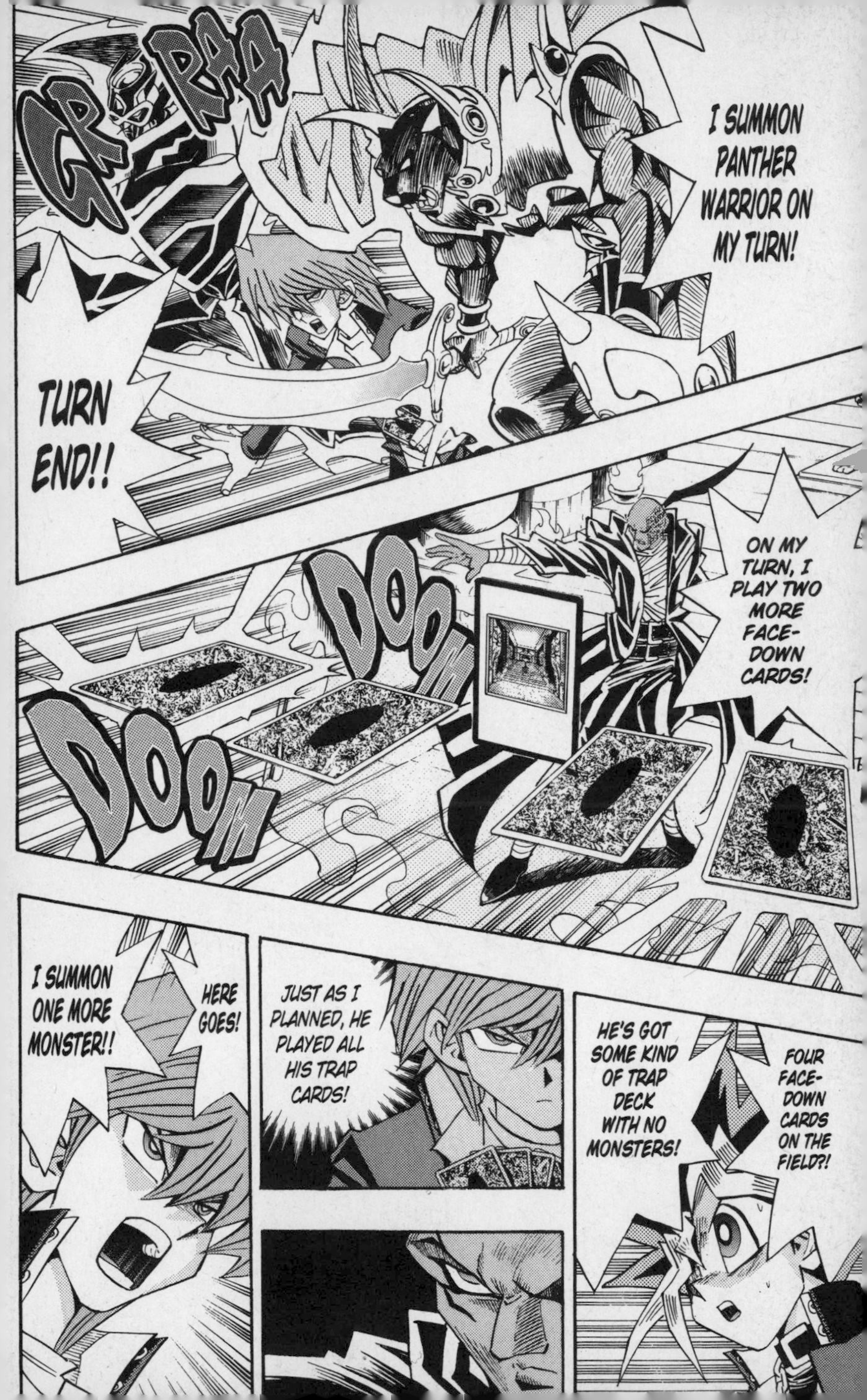
I SUMMON PANTHER WARRIOR ON MY TURN!
GR-RAA
TURN END!!
ON MY TURN, I PLAY TWO MORE FACE-DOWN CARDS!
DOOM
DOOM
FOUR FACE-DOWN CARDS ON THE FIELD?!
HE'S GOT SOME KIND OF TRAP DECK WITH NO MONSTERS!
JUST AS I PLANNED, HE PLAYED ALL HIS TRAP CARDS!
HERE GOES!
I SUMMON ONE MORE MONSTER!!

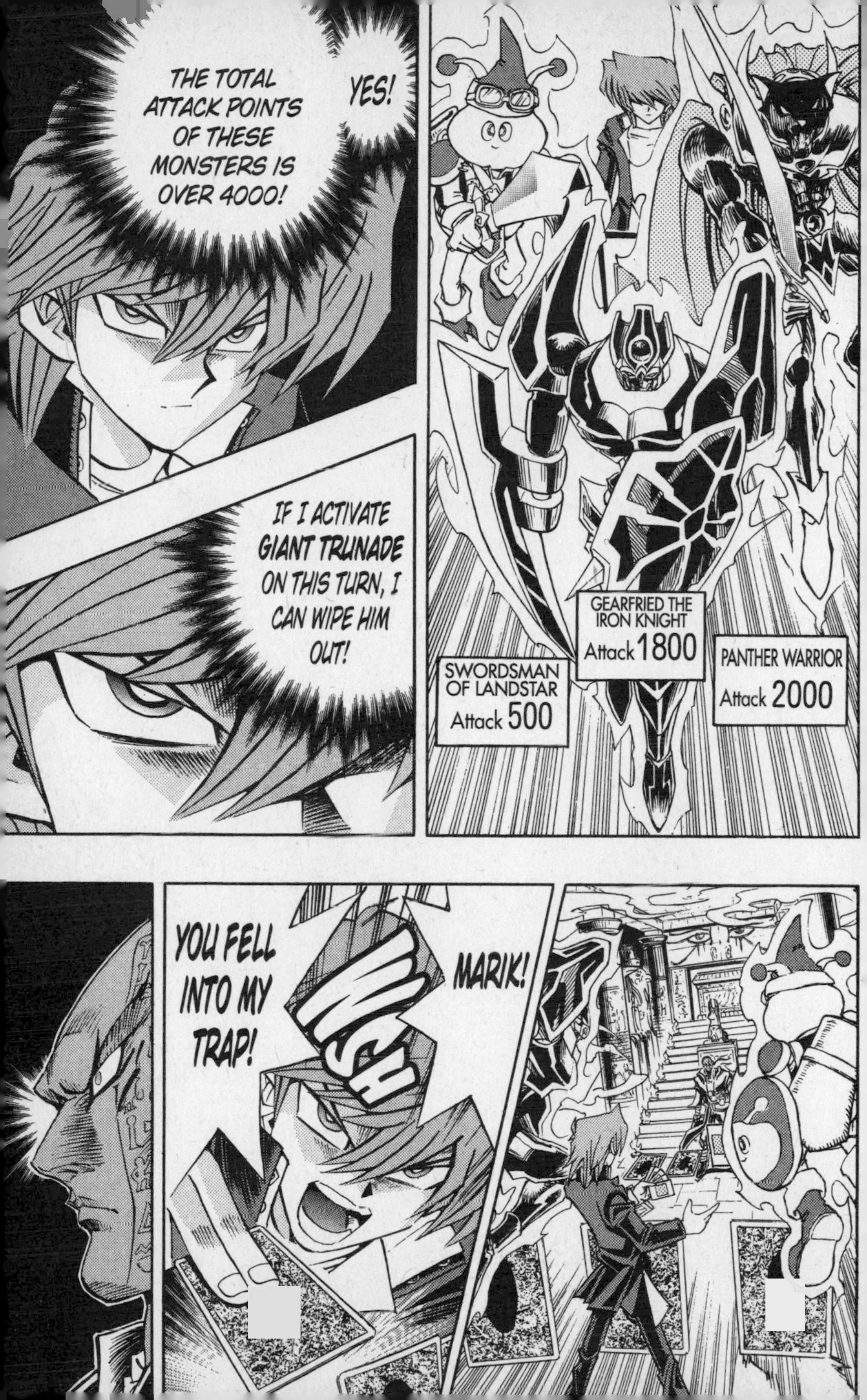
GEARFRIED THE IRON KNIGHT Attack 1800
PANTHER WARRIOR Attack 2000
SWORDSMAN OF LANDSTAR Attack 500
YES!
THE TOTAL ATTACK POINTS OF THESE MONSTERS IS OVER 4000!
IF I ACTIVATE GIANT TRUNADE ON THIS TURN, I CAN WIPE HIM OUT!
MARIK!
YOU FELL INTO MY TRAP!

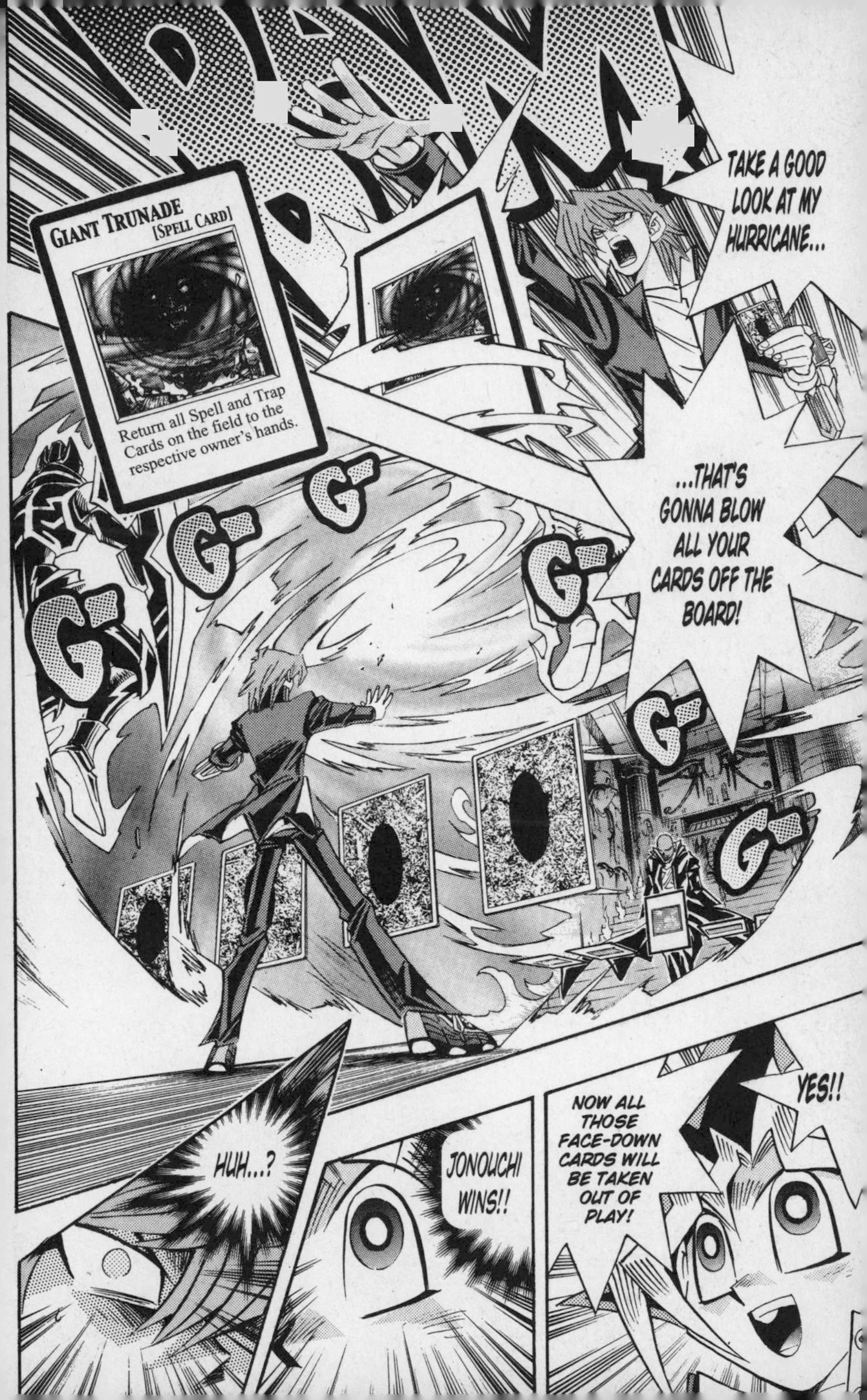
TAKE A GOOD LOOK AT MY HURRICANE...
...THAT'S GONNA BLOW ALL YOUR CARDS OFF THE BOARD!
GIANT TRUNADE
[SPELL CARD]
Return all Spell and Trap Cards on the field to the respective owner's hands.
G
G
G
G
G
G
YES!!
NOW ALL THOSE FACE-DOWN CARDS WILL BE TAKEN OUT OF PLAY!
JONOUCHI WINS!!
HUH...?

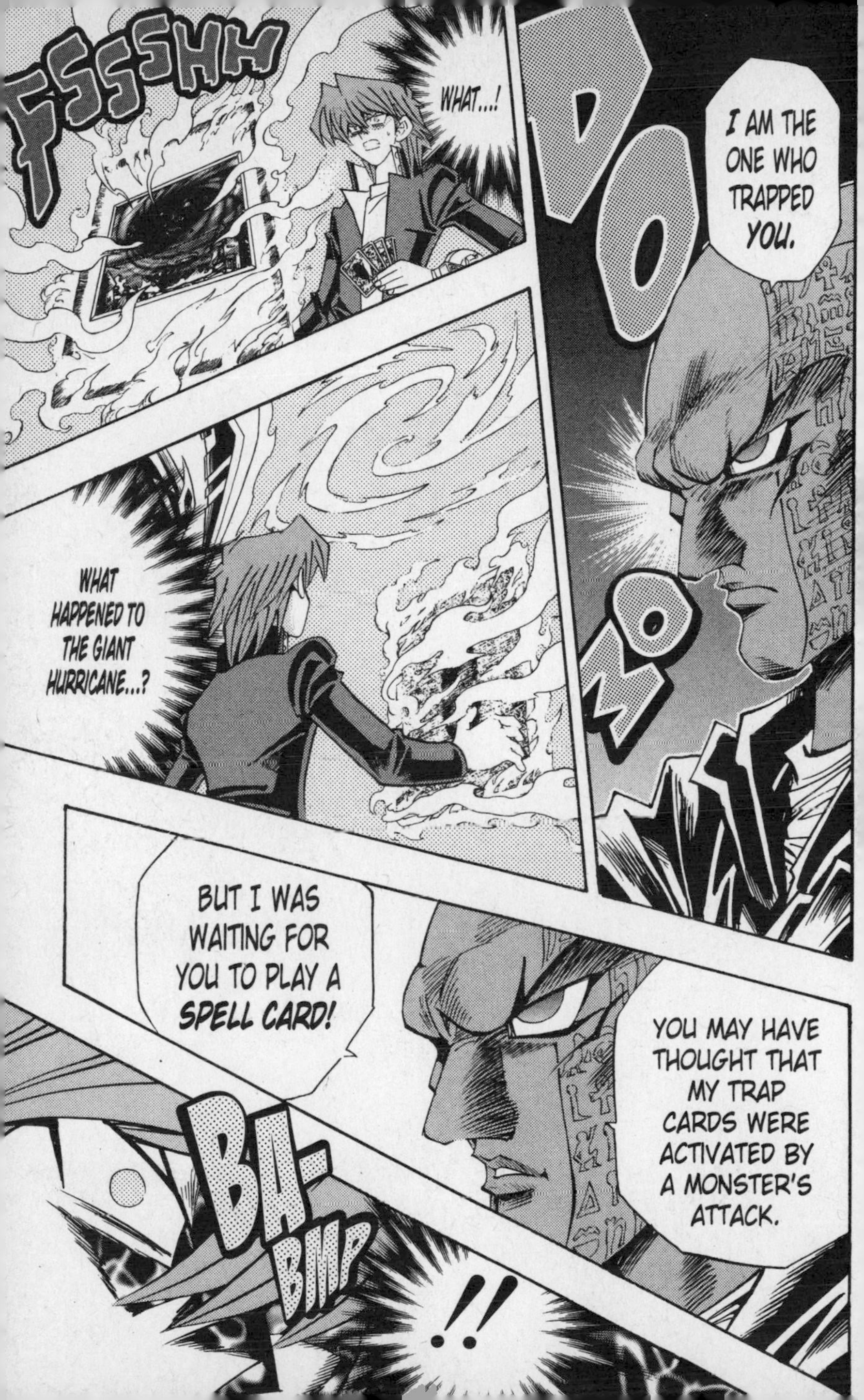
DOOM
I AM THE ONE WHO TRAPPED YOU.
FSSSHH
WHAT...!
WHAT HAPPENED TO THE GIANT HURRICANE...?
YOU MAY HAVE THOUGHT THAT MY TRAP CARDS WERE ACTIVATED BY A MONSTER'S ATTACK.
BUT I WAS WAITING FOR YOU TO PLAY A SPELL CARD!
BA-BMP
!!

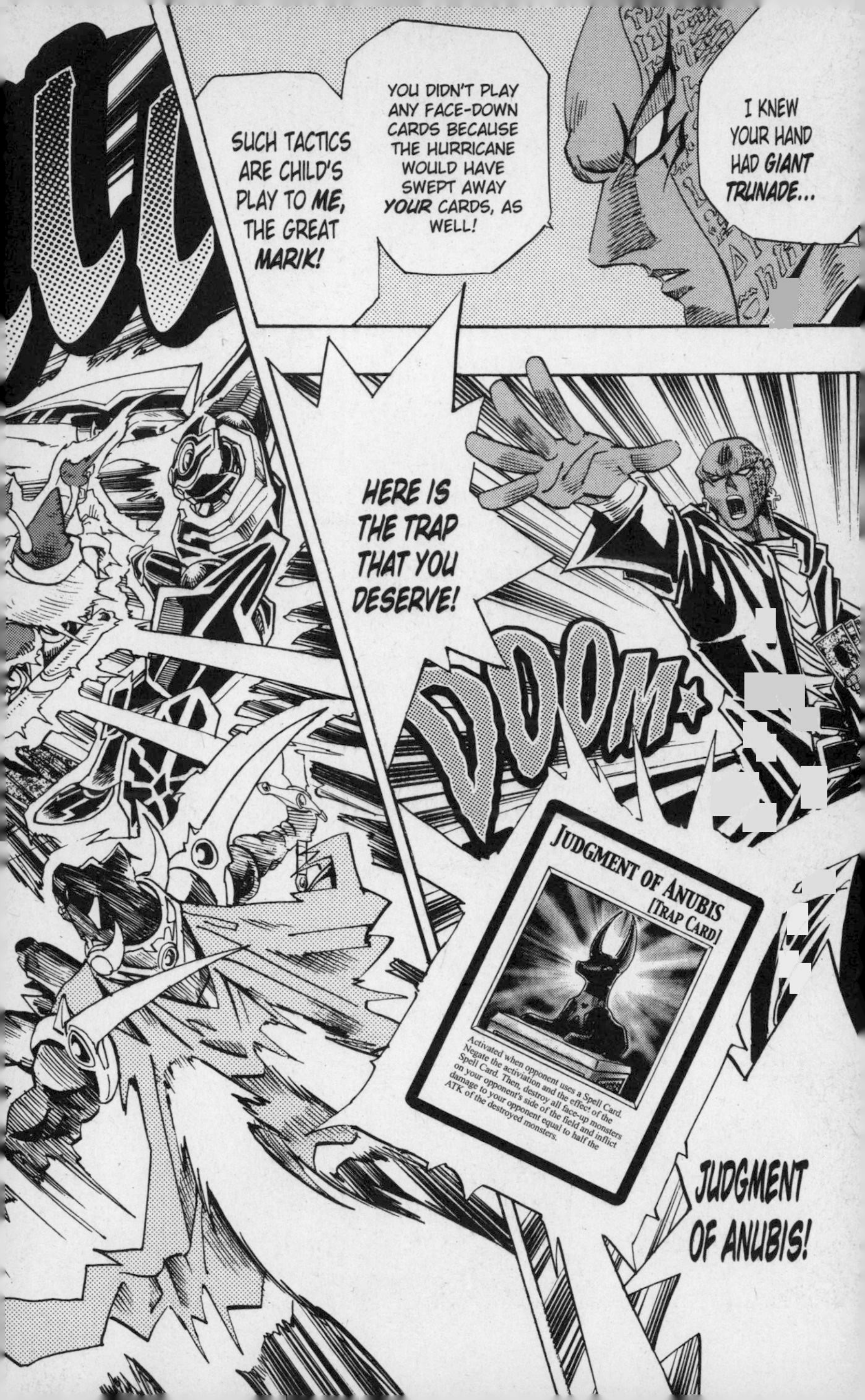
I KNEW YOUR HAND HAD GIANT TRUNADE...
YOU DIDN'T PLAY ANY FACE-DOWN CARDS BECAUSE THE HURRICANE WOULD HAVE SWEPT AWAY YOUR CARDS, AS WELL!
SUCH TACTICS ARE CHILD'S PLAY TO ME, THE GREAT MARIK!
HERE IS THE TRAP THAT YOU DESERVE!
DOOM
JUDGMENT OF ANUBIS
[TRAP CARD]
Activated when opponent uses a Spell Card. Negate the activation and the effect of the Spell Card. Then, destroy all face-up monsters on your opponent's side of the field and inflict damage to your opponent equal to half the ATK of the destroyed monsters.
JUDGMENT OF ANUBIS!

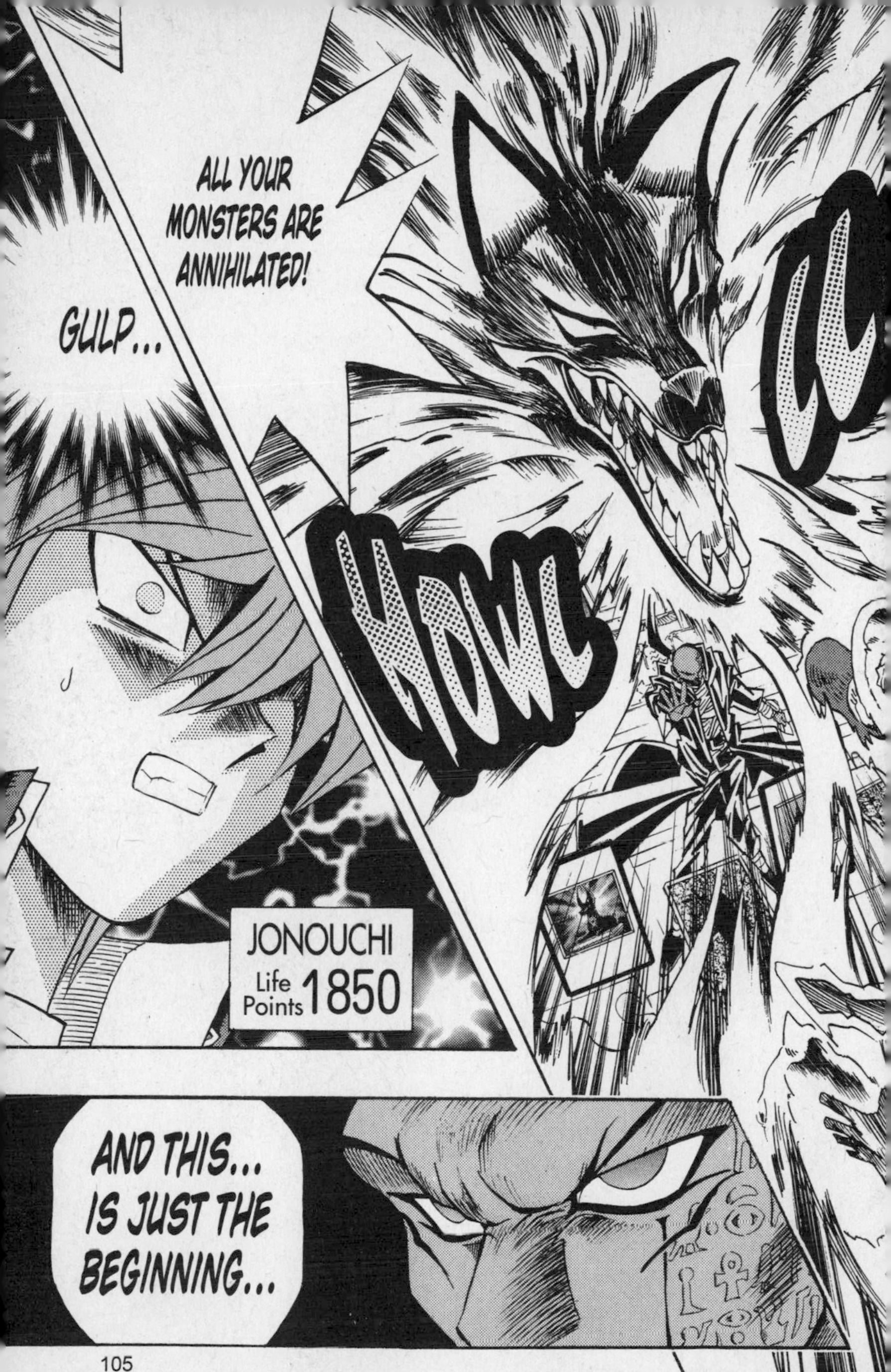
HOWL
ALL YOUR MONSTERS ARE ANNIHILATED!
GULP...
JONOUCHI Life Points 1850
AND THIS... IS JUST THE BEGINNING...

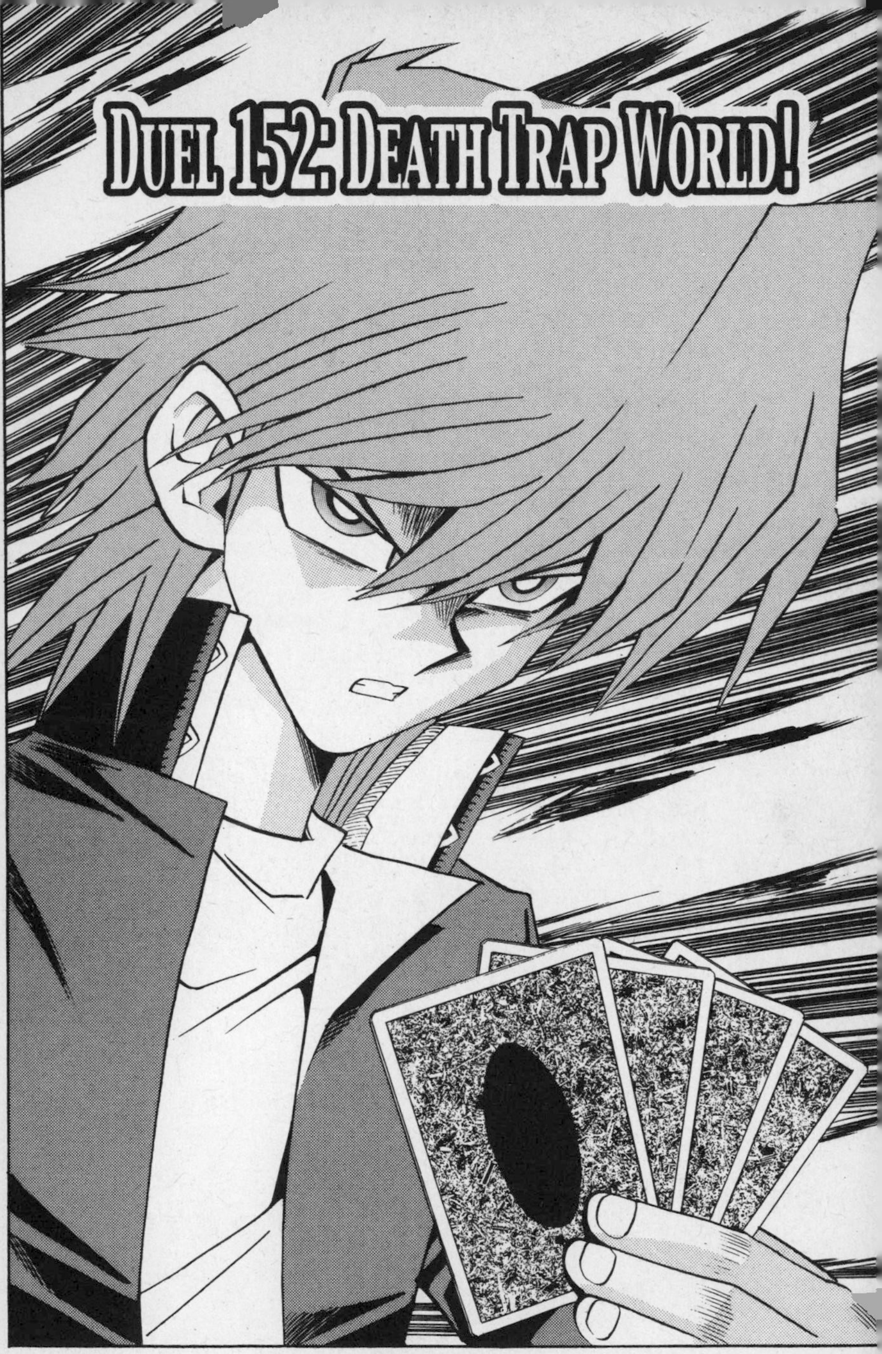
DUEL 152: DEATH TRAP WORLD!

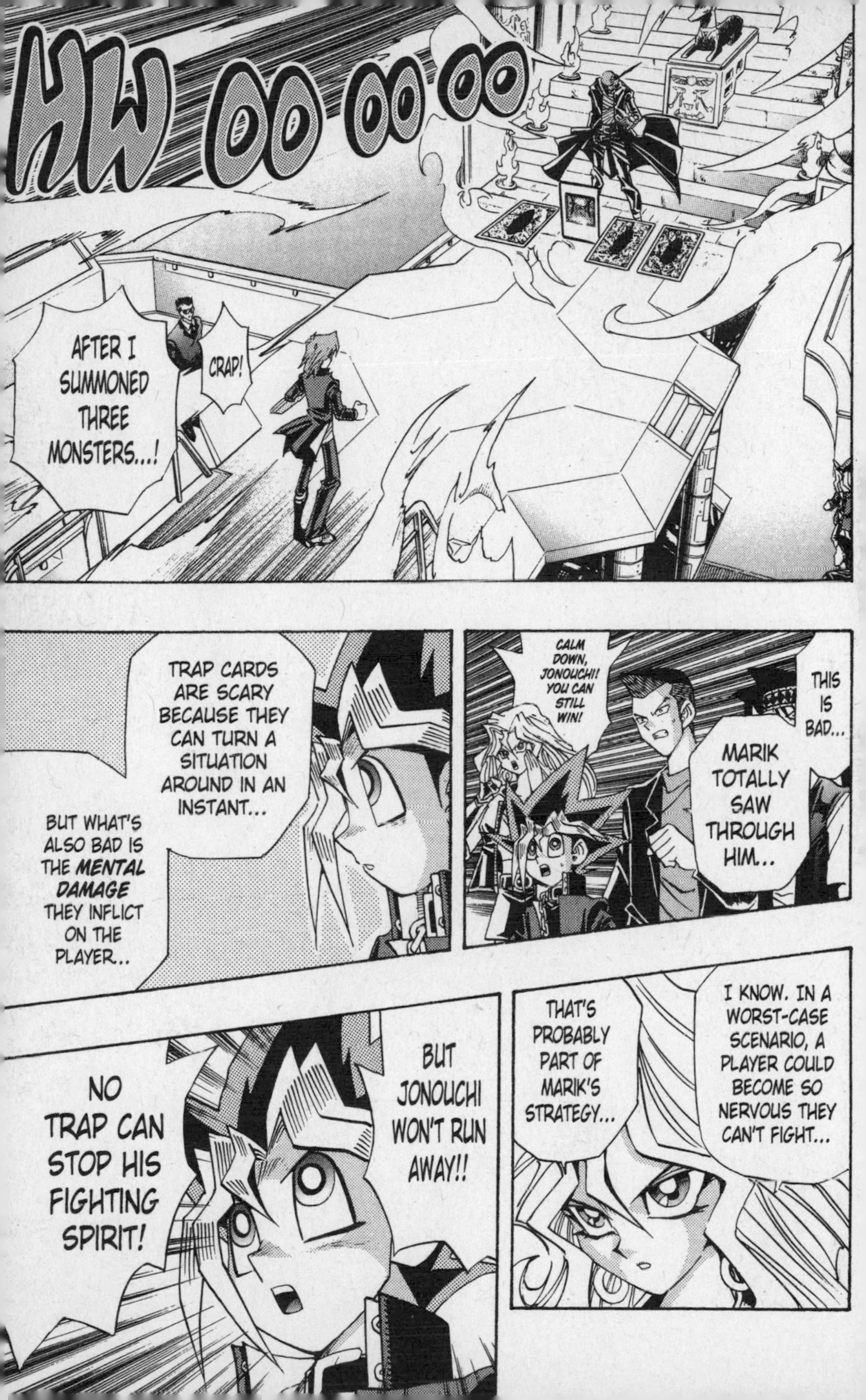
HWOOOOOO
CRAP!
AFTER I SUMMONED THREE MONSTERS...!
THIS IS BAD...
CALM DOWN, JONOUCHI! YOU CAN STILL WIN!
MARIK TOTALLY SAW THROUGH HIM...
TRAP CARDS ARE SCARY BECAUSE THEY CAN TURN A SITUATION AROUND IN AN INSTANT...
BUT WHAT'S ALSO BAD IS THE MENTAL DAMAGE THEY INFLICT ON THE PLAYER...
I KNOW. IN A WORST-CASE SCENARIO, A PLAYER COULD BECOME SO NERVOUS THEY CAN'T FIGHT...
THAT'S PROBABLY PART OF MARIK'S STRATEGY...
BUT JONOUCHI WON'T RUN AWAY!!
NO TRAP CAN STOP HIS FIGHTING SPIRIT!

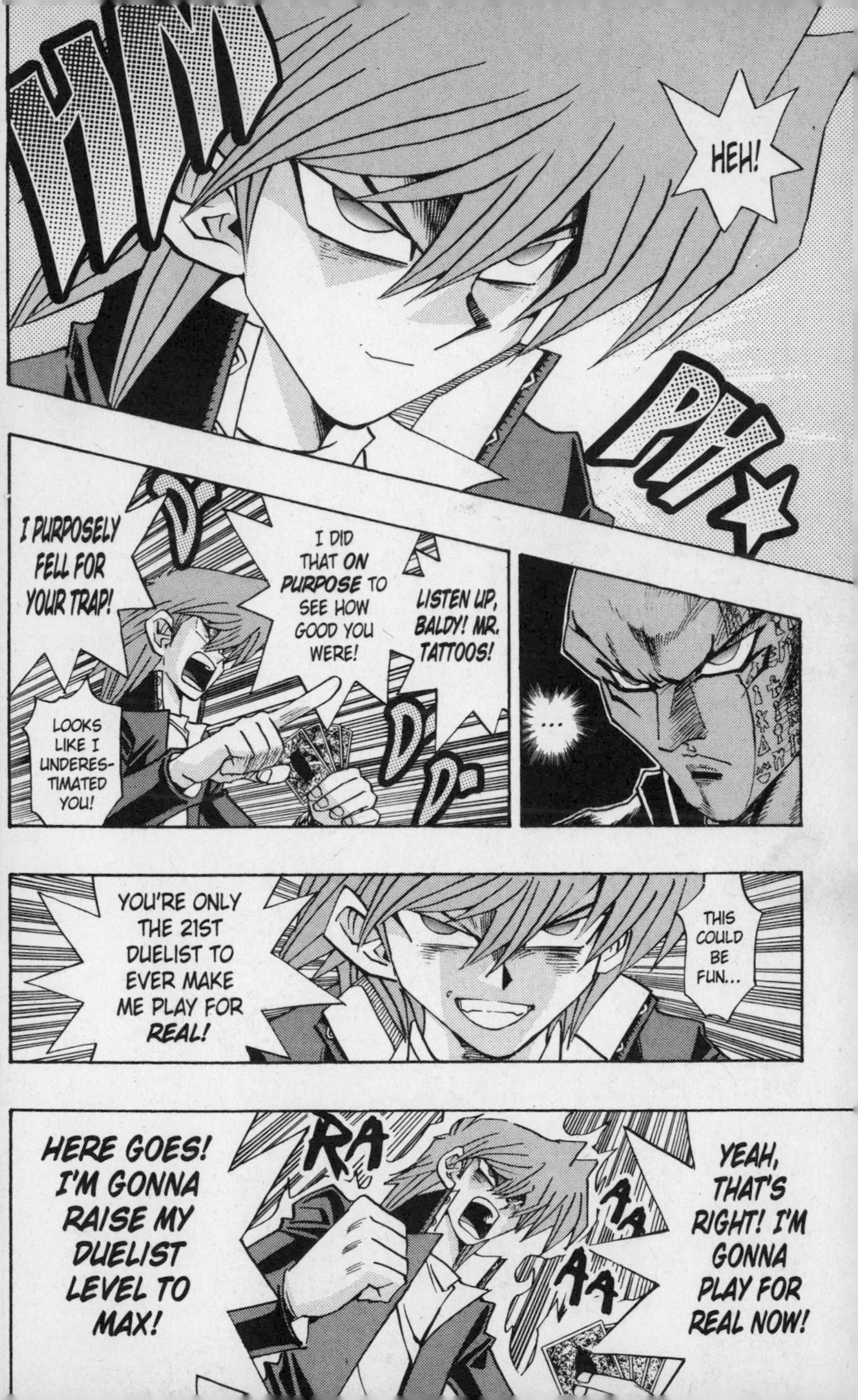
HEH!
...
LISTEN UP, BALDY! MR. TATTOOS!
I DID THAT ON PURPOSE TO SEE HOW GOOD YOU WERE!
I PURPOSELY FELL FOR YOUR TRAP!
LOOKS LIKE I UNDERESTIMATED YOU!
THIS COULD BE FUN...
YOU'RE ONLY THE 21ST DUELIST TO EVER MAKE ME PLAY FOR REAL!
YEAH, THAT'S RIGHT! I'M GONNA PLAY FOR REAL NOW!
HERE GOES! I'M GONNA RAISE MY DUELIST LEVEL TO MAX!

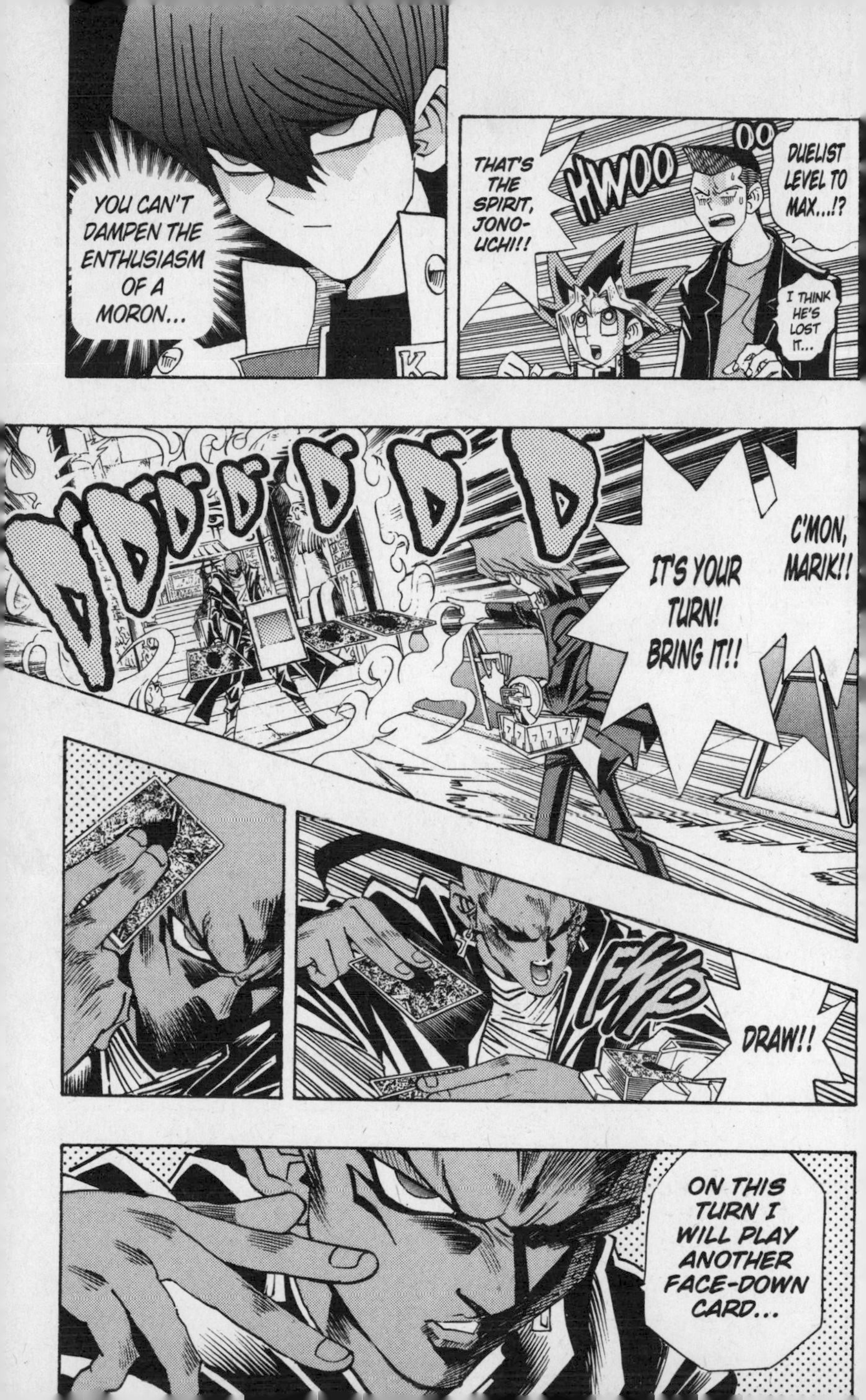
DUELIST LEVEL TO MAX...!?
HWOO
THAT'S THE SPIRIT, JONOUCHI!!
I THINK HE'S LOST IT...
YOU CAN'T DAMPEN THE ENTHUSIASM OF A MORON...
C'MON, MARIK!!
IT'S YOUR TURN! BRING IT!!
DRAW!!
FWP
ON THIS TURN I WILL PLAY ANOTHER FACE-DOWN CARD...

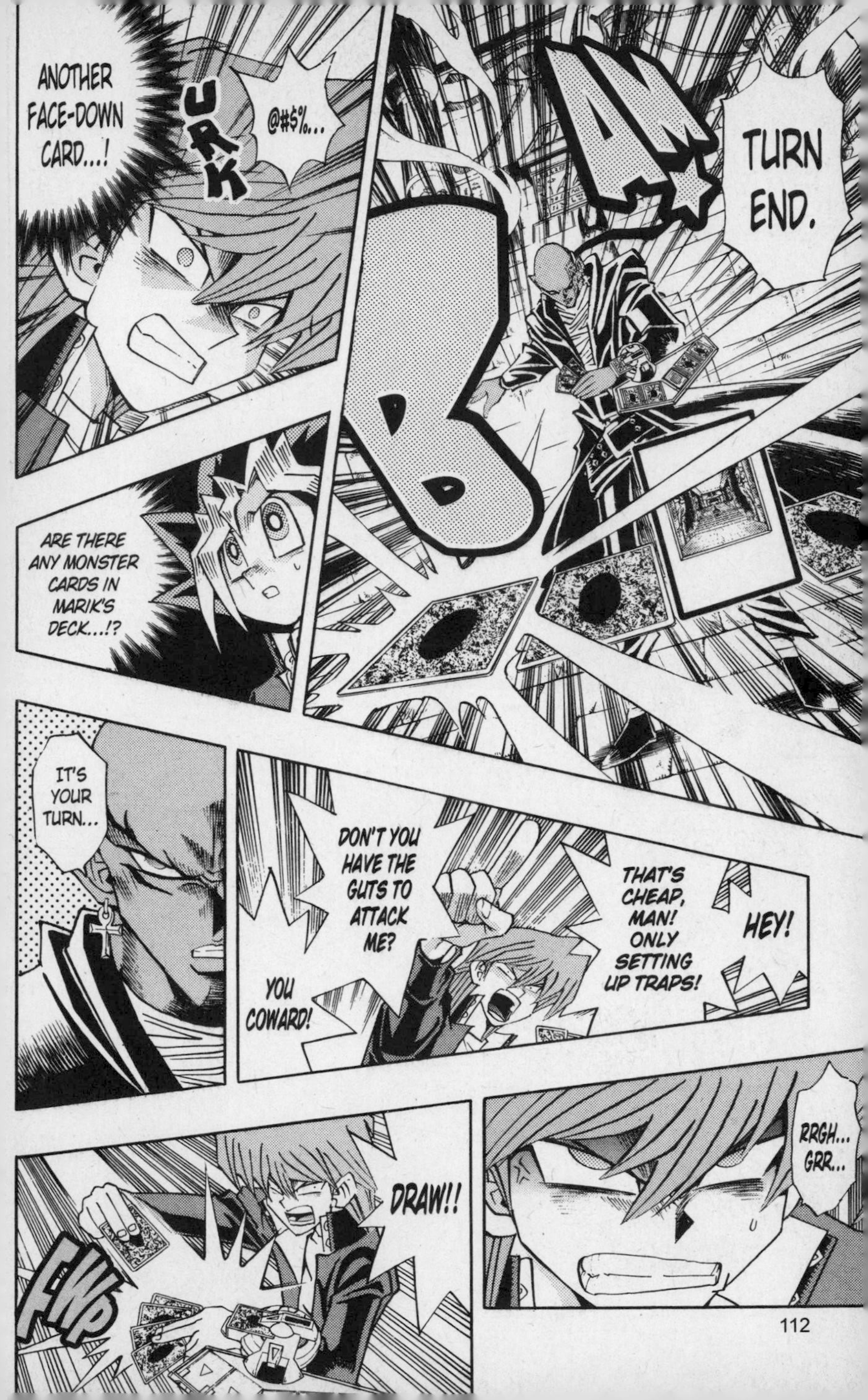
TURN END.
BAM
@#$%...
URK
ANOTHER FACE-DOWN CARD...!
ARE THERE ANY MONSTER CARDS IN MARIK'S DECK...!?
HEY!
THAT'S CHEAP, MAN! ONLY SETTING UP TRAPS!
DON'T YOU HAVE THE GUTS TO ATTACK ME?
YOU COWARD!
IT'S YOUR TURN...
RRGH... GRR...
DRAW!!
FWP

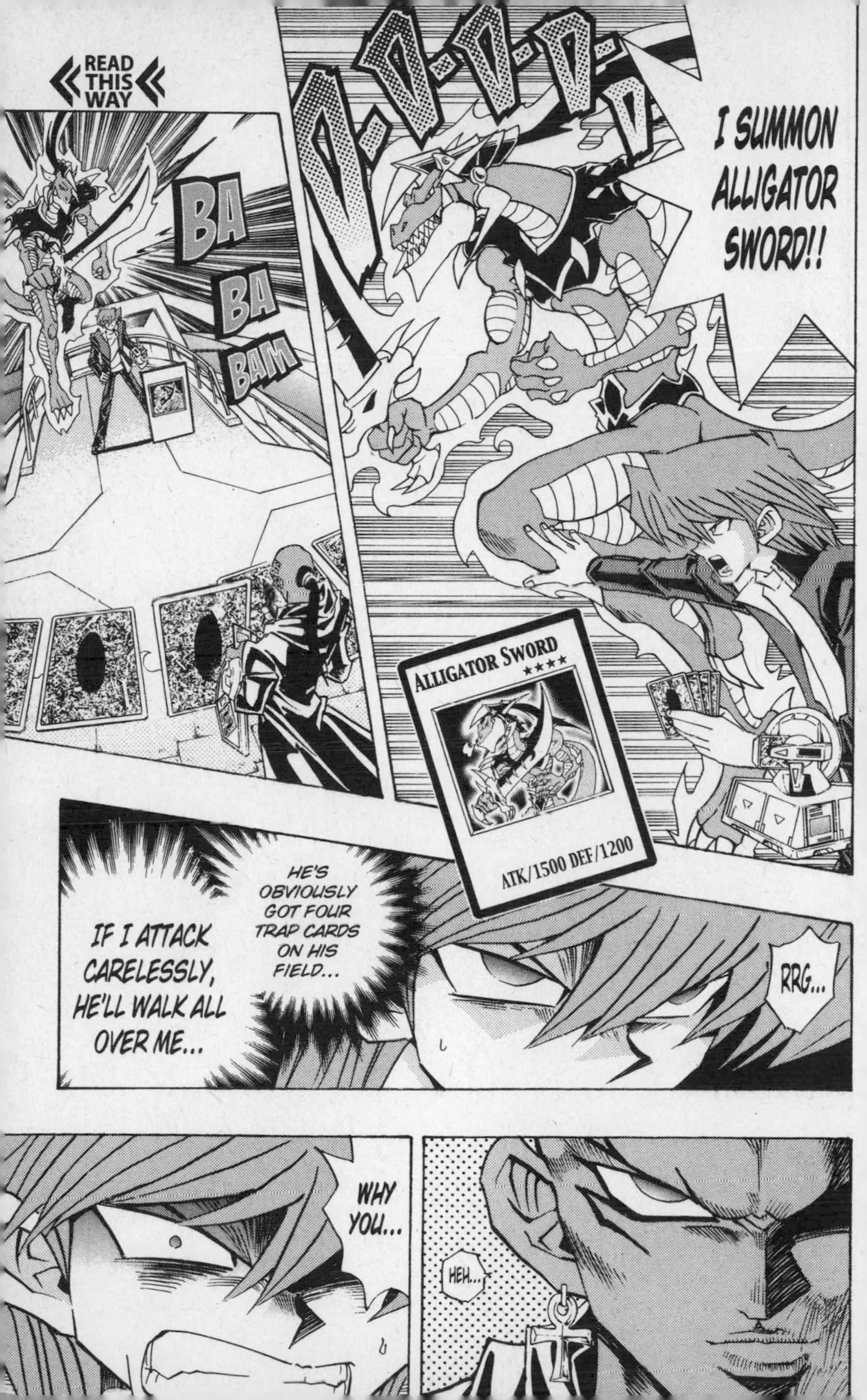
READ THIS WAY
I SUMMON ALLIGATOR SWORD!!
D-D-D-D-D
ALLIGATOR SWORD
★★★★
ATK/1500 DEF/1200
BA
BA
BAM
RRG...
HE'S OBVIOUSLY GOT FOUR TRAP CARDS ON HIS FIELD...
IF I ATTACK CARELESSLY, HE'LL WALK ALL OVER ME...
HEH...
WHY YOU...

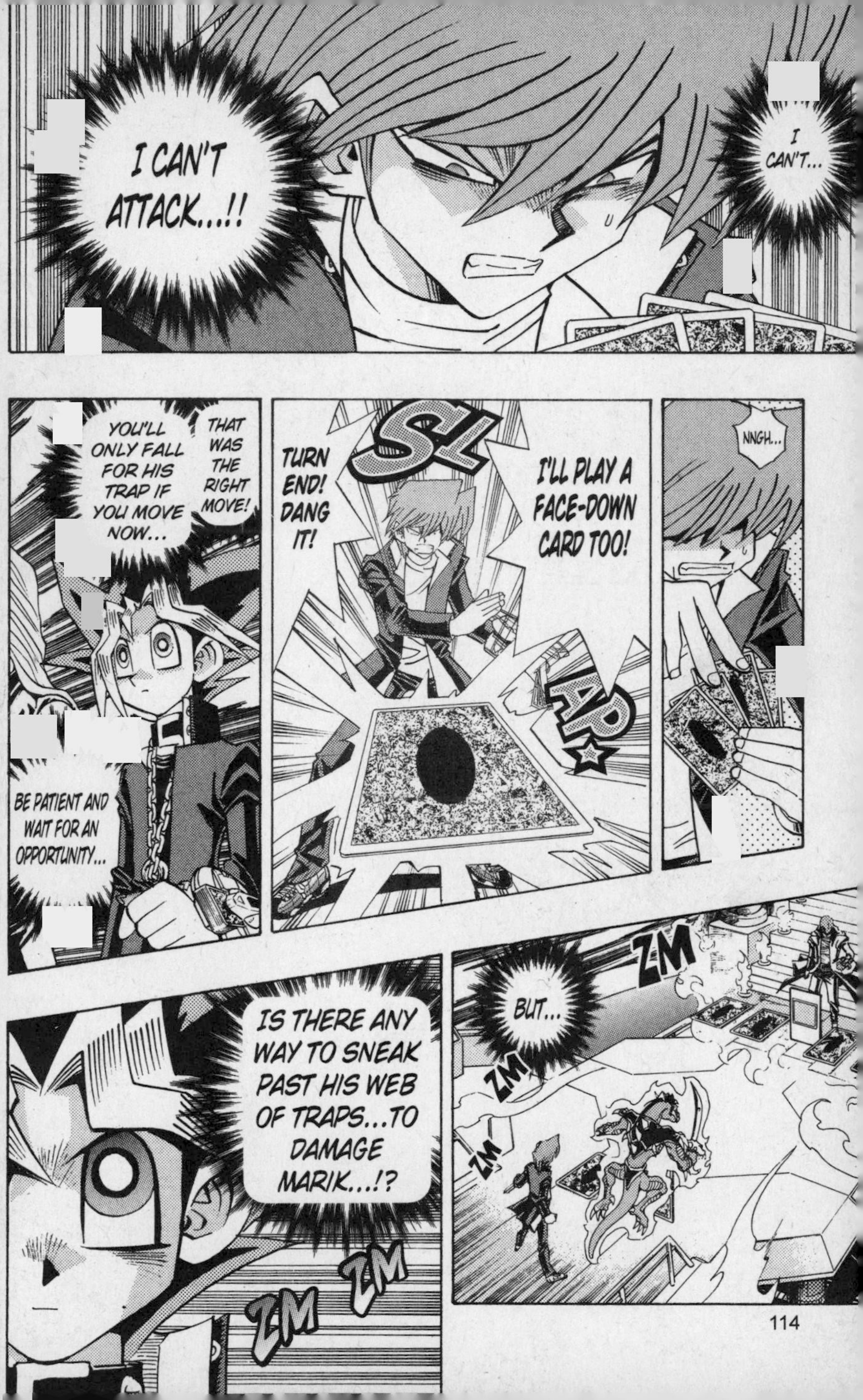
I CAN'T...
I CAN'T ATTACK...!!
NNGH...
I'LL PLAY A FACE-DOWN CARD TOO!
SL
AP
TURN END! DANG IT!
THAT WAS THE RIGHT MOVE!
YOU'LL ONLY FALL FOR HIS TRAP IF YOU MOVE NOW...
BE PATIENT AND WAIT FOR AN OPPORTUNITY...
ZM
BUT...
ZM
ZM
IS THERE ANY WAY TO SNEAK PAST HIS WEB OF TRAPS...TO DAMAGE MARIK...!?
ZM
ZM

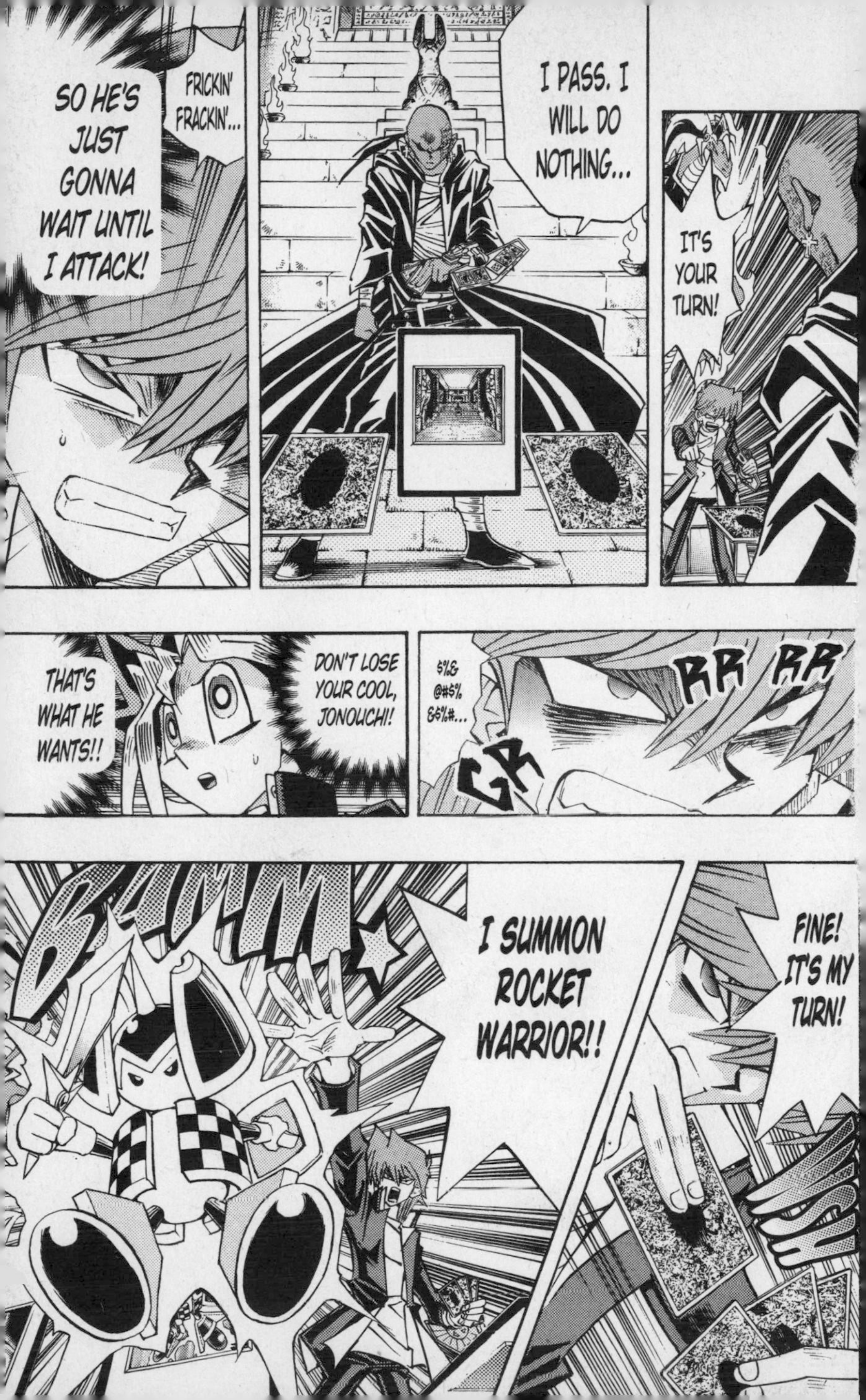
IT'S YOUR TURN!
I PASS. I WILL DO NOTHING...
FRICKIN' FRACKIN'...
SO HE'S JUST GONNA WAIT UNTIL I ATTACK!
RR RR
$%& @#$% &$%#...
GR
DON'T LOSE YOUR COOL, JONOUCHI!
THAT'S WHAT HE WANTS!!
FINE! IT'S MY TURN!
I SUMMON ROCKET WARRIOR!!
BAMM

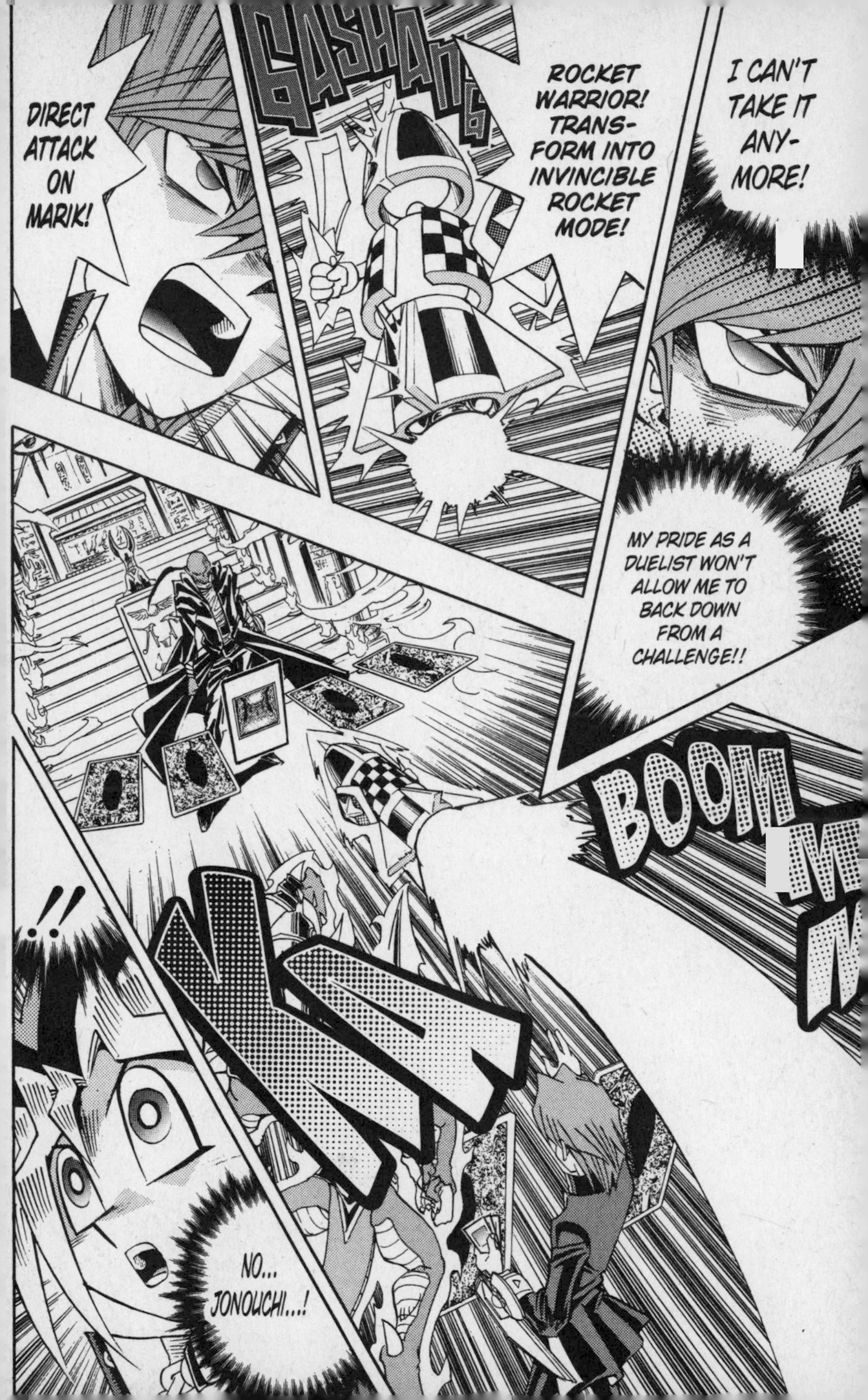
I CAN'T TAKE IT ANY-MORE!
MY PRIDE AS A DUELIST WON'T ALLOW ME TO BACK DOWN FROM A CHALLENGE!!
GASHANG
ROCKET WARRIOR! TRANS-FORM INTO INVINCIBLE ROCKET MODE!
DIRECT ATTACK ON MARIK!
BOOM
!!
NO... JONOUCHI...!

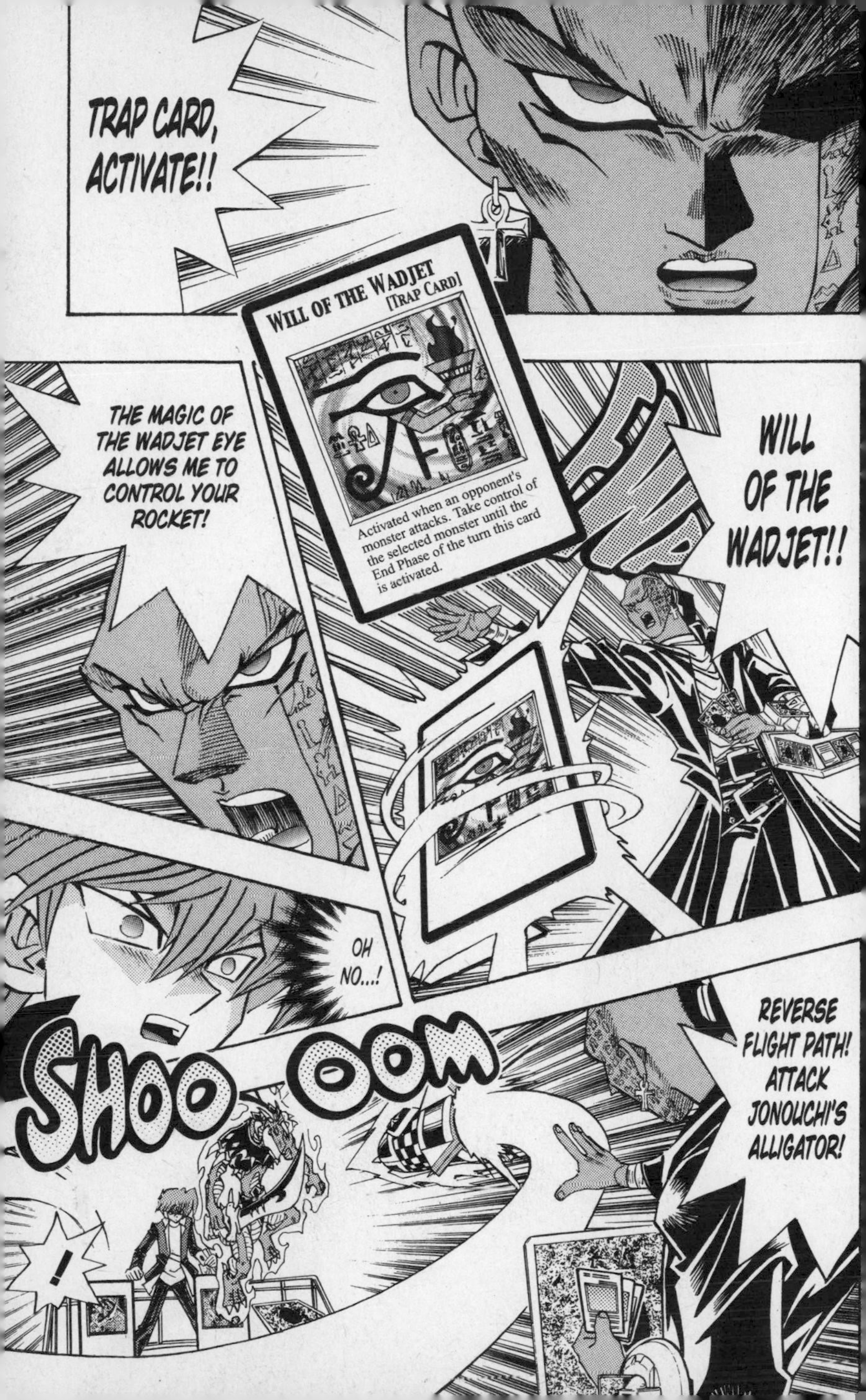
TRAP CARD, ACTIVATE!!
WILL OF THE WADJET
[TRAP CARD]
Activated when an opponent's monster attacks. Take control of the selected monster until the End Phase of the turn this card is activated.
WILL OF THE WADJET!!
THE MAGIC OF THE WADJET EYE ALLOWS ME TO CONTROL YOUR ROCKET!
OH NO...!
REVERSE FLIGHT PATH! ATTACK JONOUCHI'S ALLIGATOR!
SHOO OOM
!

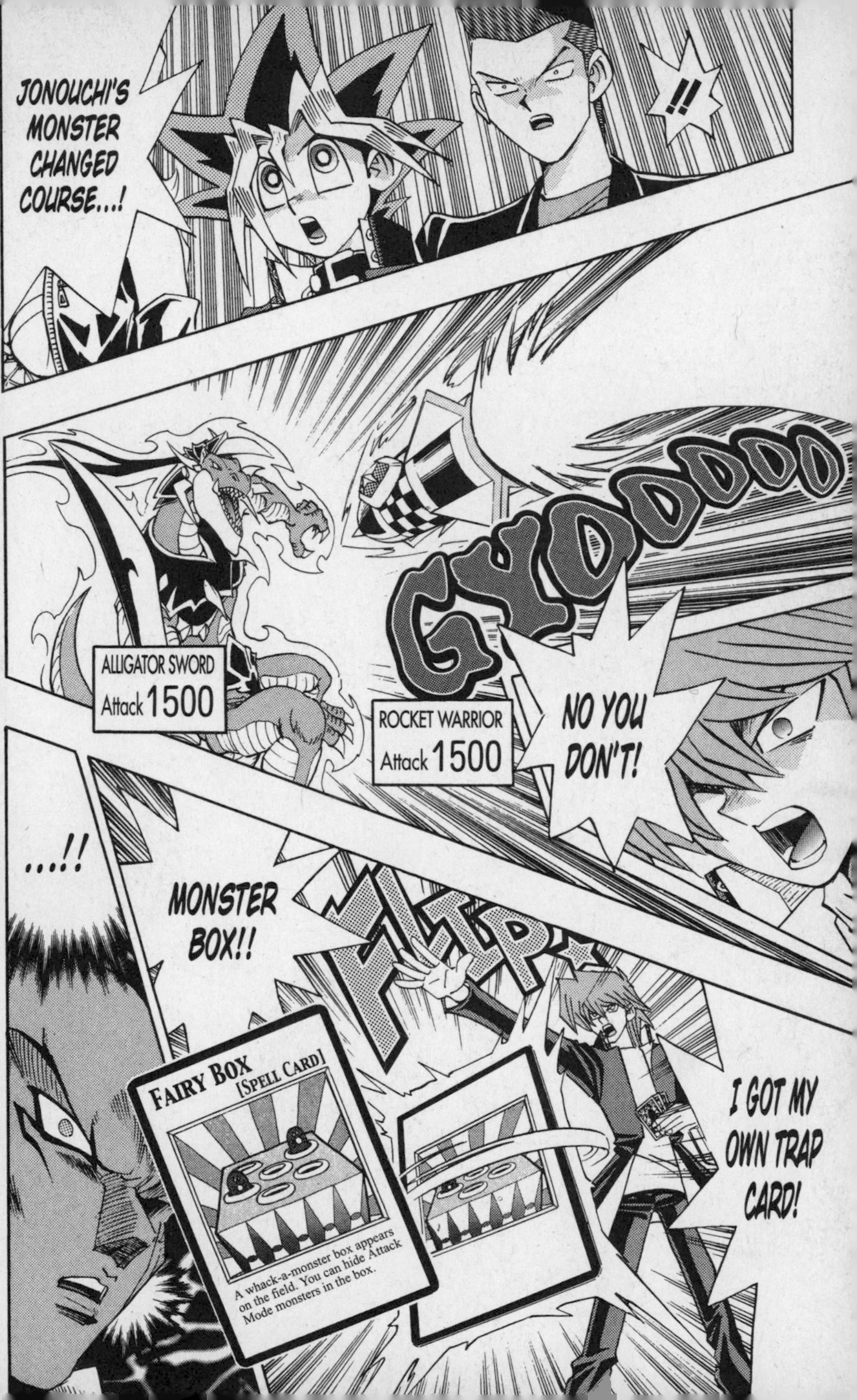
!!
JONOUCHI'S MONSTER CHANGED COURSE...!
GYODDDDD
NO YOU DON'T!
ROCKET WARRIOR
Attack 1500
ALLIGATOR SWORD
Attack 1500
FLIP
I GOT MY OWN TRAP CARD!
FAIRY BOX
[SPELL CARD]
A whack-a-monster box appears on the field. You can hide Attack Mode monsters in the box.
MONSTER BOX!!
...!!

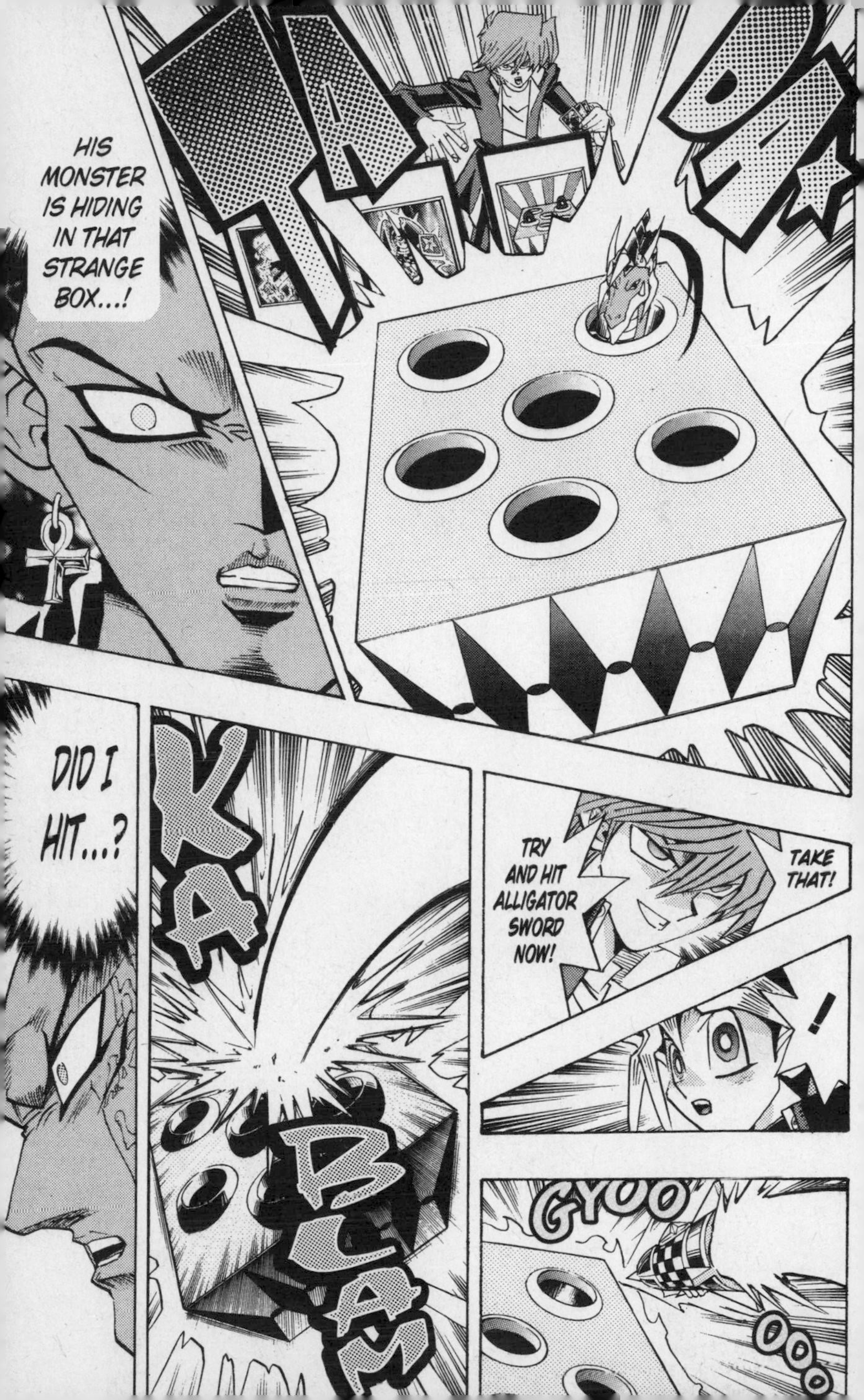
HIS MONSTER IS HIDING IN THAT STRANGE BOX...!
TAKE THAT!
TRY AND HIT ALLIGATOR SWORD NOW!
!
GYOO
OOO
KA
BLAM
DID I HIT...?

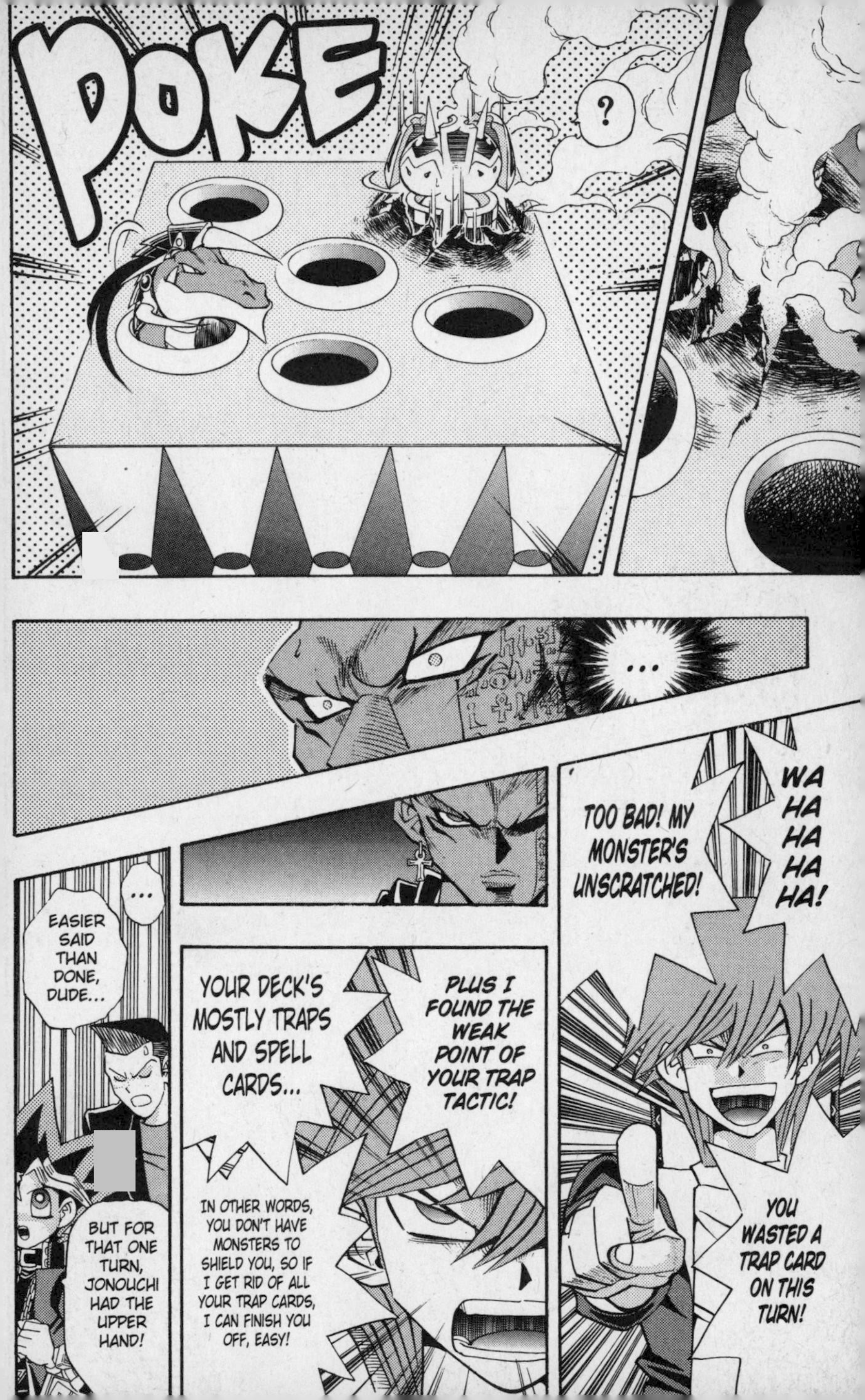
?
POKE
...
WA HA HA HA HA!
TOO BAD! MY MONSTER'S UNSCRATCHED!
YOU WASTED A TRAP CARD ON THIS TURN!
PLUS I FOUND THE WEAK POINT OF YOUR TRAP TACTIC!
YOUR DECK'S MOSTLY TRAPS AND SPELL CARDS...
IN OTHER WORDS, YOU DON'T HAVE MONSTERS TO SHIELD YOU, SO IF I GET RID OF ALL YOUR TRAP CARDS, I CAN FINISH YOU OFF, EASY!
...
EASIER SAID THAN DONE, DUDE...
BUT FOR THAT ONE TURN, JONOUCHI HAD THE UPPER HAND!

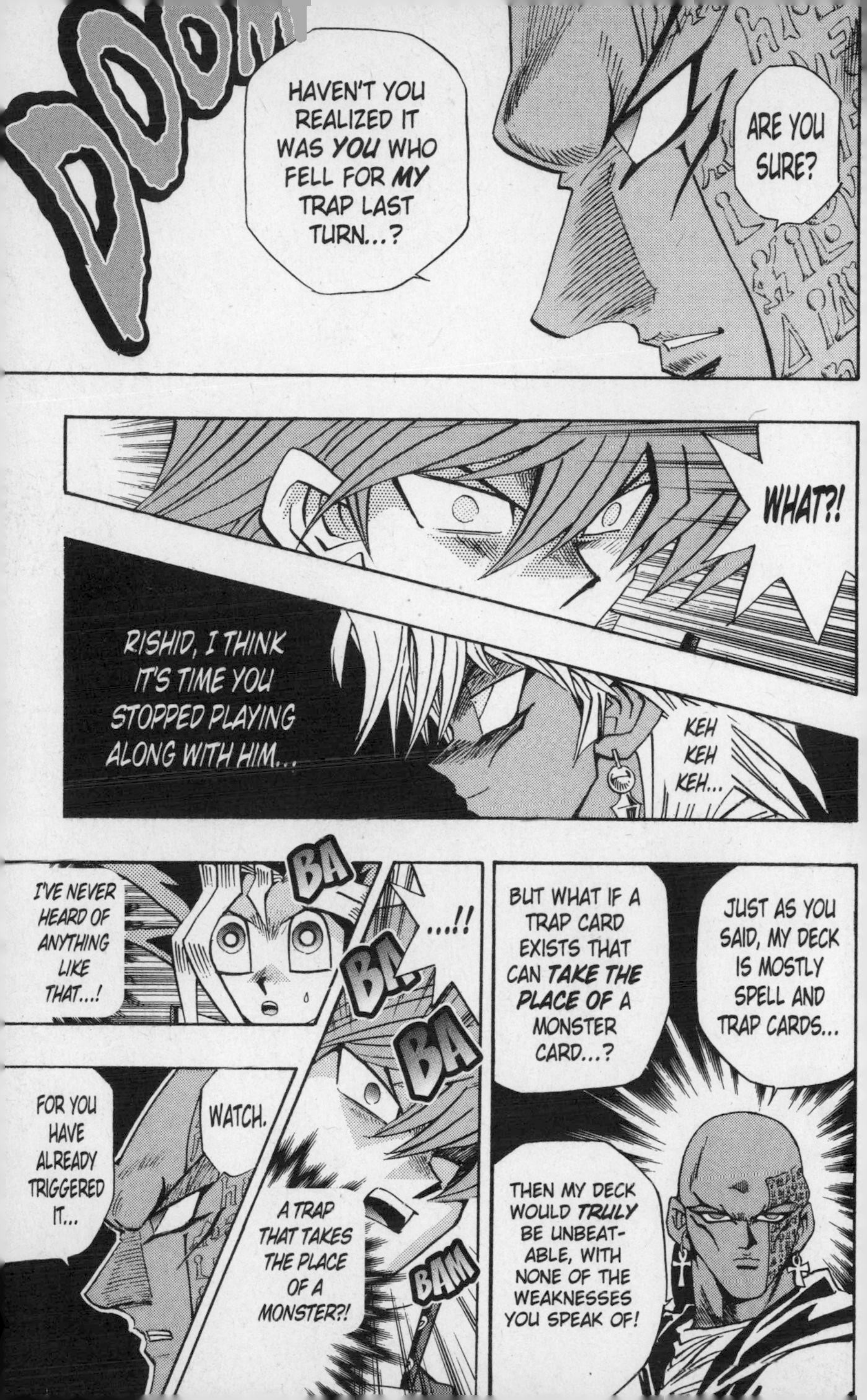
ARE YOU SURE?
HAVEN'T YOU REALIZED IT WAS *YOU* WHO FELL FOR *MY* TRAP LAST TURN...?
DOOOM
WHAT?!
RISHID, I THINK IT'S TIME YOU STOPPED PLAYING ALONG WITH HIM...
KEH KEH KEH...
JUST AS YOU SAID, MY DECK IS MOSTLY SPELL AND TRAP CARDS...
BUT WHAT IF A TRAP CARD EXISTS THAT CAN *TAKE THE PLACE OF* A MONSTER CARD...?
THEN MY DECK WOULD *TRULY* BE UNBEAT-ABLE, WITH NONE OF THE WEAKNESSES YOU SPEAK OF!
BA
BA
BA
...!!
A TRAP THAT TAKES THE PLACE OF A MONSTER?!
BAM
I'VE NEVER HEARD OF ANYTHING LIKE THAT...!
WATCH.
FOR YOU HAVE ALREADY TRIGGERED IT...

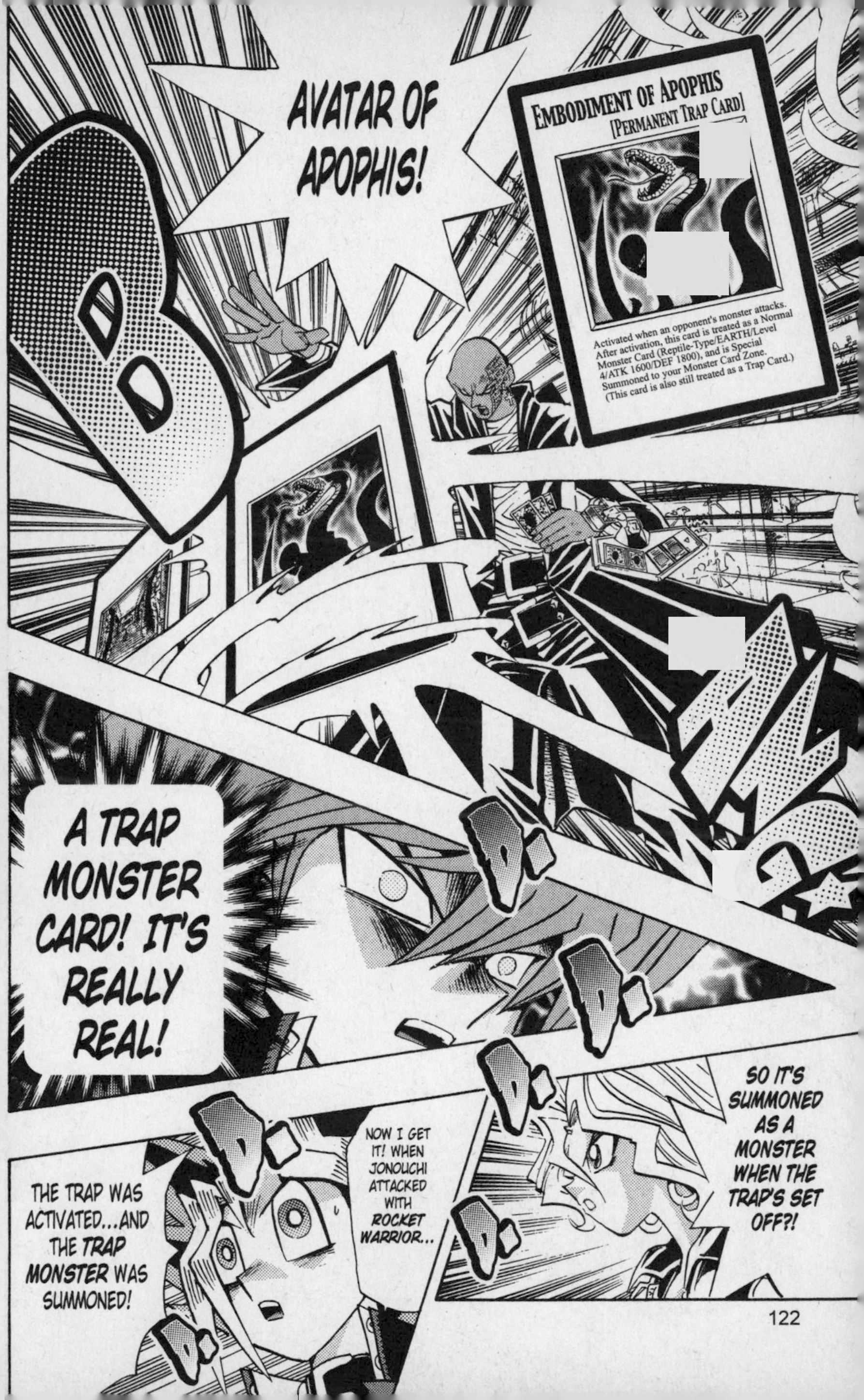
EMBODIMENT OF APOPHIS
[PERMANENT TRAP CARD]
Activated when an opponent's monster attacks. After activation, this card is treated as a Normal Monster Card (Reptile-Type/EARTH/Level 4/ATK 1600/DEF 1800), and is Special Summoned to your Monster Card Zone. (This card is also still treated as a Trap Card.)
AVATAR OF APOPHIS!
A TRAP MONSTER CARD! IT'S REALLY REAL!
SO IT'S SUMMONED AS A MONSTER WHEN THE TRAP'S SET OFF?!
NOW I GET IT! WHEN JONOUCHI ATTACKED WITH ROCKET WARRIOR...
THE TRAP WAS ACTIVATED...AND THE TRAP MONSTER WAS SUMMONED!

READ THIS WAY

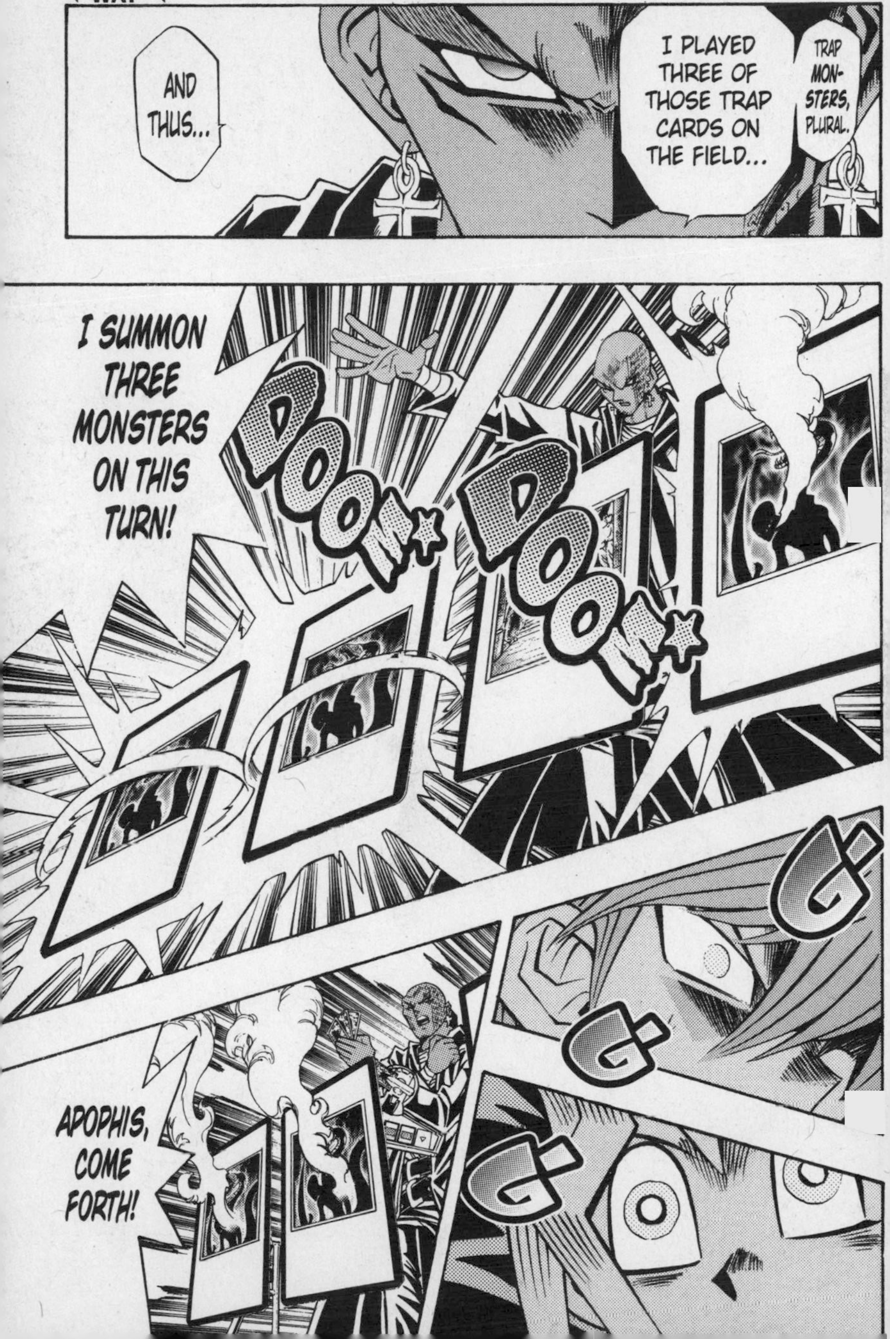
TRAP MONSTERS, PLURAL.
I PLAYED THREE OF THOSE TRAP CARDS ON THE FIELD...
AND THUS...
DOOM*
DOOM*
I SUMMON THREE MONSTERS ON THIS TURN!
G
G
G
APOPHIS, COME FORTH!

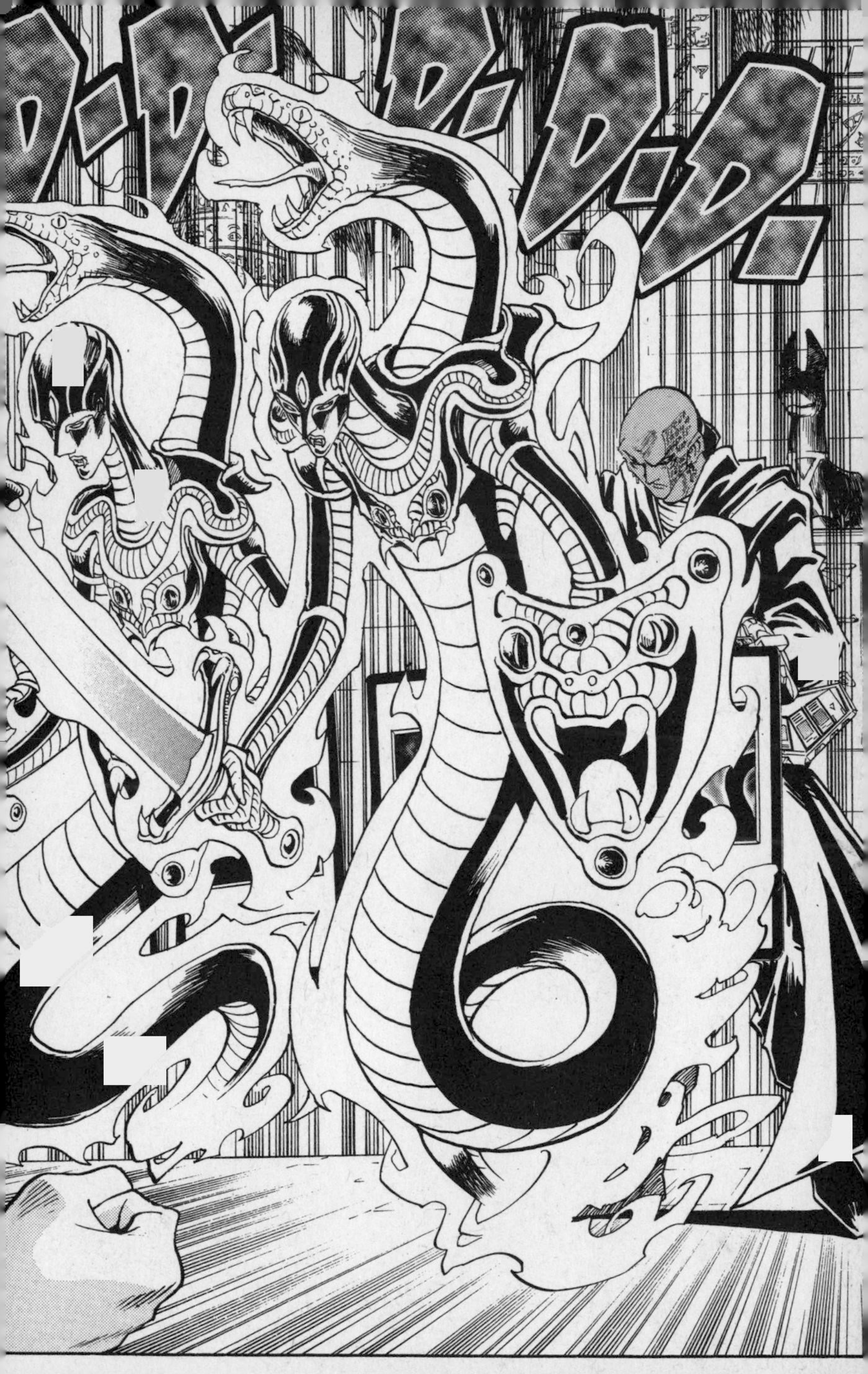
D-D-D-D-D.

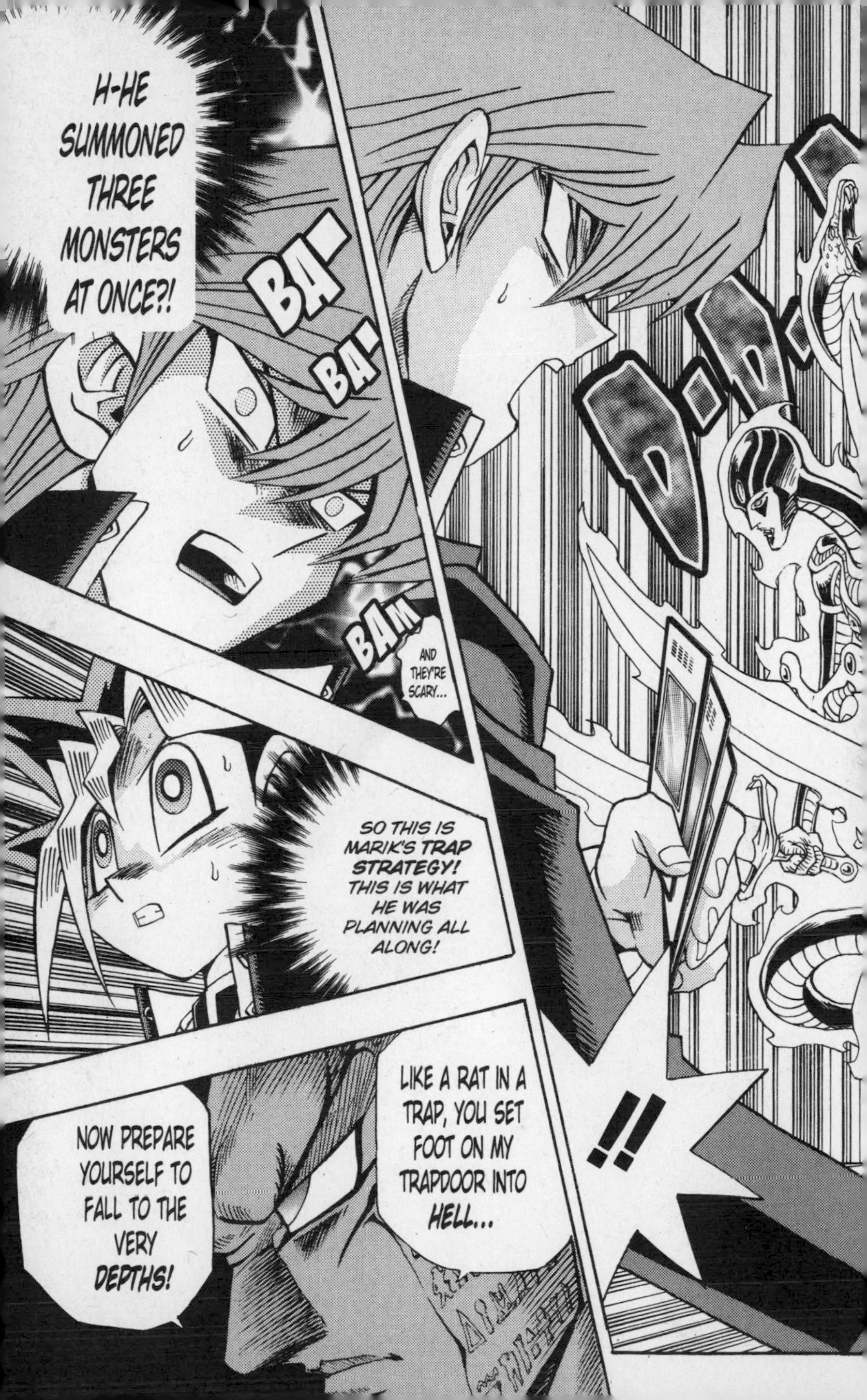
H-HE SUMMONED THREE MONSTERS AT ONCE?!
BA- BA-
BAM
AND THEY'RE SCARY...
SO THIS IS MARIK'S TRAP STRATEGY! THIS IS WHAT HE WAS PLANNING ALL ALONG!
!!
LIKE A RAT IN A TRAP, YOU SET FOOT ON MY TRAPDOOR INTO HELL...
NOW PREPARE YOURSELF TO FALL TO THE VERY DEPTHS!

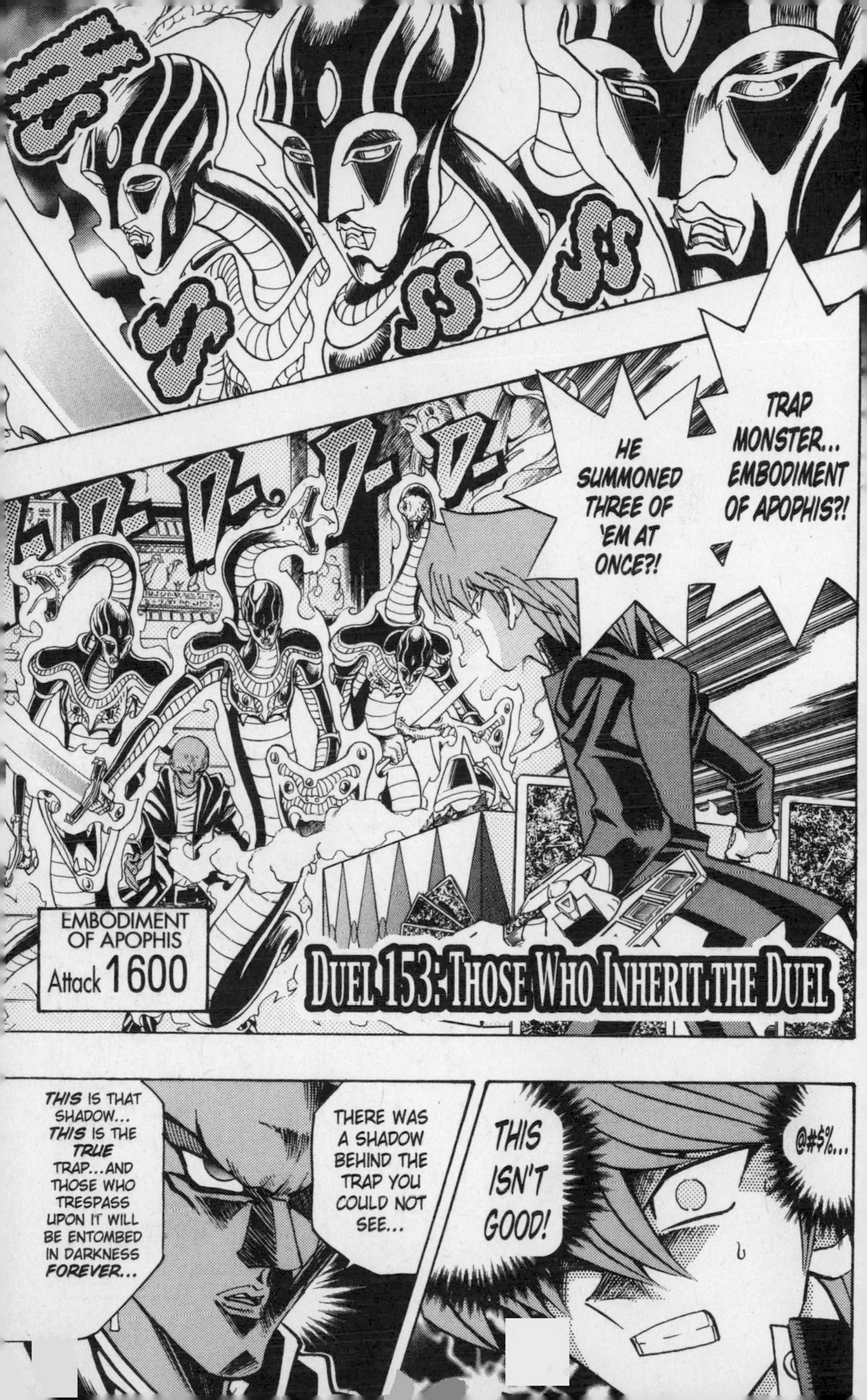
TRAP MONSTER... EMBODIMENT OF APOPHIS?!
HE SUMMONED THREE OF 'EM AT ONCE?!
EMBODIMENT OF APOPHIS Attack 1600
DUEL 153: THOSE WHO INHERIT THE DUEL
@#$%...
THIS ISN'T GOOD!
THERE WAS A SHADOW BEHIND THE TRAP YOU COULD NOT SEE...
THIS IS THAT SHADOW... THIS IS THE TRUE TRAP...AND THOSE WHO TRESPASS UPON IT WILL BE ENTOMBED IN DARKNESS FOREVER...

MARIK (RISHID)
Life Points **4000**

JONOUCHI
Life Points **1850**

DUEL 153: THOSE WHO INHERIT THE DUEL

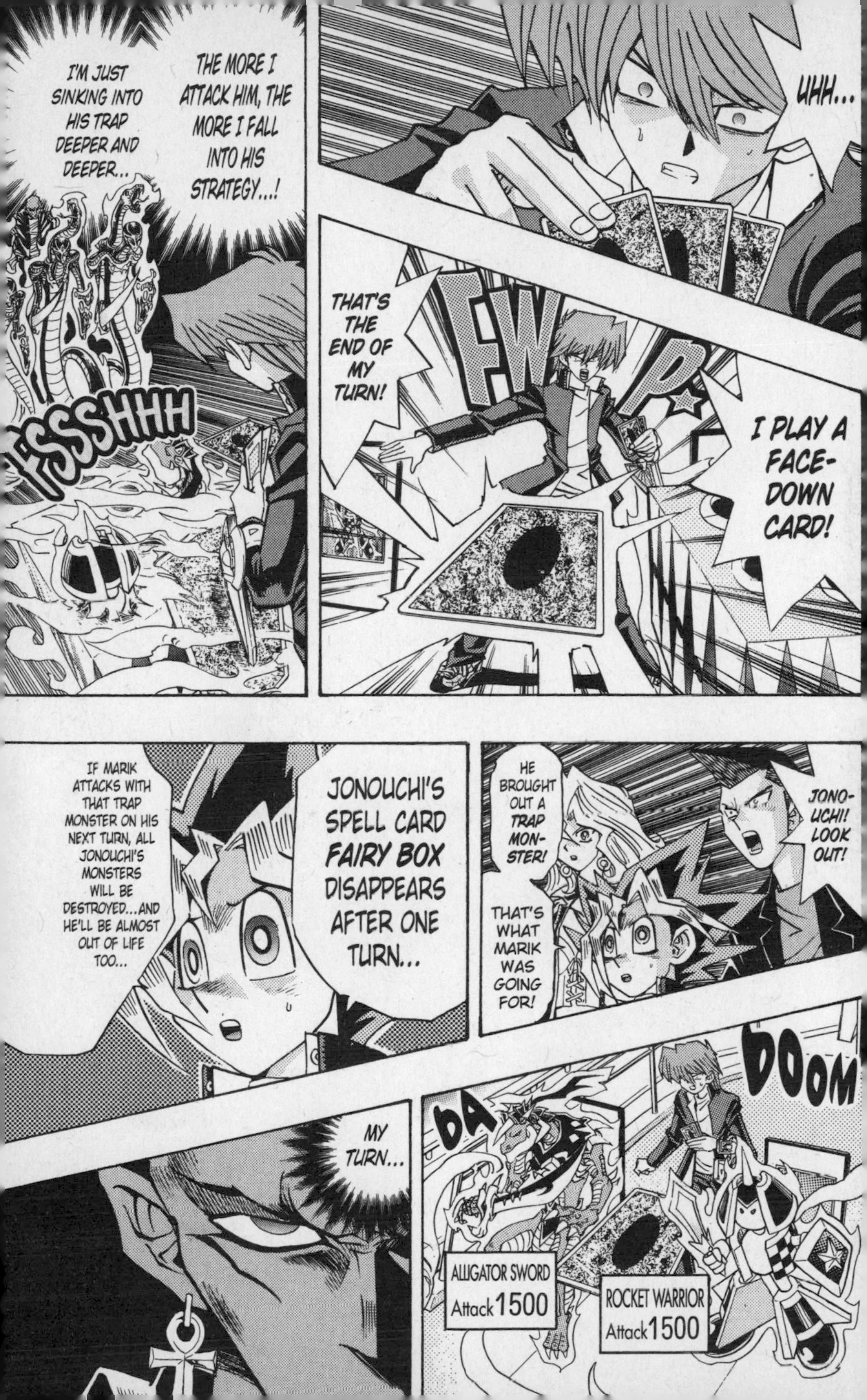
UHH...
I PLAY A FACE-DOWN CARD!
FWP
THAT'S THE END OF MY TURN!
THE MORE I ATTACK HIM, THE MORE I FALL INTO HIS STRATEGY...!
I'M JUST SINKING INTO HIS TRAP DEEPER AND DEEPER...
FSSSHHH
JONO-UCHI! LOOK OUT!
HE BROUGHT OUT A TRAP MONSTER!
THAT'S WHAT MARIK WAS GOING FOR!
JONOUCHI'S SPELL CARD FAIRY BOX DISAPPEARS AFTER ONE TURN...
IF MARIK ATTACKS WITH THAT TRAP MONSTER ON HIS NEXT TURN, ALL JONOUCHI'S MONSTERS WILL BE DESTROYED...AND HE'LL BE ALMOST OUT OF LIFE TOO...
DOOM
BA
ROCKET WARRIOR Attack 1500
ALLIGATOR SWORD Attack 1500
MY TURN...

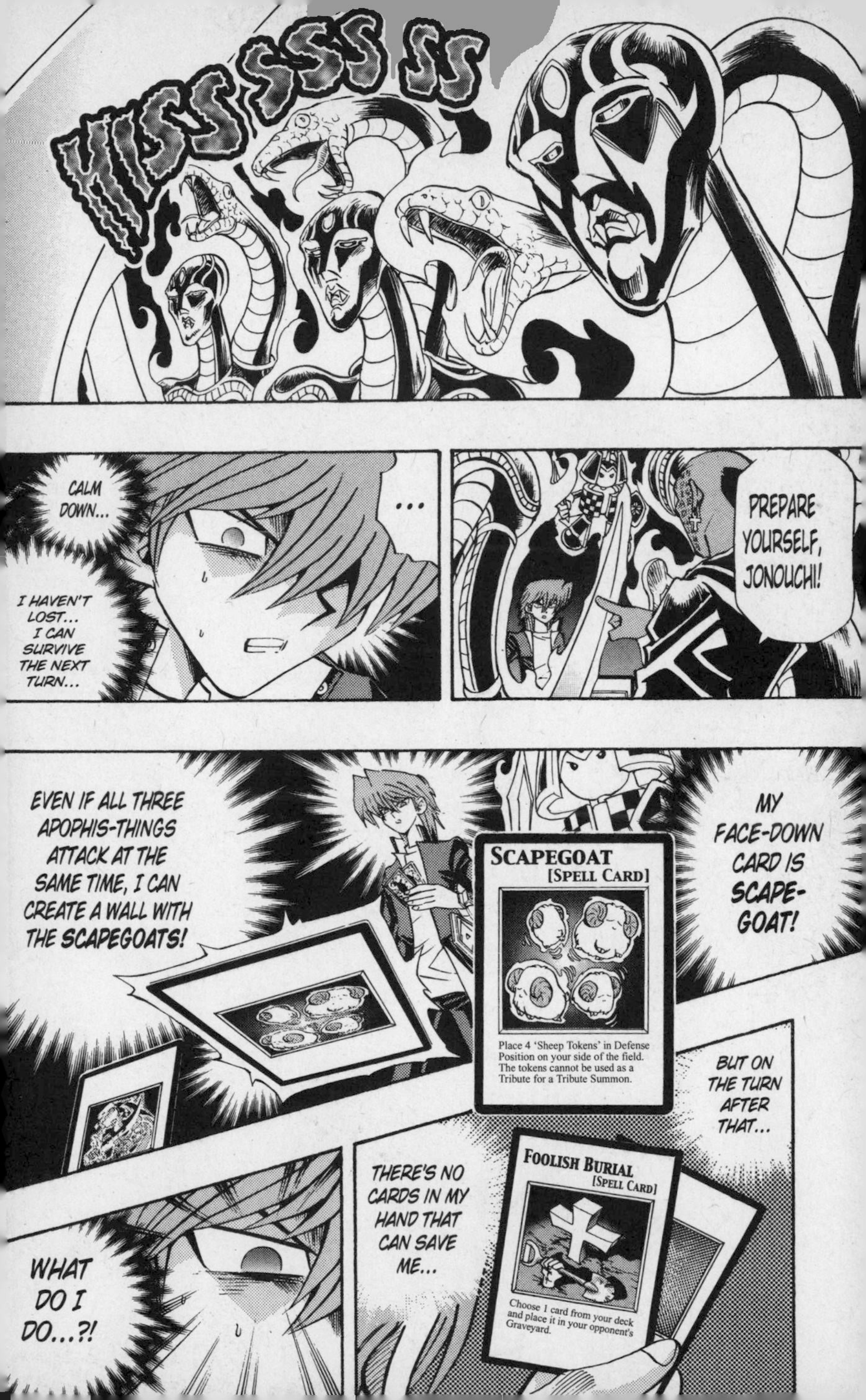
HISS SSS SS
PREPARE YOURSELF, JONOUCHI!
...
CALM DOWN...
I HAVEN'T LOST... I CAN SURVIVE THE NEXT TURN...
MY FACE-DOWN CARD IS SCAPE-GOAT!
SCAPEGOAT
[SPELL CARD]
Place 4 'Sheep Tokens' in Defense Position on your side of the field. The tokens cannot be used as a Tribute for a Tribute Summon.
EVEN IF ALL THREE APOPHIS-THINGS ATTACK AT THE SAME TIME, I CAN CREATE A WALL WITH THE SCAPEGOATS!
BUT ON THE TURN AFTER THAT...
FOOLISH BURIAL
[SPELL CARD]
Choose 1 card from your deck and place it in your opponent's Graveyard.
THERE'S NO CARDS IN MY HAND THAT CAN SAVE ME...
WHAT DO I DO...?!

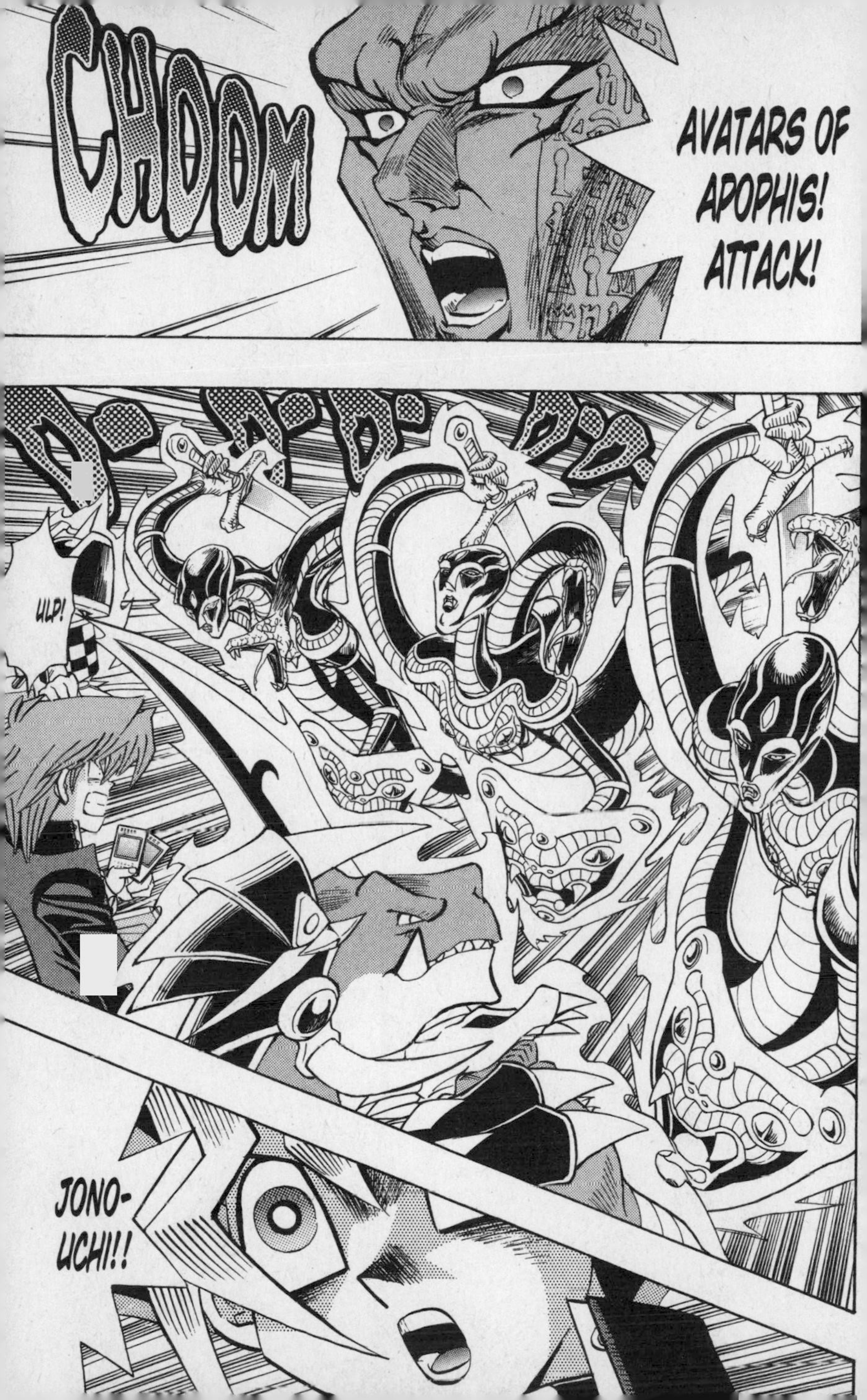
AVATARS OF APOPHIS! ATTACK!
CHOOM
ULP!
JONO-UCHI!!

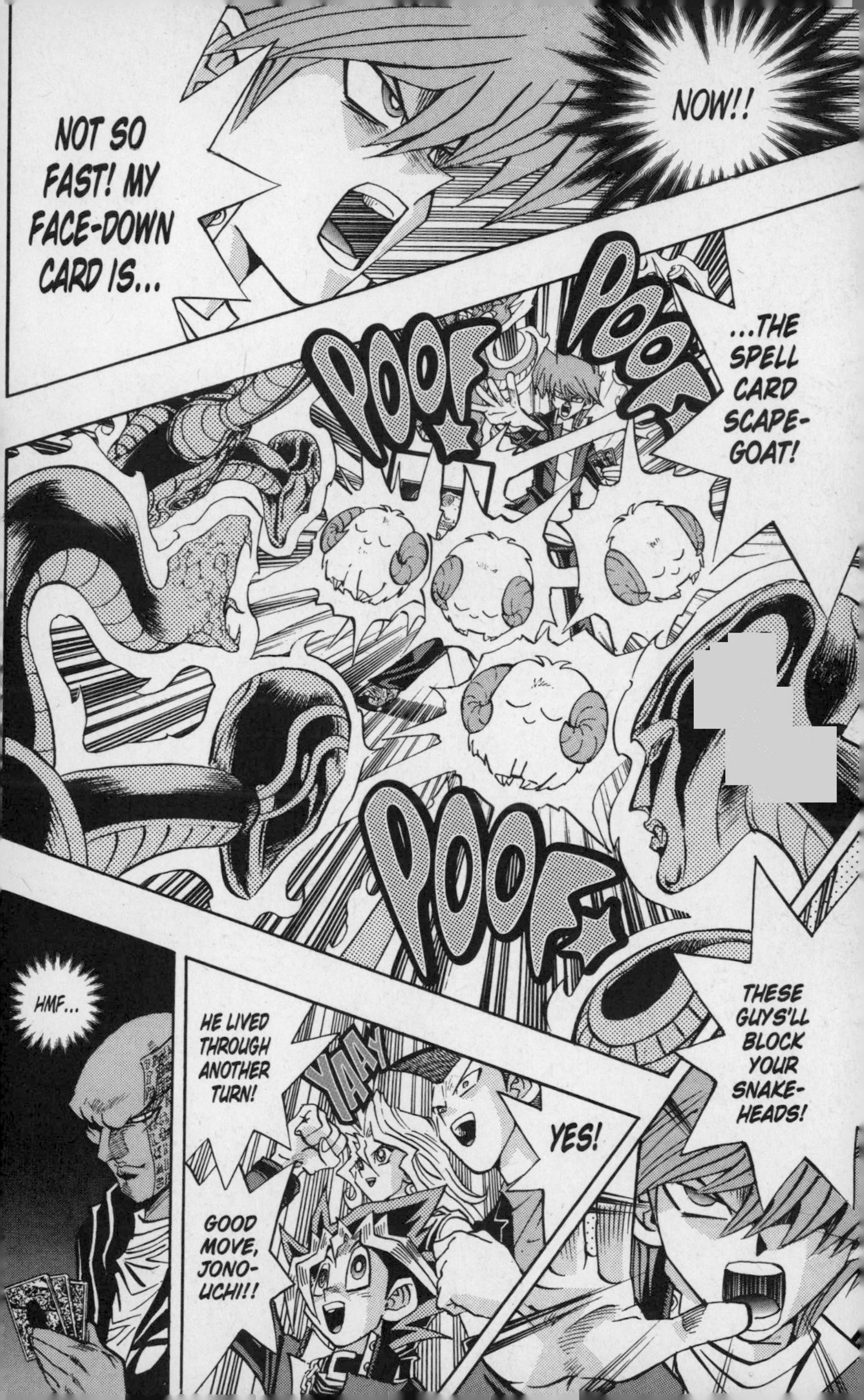
NOW!!
NOT SO FAST! MY FACE-DOWN CARD IS...
POOF
POOF
...THE SPELL CARD SCAPE-GOAT!
POOF
THESE GUYS'LL BLOCK YOUR SNAKE-HEADS!
YES!
HE LIVED THROUGH ANOTHER TURN!
GOOD MOVE, JONO-UCHI!!
HMF...

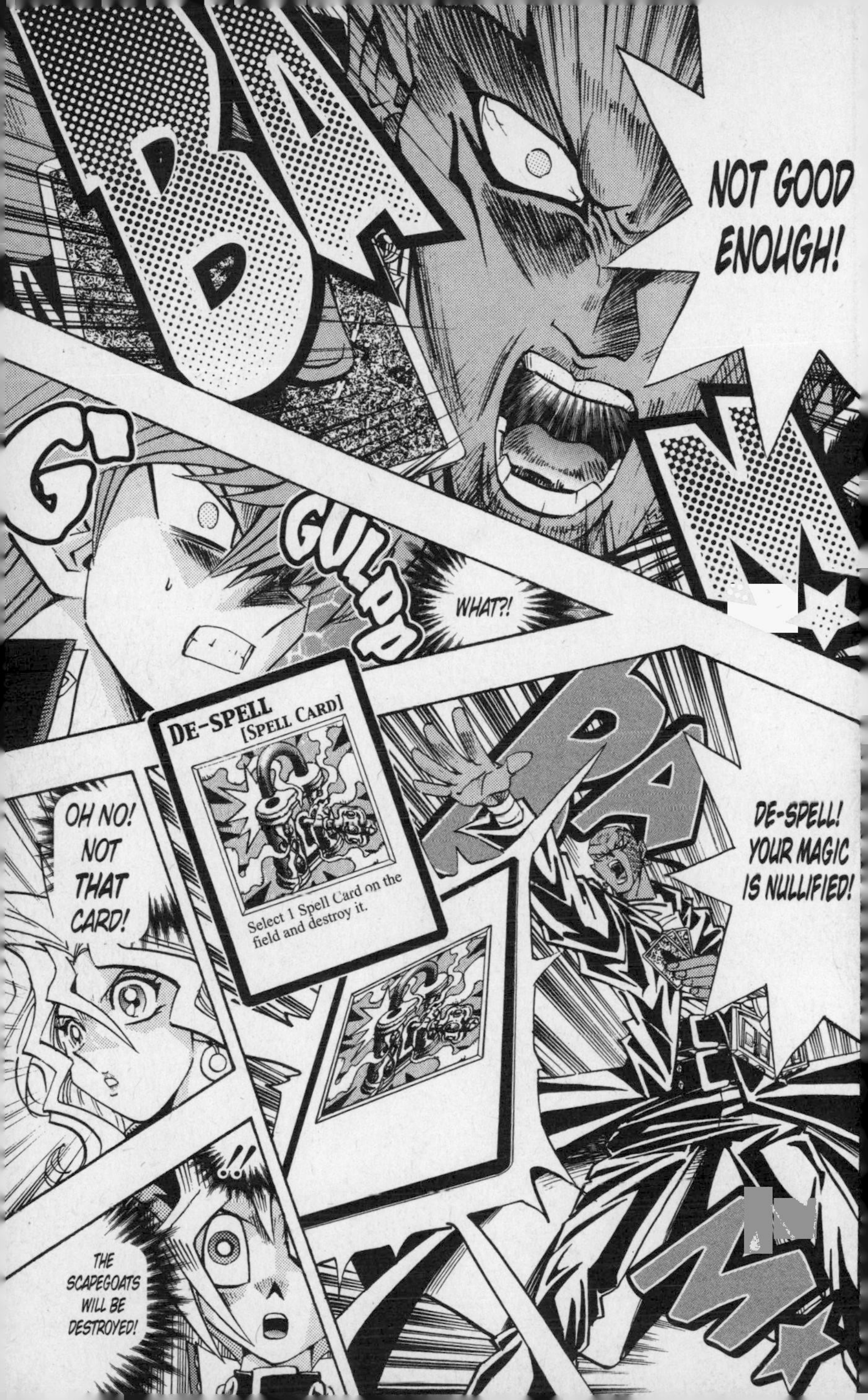
NOT GOOD ENOUGH!
WHAT?!
DE-SPELL! YOUR MAGIC IS NULLIFIED!
DE-SPELL
[SPELL CARD]
Select 1 Spell Card on the field and destroy it.
OH NO! NOT THAT CARD!
THE SCAPEGOATS WILL BE DESTROYED!

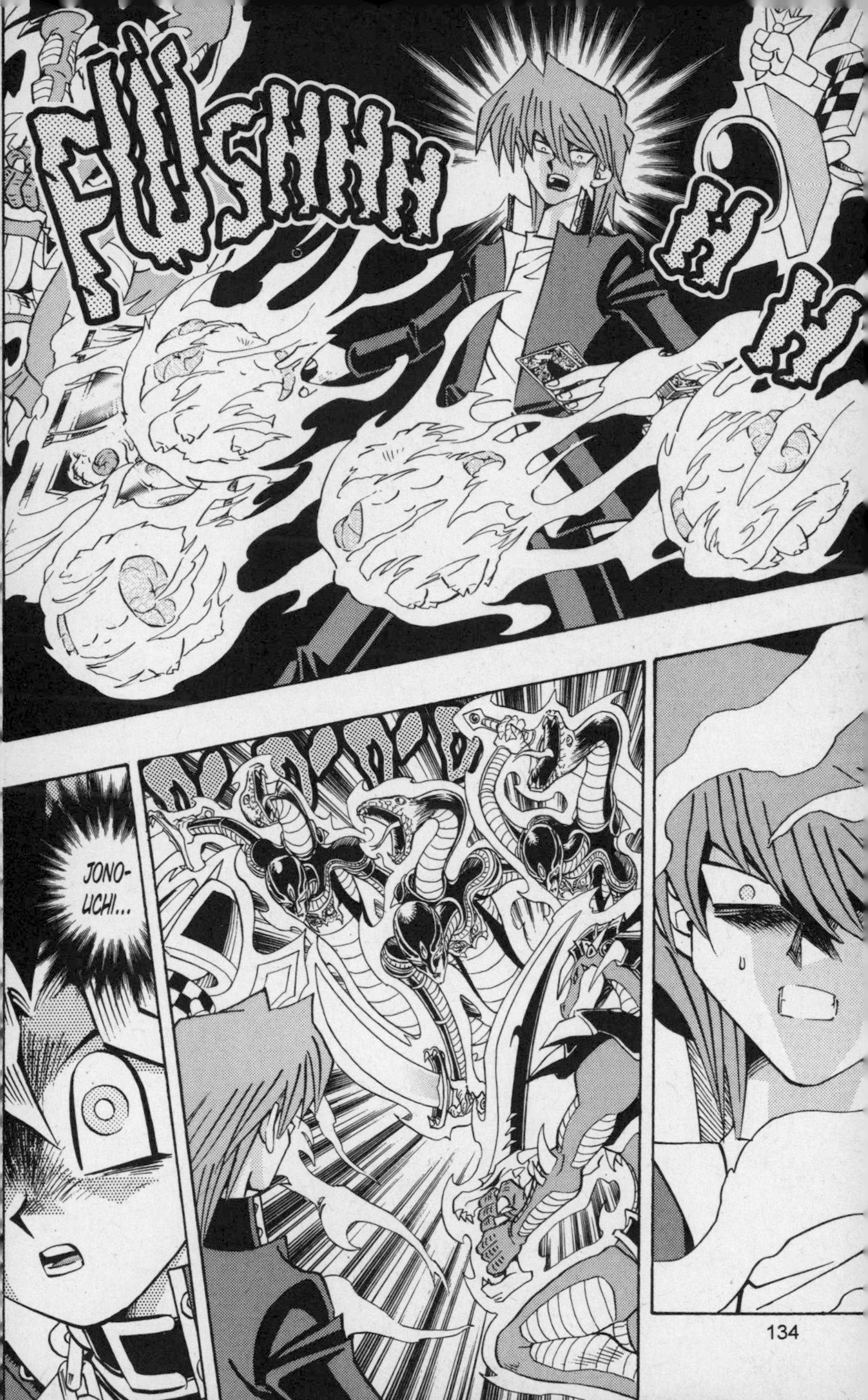
FUSHNN
JONO-
UCHI...

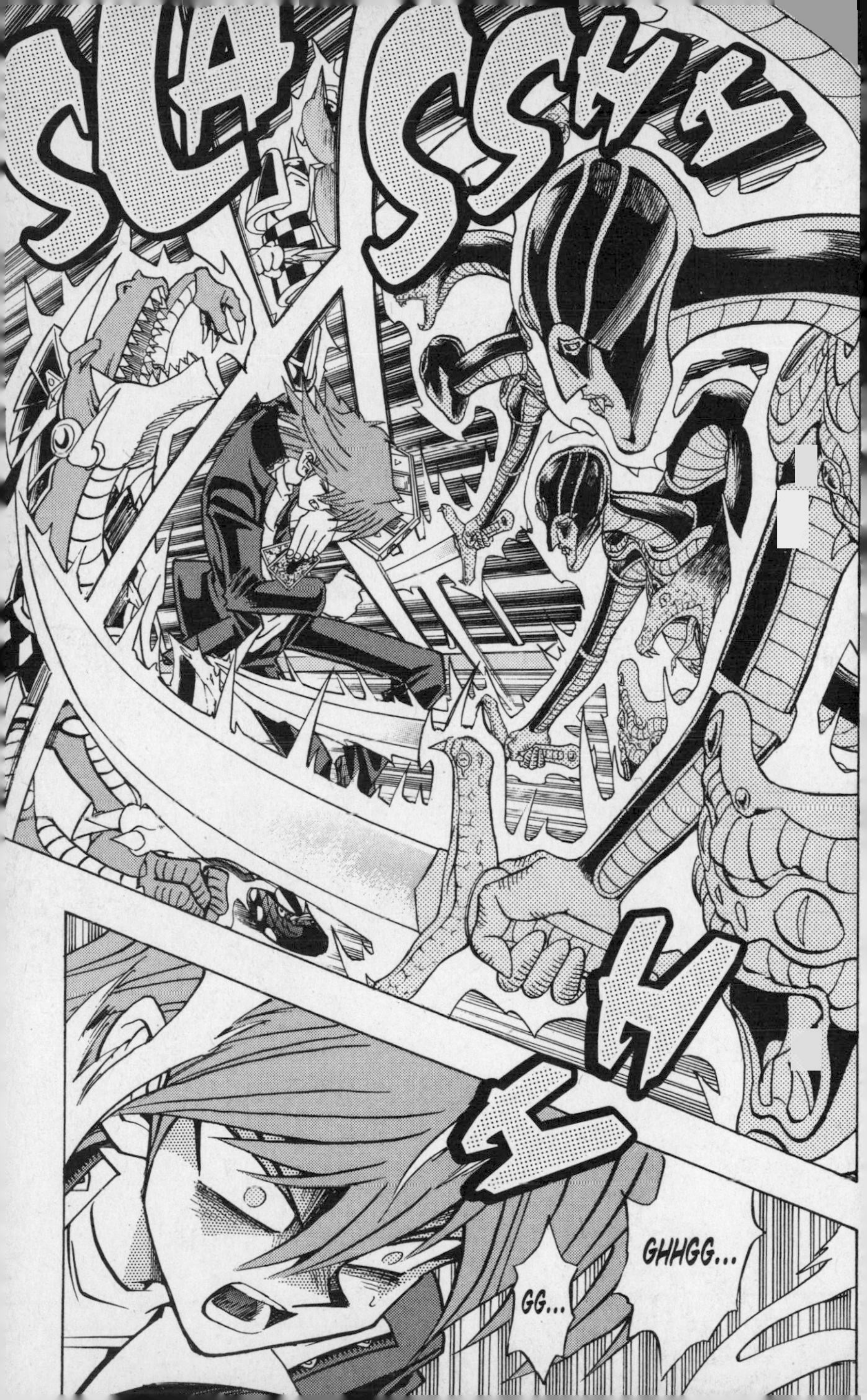
SLASSHH
GHHGG...
GG...

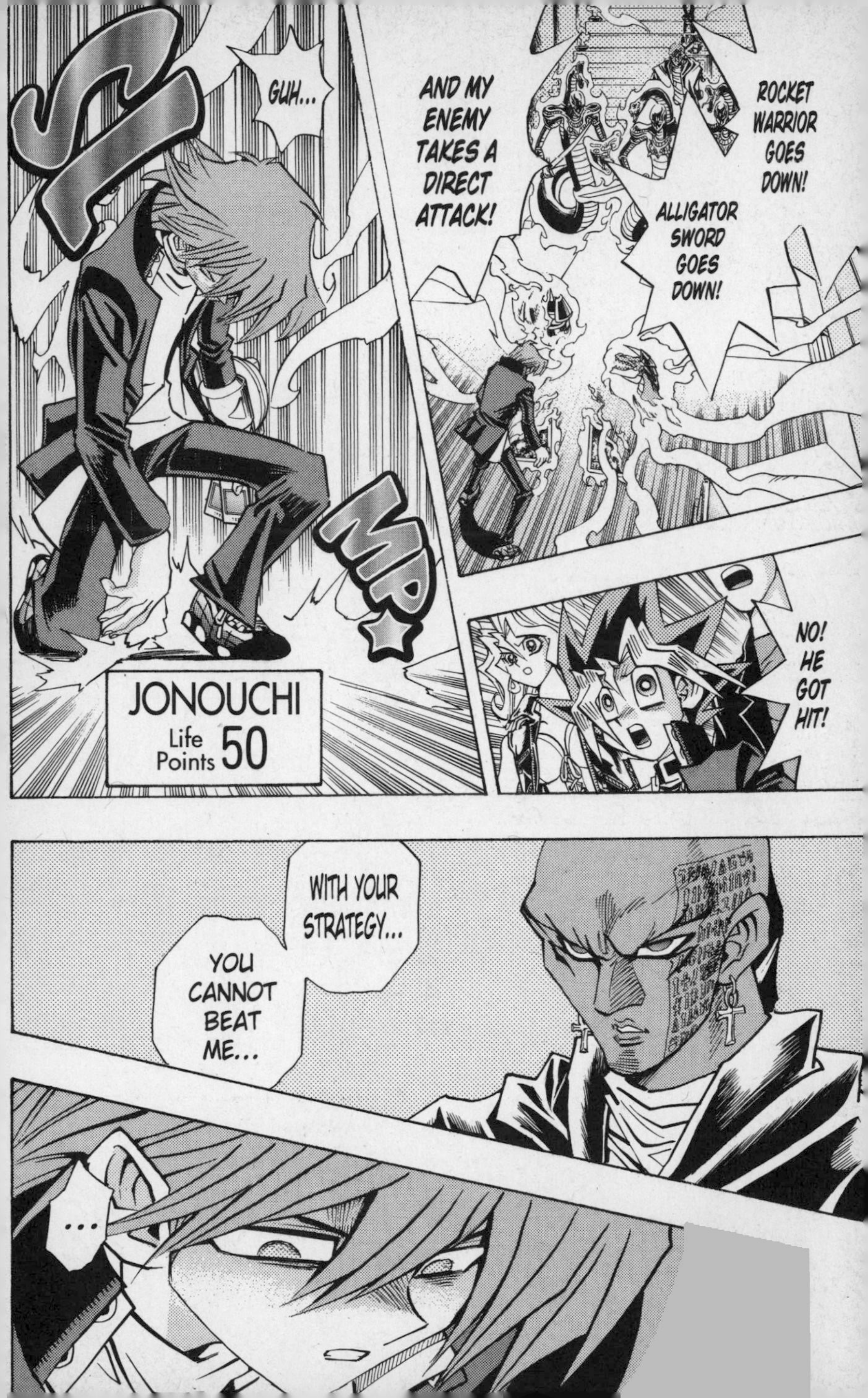
ROCKET WARRIOR GOES DOWN!
ALLIGATOR SWORD GOES DOWN!
AND MY ENEMY TAKES A DIRECT ATTACK!
NO! HE GOT HIT!
GUH...
SL
MP!
JONOUCHI
Life Points 50
WITH YOUR STRATEGY...
YOU CANNOT BEAT ME...
...

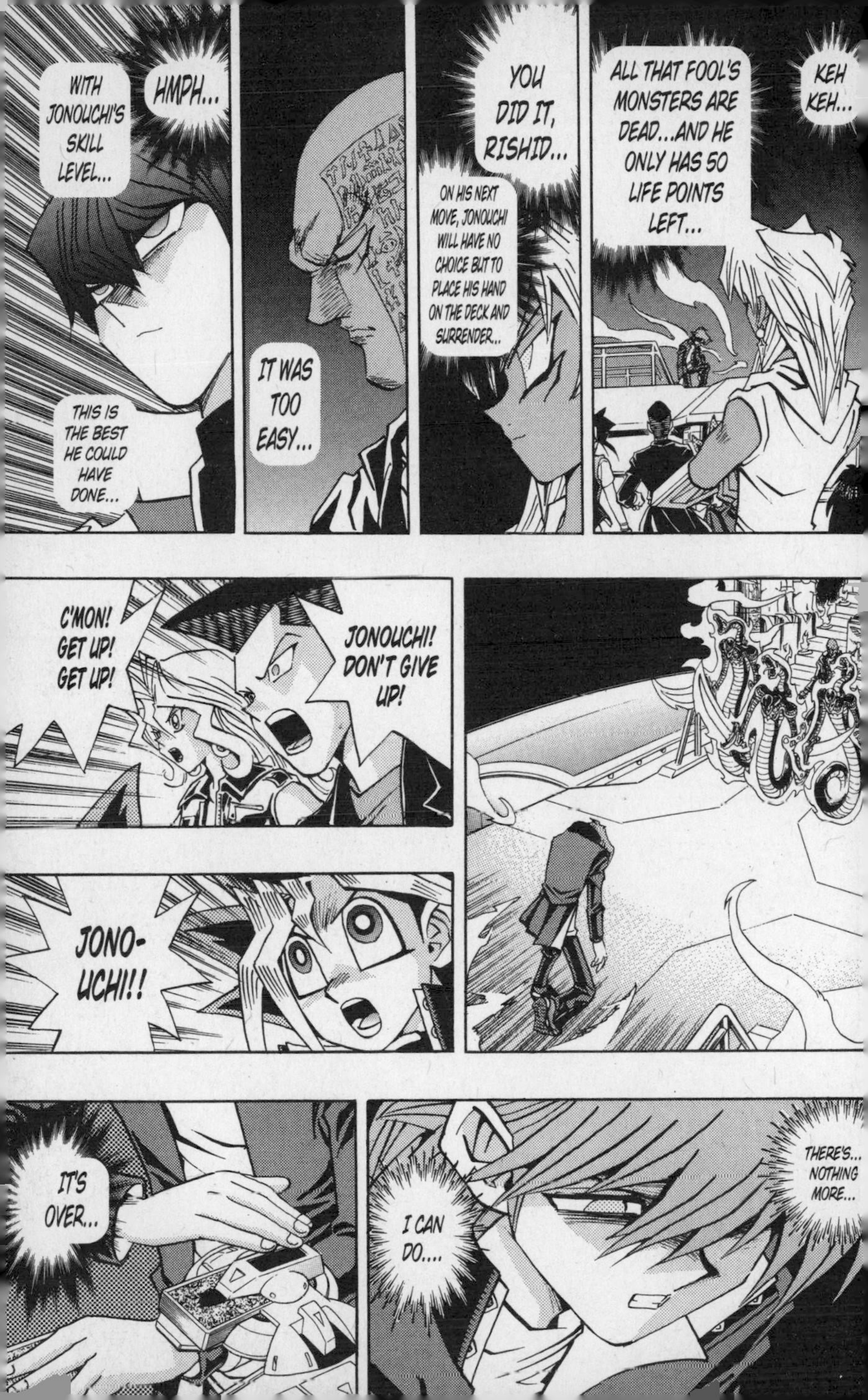
KEH KEH...
ALL THAT FOOL'S MONSTERS ARE DEAD...AND HE ONLY HAS 50 LIFE POINTS LEFT...
YOU DID IT, RISHID...
ON HIS NEXT MOVE, JONOUCHI WILL HAVE NO CHOICE BUT TO PLACE HIS HAND ON THE DECK AND SURRENDER...
IT WAS TOO EASY...
HMPH...
WITH JONOUCHI'S SKILL LEVEL...
THIS IS THE BEST HE COULD HAVE DONE...
JONOUCHI! DON'T GIVE UP!
C'MON! GET UP! GET UP!
JONO-UCHI!!
THERE'S... NOTHING MORE...
I CAN DO....
IT'S OVER...

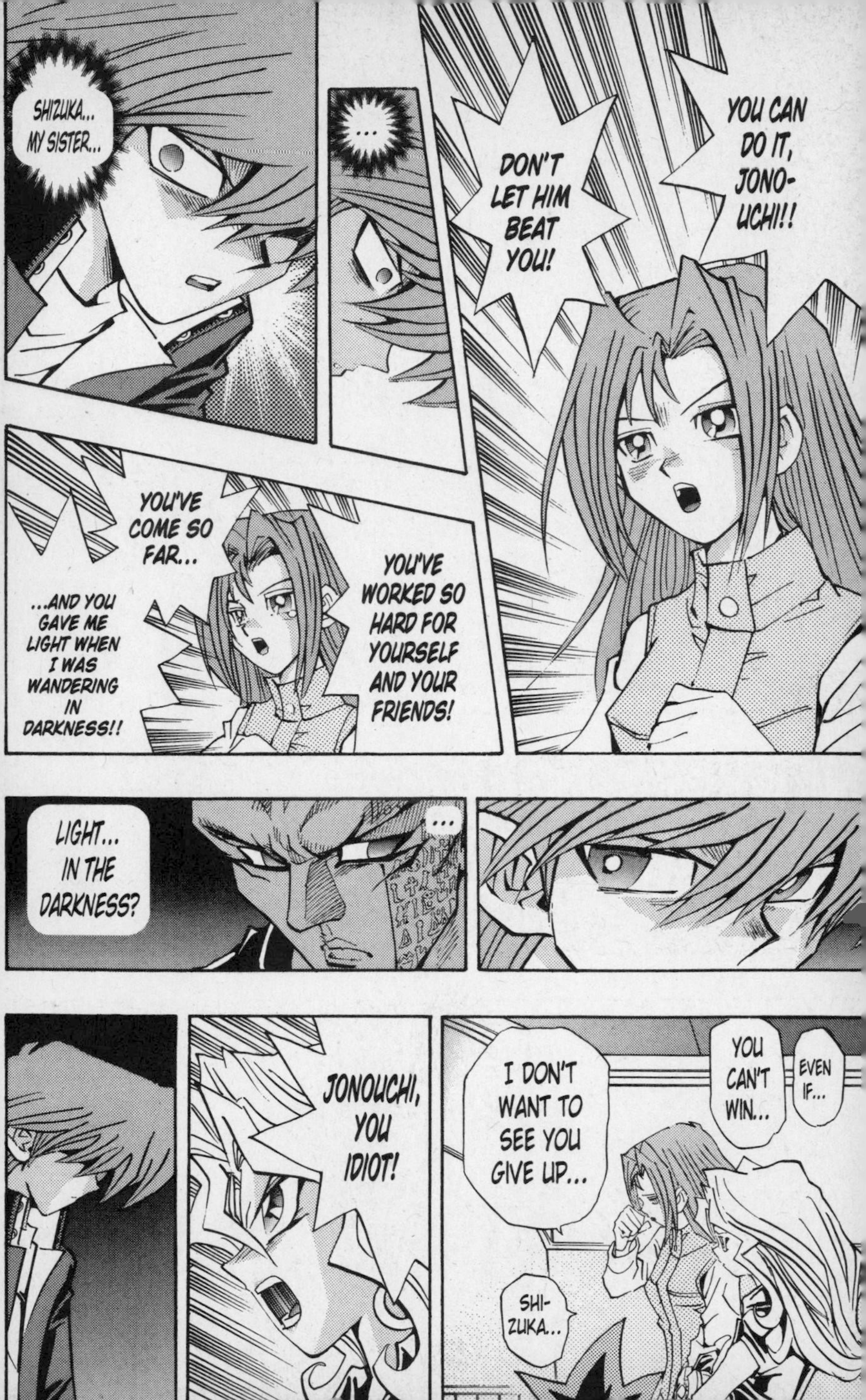

YOU CAN DO IT, JONO-UCHI!!
DON'T LET HIM BEAT YOU!
...
SHIZUKA... MY SISTER...
YOU'VE COME SO FAR...
YOU'VE WORKED SO HARD FOR YOURSELF AND YOUR FRIENDS!
...AND YOU GAVE ME LIGHT WHEN I WAS WANDERING IN DARKNESS!!
...
LIGHT... IN THE DARKNESS?
EVEN IF...
YOU CAN'T WIN...
I DON'T WANT TO SEE YOU GIVE UP...
SHI-ZUKA...
JONOUCHI, YOU IDIOT!

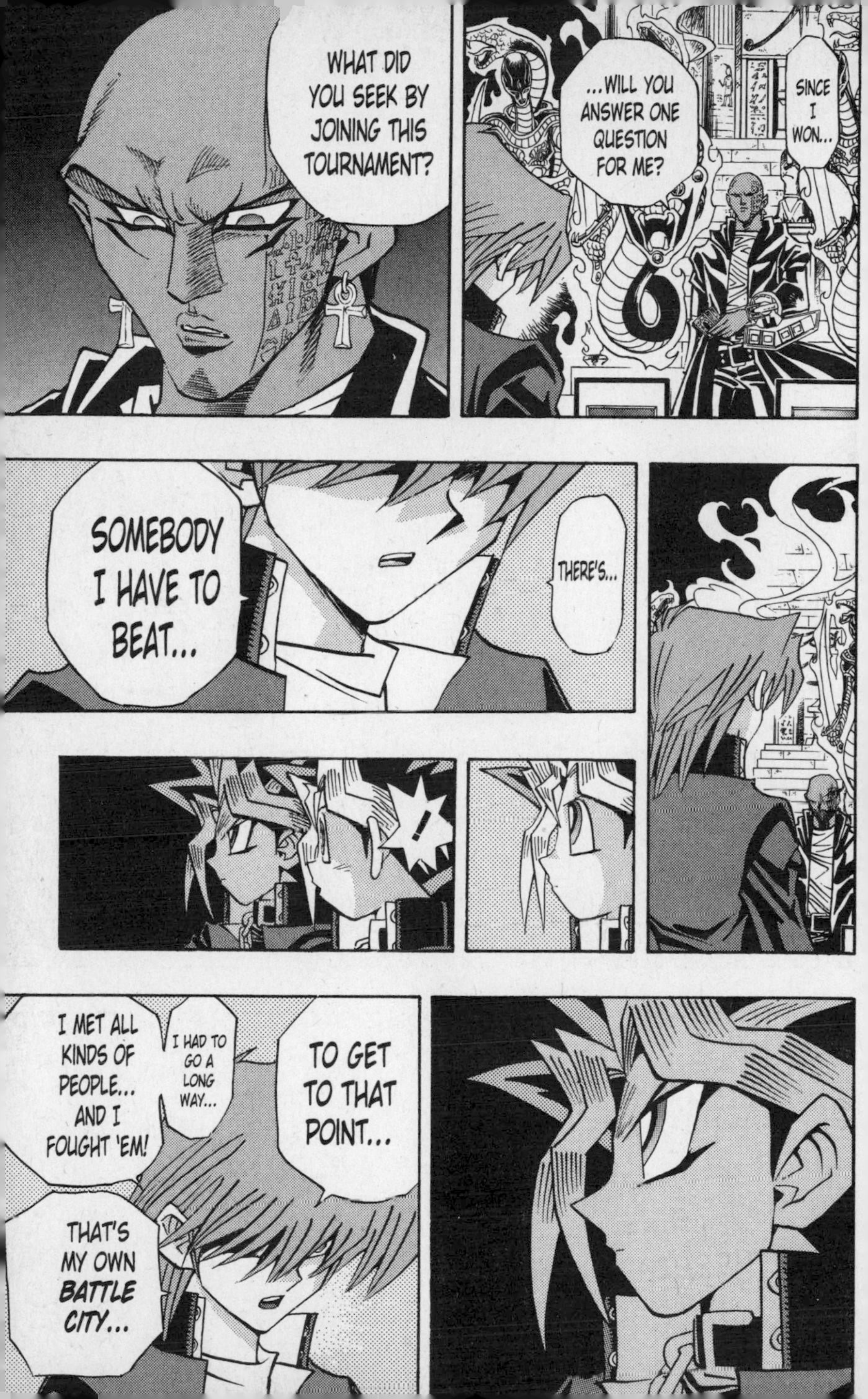
SINCE I WON...
...WILL YOU ANSWER ONE QUESTION FOR ME?
WHAT DID YOU SEEK BY JOINING THIS TOURNAMENT?
THERE'S...
SOMEBODY I HAVE TO BEAT...
!
TO GET TO THAT POINT...
I HAD TO GO A LONG WAY...
I MET ALL KINDS OF PEOPLE... AND I FOUGHT 'EM!
THAT'S MY OWN BATTLE CITY...

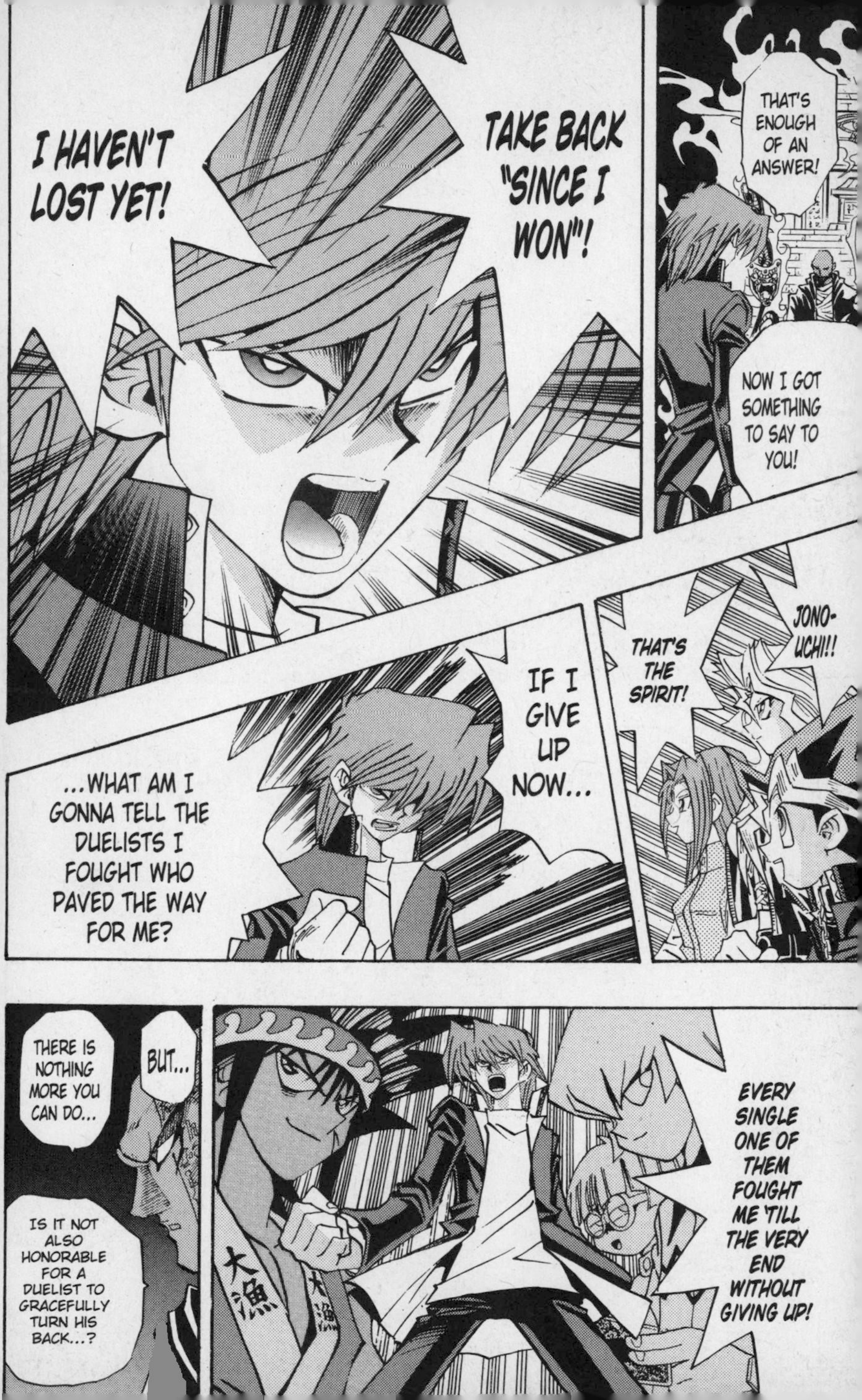
THAT'S ENOUGH OF AN ANSWER!
NOW I GOT SOMETHING TO SAY TO YOU!
TAKE BACK "SINCE I WON"!
I HAVEN'T LOST YET!
JONO-UCHI!!
THAT'S THE SPIRIT!
IF I GIVE UP NOW...
...WHAT AM I GONNA TELL THE DUELISTS I FOUGHT WHO PAVED THE WAY FOR ME?
EVERY SINGLE ONE OF THEM FOUGHT ME 'TILL THE VERY END WITHOUT GIVING UP!
BUT...
THERE IS NOTHING MORE YOU CAN DO...
IS IT NOT ALSO HONORABLE FOR A DUELIST TO GRACEFULLY TURN HIS BACK...?

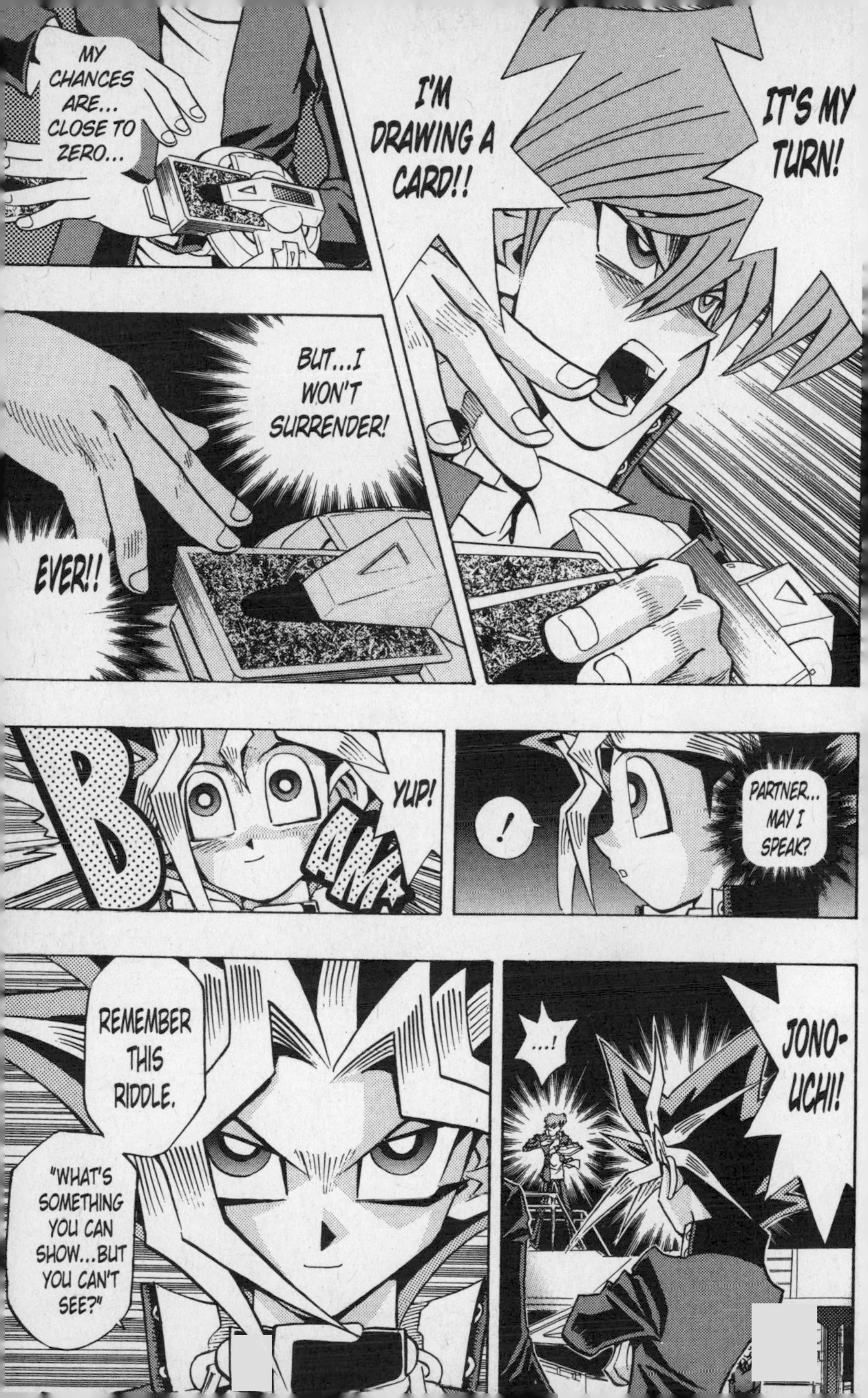
IT'S MY TURN!
I'M DRAWING A CARD!!
MY CHANCES ARE... CLOSE TO ZERO...
BUT...I WON'T SURRENDER!
EVER!!
PARTNER... MAY I SPEAK?
!
YUP!
BAM!
JONO-UCHI!
...!
REMEMBER THIS RIDDLE.
"WHAT'S SOMETHING YOU CAN SHOW...BUT YOU CAN'T SEE?"

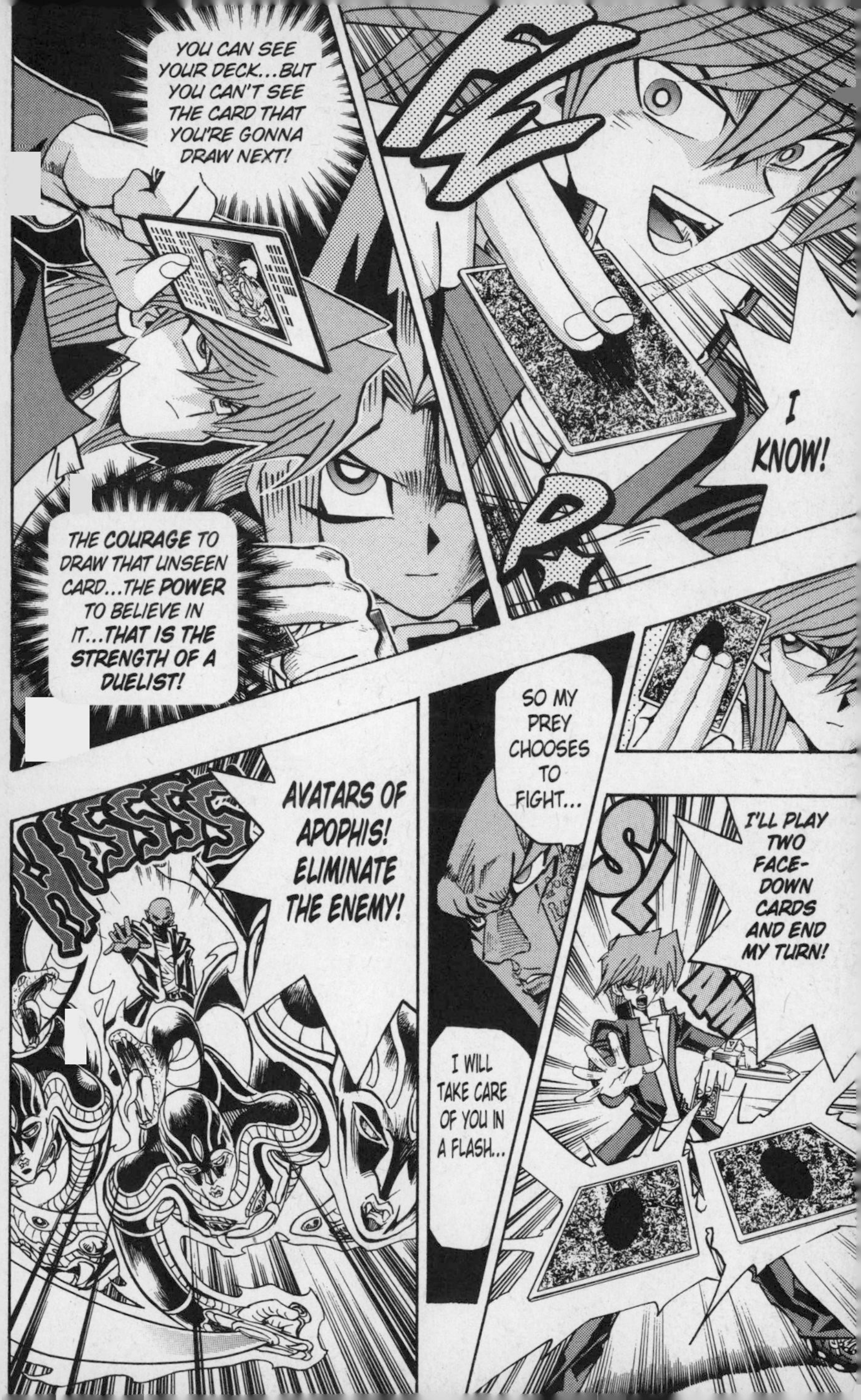
I KNOW!
YOU CAN SEE YOUR DECK...BUT YOU CAN'T SEE THE CARD THAT YOU'RE GONNA DRAW NEXT!
THE COURAGE TO DRAW THAT UNSEEN CARD...THE POWER TO BELIEVE IN IT...THAT IS THE STRENGTH OF A DUELIST!
I'LL PLAY TWO FACE-DOWN CARDS AND END MY TURN!
SO MY PREY CHOOSES TO FIGHT...
I WILL TAKE CARE OF YOU IN A FLASH...
AVATARS OF APOPHIS! ELIMINATE THE ENEMY!
HISSSS

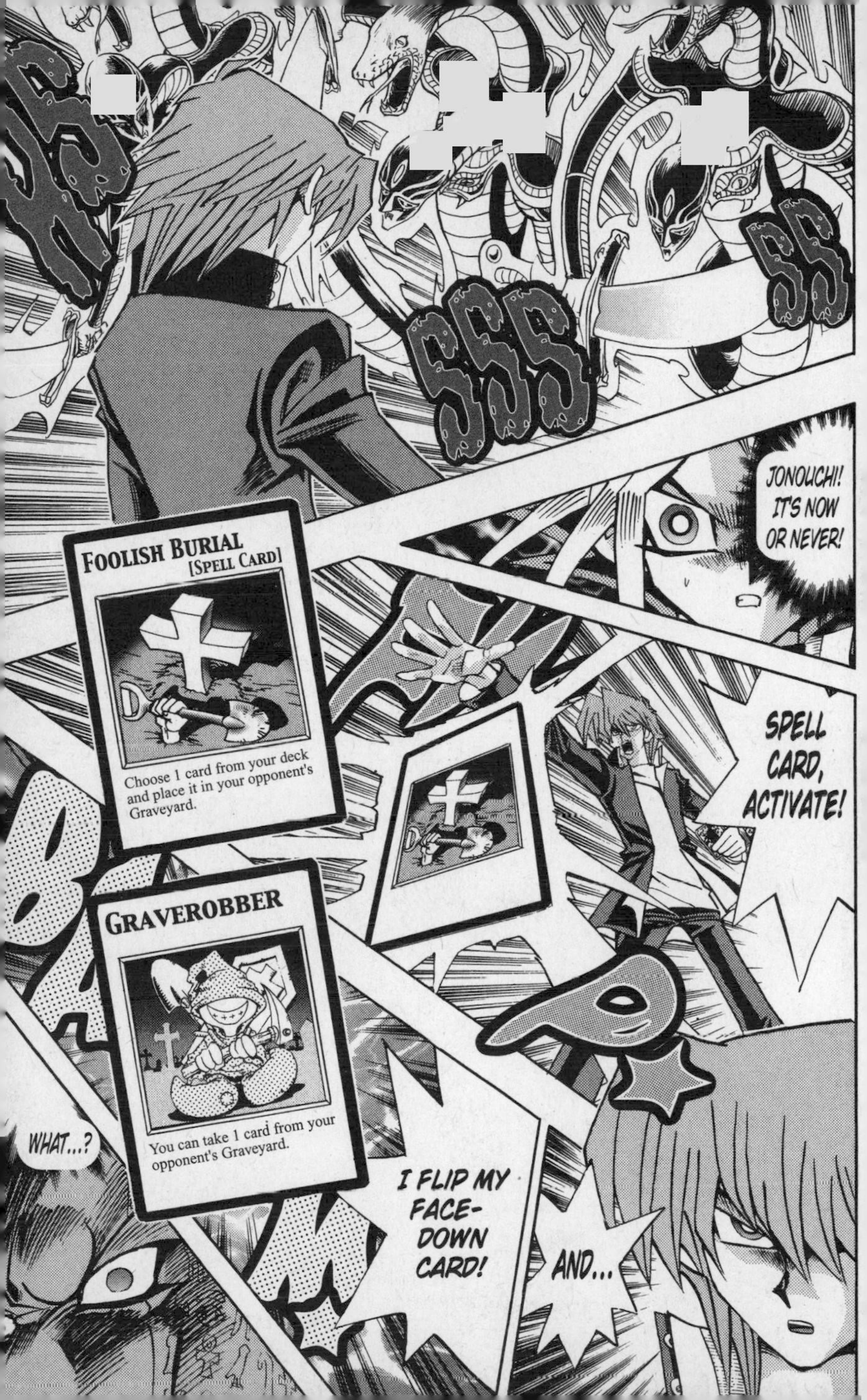

SSS
SS
JONOUCHI! IT'S NOW OR NEVER!
SPELL CARD, ACTIVATE!
FOOLISH BURIAL
[SPELL CARD]
Choose 1 card from your deck and place it in your opponent's Graveyard.
GRAVEROBBER
You can take 1 card from your opponent's Graveyard.
I FLIP MY FACE-DOWN CARD!
AND...
WHAT...?

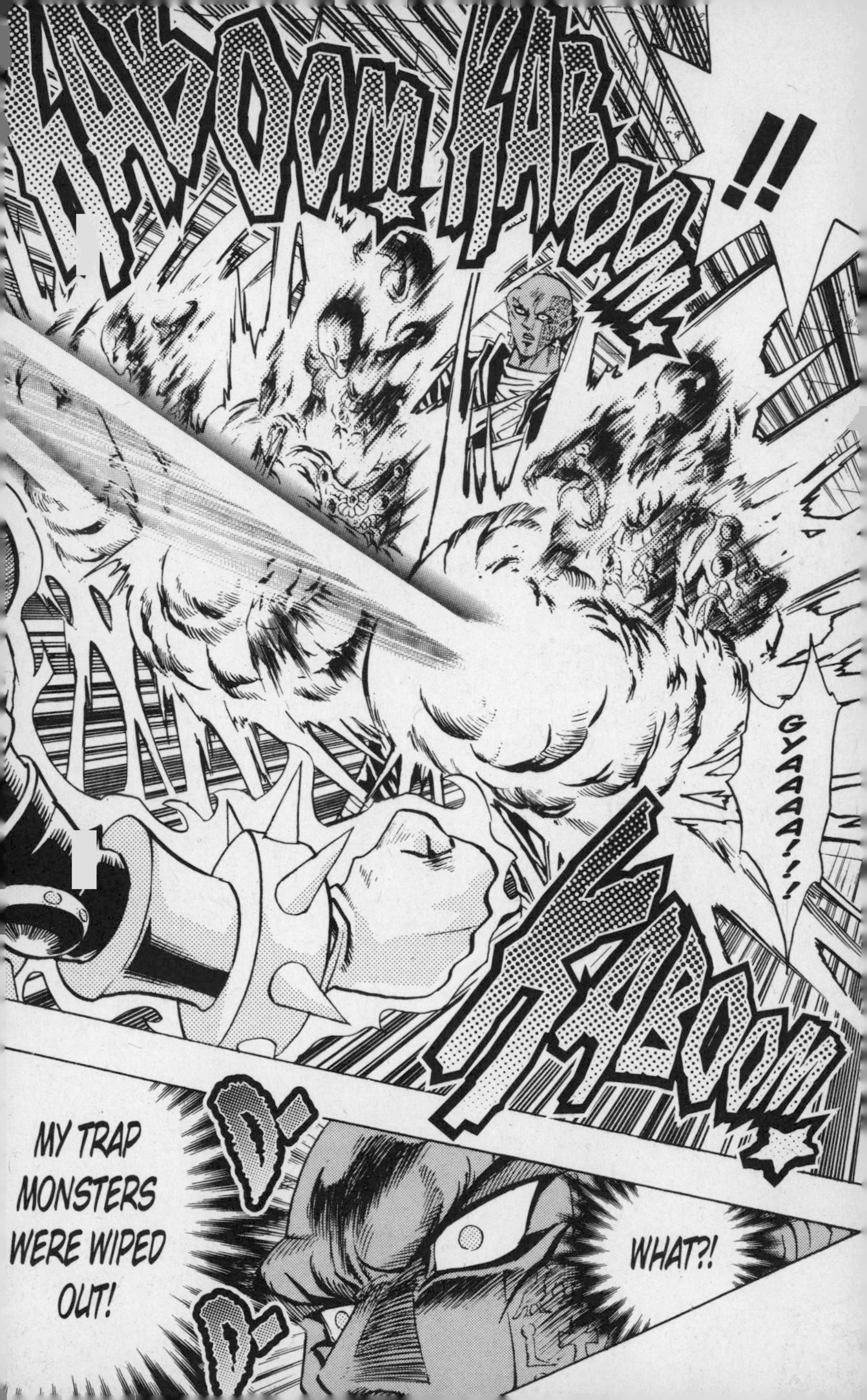
GYAAAAA!!!
WHAT?!
MY TRAP MONSTERS WERE WIPED OUT!

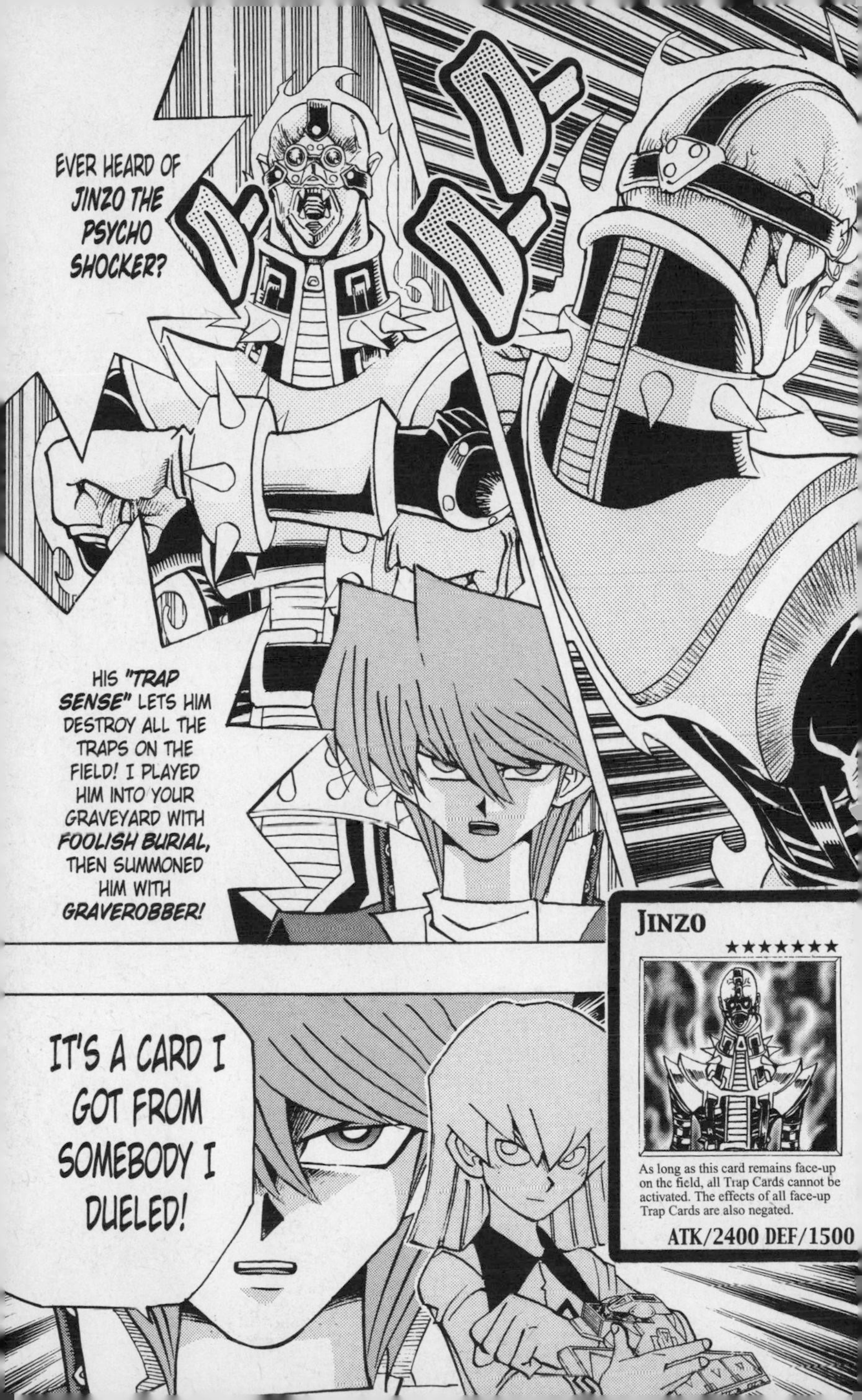
EVER HEARD OF JINZO THE PSYCHO SHOCKER?
HIS "TRAP SENSE" LETS HIM DESTROY ALL THE TRAPS ON THE FIELD! I PLAYED HIM INTO YOUR GRAVEYARD WITH FOOLISH BURIAL, THEN SUMMONED HIM WITH GRAVEROBBER!
JINZO
★★★★★★★
As long as this card remains face-up on the field, all Trap Cards cannot be activated. The effects of all face-up Trap Cards are also negated.
ATK/2400 DEF/1500
IT'S A CARD I GOT FROM SOMEBODY I DUELED!

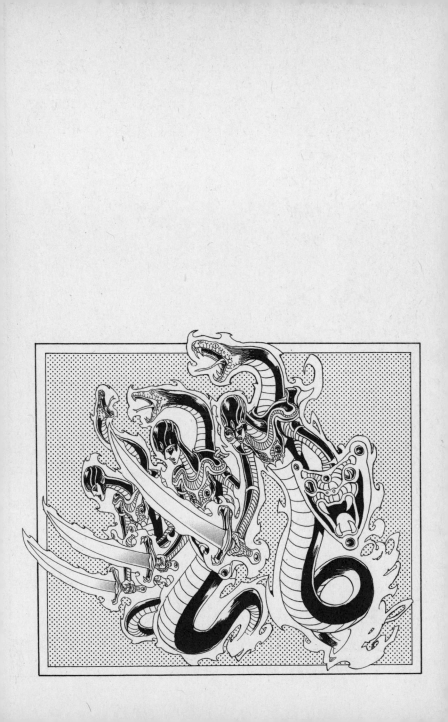

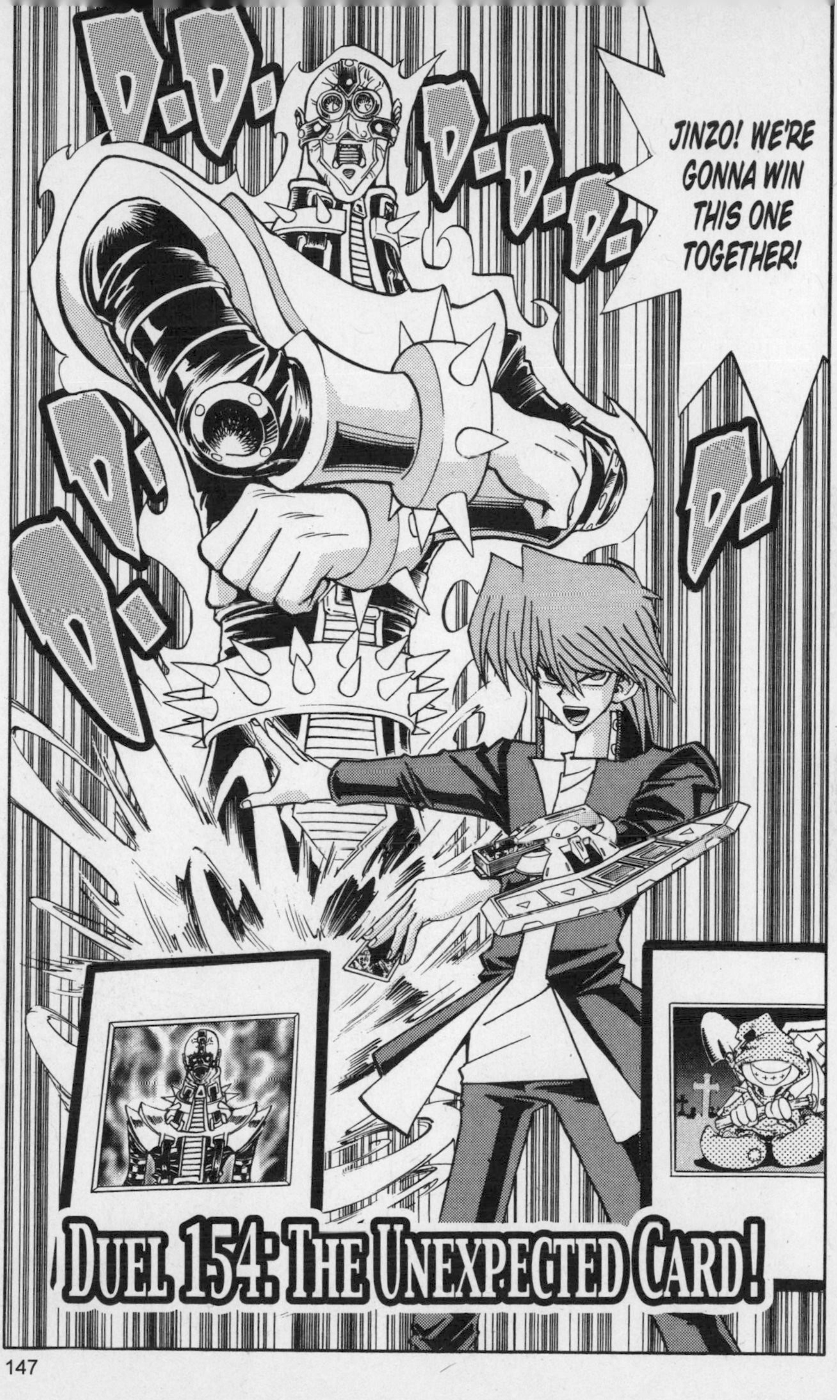
JINZO! WE'RE GONNA WIN THIS ONE TOGETHER!
D.D.D.D.
D.D.
D.
D.D.D.
DUEL 154: THE UNEXPECTED CARD!

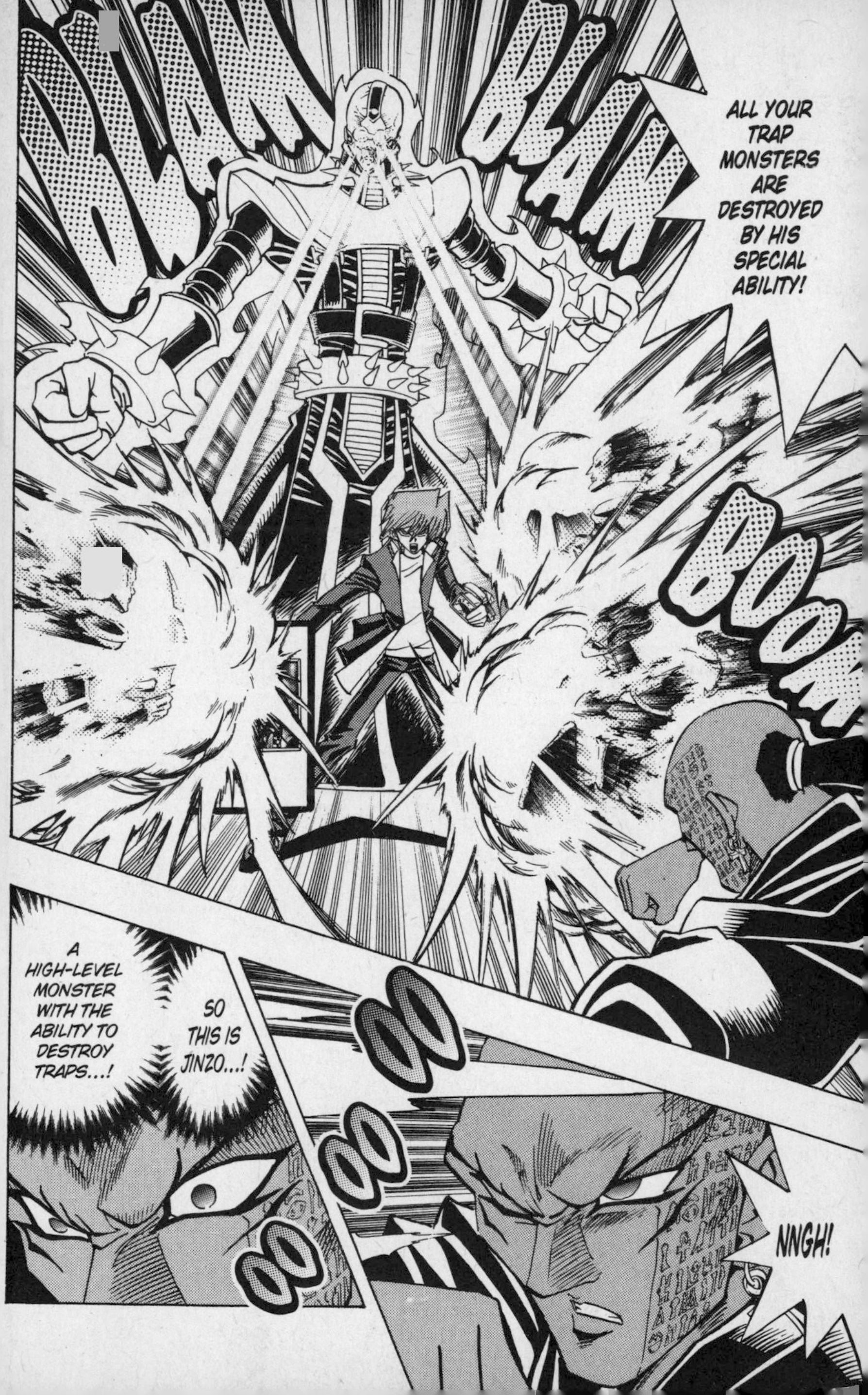
BLAM BLAM
ALL YOUR TRAP MONSTERS ARE DESTROYED BY HIS SPECIAL ABILITY!
BOOM
NNGH!
SO THIS IS JINZO...!
A HIGH-LEVEL MONSTER WITH THE ABILITY TO DESTROY TRAPS...!

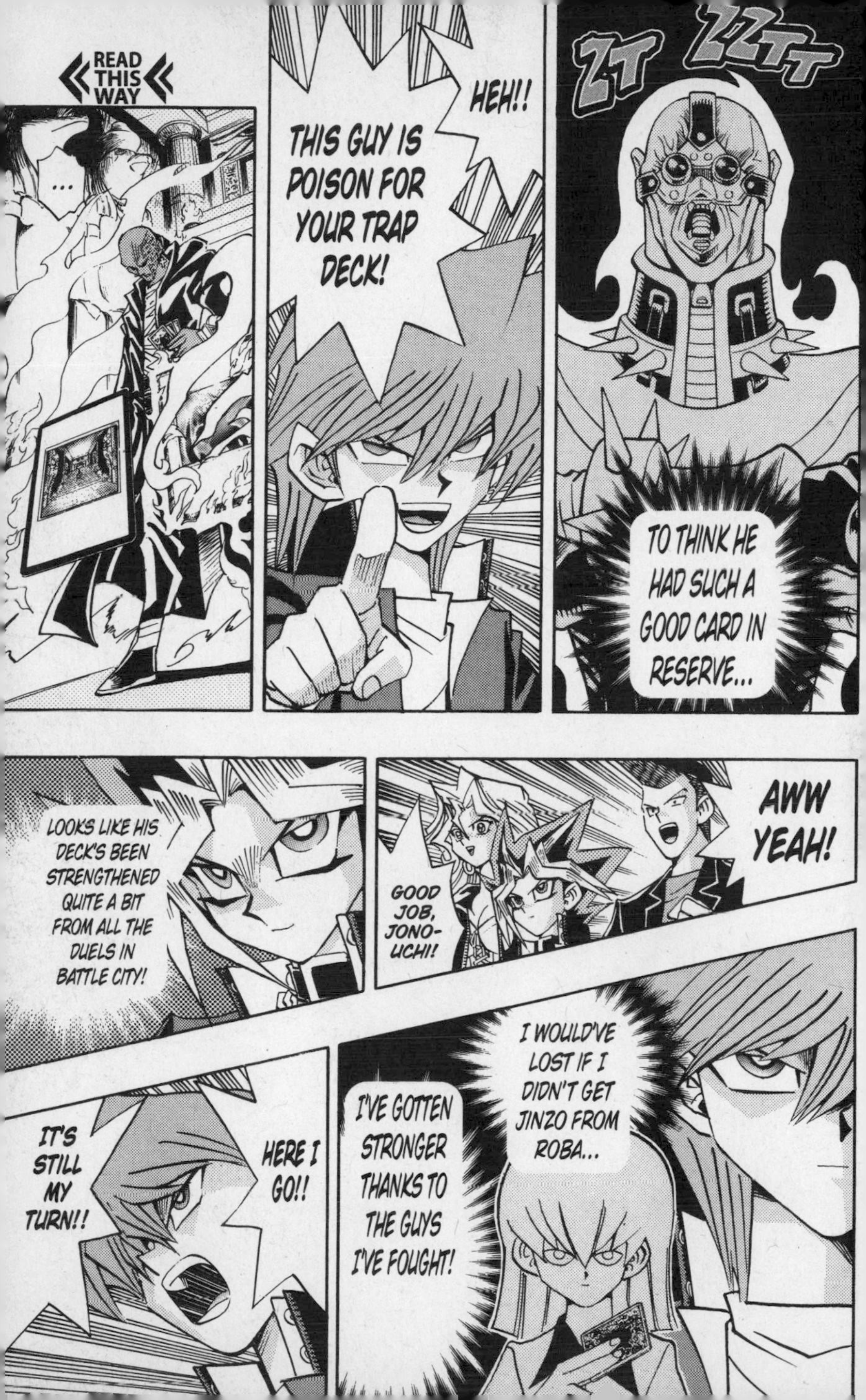
READ THIS WAY
ZT ZZTT
TO THINK HE HAD SUCH A GOOD CARD IN RESERVE...
HEH!!
THIS GUY IS POISON FOR YOUR TRAP DECK!
...
AWW YEAH!
GOOD JOB, JONO-UCHI!
LOOKS LIKE HIS DECK'S BEEN STRENGTHENED QUITE A BIT FROM ALL THE DUELS IN BATTLE CITY!
I WOULD'VE LOST IF I DIDN'T GET JINZO FROM ROBA...
I'VE GOTTEN STRONGER THANKS TO THE GUYS I'VE FOUGHT!
HERE I GO!!
IT'S STILL MY TURN!!

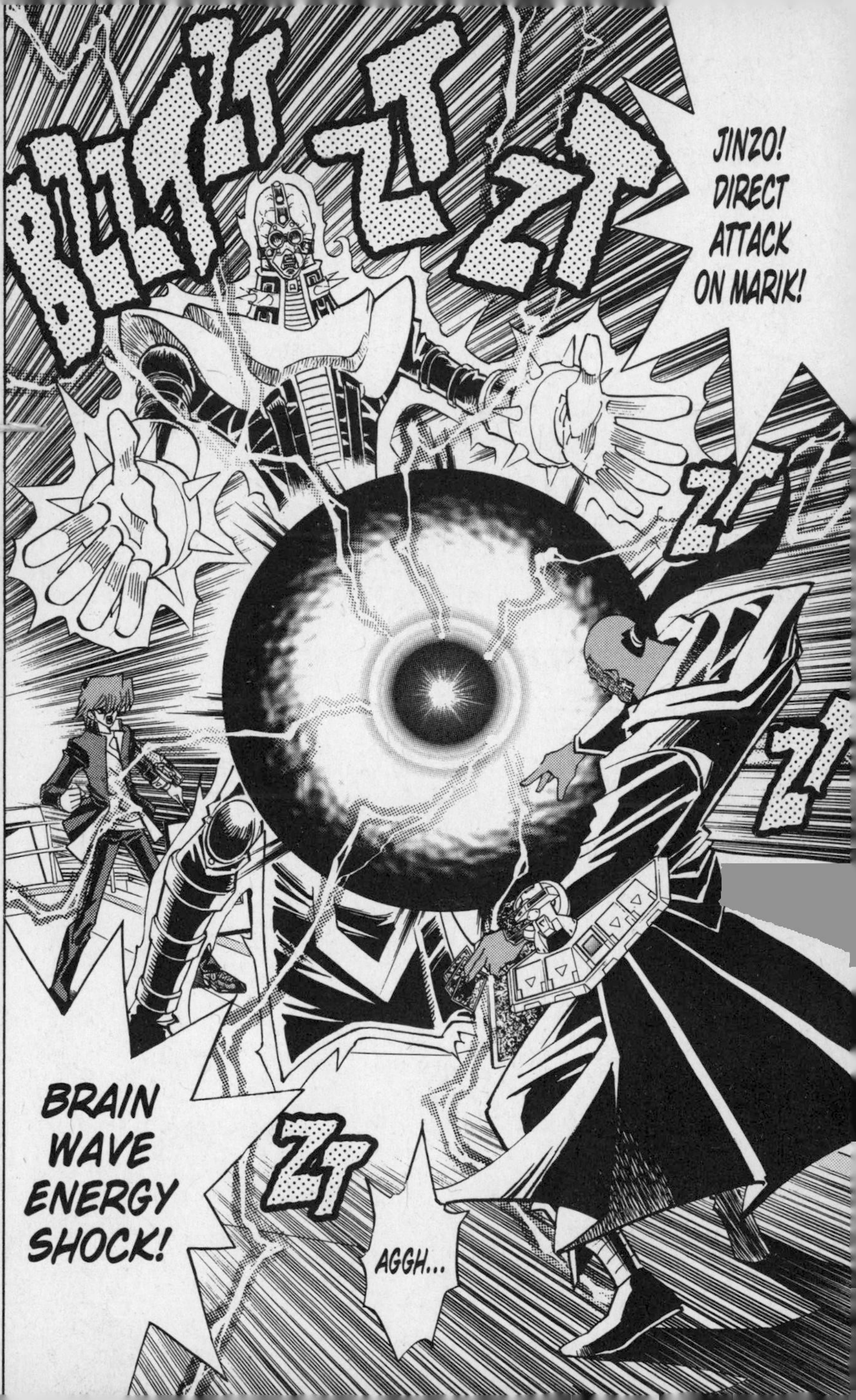
JINZO! DIRECT ATTACK ON MARIK!
BRAIN WAVE ENERGY SHOCK!
AGGH...

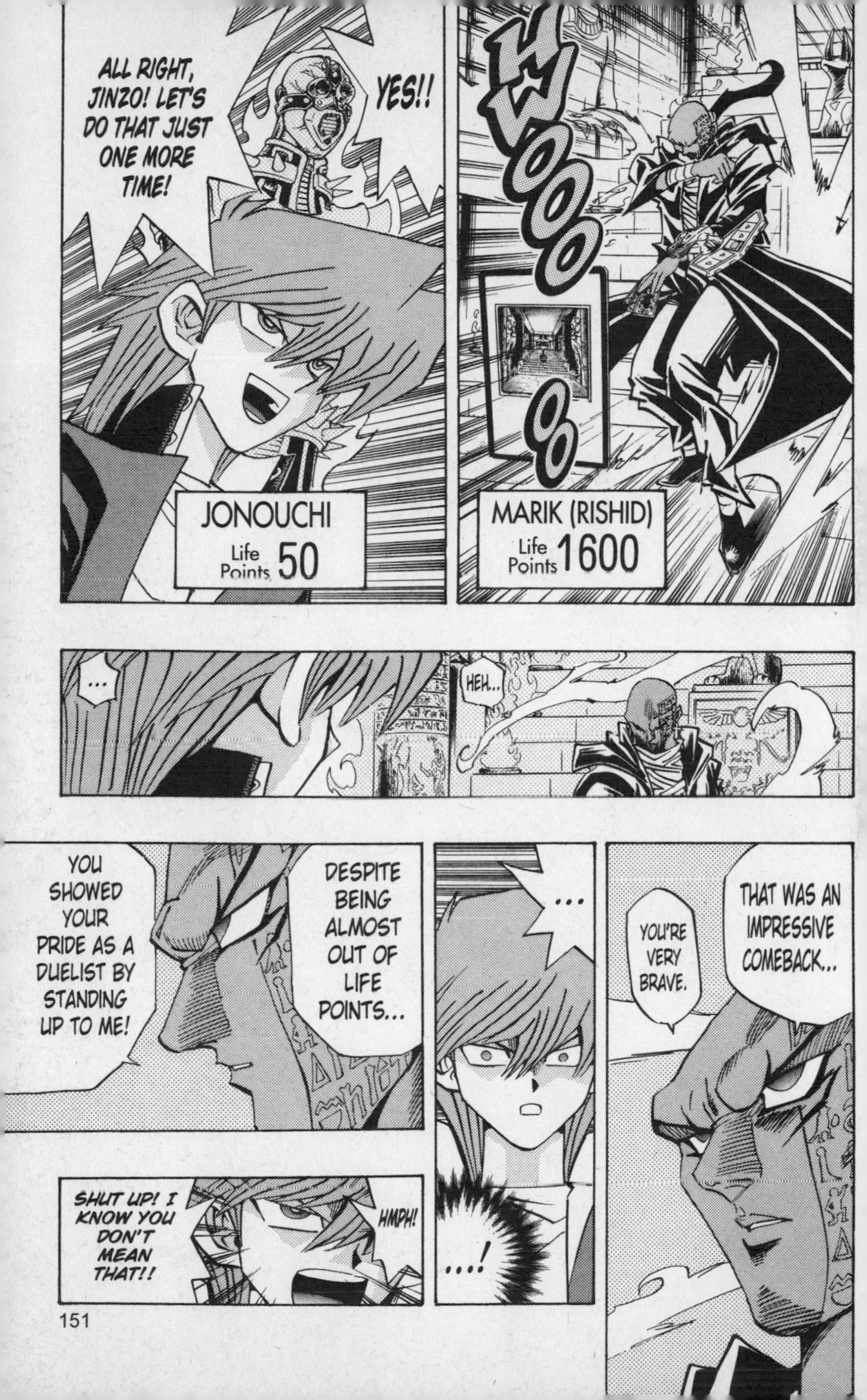
WHOOOOO
MARIK (RISHID)
Life Points 1600
ALL RIGHT, JINZO! LET'S DO THAT JUST ONE MORE TIME!
YES!!
JONOUCHI
Life Points 50
HEH...
...
THAT WAS AN IMPRESSIVE COMEBACK...
YOU'RE VERY BRAVE.
...
DESPITE BEING ALMOST OUT OF LIFE POINTS...
YOU SHOWED YOUR PRIDE AS A DUELIST BY STANDING UP TO ME!
...!
HMPH!
SHUT UP! I KNOW YOU DON'T MEAN THAT!!

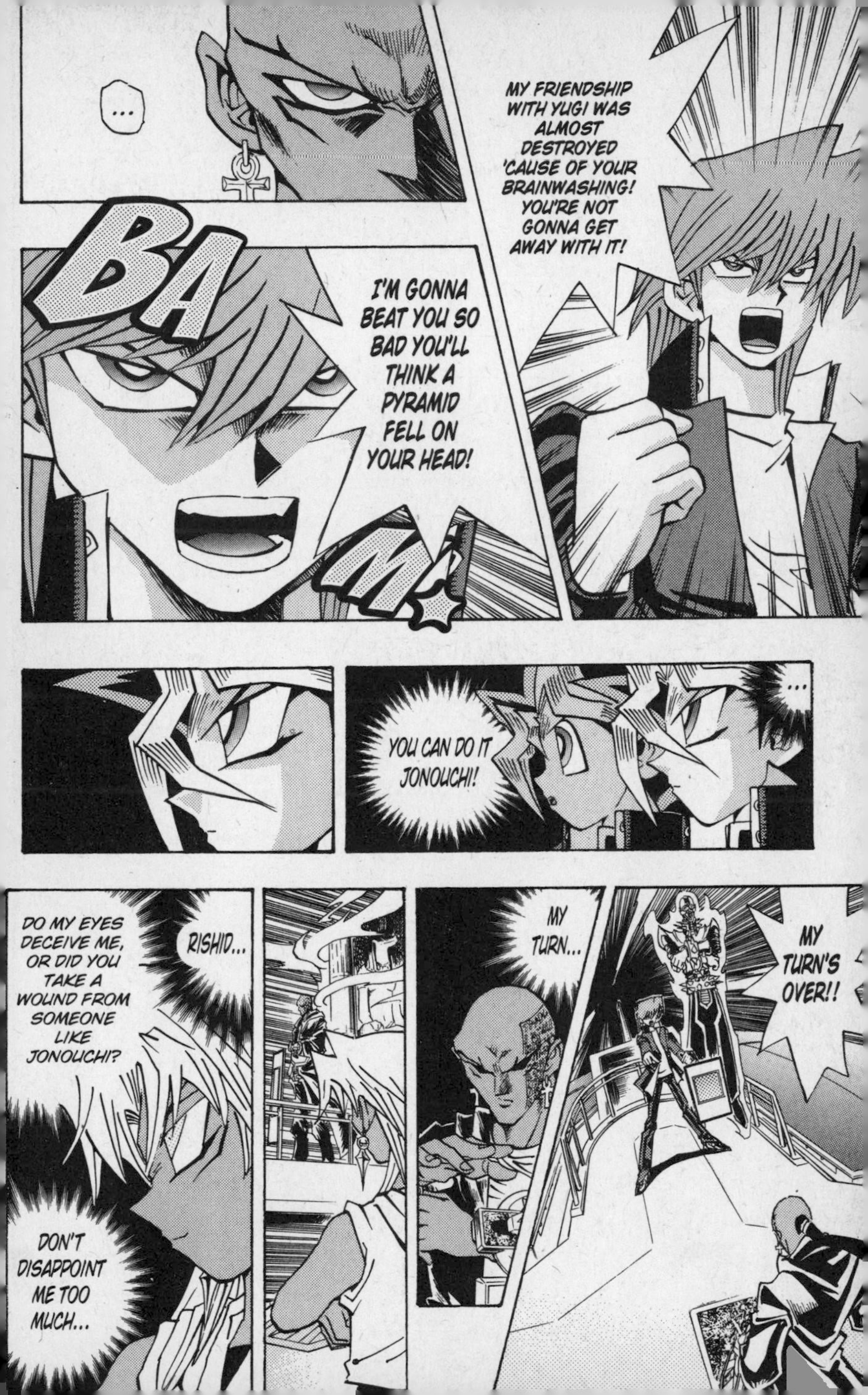
MY FRIENDSHIP WITH YUGI WAS ALMOST DESTROYED 'CAUSE OF YOUR BRAINWASHING! YOU'RE NOT GONNA GET AWAY WITH IT!
...
BA
I'M GONNA BEAT YOU SO BAD YOU'LL THINK A PYRAMID FELL ON YOUR HEAD!
M!
...
YOU CAN DO IT JONOUCHI!
MY TURN'S OVER!!
MY TURN...
RISHID...
DO MY EYES DECEIVE ME, OR DID YOU TAKE A WOUND FROM SOMEONE LIKE JONOUCHI?
DON'T DISAPPOINT ME TOO MUCH...

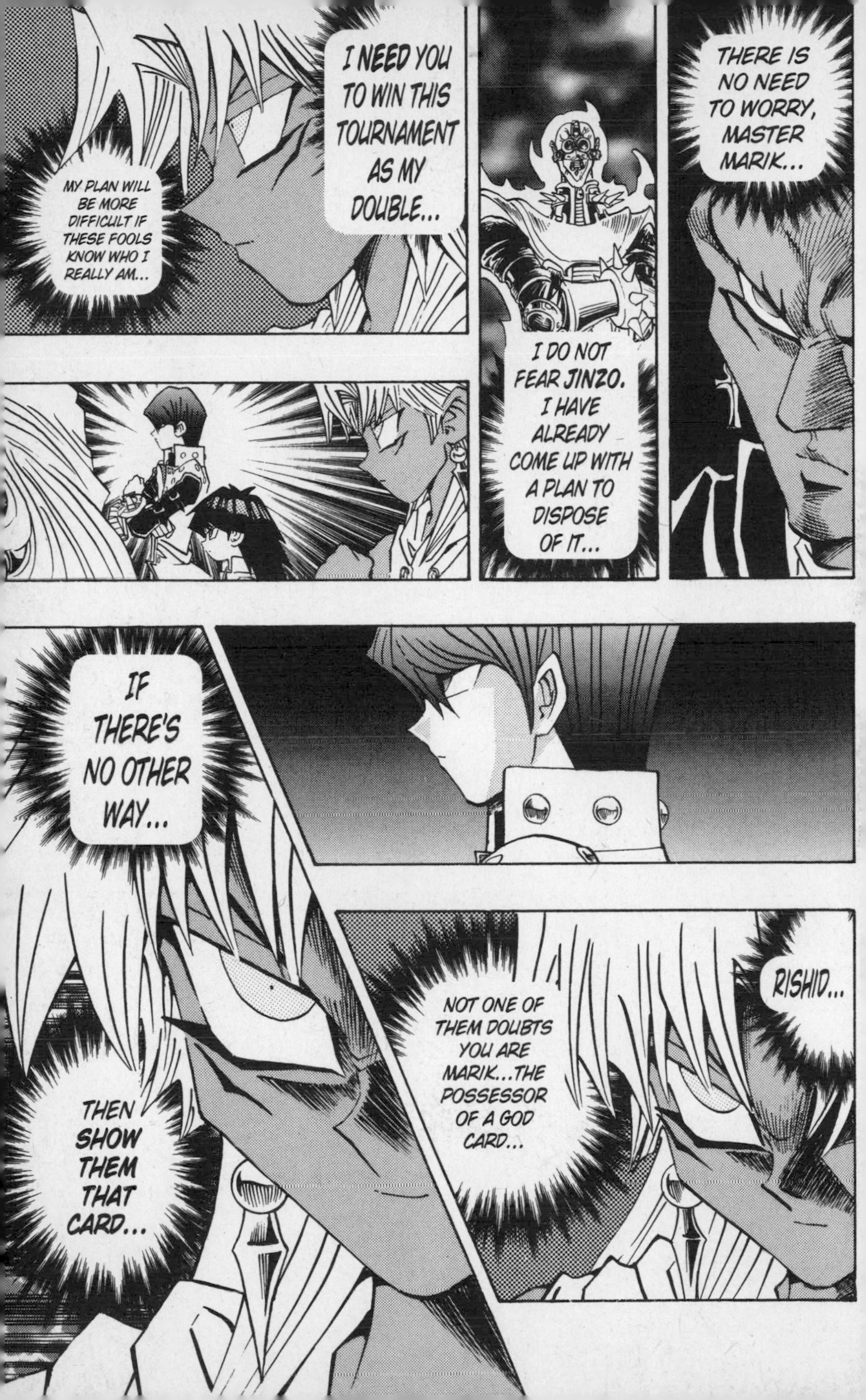
THERE IS NO NEED TO WORRY, MASTER MARIK...
I DO NOT FEAR JINZO. I HAVE ALREADY COME UP WITH A PLAN TO DISPOSE OF IT...
I NEED YOU TO WIN THIS TOURNAMENT AS MY DOUBLE...
MY PLAN WILL BE MORE DIFFICULT IF THESE FOOLS KNOW WHO I REALLY AM...
IF THERE'S NO OTHER WAY...
RISHID...
NOT ONE OF THEM DOUBTS YOU ARE MARIK...THE POSSESSOR OF A GOD CARD...
THEN SHOW THEM THAT CARD...

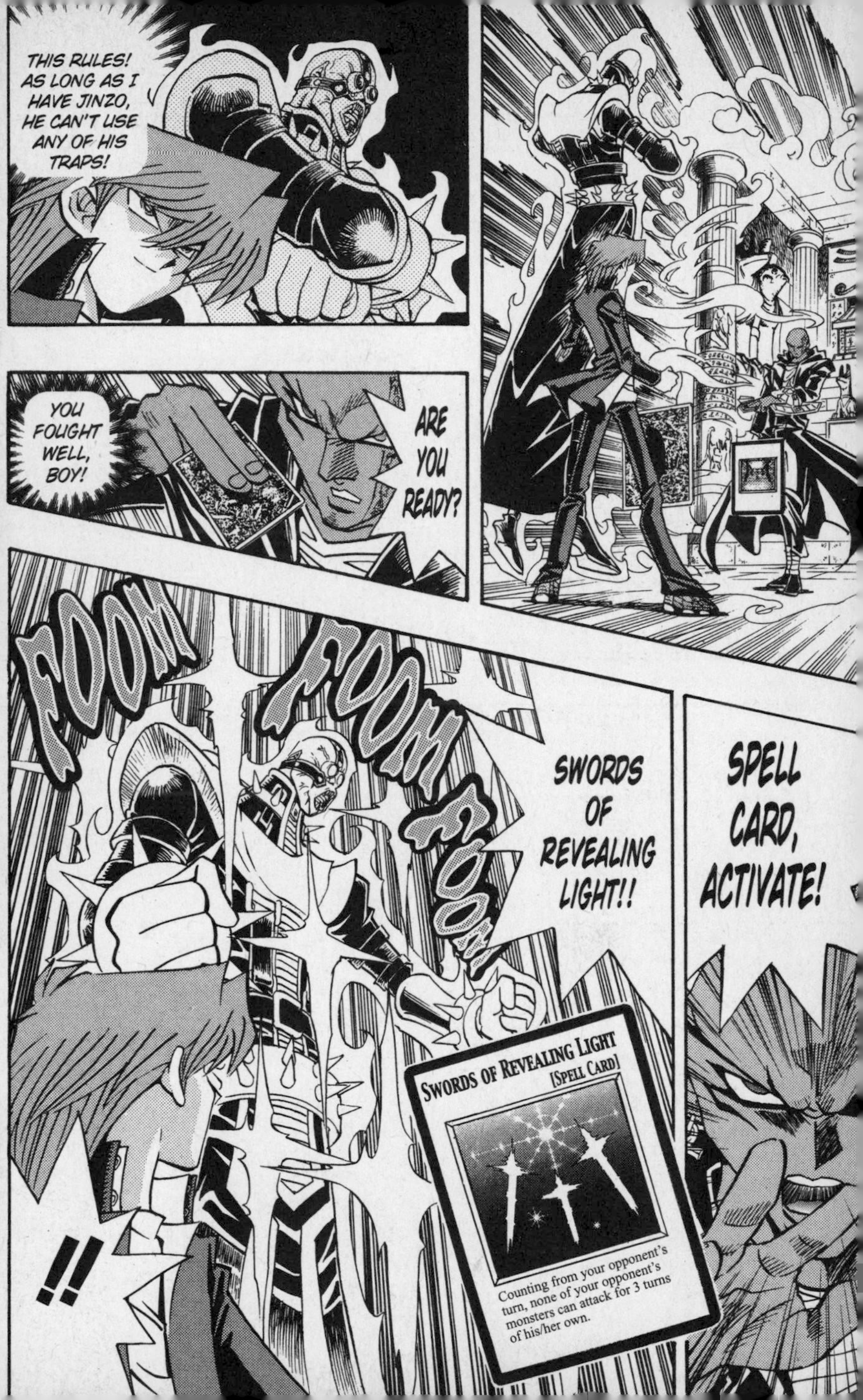
THIS RULES! AS LONG AS I HAVE JINZO, HE CAN'T USE ANY OF HIS TRAPS!
ARE YOU READY?
YOU FOUGHT WELL, BOY!
SPELL CARD, ACTIVATE!
SWORDS OF REVEALING LIGHT!!
FOOM
FOOM
FOOM
SWORDS OF REVEALING LIGHT
[SPELL CARD]
Counting from your opponent's turn, none of your opponent's monsters can attack for 3 turns of his/her own.
!!

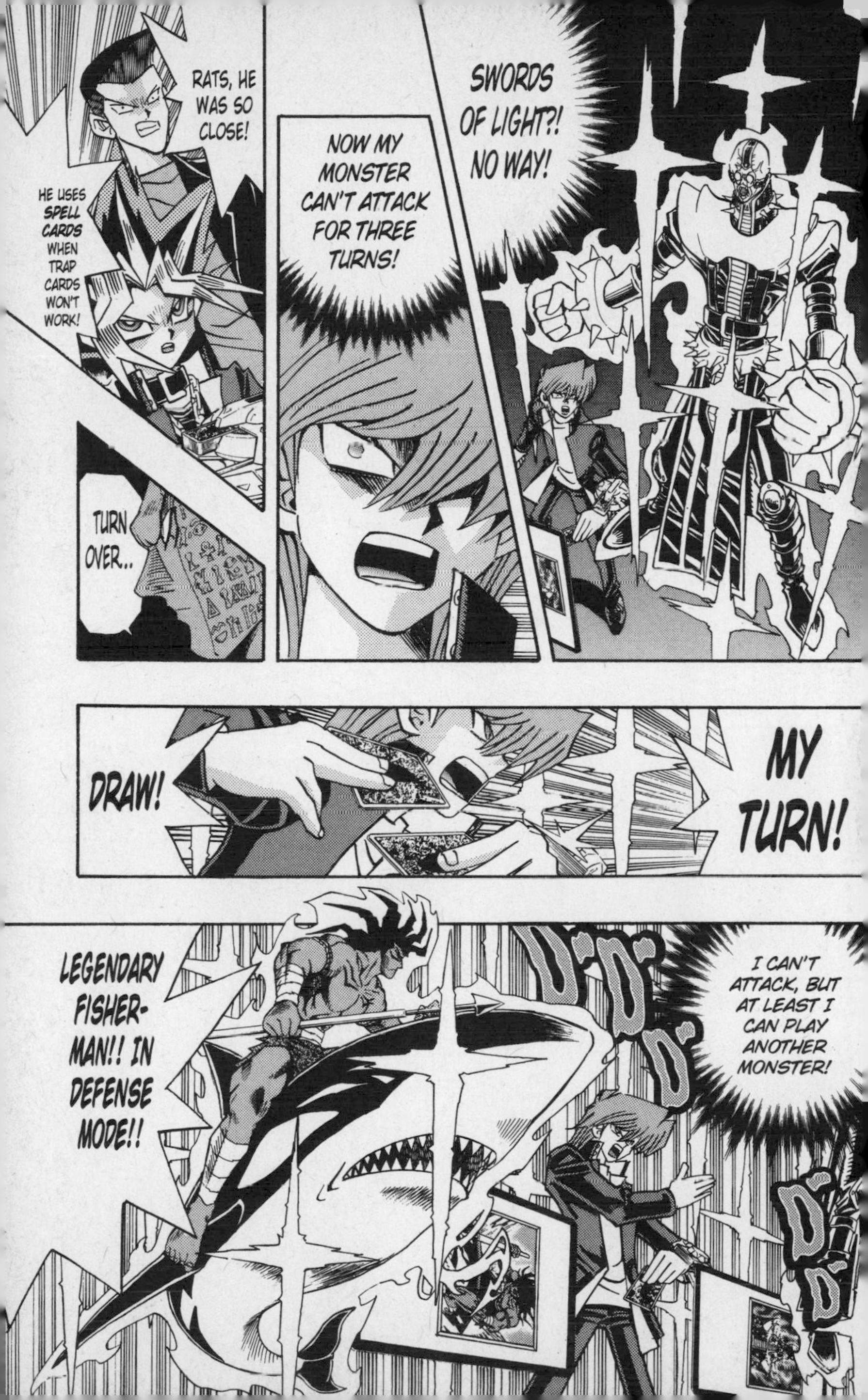
SWORDS OF LIGHT?! NO WAY!
NOW MY MONSTER CAN'T ATTACK FOR THREE TURNS!
RATS, HE WAS SO CLOSE!
HE USES SPELL CARDS WHEN TRAP CARDS WON'T WORK!
TURN OVER...
MY TURN!
DRAW!
I CAN'T ATTACK, BUT AT LEAST I CAN PLAY ANOTHER MONSTER!
LEGENDARY FISHER-MAN!! IN DEFENSE MODE!!

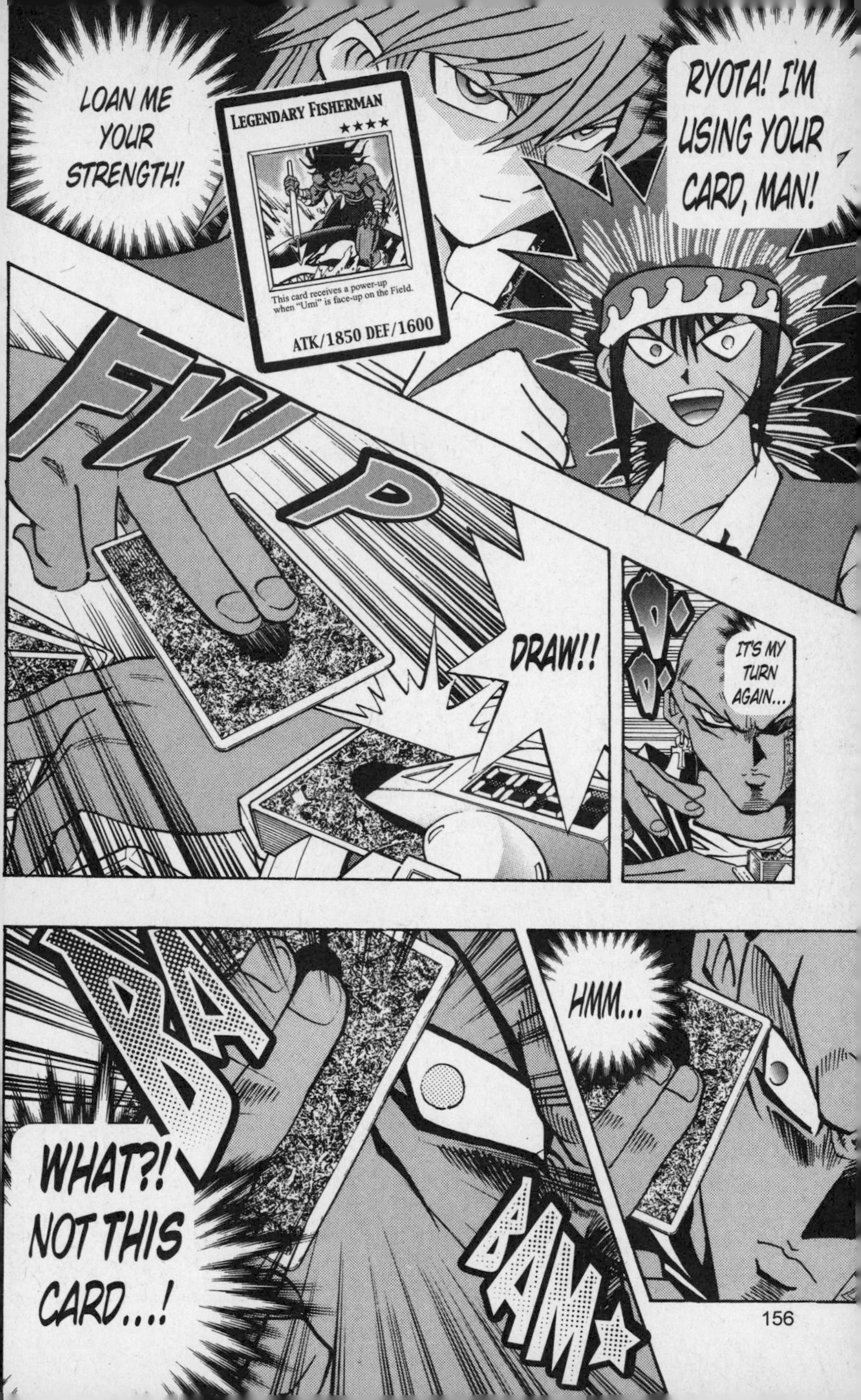
RYOTA! I'M USING YOUR CARD, MAN!
LOAN ME YOUR STRENGTH!
LEGENDARY FISHERMAN
This card receives a power-up when "Umi" is face-up on the Field.
ATK/1850 DEF/1600
IT'S MY TURN AGAIN...
DRAW!!
FWP
HMM...
BAM
BA
WHAT?! NOT THIS CARD...!

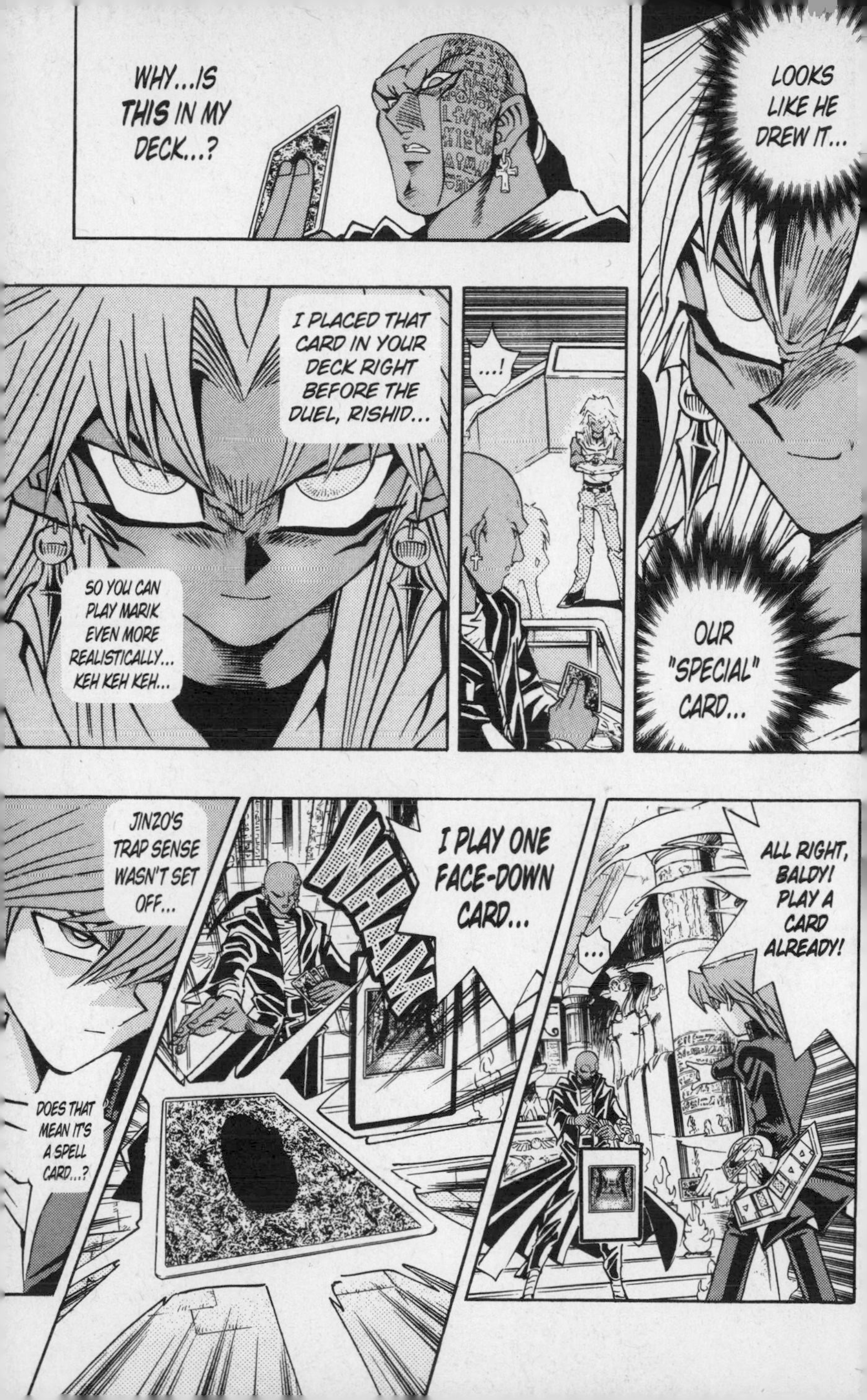
LOOKS LIKE HE DREW IT...
OUR "SPECIAL" CARD...
WHY...IS THIS IN MY DECK...?
...!
I PLACED THAT CARD IN YOUR DECK RIGHT BEFORE THE DUEL, RISHID...
SO YOU CAN PLAY MARIK EVEN MORE REALISTICALLY... KEH KEH KEH...
ALL RIGHT, BALDY! PLAY A CARD ALREADY!
...
WHAM
I PLAY ONE FACE-DOWN CARD...
JINZO'S TRAP SENSE WASN'T SET OFF...
DOES THAT MEAN IT'S A SPELL CARD...?

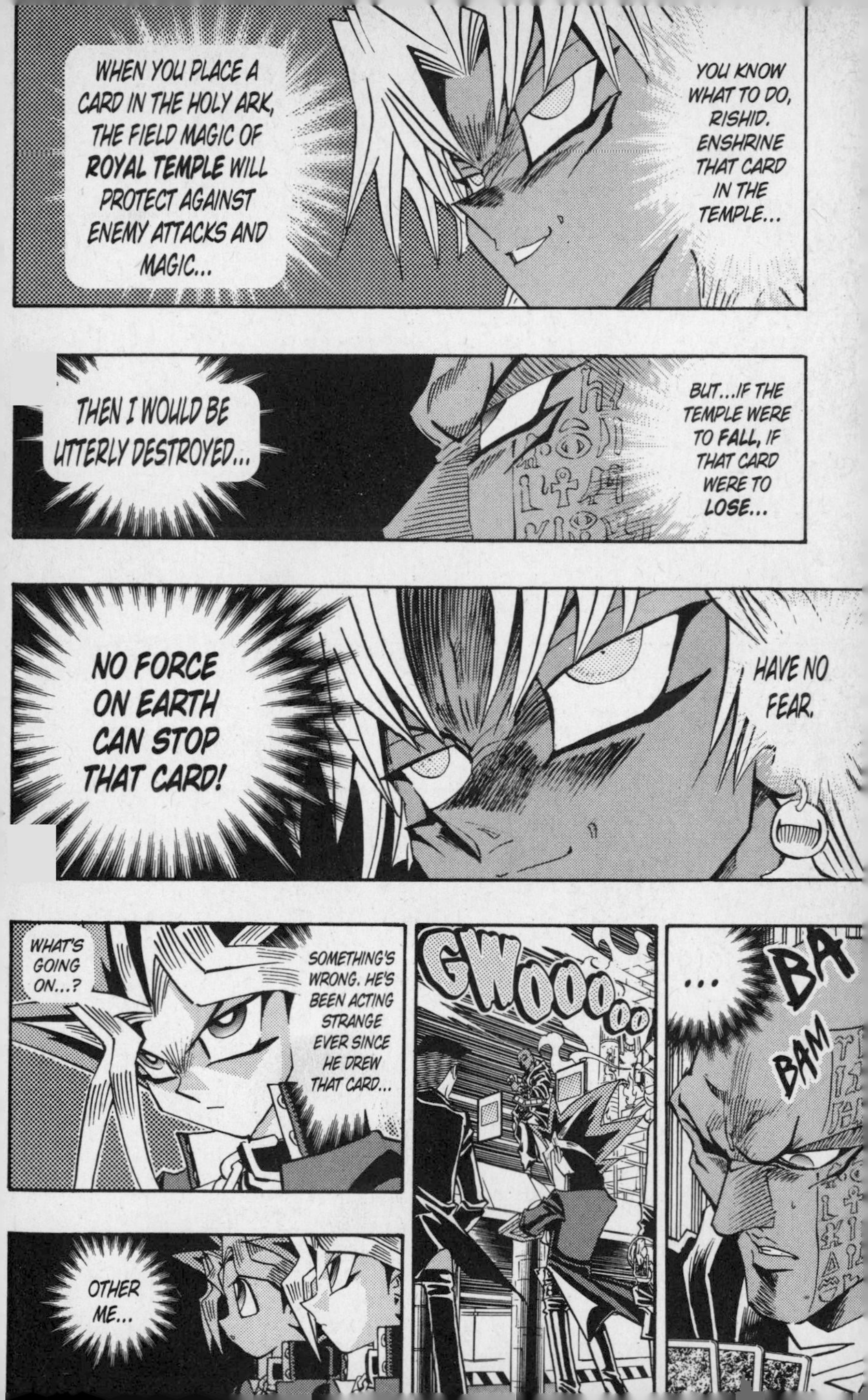
YOU KNOW WHAT TO DO, RISHID. ENSHRINE THAT CARD IN THE TEMPLE...
WHEN YOU PLACE A CARD IN THE HOLY ARK, THE FIELD MAGIC OF ROYAL TEMPLE WILL PROTECT AGAINST ENEMY ATTACKS AND MAGIC...
BUT...IF THE TEMPLE WERE TO FALL, IF THAT CARD WERE TO LOSE...
THEN I WOULD BE UTTERLY DESTROYED...
HAVE NO FEAR.
NO FORCE ON EARTH CAN STOP THAT CARD!
BA
BAM
...
GWOOOO...
SOMETHING'S WRONG. HE'S BEEN ACTING STRANGE EVER SINCE HE DREW THAT CARD...
WHAT'S GOING ON...?
OTHER ME...

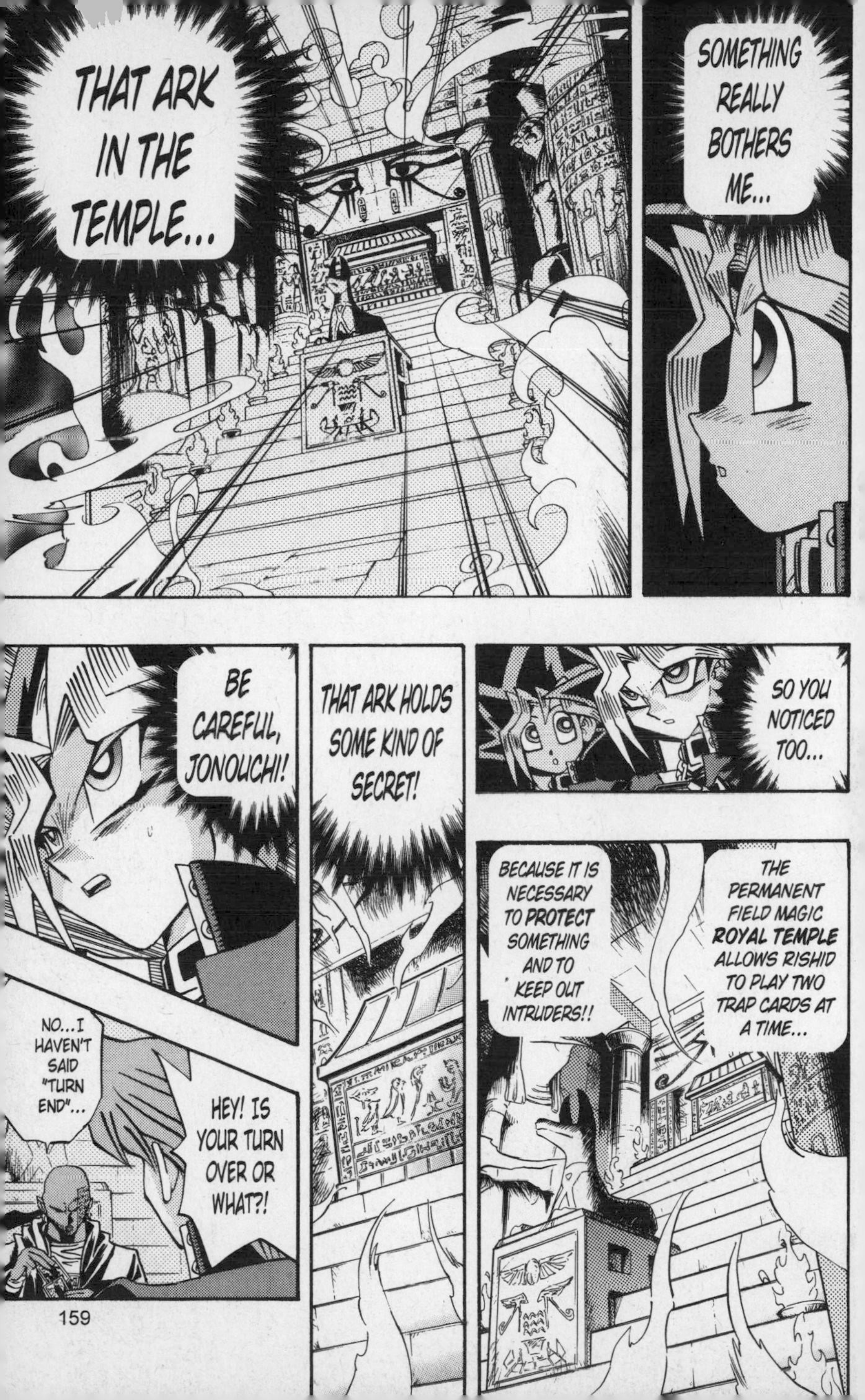
SOMETHING REALLY BOTHERS ME...
THAT ARK IN THE TEMPLE...
SO YOU NOTICED TOO...
THE PERMANENT FIELD MAGIC ROYAL TEMPLE ALLOWS RISHID TO PLAY TWO TRAP CARDS AT A TIME...
BECAUSE IT IS NECESSARY TO PROTECT SOMETHING AND TO KEEP OUT INTRUDERS!!
THAT ARK HOLDS SOME KIND OF SECRET!
BE CAREFUL, JONOUCHI!
HEY! IS YOUR TURN OVER OR WHAT?!
NO...I HAVEN'T SAID "TURN END"...

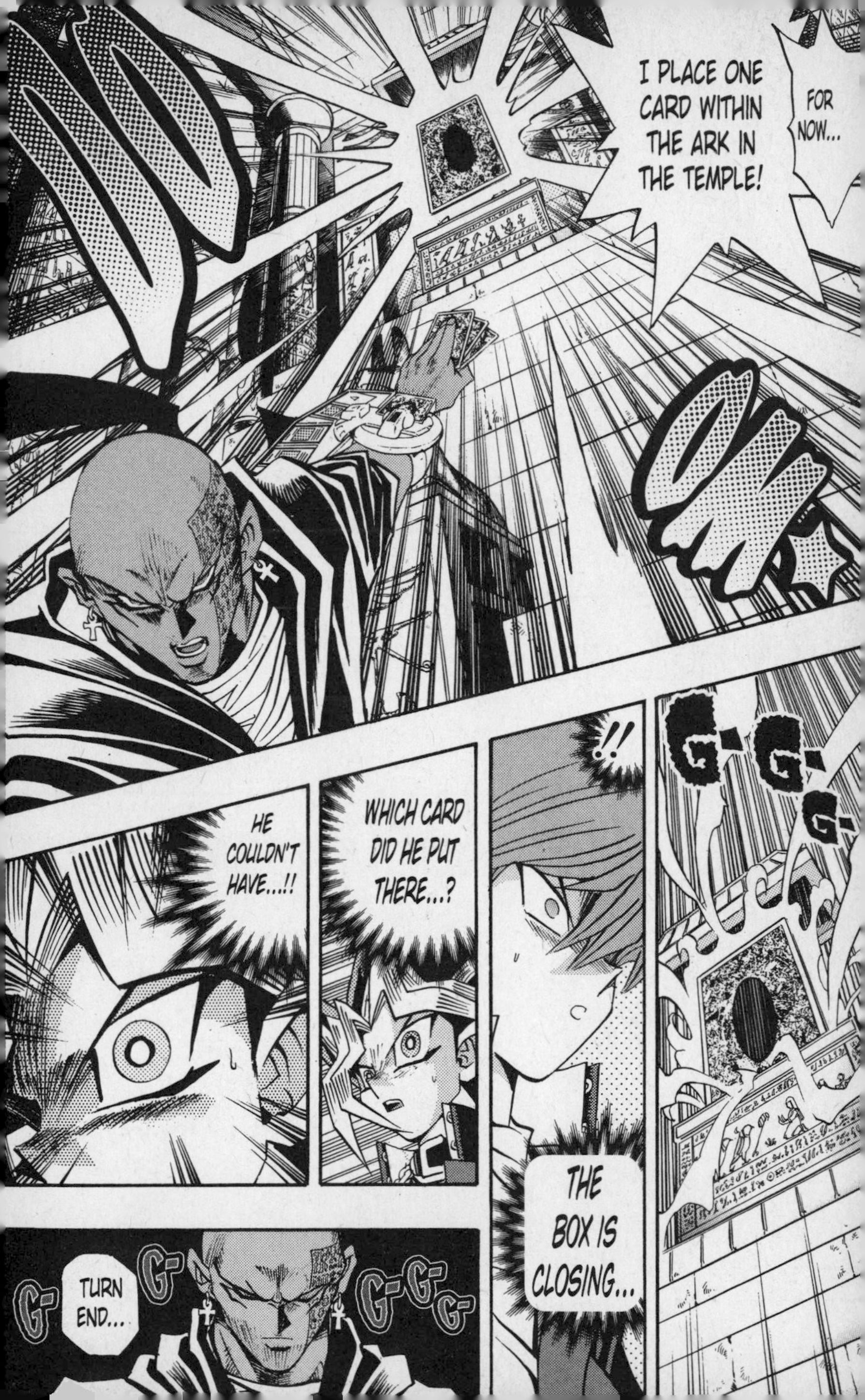
FOR NOW...
I PLACE ONE CARD WITHIN THE ARK IN THE TEMPLE!
G-G-G-G-
!!
THE BOX IS CLOSING...
WHICH CARD DID HE PUT THERE...?
HE COULDN'T HAVE...!!
G-G-G-
TURN END...
G-
G-

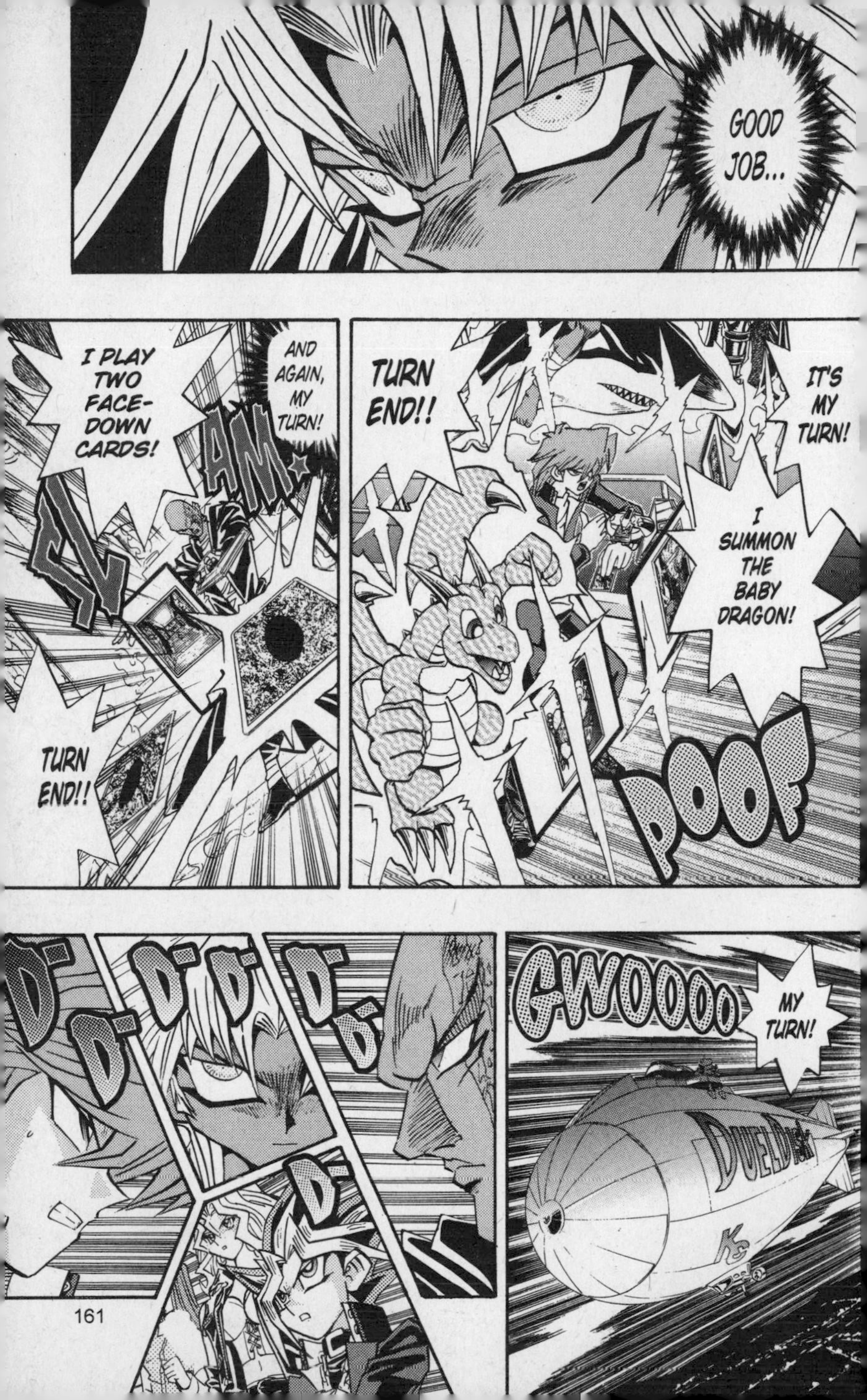
GOOD JOB...
IT'S MY TURN!
I SUMMON THE BABY DRAGON!
POOF
TURN END!!
AND AGAIN, MY TURN!
I PLAY TWO FACE-DOWN CARDS!
CLAM
TURN END!!
MY TURN!
GWOOOOO
DUELDISK
KC
D- D- D- D- D- D-

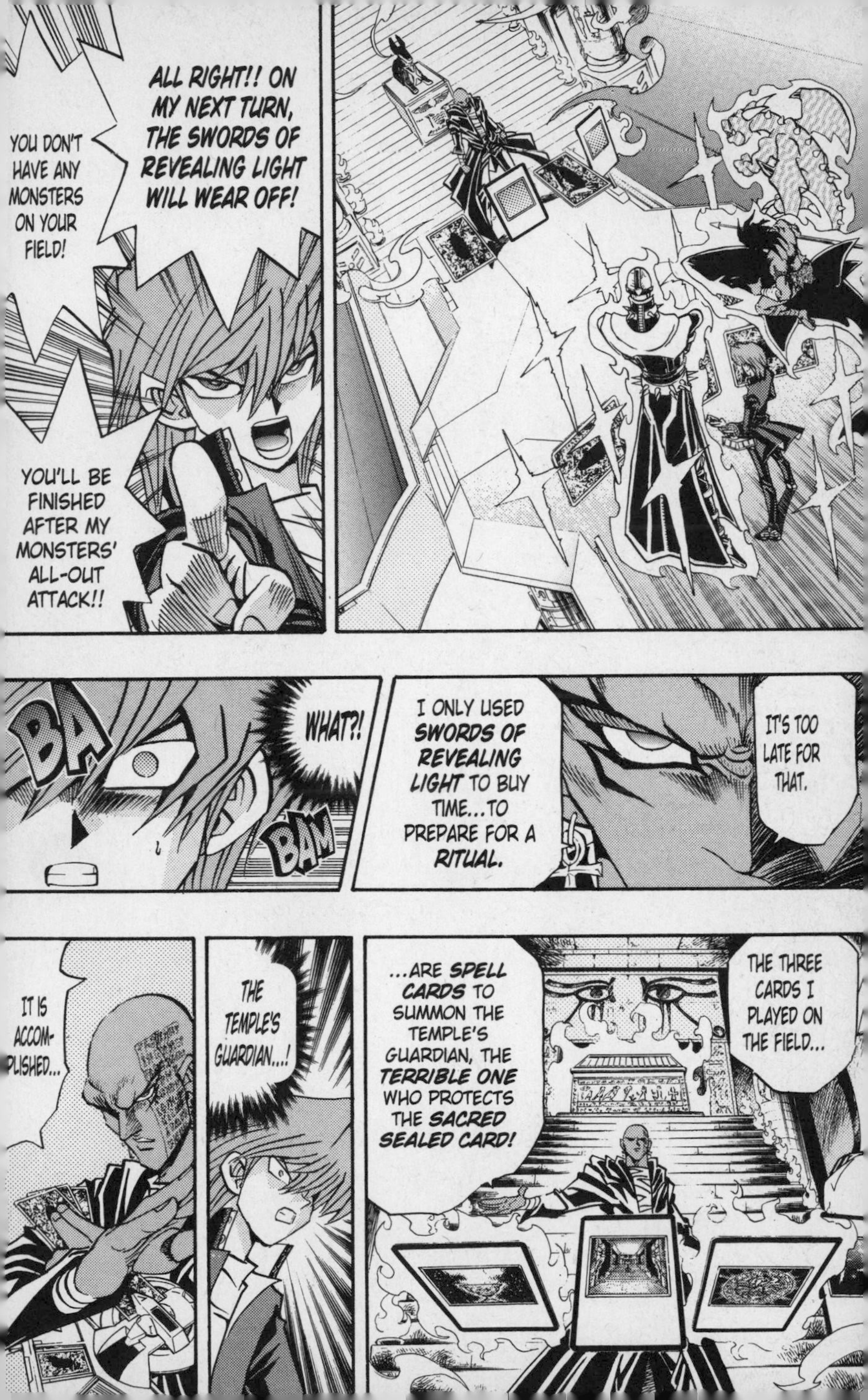
ALL RIGHT!! ON MY NEXT TURN, THE SWORDS OF REVEALING LIGHT WILL WEAR OFF!
YOU DON'T HAVE ANY MONSTERS ON YOUR FIELD!
YOU'LL BE FINISHED AFTER MY MONSTERS' ALL-OUT ATTACK!!
IT'S TOO LATE FOR THAT.
I ONLY USED SWORDS OF REVEALING LIGHT TO BUY TIME...TO PREPARE FOR A RITUAL.
WHAT?!
BA
BAM
THE THREE CARDS I PLAYED ON THE FIELD...
...ARE SPELL CARDS TO SUMMON THE TEMPLE'S GUARDIAN, THE TERRIBLE ONE WHO PROTECTS THE SACRED SEALED CARD!
THE TEMPLE'S GUARDIAN...!
IT IS ACCOM-PLISHED...

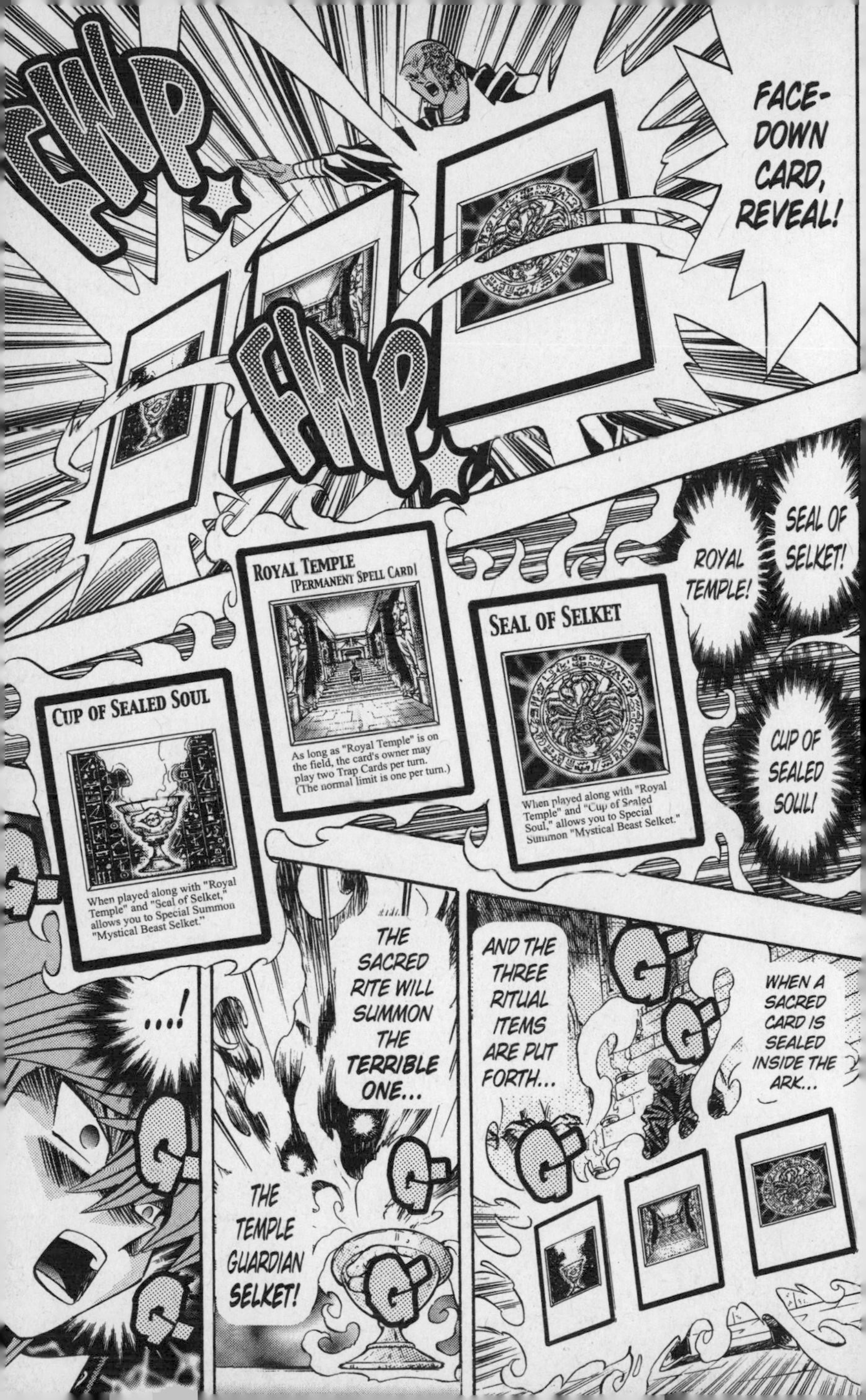
FACE-DOWN CARD, REVEAL!
FWP!
FWP!
SEAL OF SELKET!
ROYAL TEMPLE!
CUP OF SEALED SOUL!
SEAL OF SELKET
When played along with "Royal Temple" and "Cup of Sealed Soul," allows you to Special Summon "Mystical Beast Selket."
ROYAL TEMPLE
[PERMANENT SPELL CARD]
As long as "Royal Temple" is on the field, the card's owner may play two Trap Cards per turn. (The normal limit is one per turn.)
CUP OF SEALED SOUL
When played along with "Royal Temple" and "Seal of Selket," allows you to Special Summon "Mystical Beast Selket."
WHEN A SACRED CARD IS SEALED INSIDE THE ARK...
AND THE THREE RITUAL ITEMS ARE PUT FORTH...
THE SACRED RITE WILL SUMMON THE TERRIBLE ONE...
THE TEMPLE GUARDIAN SELKET!
...!

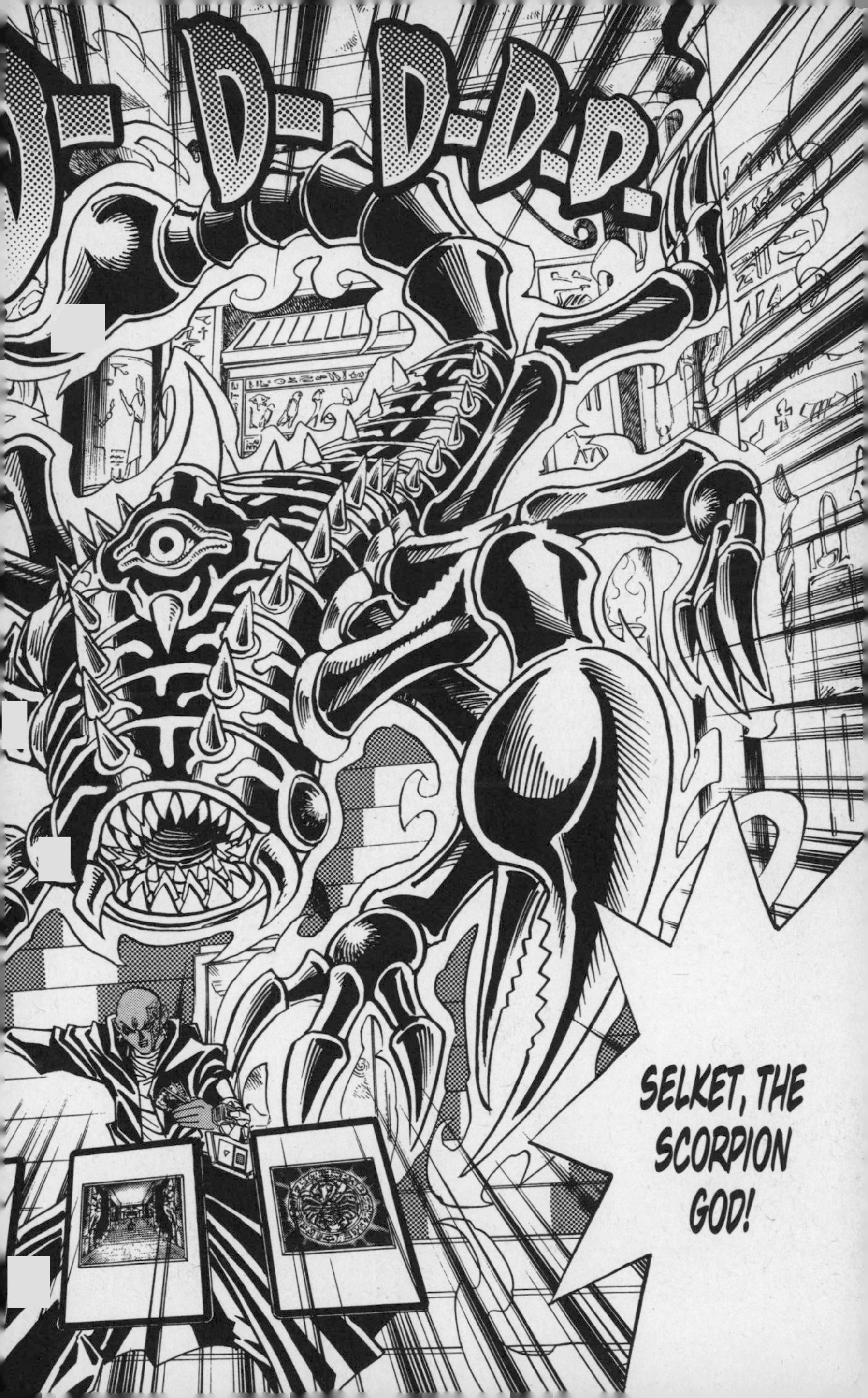
D-D-D-D-D-D!
SELKET, THE SCORPION GOD!

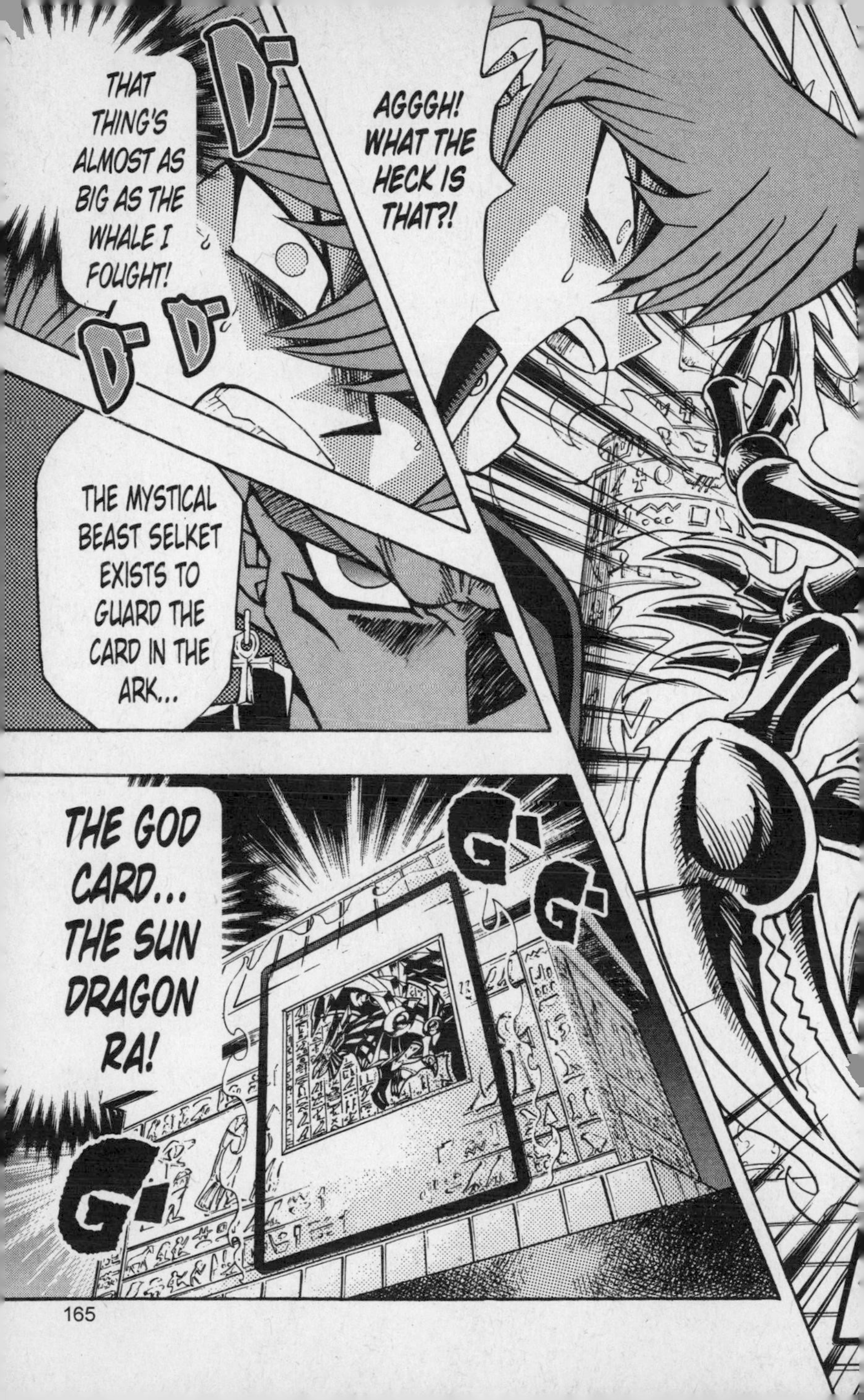
AGGGH! WHAT THE HECK IS THAT?!
D-
THAT THING'S ALMOST AS BIG AS THE WHALE I FOUGHT!
D-
D-
THE MYSTICAL BEAST SELKET EXISTS TO GUARD THE CARD IN THE ARK...
THE GOD CARD... THE SUN DRAGON RA!

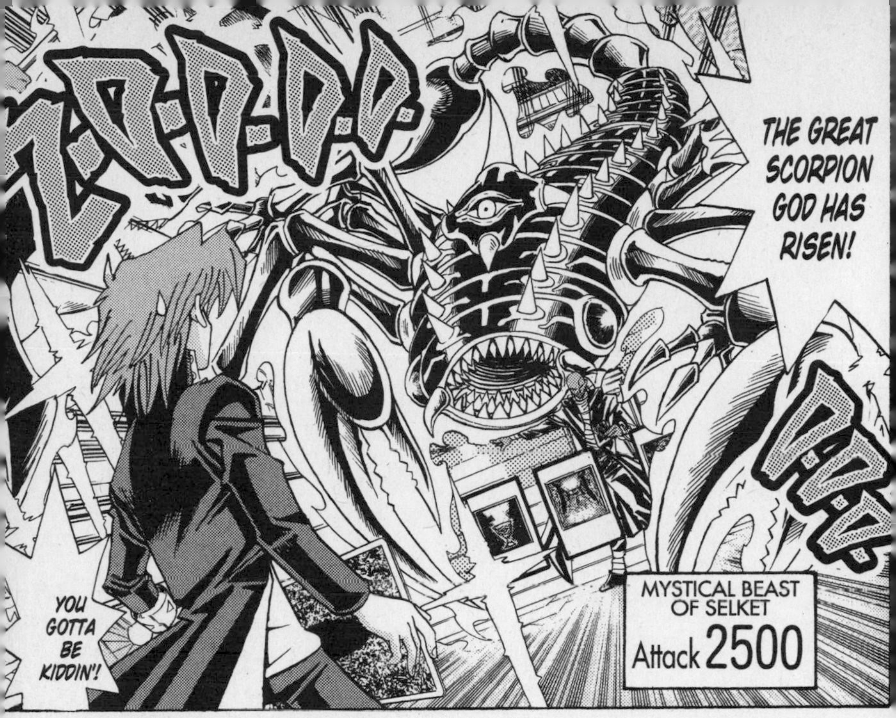
THE GREAT SCORPION GOD HAS RISEN!
MYSTICAL BEAST OF SELKET
Attack 2500
YOU GOTTA BE KIDDIN'!

Duel 155: The Cursed Bloodline!

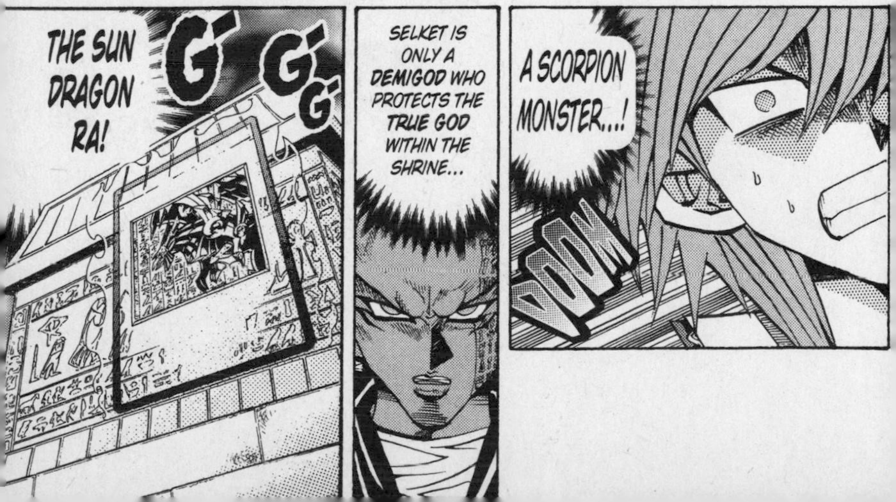
A SCORPION MONSTER...!
SELKET IS ONLY A DEMIGOD WHO PROTECTS THE TRUE GOD WITHIN THE SHRINE...
THE SUN DRAGON RA!
G G G

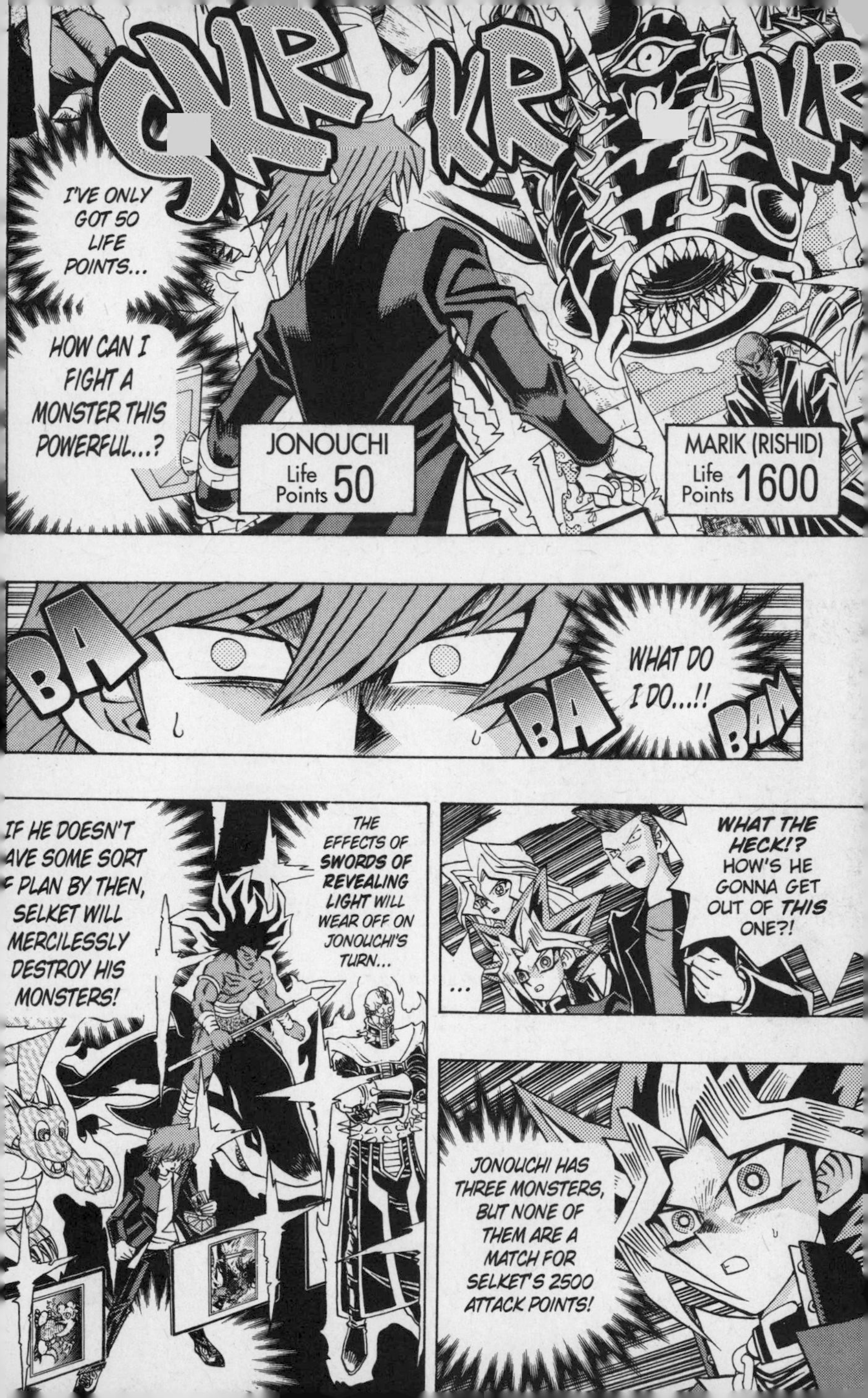
CHR KR KR
I'VE ONLY GOT 50 LIFE POINTS...
HOW CAN I FIGHT A MONSTER THIS POWERFUL...?
MARIK (RISHID) Life Points 1600
JONOUCHI Life Points 50
BAM
WHAT DO I DO...!!
BA
BA
WHAT THE HECK!? HOW'S HE GONNA GET OUT OF THIS ONE?!
...
JONOUCHI HAS THREE MONSTERS, BUT NONE OF THEM ARE A MATCH FOR SELKET'S 2500 ATTACK POINTS!
THE EFFECTS OF SWORDS OF REVEALING LIGHT WILL WEAR OFF ON JONOUCHI'S TURN...
IF HE DOESN'T AVE SOME SORT F PLAN BY THEN, SELKET WILL MERCILESSLY DESTROY HIS MONSTERS!

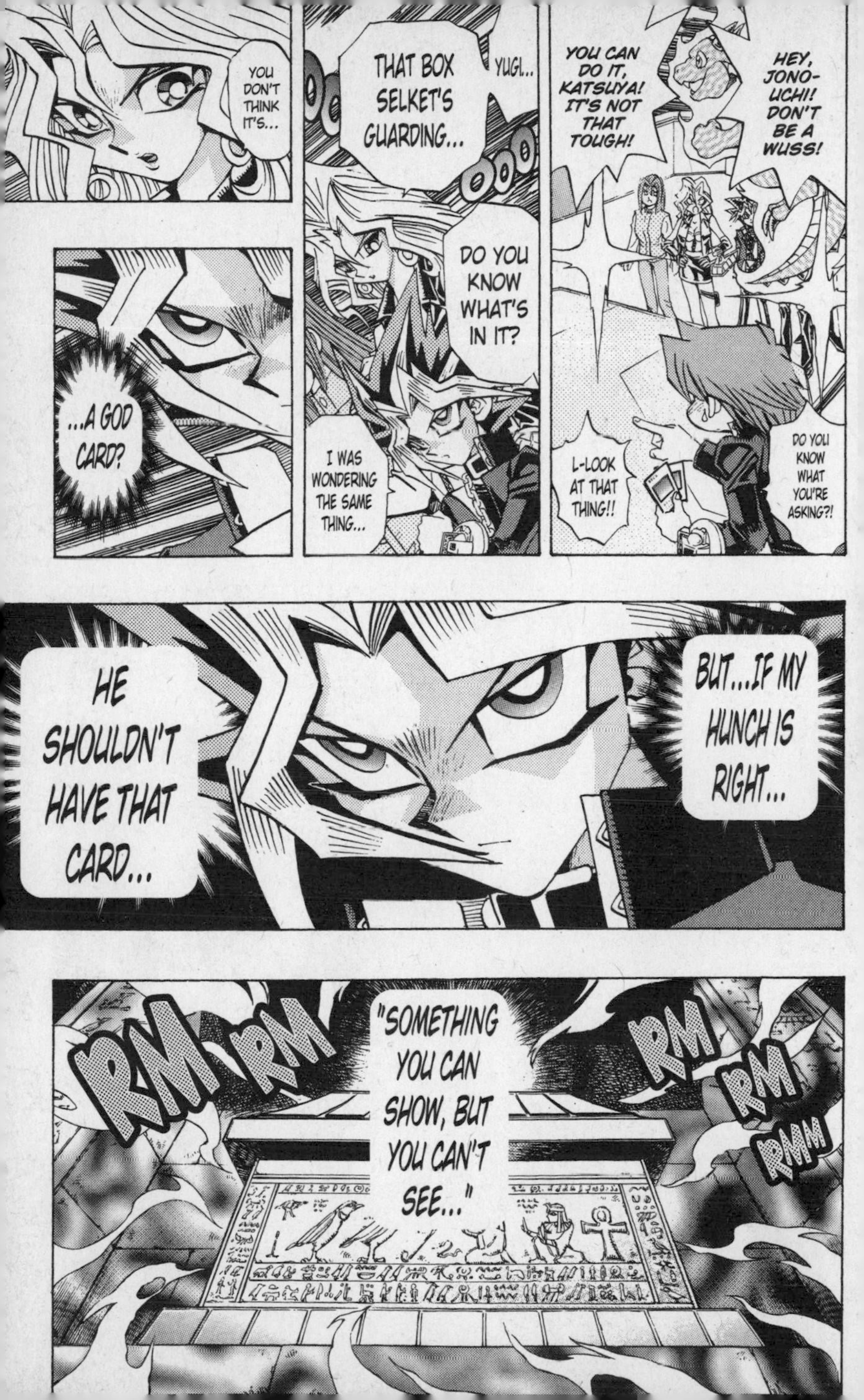
HEY, JONO-UCHI! DON'T BE A WUSS!
YOU CAN DO IT, KATSUYA! IT'S NOT THAT TOUGH!
DO YOU KNOW WHAT YOU'RE ASKING?!
L-LOOK AT THAT THING!!
YUGI...
THAT BOX SELKET'S GUARDING...
DO YOU KNOW WHAT'S IN IT?
I WAS WONDERING THE SAME THING...
YOU DON'T THINK IT'S...
...A GOD CARD?
BUT...IF MY HUNCH IS RIGHT...
HE SHOULDN'T HAVE THAT CARD...
RM RM RM RMM
"SOMETHING YOU CAN SHOW, BUT YOU CAN'T SEE..."
RM RM

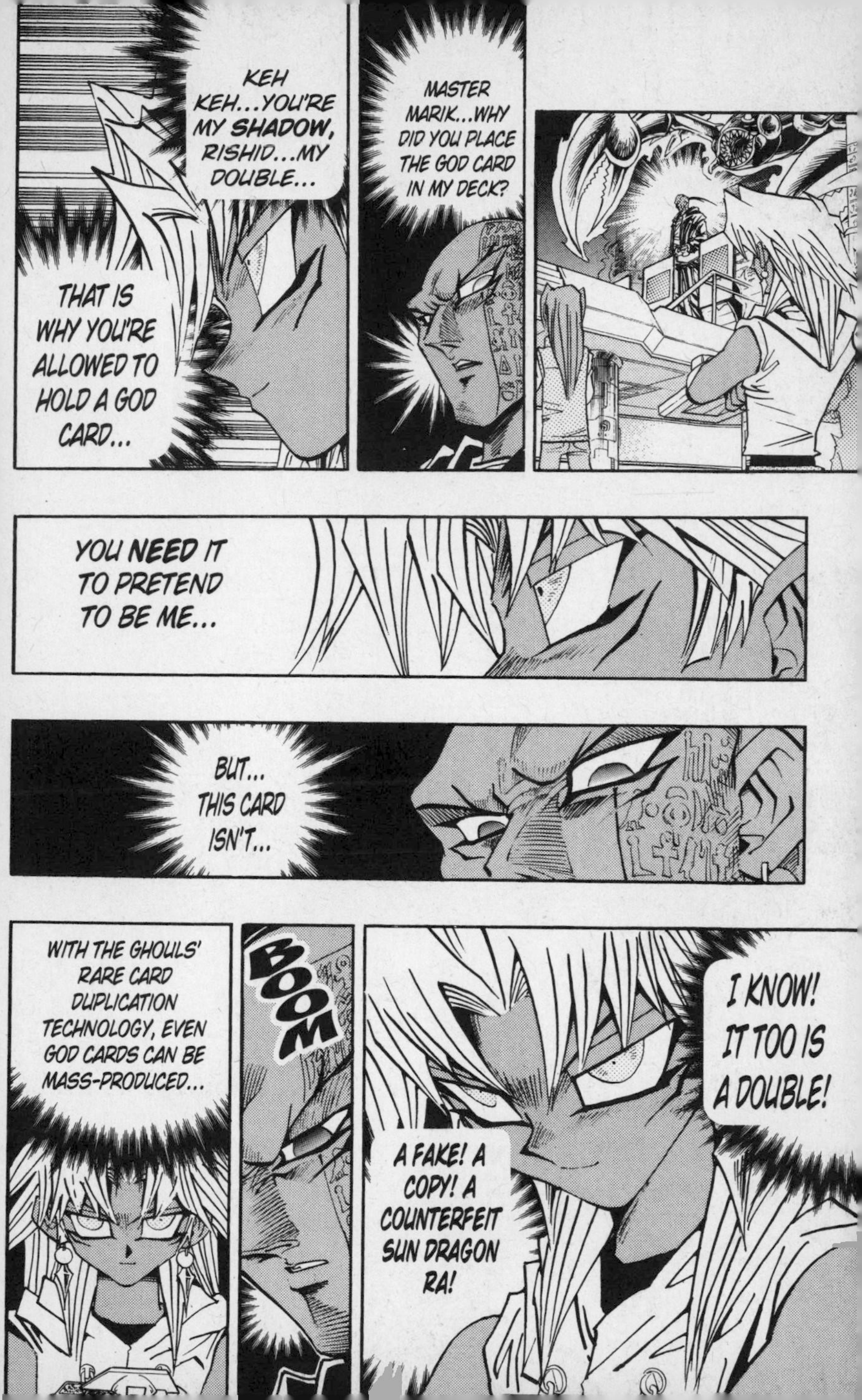
MASTER MARIK...WHY DID YOU PLACE THE GOD CARD IN MY DECK?
KEH KEH...YOU'RE MY **SHADOW,** RISHID...MY DOUBLE...
THAT IS WHY YOU'RE ALLOWED TO HOLD A GOD CARD...
YOU **NEED** IT TO PRETEND TO BE ME...
BUT... THIS CARD ISN'T...
I KNOW! IT TOO IS A DOUBLE!
A FAKE! A COPY! A COUNTERFEIT SUN DRAGON RA!
BOOM
WITH THE GHOULS' RARE CARD DUPLICATION TECHNOLOGY, EVEN GOD CARDS CAN BE MASS-PRODUCED...

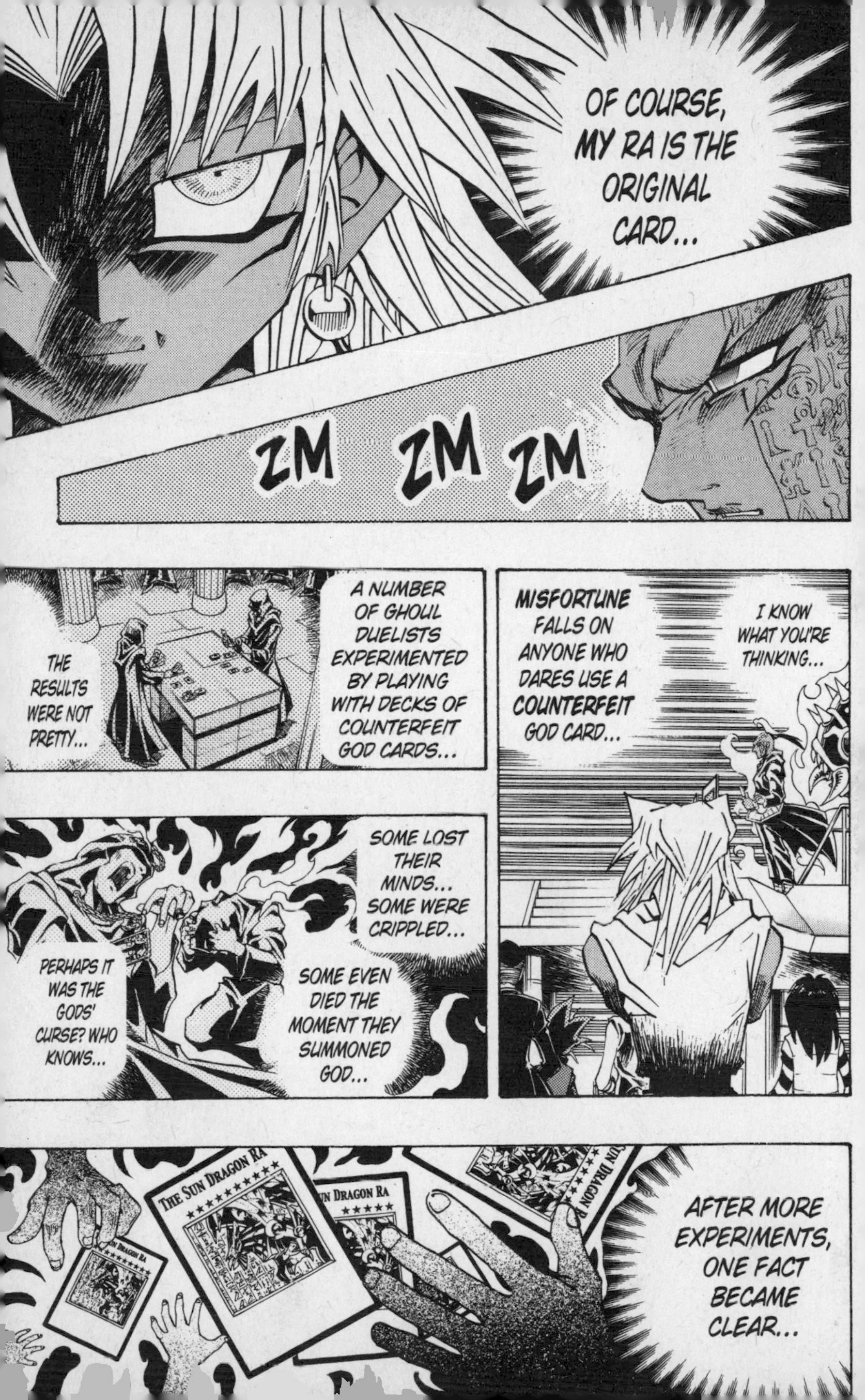
OF COURSE, MY RA IS THE ORIGINAL CARD...
ZM ZM ZM
I KNOW WHAT YOU'RE THINKING...
MISFORTUNE FALLS ON ANYONE WHO DARES USE A COUNTERFEIT GOD CARD...
A NUMBER OF GHOUL DUELISTS EXPERIMENTED BY PLAYING WITH DECKS OF COUNTERFEIT GOD CARDS...
THE RESULTS WERE NOT PRETTY...
SOME LOST THEIR MINDS... SOME WERE CRIPPLED...
SOME EVEN DIED THE MOMENT THEY SUMMONED GOD...
PERHAPS IT WAS THE GODS' CURSE? WHO KNOWS...
AFTER MORE EXPERIMENTS, ONE FACT BECAME CLEAR...
THE SUN DRAGON RA

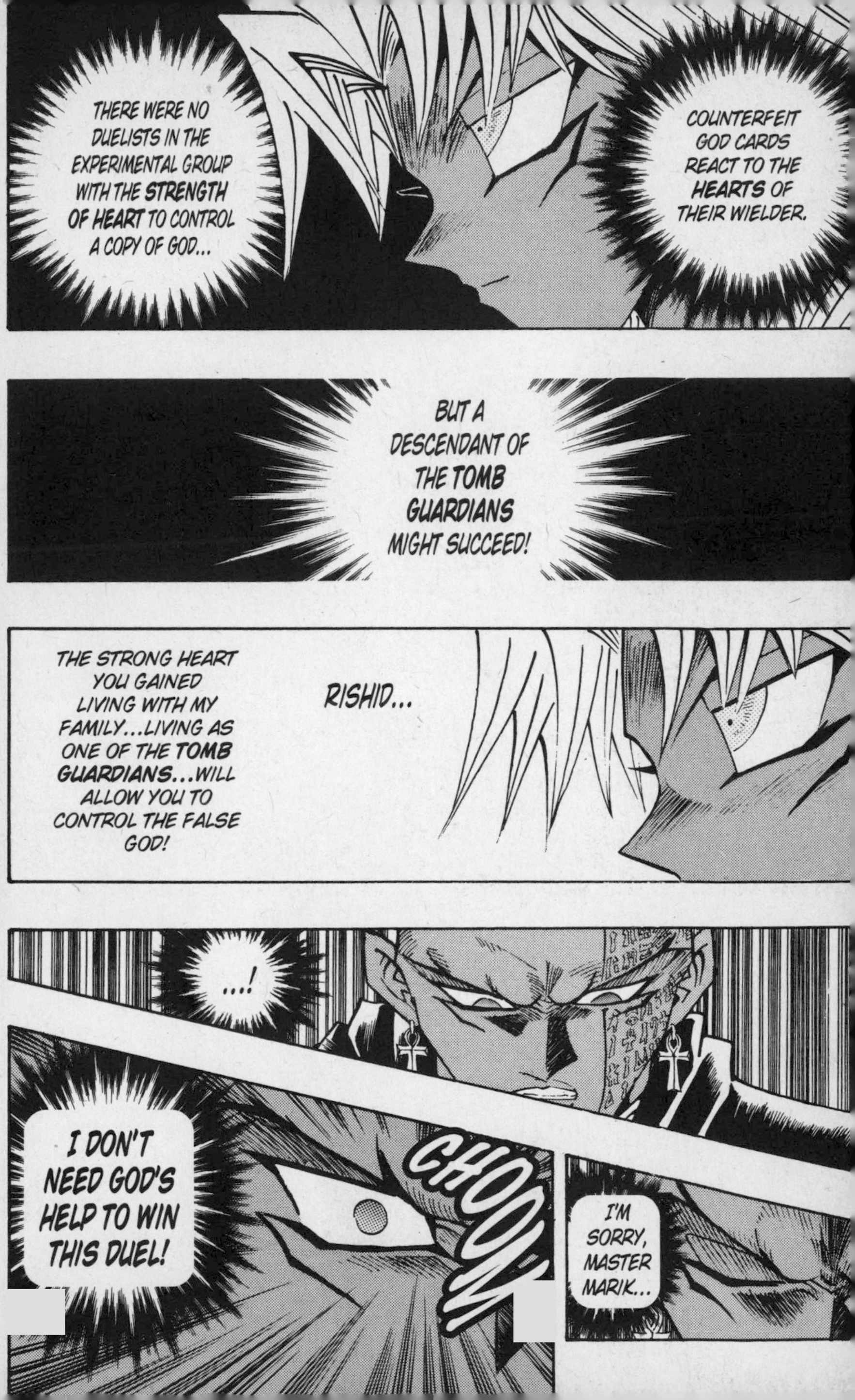
COUNTERFEIT GOD CARDS REACT TO THE **HEARTS** OF THEIR WIELDER.
THERE WERE NO DUELISTS IN THE EXPERIMENTAL GROUP WITH THE **STRENGTH OF HEART** TO CONTROL A COPY OF GOD...
BUT A DESCENDANT OF THE **TOMB GUARDIANS** MIGHT SUCCEED!
RISHID...
THE STRONG HEART YOU GAINED LIVING WITH MY FAMILY...LIVING AS ONE OF THE **TOMB GUARDIANS**...WILL ALLOW YOU TO CONTROL THE FALSE GOD!
...!
I'M SORRY, MASTER MARIK...
CHOOM
I DON'T NEED GOD'S HELP TO WIN THIS DUEL!

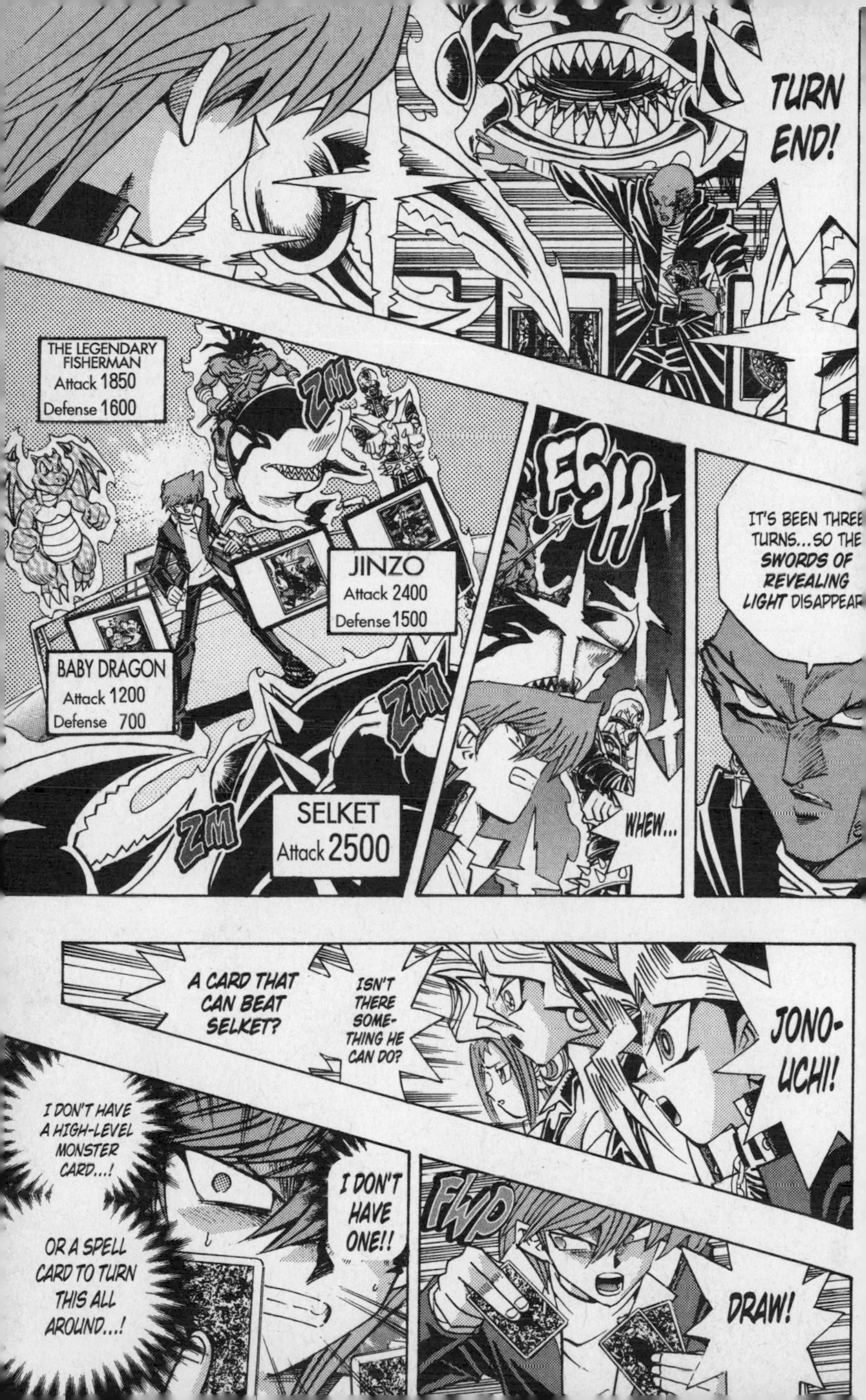
TURN END!
IT'S BEEN THREE TURNS...SO THE SWORDS OF REVEALING LIGHT DISAPPEAR
FSH
WHEW...
THE LEGENDARY FISHERMAN Attack 1850 Defense 1600
ZM
JINZO Attack 2400 Defense 1500
BABY DRAGON Attack 1200 Defense 700
ZM
ZM
SELKET Attack 2500
JONO-UCHI!
ISN'T THERE SOME-THING HE CAN DO?
A CARD THAT CAN BEAT SELKET?
FWP
DRAW!
I DON'T HAVE ONE!!
I DON'T HAVE A HIGH-LEVEL MONSTER CARD...!
OR A SPELL CARD TO TURN THIS ALL AROUND...!

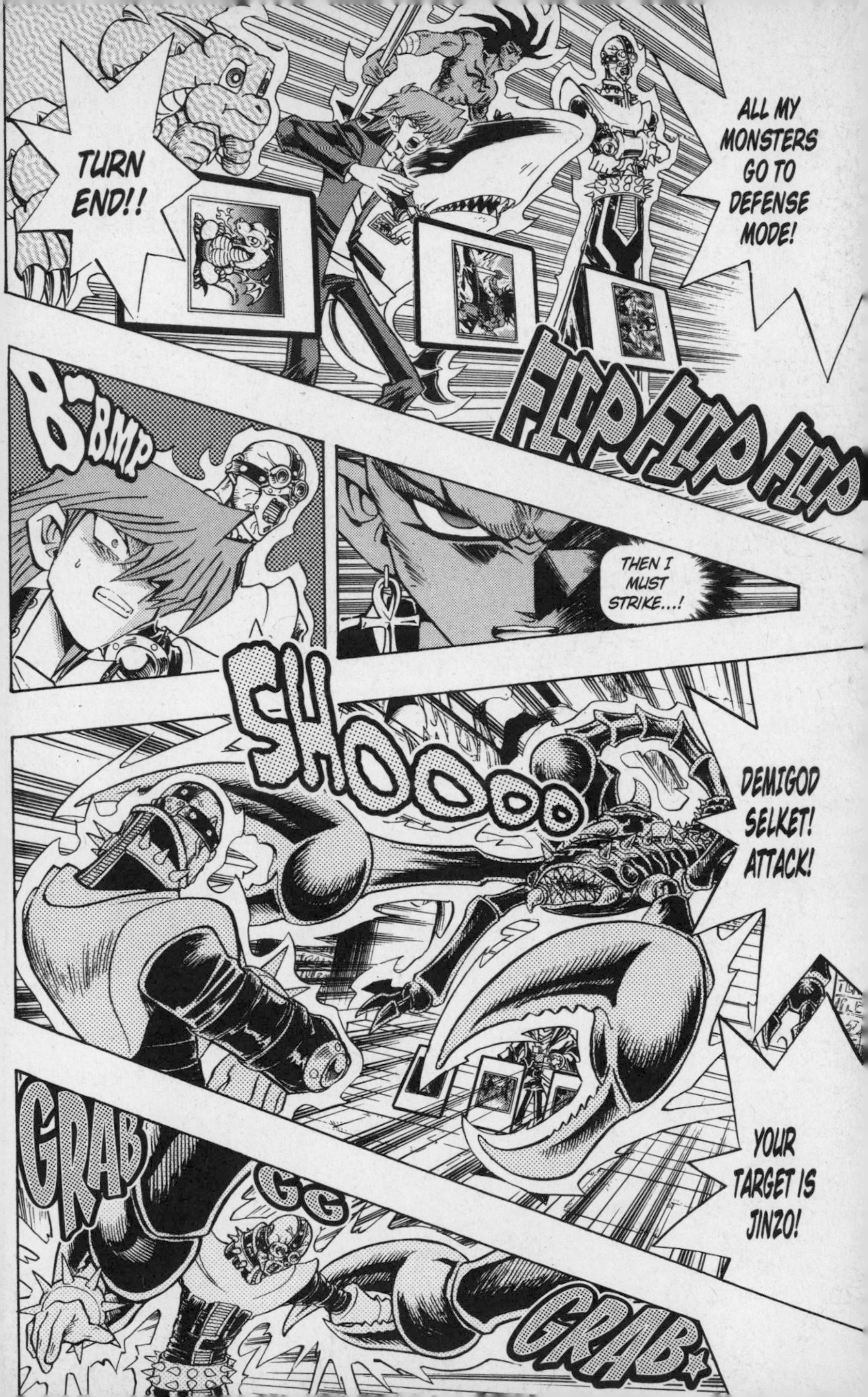
ALL MY MONSTERS GO TO DEFENSE MODE!
TURN END!!
FLIP FLIP FLIP
THEN I MUST STRIKE...!
B-BMP
SHOOOOOO
DEMIGOD SELKET! ATTACK!
YOUR TARGET IS JINZO!
GRAB
GG
GRAB

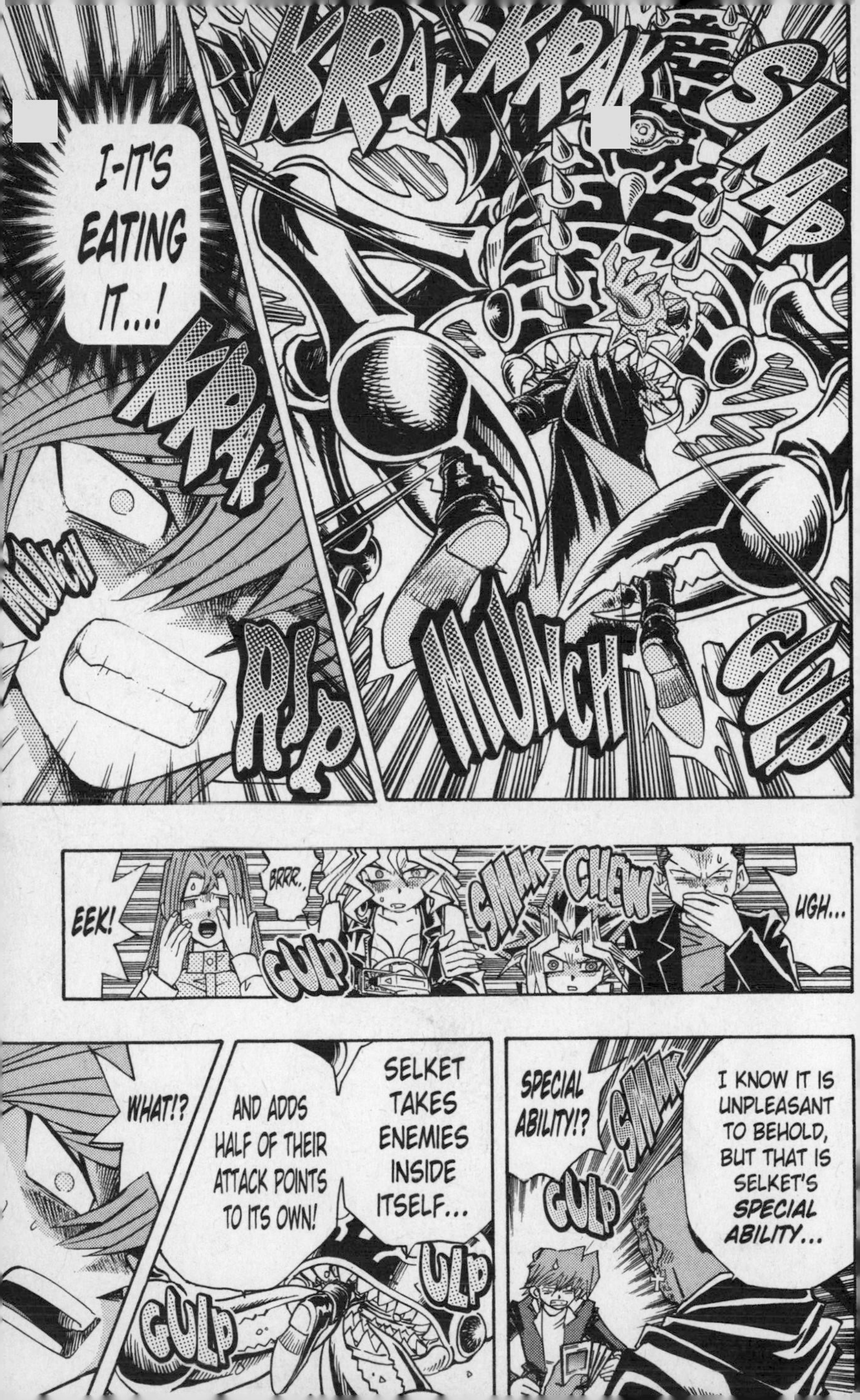
SNAP
KRAK
KRAK
GULP
MUNCH
I-IT'S EATING IT...!
KRAK
RIP
MUNCH
UGH...
CHEW
SMAK
BRRR..
GULP
EEK!
I KNOW IT IS UNPLEASANT TO BEHOLD, BUT THAT IS SELKET'S *SPECIAL ABILITY*...
SMAK
SPECIAL ABILITY!?
GULP
SELKET TAKES ENEMIES INSIDE ITSELF...
AND ADDS HALF OF THEIR ATTACK POINTS TO ITS OWN!
ULP
GULP
WHAT!?

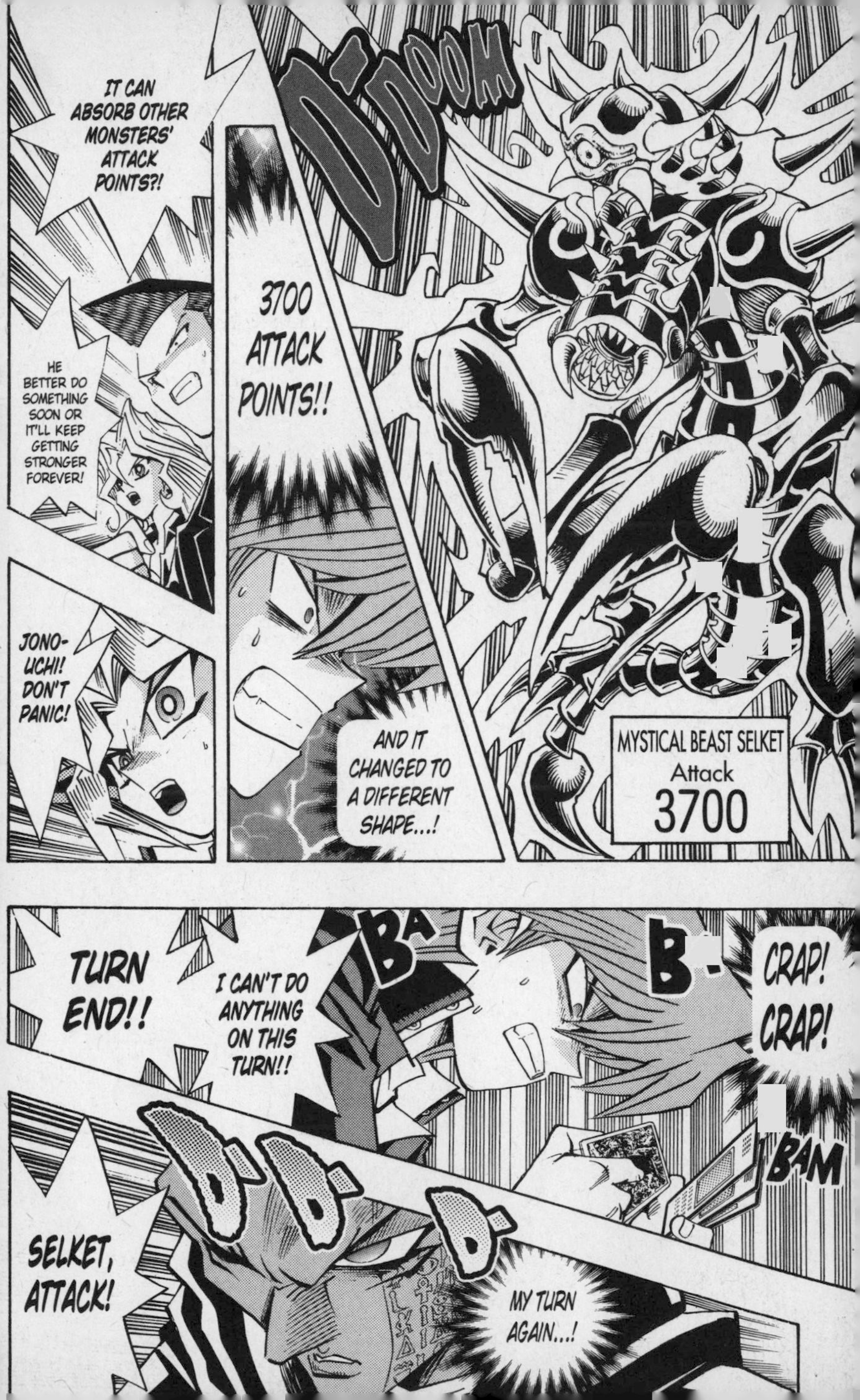
DOOOM
MYSTICAL BEAST SELKET Attack 3700
3700 ATTACK POINTS!!
AND IT CHANGED TO A DIFFERENT SHAPE...!
IT CAN ABSORB OTHER MONSTERS' ATTACK POINTS?!
HE BETTER DO SOMETHING SOON OR IT'LL KEEP GETTING STRONGER FOREVER!
JONO-UCHI! DON'T PANIC!
CRAP! CRAP!
BAM
BA
I CAN'T DO ANYTHING ON THIS TURN!!
TURN END!!
MY TURN AGAIN...!
SELKET, ATTACK!

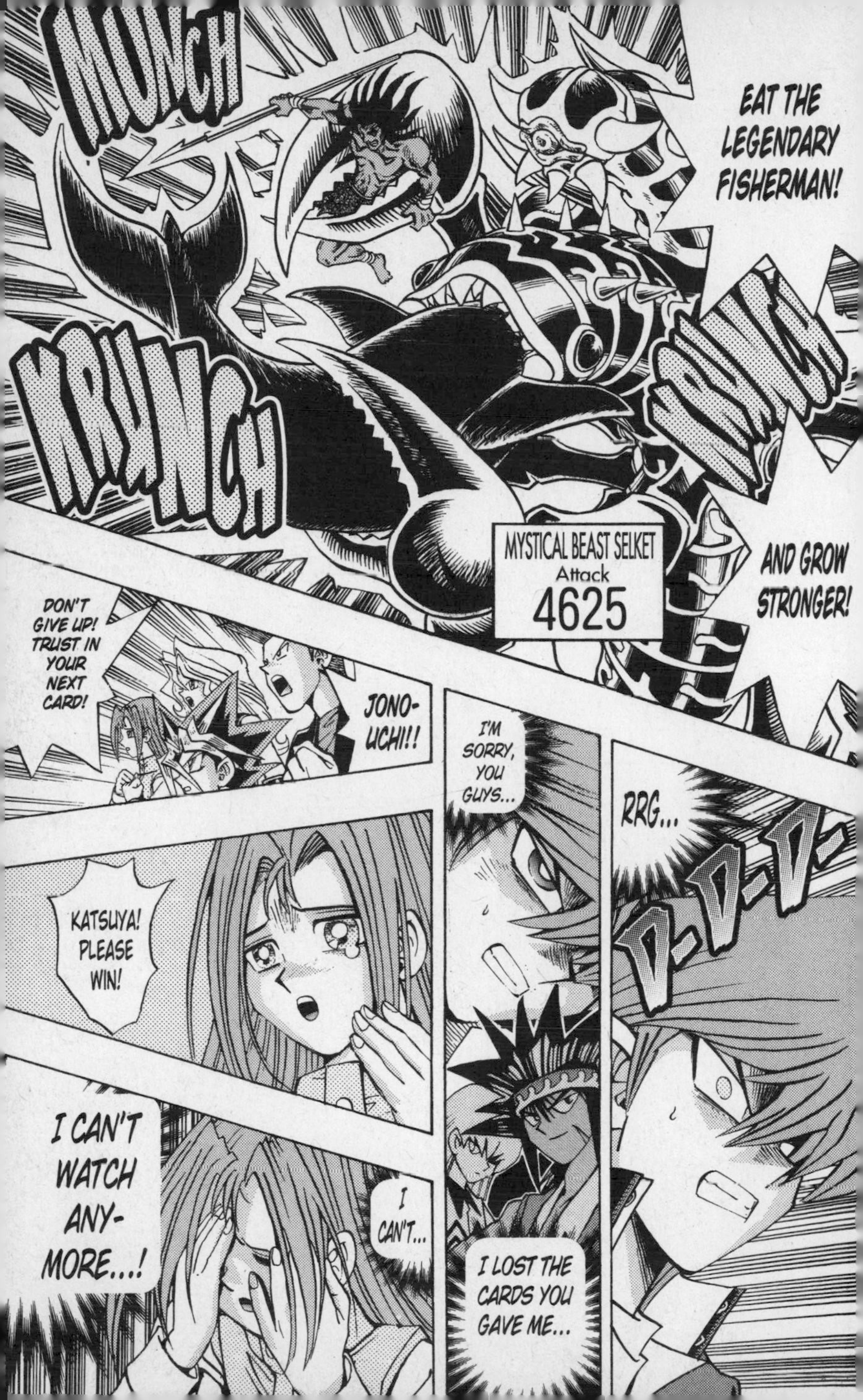
EAT THE LEGENDARY FISHERMAN!
MUNCH
MUNCH
AND GROW STRONGER!
MYSTICAL BEAST SELKET Attack 4625
KRUNCH
JONO-UCHI!!
DON'T GIVE UP! TRUST IN YOUR NEXT CARD!
RRG...
D-D-D-
I'M SORRY, YOU GUYS...
I LOST THE CARDS YOU GAVE ME...
KATSUYA! PLEASE WIN!
I CAN'T...
I CAN'T WATCH ANY-MORE...!

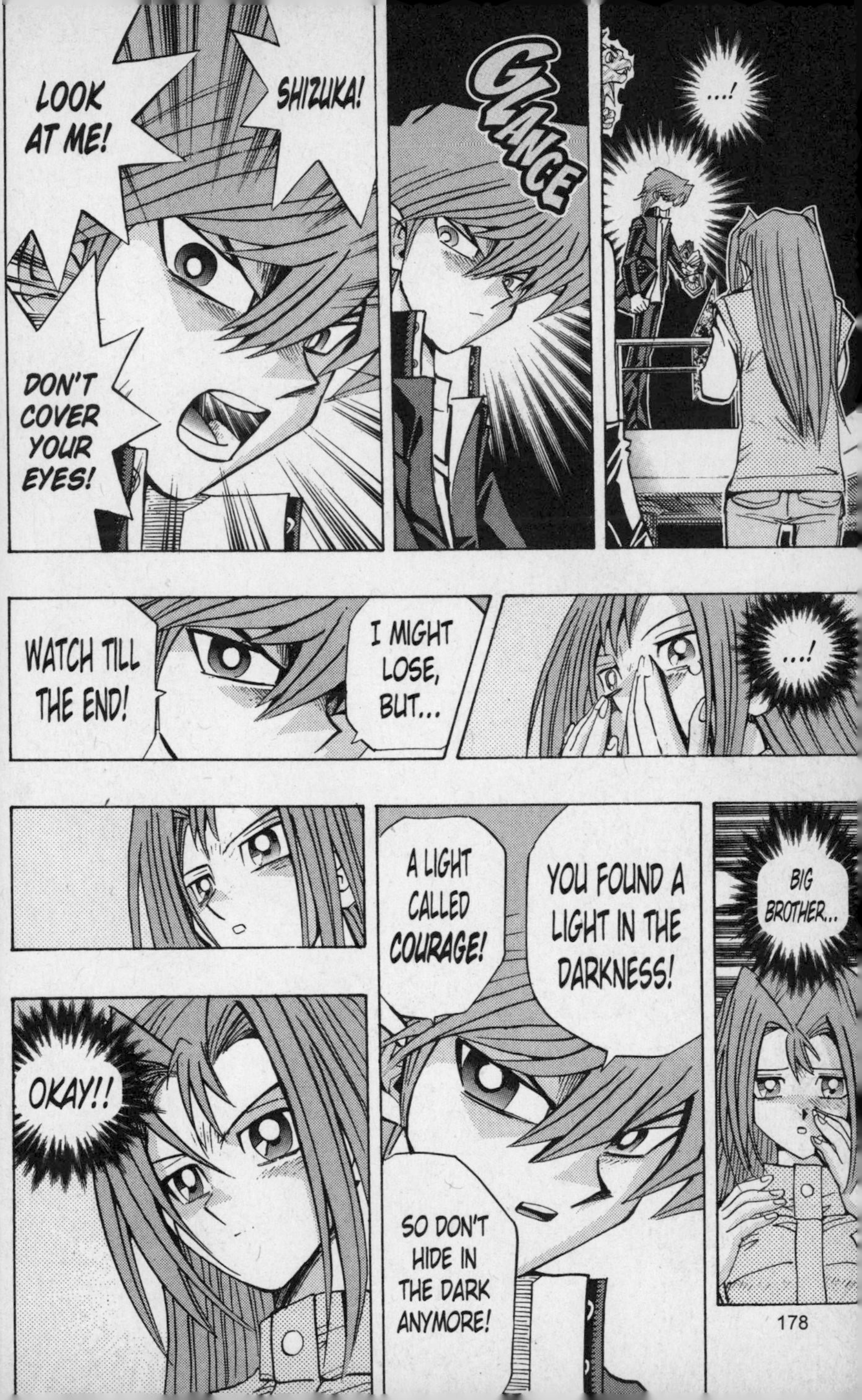
...!
GLANCE
SHIZUKA!
LOOK AT ME!
DON'T COVER YOUR EYES!
...!
I MIGHT LOSE, BUT...
WATCH TILL THE END!
BIG BROTHER...
YOU FOUND A LIGHT IN THE DARKNESS!
A LIGHT CALLED COURAGE!
SO DON'T HIDE IN THE DARK ANYMORE!
OKAY!!

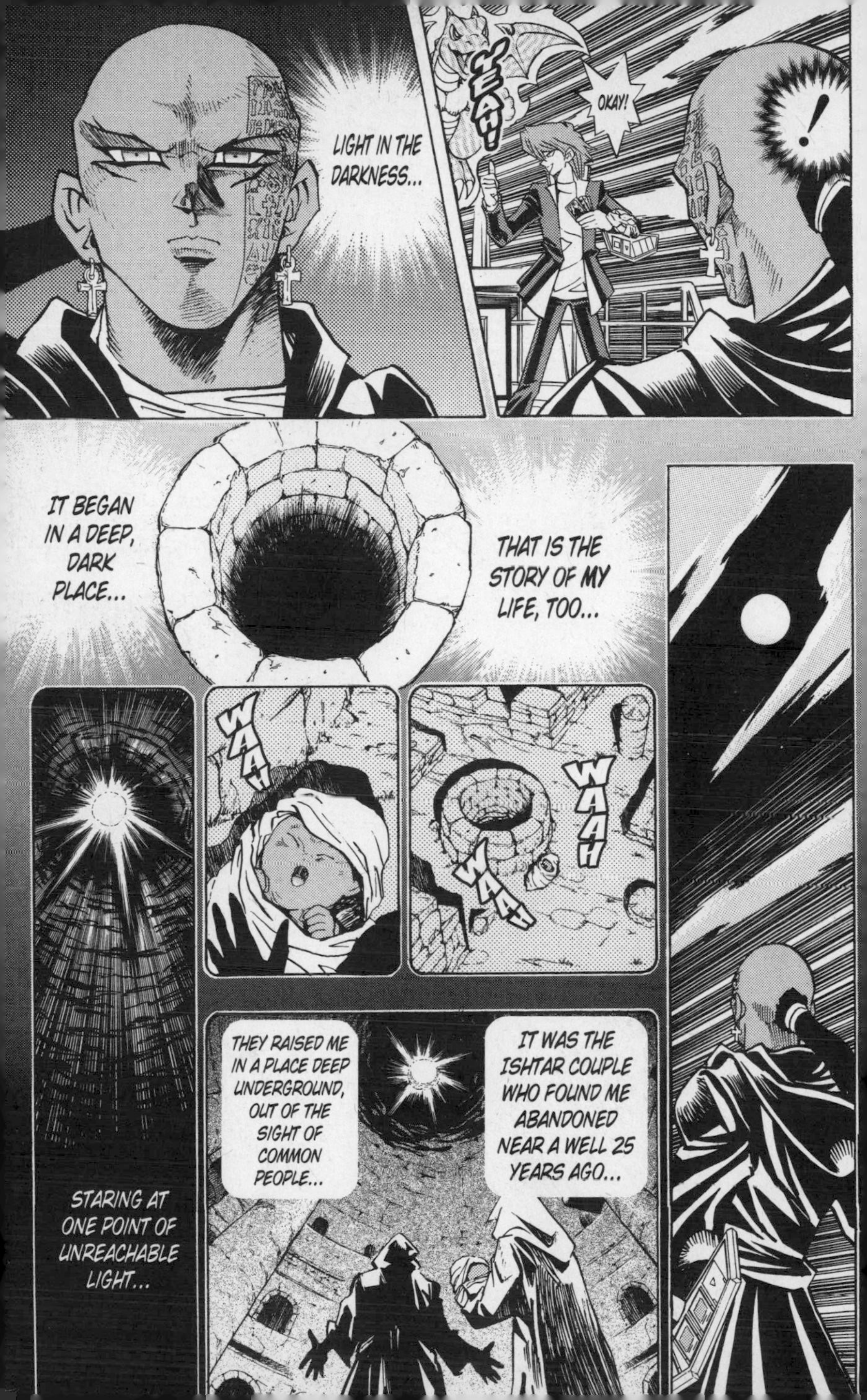

!
OKAY!
YEAH!
LIGHT IN THE DARKNESS...
IT BEGAN IN A DEEP, DARK PLACE...
THAT IS THE STORY OF MY LIFE, TOO...
WAAH
WAAAH
WAAH
IT WAS THE ISHTAR COUPLE WHO FOUND ME ABANDONED NEAR A WELL 25 YEARS AGO...
THEY RAISED ME IN A PLACE DEEP UNDERGROUND, OUT OF THE SIGHT OF COMMON PEOPLE...
STARING AT ONE POINT OF UNREACHABLE LIGHT...

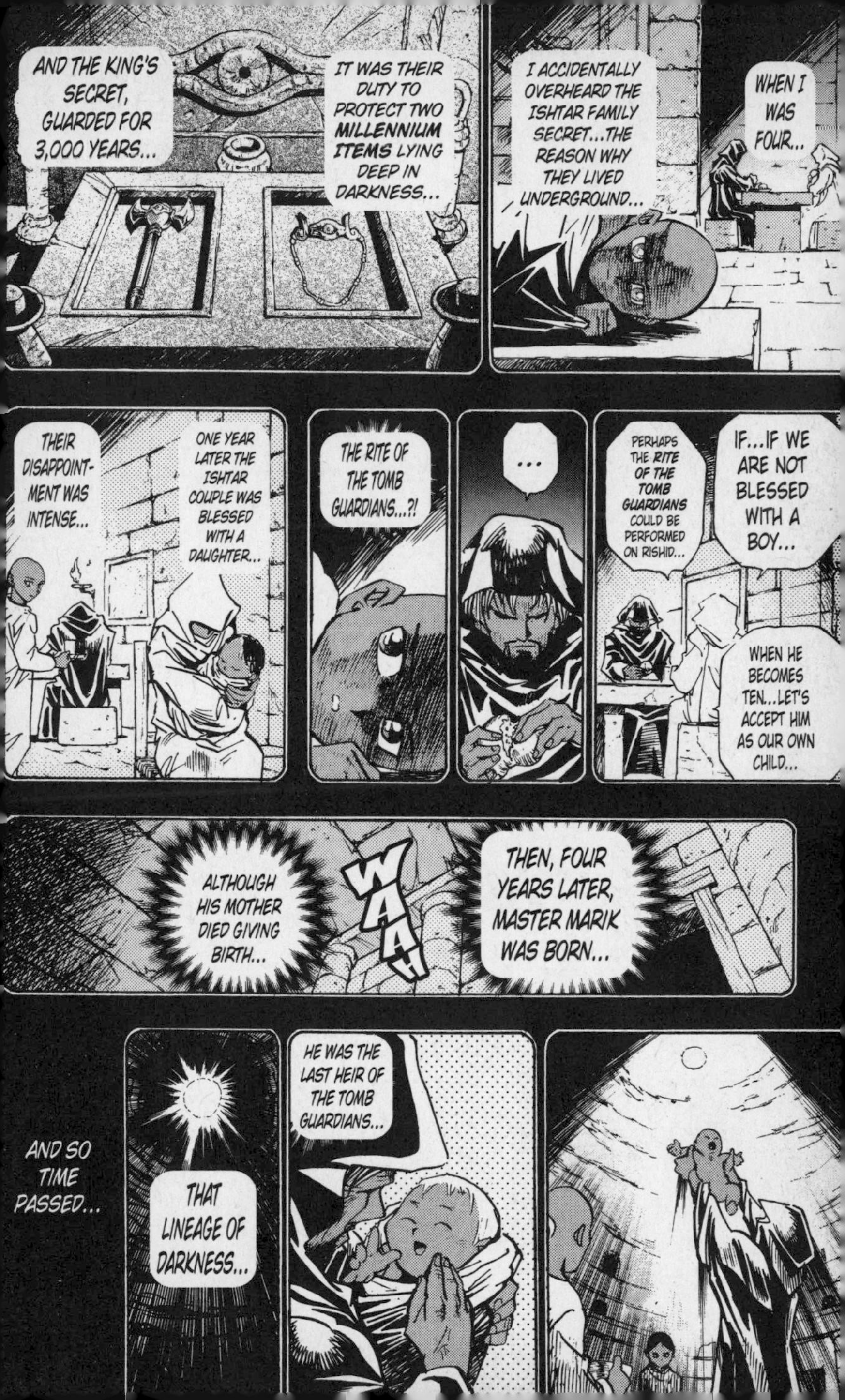
WHEN I WAS FOUR...
I ACCIDENTALLY OVERHEARD THE ISHTAR FAMILY SECRET...THE REASON WHY THEY LIVED UNDERGROUND...
IT WAS THEIR DUTY TO PROTECT TWO **MILLENNIUM ITEMS** LYING DEEP IN DARKNESS...
AND THE KING'S SECRET, GUARDED FOR 3,000 YEARS...
IF...IF WE ARE NOT BLESSED WITH A BOY...
PERHAPS THE *RITE OF THE TOMB GUARDIANS* COULD BE PERFORMED ON RISHID...
WHEN HE BECOMES TEN...LET'S ACCEPT HIM AS OUR OWN CHILD...
...
THE RITE OF THE TOMB GUARDIANS...?!
ONE YEAR LATER THE ISHTAR COUPLE WAS BLESSED WITH A DAUGHTER...
THEIR DISAPPOINT-MENT WAS INTENSE...
THEN, FOUR YEARS LATER, MASTER MARIK WAS BORN...
WAAAH
ALTHOUGH HIS MOTHER DIED GIVING BIRTH...
HE WAS THE LAST HEIR OF THE TOMB GUARDIANS...
THAT LINEAGE OF DARKNESS...
AND SO TIME PASSED...

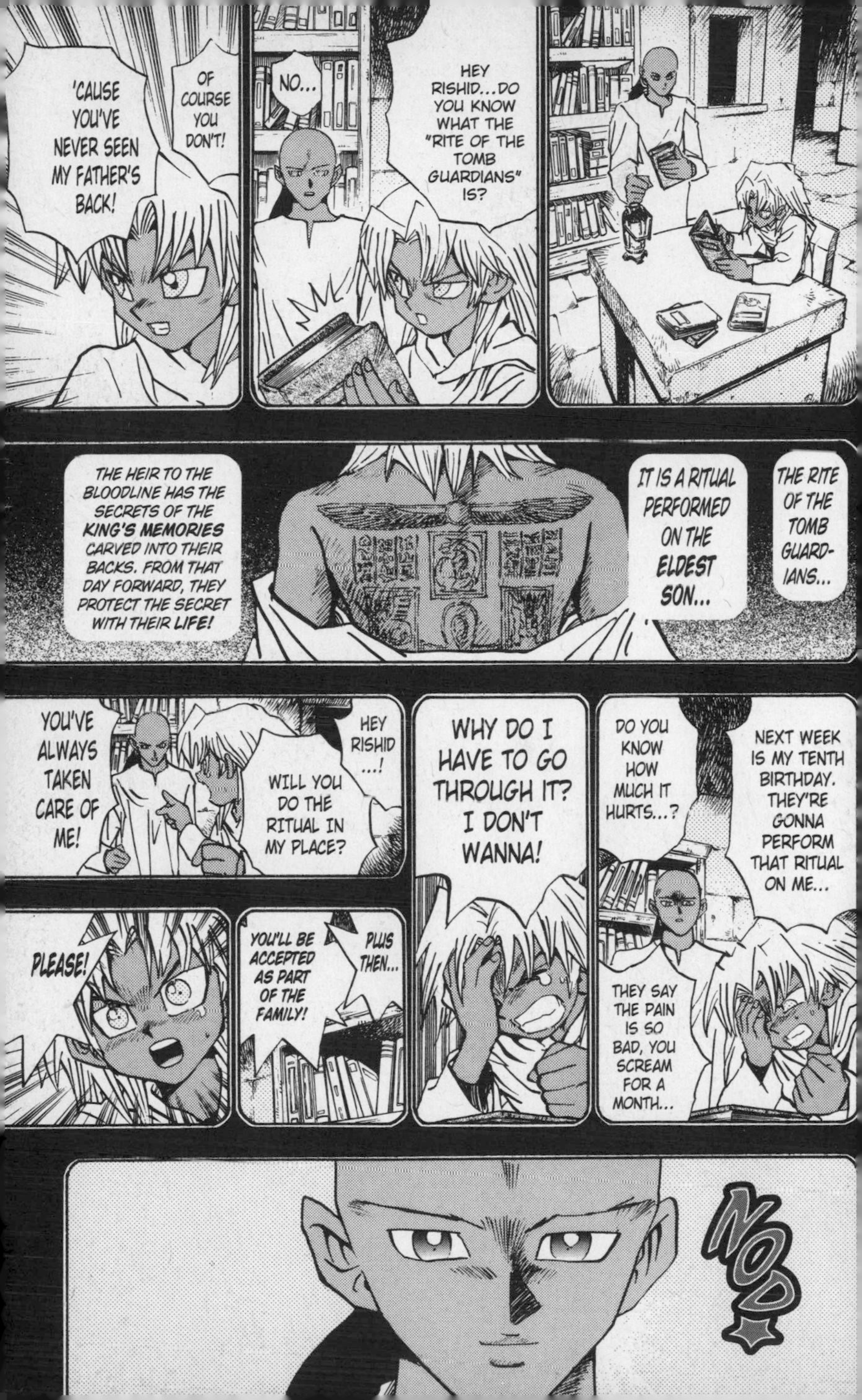
HEY RISHID...DO YOU KNOW WHAT THE "RITE OF THE TOMB GUARDIANS" IS?
NO...
OF COURSE YOU DON'T!
'CAUSE YOU'VE NEVER SEEN MY FATHER'S BACK!
THE RITE OF THE TOMB GUARD-IANS...
IT IS A RITUAL PERFORMED ON THE ELDEST SON...
THE HEIR TO THE BLOODLINE HAS THE SECRETS OF THE KING'S MEMORIES CARVED INTO THEIR BACKS. FROM THAT DAY FORWARD, THEY PROTECT THE SECRET WITH THEIR LIFE!
NEXT WEEK IS MY TENTH BIRTHDAY. THEY'RE GONNA PERFORM THAT RITUAL ON ME...
DO YOU KNOW HOW MUCH IT HURTS...?
THEY SAY THE PAIN IS SO BAD, YOU SCREAM FOR A MONTH...
WHY DO I HAVE TO GO THROUGH IT? I DON'T WANNA!
HEY RISHID ...!
WILL YOU DO THE RITUAL IN MY PLACE?
YOU'VE ALWAYS TAKEN CARE OF ME!
PLUS THEN...
YOU'LL BE ACCEPTED AS PART OF THE FAMILY!
PLEASE!
NOD

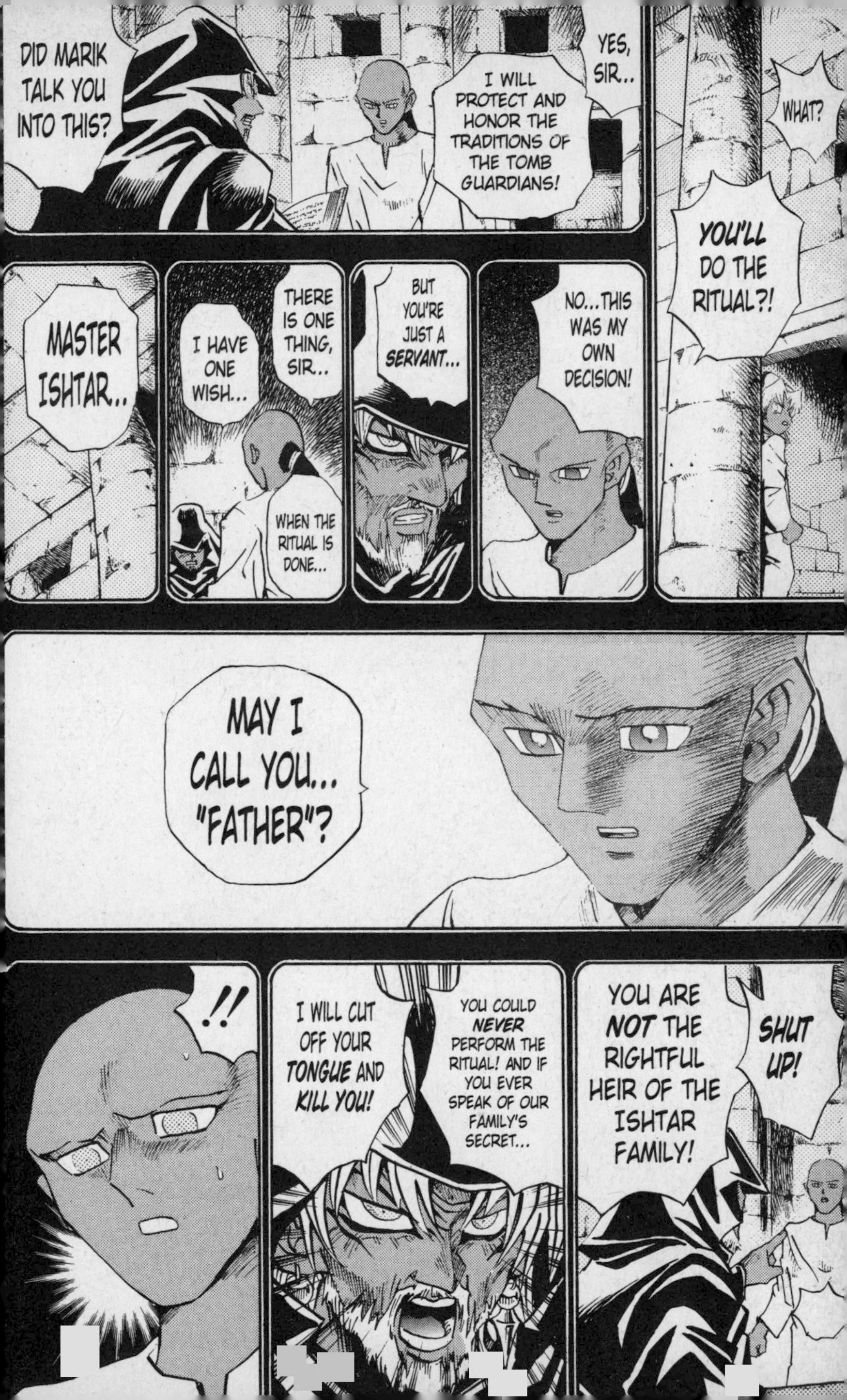
WHAT?
YOU'LL DO THE RITUAL?!
YES, SIR...
I WILL PROTECT AND HONOR THE TRADITIONS OF THE TOMB GUARDIANS!
DID MARIK TALK YOU INTO THIS?
NO...THIS WAS MY OWN DECISION!
BUT YOU'RE JUST A SERVANT...
THERE IS ONE THING, SIR...
I HAVE ONE WISH...
WHEN THE RITUAL IS DONE...
MASTER ISHTAR...
MAY I CALL YOU... "FATHER"?
SHUT UP!
YOU ARE NOT THE RIGHTFUL HEIR OF THE ISHTAR FAMILY!
YOU COULD NEVER PERFORM THE RITUAL! AND IF YOU EVER SPEAK OF OUR FAMILY'S SECRET...
I WILL CUT OFF YOUR TONGUE AND KILL YOU!
!!

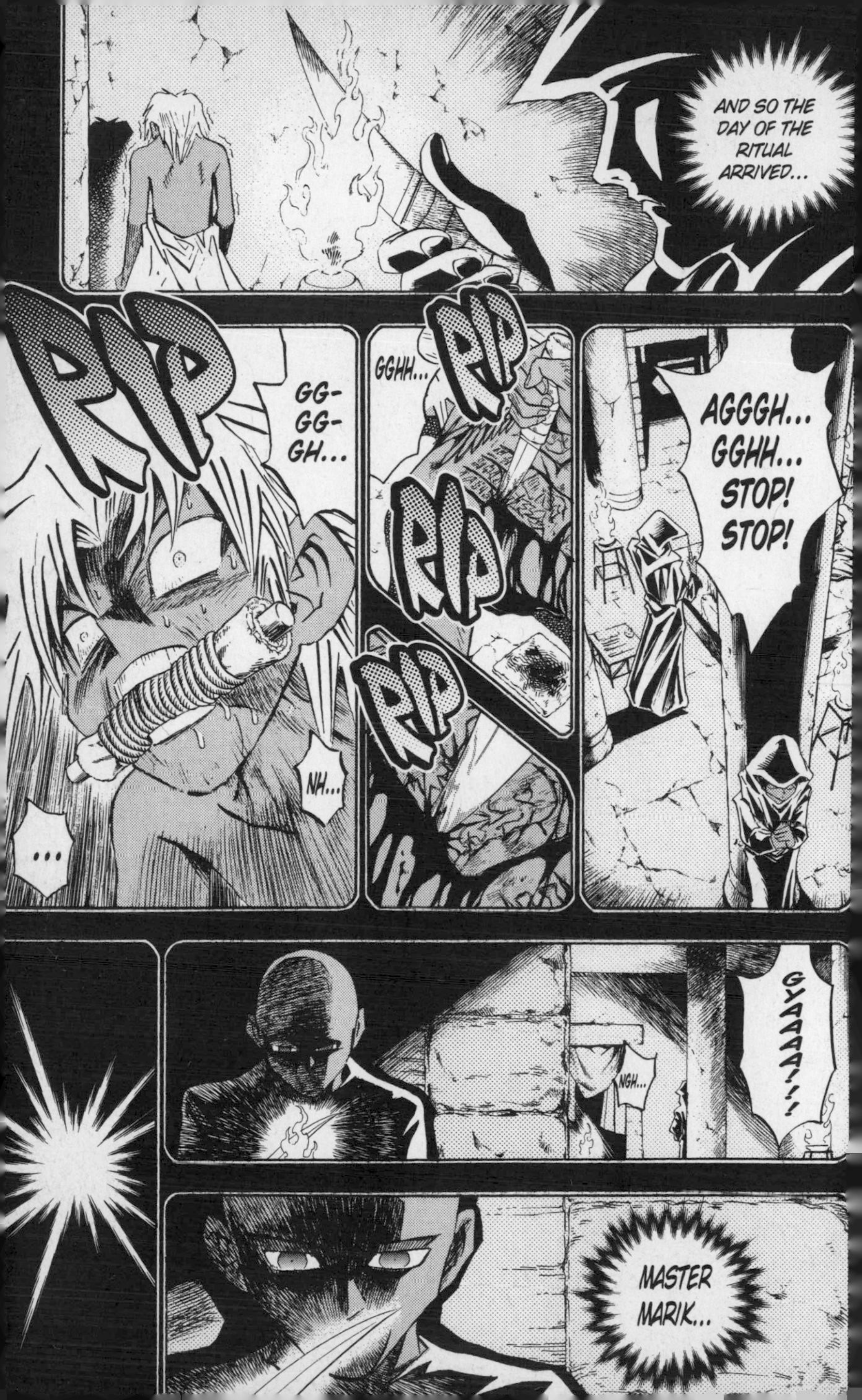
AND SO THE DAY OF THE RITUAL ARRIVED...
AGGGH... GGHH... STOP! STOP!
RIP
GGHH...
RIP
RIP
RIP
GG- GG- GH...
NH...
...
GYAAAAA!!!
NGH...
MASTER MARIK...

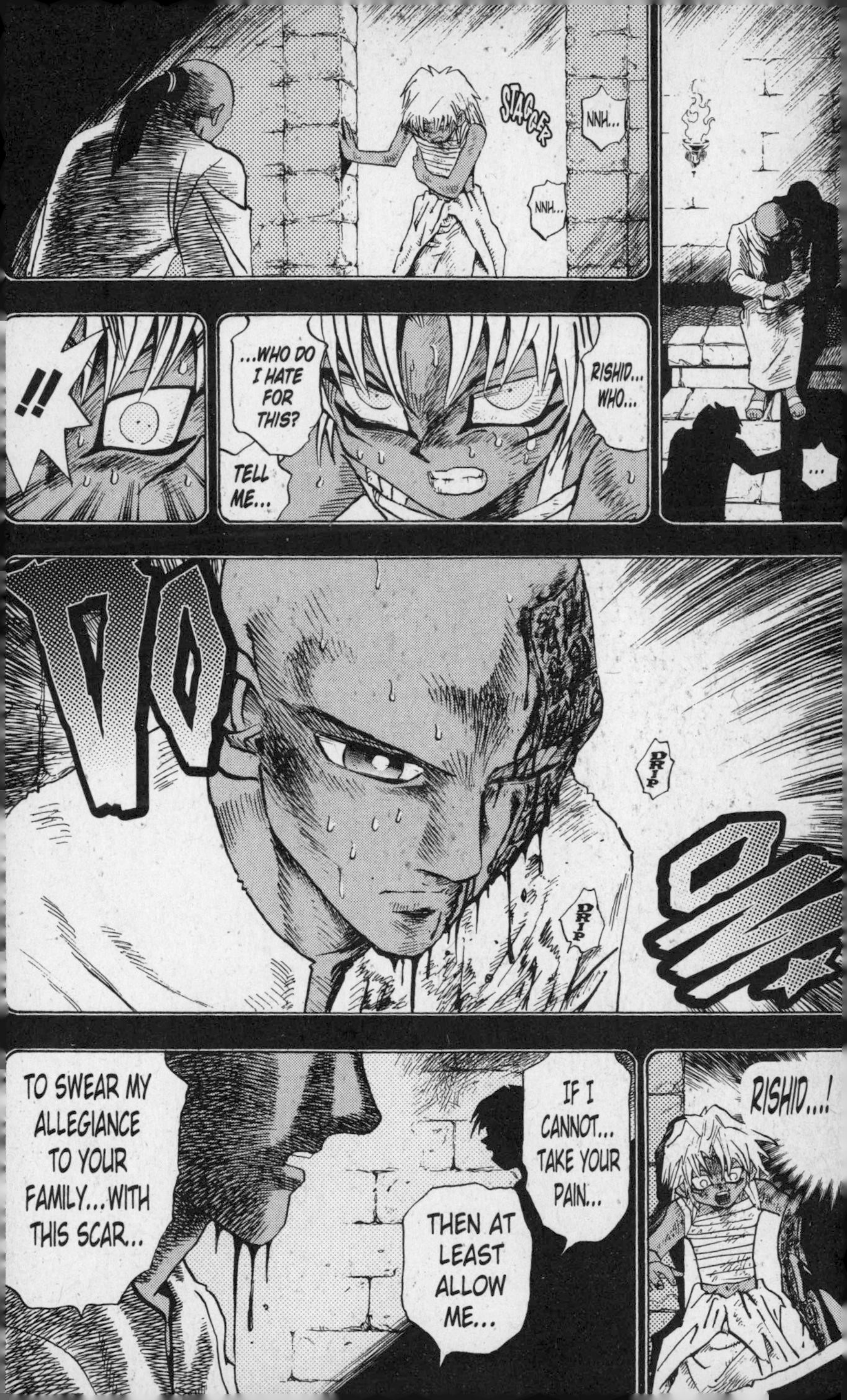
...
STAGGER
NNH...
NNH...
RISHID... WHO...
...WHO DO I HATE FOR THIS?
TELL ME...
!!
DRIP
DRIP
RISHID...!
IF I CANNOT... TAKE YOUR PAIN...
THEN AT LEAST ALLOW ME...
TO SWEAR MY ALLEGIANCE TO YOUR FAMILY...WITH THIS SCAR...

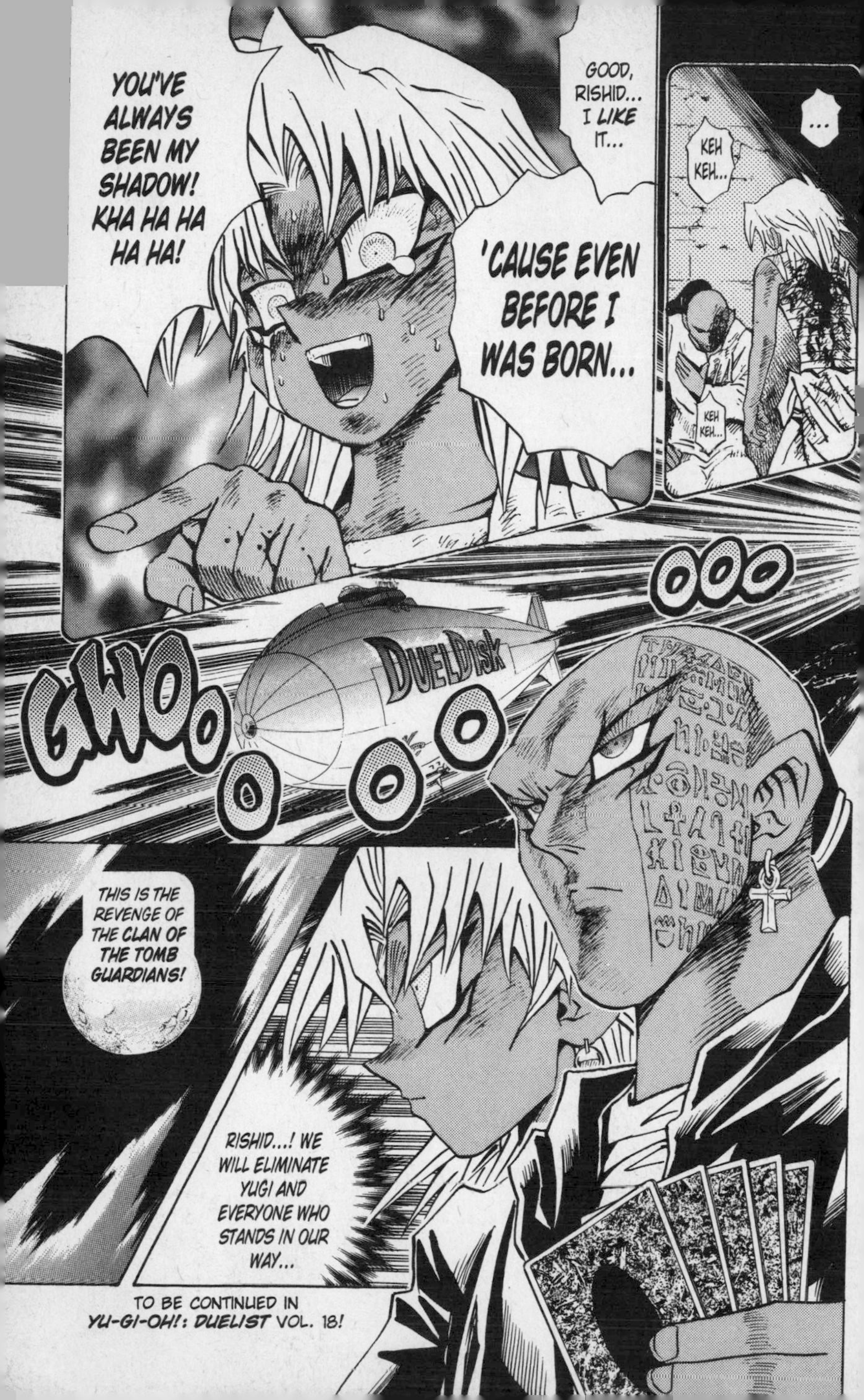
...
KEH KEH...
KEH KEH...
GOOD, RISHID... I LIKE IT...
'CAUSE EVEN BEFORE I WAS BORN...
YOU'VE ALWAYS BEEN MY SHADOW! KHA HA HA HA HA!
GWOOOOOOOO
DUELDISK
THIS IS THE REVENGE OF THE CLAN OF THE TOMB GUARDIANS!
RISHID...! WE WILL ELIMINATE YUGI AND EVERYONE WHO STANDS IN OUR WAY...

TO BE CONTINUED IN *YU-GI-OH!: DUELIST* VOL. 18!

MASTER OF THE CARDS

The "Duel Monsters" card game first appeared in volume two of the original **Yu-Gi-Oh!** graphic novel series, but it's in **Yu-Gi-Oh!: Duelist** (originally printed in Japan as volumes 8-31 of **Yu-Gi-Oh!**) that it gets really important. As many fans know, some of the card names are different between the English and Japanese versions. In case you play the game, or you're interested in playing, here's a rundown of some of the cards in this graphic novel. Some cards only appear in the **Yu-Gi-Oh!** video games, not in the actual collectible card game.

FIRST APPEARANCE IN THIS VOLUME	JAPANESE CARD NAME	ENGLISH CARD NAME
p.7	*Dark Necrofear*	Dark Necrofear
p.7	*Ouija Ban* (Ouija Board)	Destiny Board
p.7	*Ankoku no Tobira* (Door of Darkness)	The Dark Door
p.7	*Kuribo*	Kuriboh
p.7	Black Magician Girl	Dark Magician Girl
p.9	*Monster Kaishû* (Monster Withdrawal)	Monster Recovery
p.9	*Chain Destruction* (NOTE: Japanese kanji reads "Chain Destruction")	Chain Destruction
p.10	*Earthbound Spirit* (Japanese kanji reads "Jibakurei" [Earthbound Spirit])	Earthbound Spirit
p.10	*Magnet Warrior Gamma*	Gamma the Magnet Warrior
p.10	*Chinmoku no Dark Spirit* (Dark Spirit of Silence)	Dark Spirit of the Silent
p.13	*Shisha Sosei* (Resurrection of the Dead)	Monster Reborn

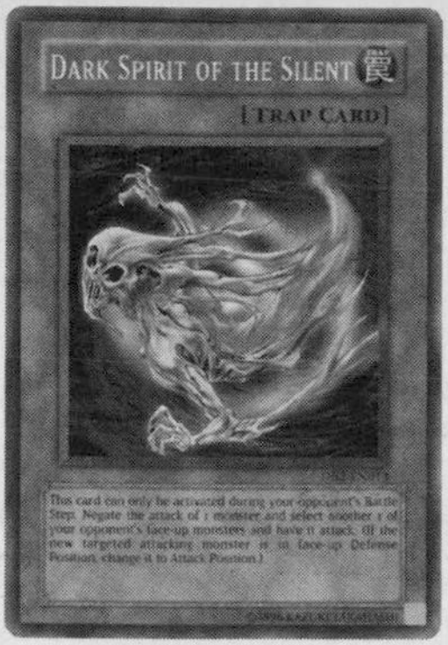
Dark Spirit of the Silent
[TRAP CARD]
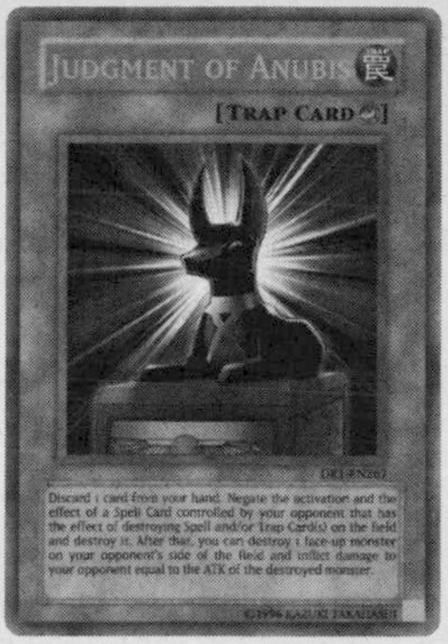
Judgment of Anubis
[TRAP CARD]
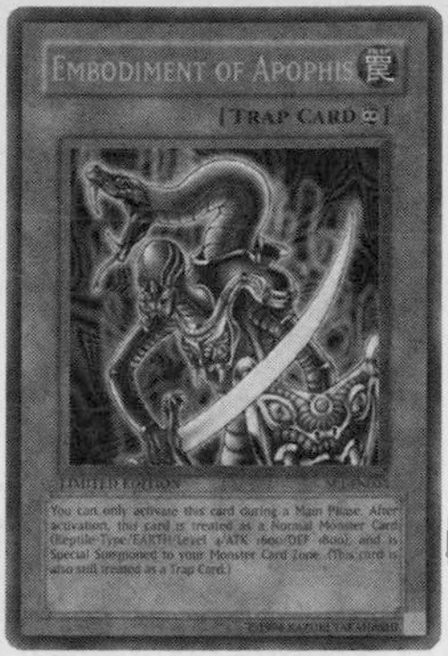
Embodiment of Apophis
[TRAP CARD]

FIRST APPEARANCE IN THIS VOLUME	JAPANESE CARD NAME	ENGLISH CARD NAME
p.30	*Shiryô Hakushaku* (Ghost Count)	The Earl of Demise
p.30	(NOTE: One of Bakura's cards is unnamed.)	(NOTE: One of Bakura's cards is unnamed.)
p.40	*Deja Vu*	Deja Vu (NOTE: Not a real game card.)
p.41	*Tefuda Massatsu* (Card Obliteration)	Card Destruction
p.41	*Yûgô* (Fusion)	Polymerization
p.44	*Osiris no Tenkûryû* (Osiris the Heaven Dragon)	Slifer the Sky Dragon
p.92	*Red-Eyes Black Dragon*	Red-Eyes Black Dragon
p.92	*Tetsu no Kishi Gear Fried* (Iron Knight Gear Fried)	Gearfried the Iron Knight
p.93	*Hurricane*	Giant Trunade
p.94	*Anubis no Sabaki* (Judgment of Anubis)	Judgment of Anubis
p.94	*Ôke no Shinden* (Temple of the Kings)	Royal Temple
p.99	*Landstar no Kenshi* (Landstar Swordsman)	Swordsman of Landstar

FIRST APPEARANCE IN THIS VOLUME	JAPANESE CARD NAME	ENGLISH CARD NAME
p.100	*Shikkoku no Hyôsenshi Panther Warrior* (Jet Black Panther Warrior)	Panther Warrior
p.113	*Wyvern no Senshi* (Wyvern Warrior)	Alligator Sword
p.115	*Rocket Senshi* (Rocket Warrior)	Rocket Warrior
p.117	*Wadjet Gan no Nenriki* (Will of the Wadjet Eye)	Will of the Wadjet Eye (NOTE: Not a real game card.)
p.118	*Monster Box*	Fairy Box
p.122	*Apophis no Keshin* (Avatar of Apophis)	Embodiment of Apophis
p.130	*Scape Goat*	Scapegoat
p.130	*Orokana Maisô* (Foolish Burial)	Foolish Burial
p.133	*Mahô Kaishô* (Magic Liquidation/Dissolution)	De-Spell
p.142	*Haka Arashi* (Graverobber)	Graverobber
p.144	*Jinzô Ningen Psycho Shocker* (Android/Cyborg Psycho Shocker)	Jinzo
p.154	*Hikari no Gofûken* (Swords of Binding/Sealing Light)	Swords of Revealing Light
p.155	*Densetsu no Fisherman* (Legendary Fisherman)	The Legendary Fisherman
p.161	*Baby Dragon*	Baby Dragon
p.163	*Fûkon no Seihai* (Chalice of Sealed/Bound Soul)	Cup of Sealed Soul (NOTE: Not a real game card)
p.163	*Selket no Monshô* (Crest of Selket)	Seal of Selket (NOTE: Not a real game card)
p.164	*Seijû Selket* (Holy Beast/Beast God Selket)	Mystical Beast of Selket (NOTE: Not a real game card)
p.165	*Ra no Yokushinryû* (Ra the Winged God Dragon) (NOTE: The kanji for "sun god" is written beside the kanji for "Ra.")	The Sun Dragon Ra (NOTE: Called "The Winged Dragon of Ra" in the English anime and card game.)

IN THE NEXT VOLUME...

Can Jonouchi overcome the massive power of the Beast of Selket?! But even as he struggles for his life, his duelist instincts tell him the truth: *Rishid isn't really Marik!* To prove "his" identity, Rishid plays his ultimate card, the fake Sun Dragon Ra! But the *real* god Ra is growing angry...and the *real* Marik is about to show his full power...

COMING DECEMBER 2006!

Tell us what you think about SHONEN JUMP manga!

Our survey is now available online.
Go to: www.SHONENJUMP.com/mangasurvey

Help us make our product offering better!

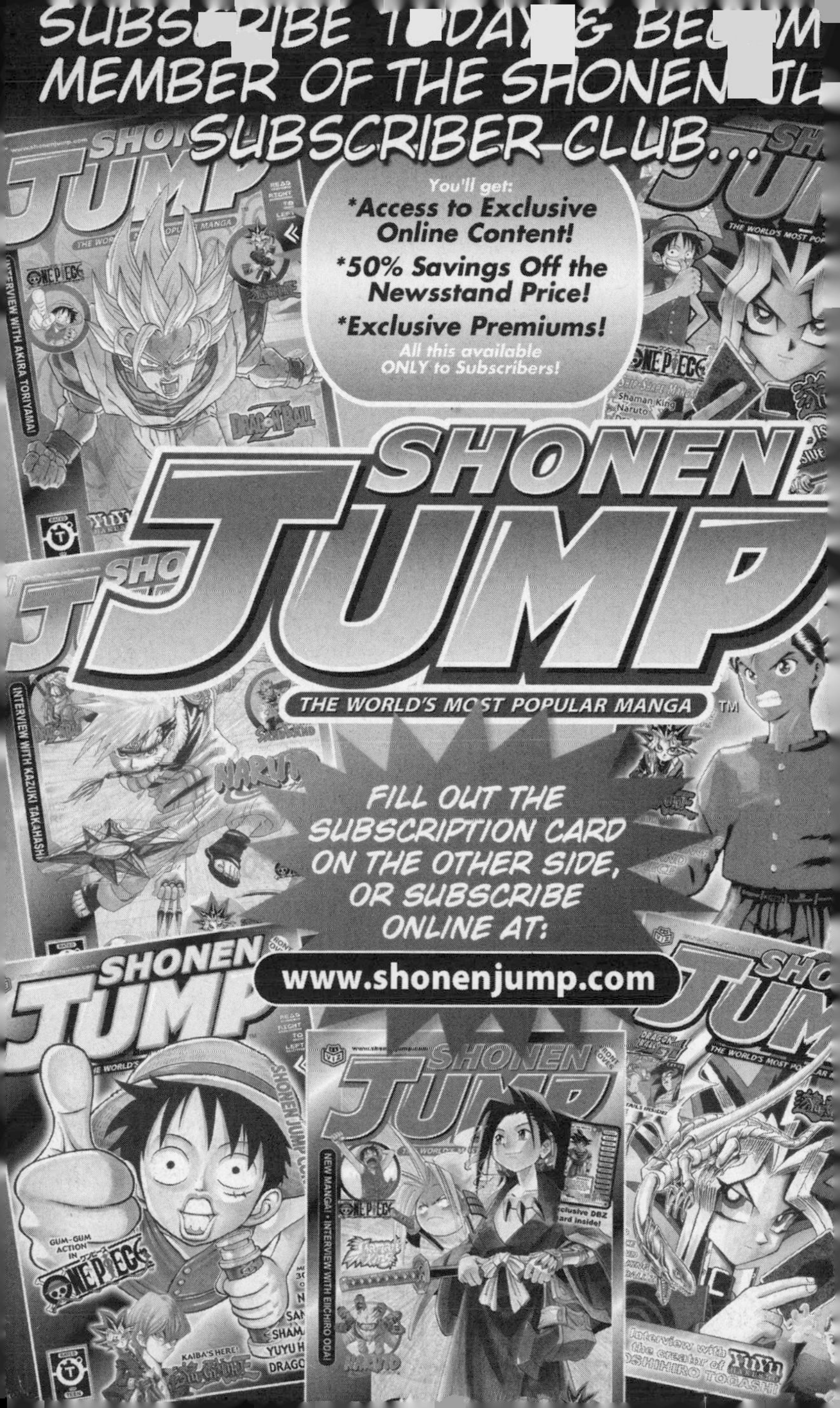
SUBSC RIBE T DAY & BEC M
MEMBER OF THE SHONEN JL
SUBSCRIBER CLUB...
You'll get:
*Access to Exclusive Online Content!
*50% Savings Off the Newsstand Price!
*Exclusive Premiums!
All this available ONLY to Subscribers!
SHONEN JUMP
THE WORLD'S MOST POPULAR MANGA ™
FILL OUT THE SUBSCRIPTION CARD ON THE OTHER SIDE, OR SUBSCRIBE ONLINE AT:
www.shonenjump.com
INTERVIEW WITH AKIRA TORIYAMA!
INTERVIEW WITH KAZUKI TAKAHASHI
NEW MANGA! · INTERVIEW WITH EIICHIRO ODA!
GUM-GUM ACTION IN ONE PIECE
KAIBA'S HERE!
Exclusive DBZ card inside!